ELECTRONIC COMMERCE AND THE REVOLUTION IN FINANCIAL MARKETS

MING FAN

SAYEE SRINIVASAN

JAN STALLAERT

ANDREW B. WHINSTON

SOUTH-WESTERN

THOMSON LEARNING™

Australia • Canada • Mexico • Singapore • Spain • United Kingdom • United States

Acquistions Editor: Mike Reynolds
Development Editor: Lauren Feldman
Marketing Strategist: Charlie Stutesman
Project Editor: Jim Patterson
Art Director: Brian Salisbury
Production Manager: Suzie Wurzer
Manufacturing Manager: Lisa Kelley

Picture & Literary Rights Editor: Linda Blundell
Copy Editor: Donna Regen
Cover Designer: Brian Salisbury
Cover Printer: Transcontinental Best Book
Compositor: Progressive Information Technologies
Printer: Transcontinental Best Book

Printed in Canada

1 2 3 4 5 6 7   05 04 03 02 01

ISBN: 0-03-032993-0

Library of Congress Catalog Card Number: 2001094387

For more information about our products, contact us at:
Thomson Learning Academic Resource Center
1-800-423-0563

For permission to use material from this text, contact us by:
Phone: 1-800-730-2214
Fax: 1-800-730-2215
Web: www.thomsonrights.com

Asia
Thomson Learning
60 Albert Complex, #15-01
Albert Complex
Singapore 189969

Australia
Nelson Thomson Learning
102 Dodds Street
South Street
South Melbourne, Victoria 3205
Australia

Canada
Nelson Thomson Learning
1120 Birchmount Road
Toronto, Ontario M1K 5G4
Canada

Europe/Middle East/South Africa
Thomson Learning
Berkshire House
168-173 High Holborn
London WC1 V7AA
United Kingdom

Latin America
Thomson Learning
Seneca, 53
Colonia Polanco
11560 Mexico D.F.,
Mexico

Spain
Paraninfo Thomson Learning
Calle/Magallanes, 25
28015 Madrid, Spain

PREFACE

Financial markets have been going electronic for the past quarter century. The birth of the Web has resulted in a dramatic increase in both the speed and the breadth of change. The process described in this book appears nothing short of a revolution. It is a revolution because the Internet has transformed the manner in which individual investors manage their finances. It is a revolution because exchanges like the New York Stock Exchange (NYSE), a stoic believer in floor-based, manual trading processes, are in the process of implementing an electronic trading system. It is a revolution because the organization of financial markets in many parts of the world is being transformed beyond recognition.

The changes that have taken place in the financial world these past couple of decades are unprecedented. And the revolution has barely begun. Financial innovations, changing regulatory environment, and advances of technology have all contributed to this revolutionary process. Advances in financial innovation, regulation, and institutional structures have always played a leading role. Technology has traditionally been viewed as an enabler for financial institutions to develop new products and services. But the explosive development of the Internet has seen technology taking over the mantle of the main catalyst of change. Information technology has fundamentally changed the way financial products are developed and processes are designed. Information technology has drastically altered the competitive picture of the financial industry. Firms armed with cutting-edge technologies have made entries in this traditionally highly regulated industry and given the incumbent firms no choice but to innovate and compete vigorously. Regulators are grappling in the dark. They are trying to get a handle over a constant stream of innovations that continually change traditional definitions of products, institutional roles, and responsibilities. To complicate matters, various regulatory authorities find that their erstwhile well-defined jurisdictions are no longer valid. With this in mind, we wrote this book to take an integrated view at technologies, financial markets and institutions.

Writing this book has been a challenge. By the late 1990s, the pace of change in the industry and in technology was so substantial that we had to make frequent rewrites of complete chapters. A classic example of this pressure is the Nasdaq market. Given the intense competition in the business of trading stocks and bonds, firms tend to make every effort to promote their own interest. To complicate things further, financial markets are highly regulated. So any innovations, even simple modifications to current systems, have to be approved by regulators. All these influences have been playing out at the Nasdaq market. One result of this has been the submission of new proposals to change its market structure nearly every six months. This book has been in the making for over two years now, and just the Nasdaq chapter has been rewritten at least half a dozen times.

Attempting to describe an ongoing revolution is a risky venture. The process described in this book is still going on and is nowhere near completion. The main problem is that by the time the book reaches the printing press, some parts might already be outdated. But we hope that the reader of this book will gain an insight into the dynamics of the most important markets in the world. An earnest attempt has been made to provide up-to-date information on the ongoing revolution. In telling this story, we have consciously tried to focus on the functions of various firms and their attempts to stay relevant and competitive.

A quick review of the list of contents of different chapters will indicate that the book is implicitly divided into three parts. Chapters 1 to 3 give an overview of the broad changes that are taking place in the financial world at the age of the Internet and electronic commerce. The following seven chapters (Chapters 4 to 10) examine the ongoing changes in some of the largest financial markets in the world. Chapters 11 to 13 take a look at the innovations in other unconventional markets, the underlying technologies that are changing the shape of the financial world, and the never stationary process of creative destruction.

We will use the Web to provide updated contents and supporting materials for this book. We encourage readers to visit the book's Web site at *http://crec.bus.utexas.edu/ecfm.html*.

We are grateful to Robert Schweitzer (University of Delaware), Elizabeth Cooperman (University of Colorado, Denver), and Larry White (Mississippi State University), who read a draft the book and provided many useful comments and suggestions. We would also like to thank Susan Kutor for her suggestions and corrections of the manuscript. Finally, we thank Michael Roche and Mike Reynolds for their encouragement and support in this project. The views expressed in the book are those of the authors and not of the various institutions the authors are affiliated with, including the Chicago Mercantile Exchange, Inc.

Ming Fan
Mendoza College of Business
University of Notre Dame

Sayee Srinivasan
Chicago Mercantile Exchange, Inc.

Jan Stallaert
Marshall School of Business
University of Southern California

Andrew B. Whinston
Center for Research in Electronic Commerce
McCombs School of Business
The University of Texas at Austin

To Limin and Adrian
—M.F.

To Sashi
—S.S.

To Sulin
—J.S.

To Veronika
—A.B.W.

BRIEF CONTENTS

CONTENTS

CHAPTER 3: TOWARD A DIGITAL MARKETPLACE   59

CHAPTER 4: FINANCIAL MARKETS IN A NUTSHELL   89

CHAPTER 5: NEW YORK STOCK EXCHANGE   115

1

ELECTRONIC COMMERCE AND THE ORGANIZATION OF FINANCIAL MARKETS

In only a few years, the Internet and the World Wide Web (WWW) have revolutionized the way individuals invest. Rapid advances in technology and financial innovation, along with an ever-changing regulatory environment, are reshaping the future of the financial services industry. Financial institutions are striving to become more competitive and efficient in this time of new technologies and of a more integrated global economy. As a result, the current organization of the financial sector will be fundamentally changed in the next few years.

This book aims to show the roots of tomorrow's online financial sector, highlighting what we see as keys for success in this new business paradigm. This first chapter lays the foundation for our analysis of the financial services industry and its firms. In general, two models exist for looking at the global financial system: a functional approach and an institutional approach. We take the view from Crane *et al.* that the underlying functions of the global financial system, such as providing information and allocating resources, are required in all economies, whether past or present, Eastern or Western, and are thus more stable than the institutions themselves.[1] The institutional arrangements of the financial system that fulfill these functions are more dynamic than the underlying functions and, as a consequence, are more vulnerable to change. We focus more intensely on the current and future institutions, the organization of which defines the structure and transaction efficiency of the market. Without a doubt, information technology is one of the most important factors changing the ground rules of the financial sector; therefore, we examine the dynamics of financial institutions in an environment of technological changes.

In our opinion, complete dis-intermediation (i.e., the elimination of all intermediaries in the financial system) is unlikely to occur. Traditional intermediaries may disappear, but new types of intermediaries with more efficient business models will emerge. Financial markets and intermediaries, which serve to provide market information, reduce risk, allocate resources, and settle transactions, will have to redefine their businesses in the coming digital revolution. We use the value chain model to look at the competitive strategies for firms, which not only have to digitize their businesses but also redefine and reinvent their whole value chains. Technology, competitive forces, and business models will be quite different in the digital age. Now and in the future, firms will have to understand their customers' changing needs and develop competitive advantage by using innovative online strategies, several of which are introduced briefly in this chapter. Finally, we discuss the development of financial supermarkets and compare the business models of E*Trade, the Internet pioneer, and Citigroup, the industry giant. We conclude the introductory overview with a glimpse at the future ramifications of all these developments for today's financial exchanges.

1.1 THE INTERNET AND THE DIGITAL REVOLUTION

The Internet, simply put, is an intermeshing network of local area networks, wide area networks, and communication backbones over which a rapidly increasing range of applications is reaching thousands of new users every day. Even a thumbnail sketch of its history shows that a single innovation can truly transform the world as we know it.

The Internet's first linked network, ARPANET, started as a project of the Advanced Research Projects Agency (ARPA) of the U.S. Department of Defense in late 1960s. The goal of ARPANET was to create a network that enabled safe transmittal of data between military computers at different sites through redundant communication routes. In 1986, NSFNET, the backbone of the Internet, was created by the National Science Foundation (NSF). At that time, the Internet was primarily used by academic and research institutions and had virtually no commercial usage. A major milestone of Internet development took place in 1991, when the NSF allowed commercial traffic onto the Internet, opening the floodgates for the explosive growth of electronic commerce. Another milestone was the development of the WWW. Designed by Tim Berners-Lee at CERN (Conseil Europeen pour la Recherche Nucleaire, or European Laboratory for Particle Physics), the WWW immediately became the uniform interface for accessing information and applications that are stored on different computer platforms linked by the Internet. The WWW has succeeded in integrating not only diverse software products and hardware platforms but also entire industries that were once distinct. Today's users can use a multitude of communication devices, including computers, palm pilots, and cellular phones, to access multimedia information over the Internet.

The Internet is perhaps the most important innovation in modern computing and communication. Its open communication standards have facilitated the decentralized growth of information. Today, the Internet, with the potential of connecting every single computer in the world, has become the largest communication network humanity has ever built. According to the Internet Domain Survey produced by Network Wizards, there were more than 109 million hosts on the Internet in January 2001, compared with only 9.5 million in January 1996 and 1.3 million in January 1993.[2] Over the Internet's WWW, multimedia information content can be distributed to any place at any time. Applications that were developed using different tools and languages on different computer platforms can all be accessed through the Web. With the coming convergence of television, telephone, wireless communication, and high-speed computing, future applications of the Internet are without exaggeration limited only by human imagination. The growth of the Internet has surpassed even the most optimistic original estimations.

The impact on commerce and society of the Internet has been profound, enlarging reaches and erasing geographic barriers. Through the Internet, a student in a small village in India can read the *New York Times* or watch BBC news in video. Investors from many parts of the world can access real-time information and trade U.S. stocks as if they were on Wall Street in person. Companies can reach millions of customers in a way they never could before without building brick-and-mortar retail stores. Behind all this is the ability of the Internet to transmit information, with its foundation of common standards, at the speed of light to every nook and cranny of the world.

The growth of the Internet is rooted not just in its potential as a new communication channel that connects traditional businesses, institutions, and individuals. Rather, with the digital technology it brings together, the Internet is revolutionizing and reorganizing the structure of every single business. To succeed in this new information age, companies have to rethink their business strategies and operations. Companies begin to realize that it is not enough just to set up web pages with fancy graphics in order to be successful in e-business. Companies will have to create new business models and processes in order to take full advantage of the convergence of communication and computer technologies. Although open communication standards have created greater efficiencies in the global world of commerce, the digital economy will *redefine* the world of commerce.

In traditional commerce, we have physical stores, physical products, and physical processes. In the age of electronic commerce, each of these elements is rapidly being digitized (Figure 1.1). In the financial services industry, for instance, investors traditionally receive information such as prospectuses and transaction confirmations through the mail, and transactions are often settled by using checks. All these are changing quickly. Soon, an investor will be able to access online investment information, track his or her investment portfolio and historic transactions through the net, and transfer funds between banks and his or her broker's account electronically, foregoing the agony of waiting for the snail mail, reading the delayed transaction report, and sending paper checks. Digitizing those processes is relatively easy because financial products such as stocks, loans, and insurance plans are in effect nothing but digital notations stored at the customers' custodian accounts. Every single financial business process, ranging from product development and production to marketing, sales, customer

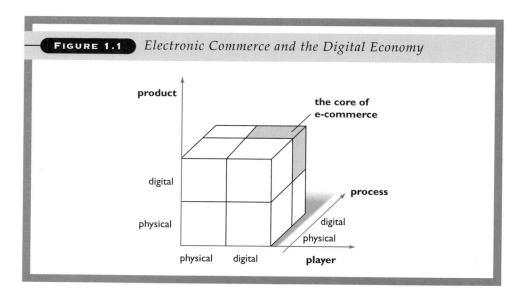

FIGURE 1.1   *Electronic Commerce and the Digital Economy*

support, trading, and settlement, can be digitized by using computers and communication networks. With this in mind, companies can bypass all traditional physical processes and develop bold new business models. In the next few sections, and throughout this book, we take a look at the world's fast-changing financial services industry and the direction it is evolving.

1.2 FINANCIAL MARKETS IN THE 21ST CENTURY: FUNCTIONS AND INSTITUTIONS

1.2.1 A Functional Analysis

Today, the landscape of the financial services industry is rapidly changing. Technology, new regulatory environment, and increasing globalization are three of the reasons for these changes. Nevertheless, the underlying functions of financial systems have changed little. The six fundamental functions of financial systems as defined by Crane *et al.*[3] are as follows:

1. Providing price information to help coordinate decentralized decision making in various sectors of the economy. For example, interest rates and asset pricing are the information that individuals and firms rely on to

make decisions regarding spending and investment. However, not everybody has equal access to this market information.

2. Pooling resources to invest in large-scale projects. The resource pooling function applies both to businesses and to individual households. Security markets and other financial intermediaries, such as banks and mutual fund companies, provide the function of aggregating resources from individuals and investing in various securities, such as stocks, bonds, and mortgage-backed securities.

3. Transferring resources across time and space. This function is related to resource pooling: By aggregating resources, it becomes possible for financial intermediaries to transfer resources across time and space. For families or individuals, the financial services industry provides the means to allocate household consumption and investment efficiently throughout the life cycle. On a global scale, financial markets supply emerging markets with capital from developed nations and regions. Banks, insurance companies, pension funds, and mutual funds are all involved in the function of matching the providers of financial resources with those who need those resources.

4. Managing risk. With rapid globalization, companies are being exposed to new risks. A well-developed financial system should facilitate an efficient allocation of risks that is beneficial both to individuals and society as a whole. Financial innovations such as derivative securities and securitization have provided different low-cost ways for individuals and firms to manage their risk.

5. Clearing and settling payments to facilitate the exchange of goods, services, and assets. In today's global economy, the payment system that facilitates trade and exchange among firms and consumers in both product markets and capital markets is of crucial importance. Payment and settling services are primarily provided by banks and are typically regulated by a central bank as an important adjunct to implementing monetary policy. Banks provide this service with cash, checks, credit cards, and wire transfers. Because a payment system involves both cost and risk, an efficient payment and clearing system is critical to the maintenance of an efficient market economy.

6. Dealing with incentive problems. The incentive problem arises because parties in the market have asymmetric information and cannot observe the actions of one another. This situation is sometimes referred to as "adverse selection" or "moral hazard" problems. Such problems could result in market breakdowns when parties with asymmetric information fail to reach mutually beneficial transactions. Banks solve incentive problems by providing intermediary functions between lenders and borrowers because banks are typically more efficient at evaluating and monitoring borrowers. This efficiency is acquired over time as the institution accumulates knowledge and expertise.

These six functions provide a framework to study the institutions that make up the fast-changing financial services industry. As technology and customer needs change, a new institutional structure that functions more efficiently will emerge. Instead of simply cementing the structure of existing financial institutions and creating their equivalents on the Internet, the functions performed by today's institutions will be "unbundled" and "rebundled" to form new institutions that will improve the performance of the financial system.

1.2.2 Institutions

Financial institutions differ from ordinary organizations in that they provide intermediary services to buyers and sellers. Although they do not produce tangible products, financial institutions are critical to the economy because they define the organization of the market and the "rules of the game" in the marketplace. An efficient financial system is essential to the success of the modern economy. As seen above, financial institutions affect the performance of the overall economy by providing information, matching buyers and sellers, and reducing uncertainties and risks.

The financial system, generally referred to as financial markets, comprises both capital markets and financial intermediaries. Capital markets include the money, fixed-income, and equity markets, along with the new and growing derivative markets. These markets match buyers and sellers and provide a price discovery function for the traded instruments. Financial intermediaries, which include commercial banks, investment banks, mutual fund companies, brokers, dealers, and insurance companies, also provide some of the functions of capital markets (Figure 1.2). Typically, investors do not participate in capital markets directly but rather through financial intermediaries such as brokerage firms or mutual fund companies. Although capital markets, as represented by organized exchanges, provide a central place to aggregate buyers and sellers, financial intermediaries play another important role in financial markets by providing customized products and services. Financial intermediaries, such as dealers and brokers, can sell the same financial securities to fund surplus units (buyers) that they have purchased from fund deficit units (sellers). Intermediaries facilitate the trade in this process, but they can also be asset transformers. Banks, for example, purchase loans from borrowers and sell to bank customers in the completely different form of deposits.

Although many financial institutions differ in terms of their core businesses, they are increasingly engaging in services traditionally offered by others. For example, mutual fund companies, which traditionally only offer asset management services, now provide money market funds and check-writing services to their investors, competing with banks for cash deposits. Insurance and reinsurance companies face competition from exchanges markets. For example, insurance companies can now use derivative instruments traded in organized exchanges to protect from excessive losses due to natural disasters instead of having to purchase reinsurance contracts directly from reinsurance companies.

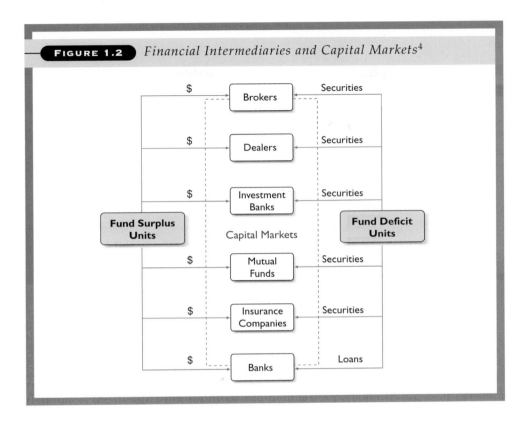

FIGURE 1.2   *Financial Intermediaries and Capital Markets*[4]

These ongoing changes have made it difficult to pigeonhole financial functions into the narrowly defined roles traditionally ascribed to a particular type of financial institution. We expect to see even more fundamental changes in the organization of financial markets driven both by new technology and financial innovations.

Information technology is a significant driving force in this process of institutional change. Advanced communication technologies have linked the world more closely together. Financial information is available on virtually everyone's desktop computer all over the world, creating the potential for the development of new financial products and new investment opportunities. In addition, information technology, particularly the Internet and electronic commerce, has provided revolutionary ways of developing, bundling, and selling financial products to customers. Therefore, customers can now get better services and pay lower prices. New information technologies have also transformed the competitive framework for current financial services companies, dictating new e-business strategies, which are discussed in later sections and chapters.

Financial innovation is another force driving the shakeup in the current financial institutional structure. Broadly speaking, financial innovation not only includes the creation of new types of securities but also the development and evolution of new financial organizations.[5] Thus, institutional change is an integral part of the financial innovation process. This process of financial innovation has led to revolutionary changes in the world's financial system. We have new financial instruments such as swaps, options, futures, and mortgage-backed securities. We have seen the development of electronic fund transfer systems, fully automated trading and execution systems such as the Toronto Stock Exchange's CATS (Computer Assisted Trading System), and other recent Web-based trading systems. An advanced understanding of economics, finance, and the mechanics of markets, together with information technology innovations, have all contributed to the profound development in asset securitization, pricing, and trading mechanisms. The financial innovation process improves market performance by establishing a more transparent market and lowering transaction costs.

1.3 DIS-INTERMEDIATION OR RE-INTERMEDIATION?

Driven by technology and financial innovation, the institutional structure of the global financial markets is experiencing profound transformations. The Internet, with its capability to communicate at the speed of light and the wealth of information available, has become a global electronic marketplace where individuals can meet and make exchanges. The question from the financial markets' standpoint is whether buyers and sellers will meet directly. Are we going to have a dis-intermediation process that will eliminate all the middlemen? In our opinion, the functions of financial intermediaries will still be required even in the digital age and will thus remain despite the changes in technology and institutions. However, the Internet will certainly reduce the number of intermediaries and change the organizational structure of the traditional intermediaries. We call this a re-intermediation process.

The current institutional structure will be greatly reshaped with the advent of the Internet, and more efficient intermediaries will emerge. Compared with traditional markets, the Internet marketplace resembles the perfect markets that economists talk about, in which a large number of buyers and sellers can access the market without geographic barriers. In this scenario, the price is determined more efficiently by the direct interactions between buyers and sellers. However, the dis-intermediation process is unlikely to happen because there are certain fundamental functions that can only be performed by intermediaries rather than by the market itself.

First, intermediaries serve the function of quality guarantors; they reduce the risks and uncertainties in the marketplace. Although data and information are available over the Internet, a large number of consumers are unable to discover the quality of a product if the quality evaluation is complicated and requires special expertise. Besides, the time and effort required for the quality research may be too costly for an individual consumer. For example, research on individual stocks requires enormous expertise and continuous monitoring, both of which are costly. Therefore, it is often more cost-effective for investors to consult professional sources to get the information they need. Individuals are assured of the truthfulness and quality of the information they get from companies with superior reputations, such as Citicorp, CNN, and *New York Times*.

Second, intermediaries provide authentication, clearing, and settlement services to ensure smooth electronic market transactions. This is crucial because individuals can easily change their identities in cyberspace, which lacks an established way to verify their physical identities. How then can one authenticate the identities of both buyers and sellers? How can one subsequently collect the payment from the buyer and transfer the financial assets from the seller to the buyer? These are digital logistics that have to be dealt with for the market to function properly. It is logical to link the business of authentication with the clearing and settlement process. A market intermediary such as a pure certification company, a brokerage firm, or a bank can serve as a certification authority that issues digital certificates for its customers. Using modern encryption technologies, digital certificates can ensure the identity and integrity of the transactions submitted to the marketplace.

The third function of the intermediary is related to the market's inability to function properly when there is a large imbalance in supply and demand. Market imbalances occur from time to time, resulting in dramatic fluctuation of market prices. This calls into account the issue of market liquidity. Generally, the larger the market size, the better the liquidity. In some less liquid markets, buyers and sellers will have to pay a high price if they want to trade immediately. Intermediaries such as dealers can provide liquidity to the market and guarantee the continuous fluctuation of market prices.

Even with a near-perfect market, financial intermediaries will clearly still be necessary to perform the aforementioned functions. But who the dominant players will be remains to be seen. Will traditional financial intermediaries survive this transformation? What are winning strategies for financial services companies in this Internet age? We discuss these issues in the following sections and throughout the book. The discussions so far have been at the industrial level and are from the perspective of market welfare—that is, how to better match the buyers and sellers and facilitate efficient transactions. Financial firms are the fundamental components in this dynamic change. To better understand the organization of financial markets, we base our subsequent analysis at the individual firm level.

1.4 VALUE CHAIN MODEL

Electronic commerce has created tremendous opportunities as well as challenges for the financial services industry. We expect to see enormous reorganization and consolidation in the next few years as the sector responds to this. It is too early to say who the winners and who the losers will be following this shakeup. However, the ultimate success of a player in any industry depends on how it formulates and executes its strategies. In this section, we take a look at competitive strategies as related to traditional firms using the value chain model and then discuss basic tenets of the application of this model to the new technological environment of the Internet.

The value chain model was first described by Michael Porter.[6] According to him, a firm's competitive advantage accrues fundamentally out of the value a firm is able to create for its buyers. It may take the form of lower prices for equivalent benefits or unique benefits that more than offset a premium price.

A value chain disaggregates a firm into its strategically relevant value activities to better understand the behavior of costs and the existing and potential sources of differentiation from other firms (Figure 1.3). A firm gains competitive advantage by performing these strategically important activities more cheaply or efficiently than its competitors. The value chain model is based largely on the physical production and distribution process and describes a firm as a collection of value activities that includes inbound logistics, operations, outbound logistics, marketing and sales, and customer service. This analysis can be done to firms in the financial sector as well.

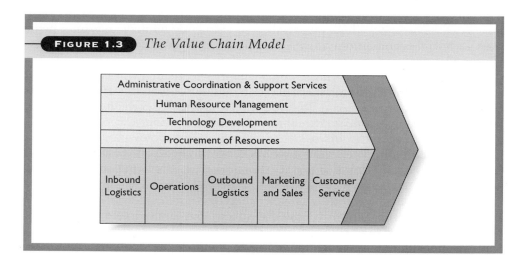

FIGURE 1.3   *The Value Chain Model*

Administrative Coordination & Support Services
Human Resource Management
Technology Development
Procurement of Resources

| Inbound Logistics | Operations | Outbound Logistics | Marketing and Sales | Customer Service |

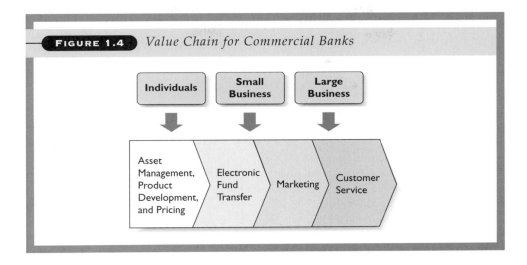

FIGURE 1.4 *Value Chain for Commercial Banks*

Let us look at the example of a retail bank. Most of today's retail banks serve as intermediaries among individuals, small businesses, and large businesses. The core value activities are to aggregate deposits, manage bank assets, and develop and sell products such as loans to individuals and businesses. In return, banks provide financial services to customers that include transaction and account management, bill payment, and funds transfer (Figure 1.4). The banking industry is special, as its product centers on money. Banks have long been pioneers in applying information technology to the management of their business. In the age of electronic commerce, money will be digitized, making this a product to which information technology can readily be applied. In the past several decades, banks have automated their account and transaction management processes. Advances in computer networking and processing have allowed banks to reduce their operating costs significantly, making the largest cost of a bank today its distribution channels: personnel and bank branches.

Further advances in information technology, especially the introduction of private and commercial Internet usage, will change the cost structure of banks even more. The Internet and the WWW are already changing the way banks interact with their customers. In the future, virtual banks on the Internet will replace glamorous high-rise bank buildings. Up-to-date online pages will make paper copies of bank information brochures obsolete. Customers will be able to log into their home banking terminals and check their balances, pay bills, download cash to their e-wallets, make fund transfers, and apply loans. Technology will continue to reduce the banks' operating costs, while providing even better and more convenient services to customers.

Ultimately, the entire value chain of banks will be completely digitized, becoming a truly virtual value chain. Many Internet banks as well as regular banks are now trying to operate in this way, encouraging customers to interact with them digitally. But is a simple digitization process enough for a bank to sustain its competitive advantage through this e-business revolution? The answer is no.

The value chain of banks already faces the danger of being pirated by others. Today, we see an increasing number of nonbanking businesses, such as mutual fund companies and brokerage firms, providing services traditionally offered only by banks. Meanwhile, with the emergence of new financial instruments, capital markets are also taking over some of banks' traditional functions. If digitization means just replacing physical processes with digital processes, this will not be enough to maintain a competitive edge in the new electronic marketplace. In other words, doing the same business cheaper and faster is not adequate. Banks, as well as other financial institutions, have to find ways to invent a totally new value chain to compete successfully.

1.5 REINVENTING THE NEW VALUE CHAIN

One of the early lessons of the Internet age is that change is taking place far more quickly and on a far larger scale than ever before. Companies without a clear Internet strategy will soon wake up to the fact that it's no longer "business as usual" for anyone—no matter how large a business it is. Companies that are just now rushing to develop a Web strategy will find that they have a lot of catching up to do. Reality shows that this can happen to any business. For example, it wasn't until Merrill Lynch began to lose business to Charles Schwab and E*Trade that it started to develop its online strategy. To stay successful in this digital revolution, companies have to reinvent their business value chains, starting from redefining their relationship with their customers and understanding their changing demands, to exploring the scale and scope of the economy that a successful online business model requires.

1.5.1 Customers Take Control

In the relationship between firms and their customers, the digital revolution has unquestionably shifted the balance of power to the latter. With almost perfect information available on the Internet, consumers today can search for products, compare prices, and find review information. For the first time ever, the electronic market has been turned into a "perfect" competitive marketplace, with product prices being driven to competitive level. Internet-based e-commerce is a global marketplace without geographic barriers. If Amazon.com sells a book at a lower price, customers will not hesitate to bypass the local Barnes & Noble bookstore and shop online at Amazon. An individual who wants to take out an auto loan can simply search the net and choose the loan with the lowest interest rate.

Despite the fact that customers are taking control, are we really entering the stage at which price becomes the only factor in the competitive equation? Are we going to see customers switch from one bank to another for a better interest rate every few days? Answering yes would grossly oversimplify the new marketplace. In such a scenario, price resulting from competition would converge to marginal cost, and firms would not be able to make any profits. In reality, it will be far more complex.

For standard products price will always be an important factor in competition. However, online companies have to compete in areas beyond product price, such as service and product quality. For specialized products, such as personal asset management, companies have to provide customers with special value to charge a premium price. The Web can itself be a tool to help them achieve this.

The net provides online firms with unprecedented levels of reach to customers, the opportunity to build a brand name and to find out the needs of the customers. By collecting valuable consumer information, online companies can deliver products and services that customers value. Among the many booksellers on the Internet, for example, Amazon's retail model offering both quantity and quality has been successful. Customers can search millions of books, and Amazon also recommends new books based on customers' taste. In a recent report, repeat customer orders at Amazon represented about 76 percent of all orders during the first quarter of 2000.

1.5.2 Understanding Customers' Value Chain

Understanding customers' needs has always been critical to delivering products and services that customers will value highly. With changing technologies and shortened product cycles, keeping up with consumers is not an easy task. Understanding the buyers' value chain is a starting point. Although the traditional value chain looks at the customer's sale as the final step, from the buyer's perspective this is just the beginning. The purchased product represents the input into the buyers' own value chain. To an individual household, financial products and services provide the financial resources and security that are the start of an individual's chosen future. Different individuals may have different ways to manage their financial assets, and online financial firms have to relate their business to the individual buyer's value chain. Segmenting the market and targeting different buyers with customized products and services is, in effect, a process of creating value for different customers by having a direct effect on each customer's value chain.

According to a recent Forrester research project, there are two types of online buyers—those who are convenience focused and those who are value focused (Figure 1.5). The convenience-focused segment represents 45 percent of online buyers. These consumers pay extra for convenience, buy throughout the year, and are not price sensitive. The value-focused buyers seek high quality for less money and will go out of their way to find it. The products and services

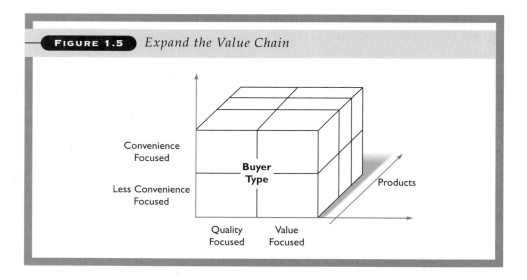

FIGURE 1.5   *Expand the Value Chain*

demanded by these two types of customers are different and require distinct online strategies. This process of understanding the customer better can be a source of competitive advantage for online firms.

1.5.3 Digitizing the Value Chain

Digitizing one's business is the first step in the transformation to the new digital business model. In Porter's value chain model, technology is considered one of the support activities for the core business. In electronic commerce, this model has to change. The digitization process is not just about using computers to support the company's core business (e.g., data processing and automation of certain business steps). Rather, companies have to consider digitizing to be the core business of their value chain. Kodak, for example, is adapting quickly to the realization that the traditional process of developing pictures by using films and chemicals is soon to be replaced with digital cameras that contain memory, computers, and image processing software. This is not merely a process of using information technology to improve the current business; rather, Kodak's business IS digital photography. Shifts of this magnitude represent a completely new paradigm for consumers, as well as for the manufacturers and service companies.

The effects of digitization of business processes go deeper than many of us originally presumed. Digitization affects every dimension of businesses, including products, processes, and even agents who operate those businesses. Turning to the financial markets, let us look at the example of organized exchanges. Although almost all exchanges now have automated systems that allow their members to route orders electronically to the exchange floor, this exists alongside traditional communication methods on the trading floor such as hand signals and telephones. Digitization is slowly changing the way exchanges are organized. On a typical day at the New York Stock Exchange (NYSE), an army of 6,000 floor brokers, specialists, computer technicians, and miscellaneous clerks is required to keep the vast trading floor running smoothly. Recently, the American Stock Exchange (AMEX) and the Chicago Board of Options Exchange (CBOE) have disclosed their plans to offer hand-held trading terminals to their members. In the long run, traders will be able to submit orders through their computer terminals without even maintaining a presence on the trading floor of the exchanges. More importantly, computers will replace humans as market makers. Although fully automated order execution systems have gained ground today, the world's most recognized exchanges such as NYSE still use human agents (specialists) to match orders. Soon, the market will become so fast moving, the rules will become so complicated, and volume will become so large that human agents will become inadequate in performing stock matching. Computerized and fully automated order transmission and execution systems in the exchanges will not only match orders faster and have less errors but also speed up the clearing and settlement process. This will, in turn, lead to a more transparent and liquid market, important factors in intermarket competition.

1.5.4 Creating a Value Web

Merely digitizing one's value chain is not enough. In the physical world, companies are limited in both scale and scope by the constraints of fixed and variable costs in making production decisions. To increase their revenues, companies have to first experience decreased production costs because fixed costs such as equipment and personnel are shared. Later, however, costs increase as it becomes more and more inefficient for companies to push the production beyond the optimal level. Therefore, in traditional value chain analysis, firms have to focus on their market segments to gain competitive advantages. By contrast, companies with digital products have a close to zero variable cost because digital products can be easily copied and regenerated once the initial investment is made. These fundamental characteristics of digital products allow a company that produces digital products with digital processes to take full advantages of economies of scale and scope and create a value web with its customers.

Freed of the above production constraints in an economy of scale, companies can try to capture as many customers as possible for a particular market segment. For example, online financial information companies such as CBS MarketWatch and TheStreet.com will want to increase the number of subscribers aggressively, because each additional user means added revenue with a near-zero marginal cost. The same strategy also works for banks, insurance companies, and brokerage firms. The nature of digital companies is that an increase in scale results in a decrease in average cost. It is therefore beneficial for financial intermediaries to expand their customer base. Many online firms can also reap the benefits of an economy of scale by expanding their markets geographically. Charles Schwab's

U.K. site, for example, has allowed British clients to trade U.S. stocks. Similarly, Ameritrade, through an agreement with Deutsche Bank, launched U.S. equity trading for clients in Germany.

Financial intermediaries cannot only increase the number of customers for a particular market segment but also expand into other market segments. For each market segment, the demand for services could be totally different. Thus, companies could provide differentiated services and could be able to charge differentiated prices. For online investors, value-focused customers who are price sensitive do not expect full financial services if paying only $10 per trade. By contrast, investors who are looking for top quality in services may need a lot of attention and consulting services. The key to success, then, is differentiation. It is possible that a single brokerage firm can serve both types of investors well. If necessary, the firm can create a separate Web site and use a different user interface to serve the needs of different groups of consumers. National Discount Brokers, for example, offers online trading both to retail traders and institutional investors. Different user groups can still share many parts of the infrastructure and expertise that the online firm has invested.

Meanwhile, a company could explore economies of scope by offering a wide range of products and expanding its value chain. Online brokerage firms traditionally only offer stocks and options trading. Once the trading infrastructure is established, however, they can easily expand trading services and include bonds and mutual funds for trading. The online brokerage firm E*Trade is aggressively expanding its products and services into areas including mortgage, insurance, credit cards, and checking accounts. If other financial intermediaries do not want to participate in online commerce, firms such as E*Trade just might end up pirating those firms' value chains.

By exploring both the economy of scale and the economy of scope, an online company can, in fact, build a value web by developing new relationships with existing customers, acquiring new customers, and expanding into new markets. If expanding the current value chain requires a new set of expertise or a significant investment, companies can form virtual alliances and still get the benefit of the economies of scale and scope. As discussed earlier, Ameritrade, for instance, reaches foreign markets through an alliance with Deutsche Bank. Language, regulatory environment, and customer service are some of the barriers that could slow down the global pace of existing online companies, but forming virtual alliances is a growth strategy that online firms could adopt if they want to quickly acquire expertise and a broad customer base.

1.5.5 Acquiring a Critical Mass

The vital significance of the economy of scale and scope makes winning customers absolutely critical to the success of online financial firms. Without a large number of customers, an online company will not be able to execute its strategies in creating its value webs. In addition, the cost of introducing a large spectrum of products cannot be recouped without enough customers.

The necessity of a broad consumer base is also related to network externalities that suggest that the value of a product or service increases as more persons use it. Examples of products with network externalities range from software products to financial exchanges. In the case of software, for instance, a larger number of users means a larger base of compatible software, an increased likelihood of future upgrades, and more and better services. In the financial world, network externalities play an important role. In the stock exchange, the more investors that trade, the better off all the investors are because of the increased liquidity, which benefits all market participants.

An online company's strategy for achieving critical mass in its customer base hinges on a number of factors. First is the ability to create positive experiences for first-time users. To achieve this, the interface design has to be intuitive and simple to use. It is definitely necessary to make sure the online application has all the functions investors could have through regular channels. Reliability is clearly a critical factor. Three straight days of breakdowns at E*Trade in February 1999 was very damaging to the online brokerage. Companies also have to keep growth and quality in balance. Before doing a big campaign to attract more traffic, the company has to make sure the network and computer facilities are adequate to handle the traffic. Otherwise, the endeavor will do more harm than good.

As in all lines of business, a positive repeat experience is the key to winning customers' trust and building a good reputation. Research in behavior studies has shown that repeated interactions help to build trust between people. This works in the physical world and is even more important in the online world given the lack of face-to-face interactions. Only through repeat positive experiences can customers develop loyalty to online companies.

Finally, companies need to make sure that they deliver value-added services to customers. For many investors, real-time quotes, fundamental and technical analysis, and order execution monitoring are worth paying a high premium. National Discount Brokers has launched NDB University, delivering electronic investment lessons to its current and potential customers. This company's willingness to go that extra step creates a great positive experience for customers. In summary, trust and added value are the tools that online companies have to use to win and retain their customers. That said, many customers in the online financial markets are, in fact, more loyal than expected. Because financial transactions involve a large sum of money, a discount of a few dollars might not be enough to lure customers away from existing services. Also, the hidden switching cost creates an entry barrier for latecomers. Switching to a new brokerage firm often means learning new interface and features of an online trading system. The incentive for customers to remain loyal makes acquiring customers all the more critical to an online financial services company.

But how far should online financial firms go to win customers? It has been reported that some online firms are even willing to take an initial loss to get customers. Online brokerage firms including E*Trade, Charles Schwab, and Ameritrade spent hundreds of millions of dollars on advertising. Customer acquisition costs skyrocketed above $300 per customer account. Depending on the offer,

10,000 frequent-flier miles, $75 cash, or hotel frequent-stay points can be received when opening an account at E*Trade. Companies are clearly looking beyond the immediate financial gain and are focusing on the lifelong value of customer loyalty. Much like Microsoft's strategy of offering its Office software to college students for $5, companies assume that they can more than recover from the initial losses if they can keep the customers and do follow-on sales.

1.5.6 Mass Customization

Traditionally, there is a tradeoff between the level of customization and the size of customer base. With a large number of customers, companies have to rely on mass production to serve their customers. Companies deliver products based on average consumer statistics. Customers may not get a 100 percent customized product, but they don't pay an outrageous price either. The digital economy may well change this scenario for the better. The extraordinary characteristics of digital products and digital processes makes it possible for companies to develop fully customized products and still charge a mass production price. *The Wall Street Journal* interactive version, for example, customizes its contents based on the reader's preferences. The user specifies a set of categories that interest him or her. Every time the reader browses the paper, the server will automatically deliver news and stories belonging to the preselected categories. Internet portals such as Excite and Yahoo! also deliver fully customized pages to their registered customers. In an online financial market, with no brochure to print and no regular paper mail to send, customer account information could be updated instantly. Using this valuable customer information, companies will aim to provide individualized, short-lived, information-rich goods and services of endless variety—the ultimate level of customization.

One technique that is frequently used in customization is called bundling. In the physical world, products are often bundled and sold together. A newspaper is a bundle of all sorts of news and other information. Cable services bundle different programs together and provide subscription service to users. Banks try to cross-sell a bundle of financial products such as loans and saving plans to their customers. Traditional bundle services offer limited choices to consumers because precise information about users is not typically available in a timely fashion and the technology to provide customized services on demand is not sufficiently developed. Thus, the traditional bundling mechanism is a flat-fee subscription model. Users receive basically the same product and dispose of those parts that they do not need.

In the digital world, although the subscription model may still work, more sophisticated and specified bundling techniques are now feasible. Users are able to specify the elements they want, and companies can meet the demand and offer customized products at customized prices. Convenience-focused customers often look for a one-stop solution to their financial needs that include banking, insurance, and financial planning. Financial companies can have a spectrum of products and be ready to provide a bundled service package to the user. The result is increased business and customer loyalty.

1.6 FINANCIAL SUPERMARKETS

Offering a one-stop solution to customers is becoming an interesting business model for financial services firms. To customers, it is convenient to have one firm to manage all the customers' financial needs. Customers can easily manage their assets from one source and easily transfer funds from one source to another. To companies competing in the Internet environment, customer acquisition and retention are the key to success. As firms establish their brand names, they can try to retain customers by offering customized bundled services to individual customers and take full advantage of economy of scale and economy of scope. Here, we discuss two of these companies that try to create a financial supermarket over the Internet.

1.6.1 E*Trade

Founded by Christos M. Cotsakos, a former executive at A.C. Nielsen Inc., E*Trade Group (Figure 1.6) has become one of the most recognizable names in online trading since it started to offer Internet trading in February 1996. The company's initial aim was to replicate a full-service brokerage firm's spectrum of services electronically without using human brokers or building branches. Currently, the company is moving aggressively away from just providing discount trading. It now aims to become the premier financial center on the Internet. The following are some of the businesses in which E*Trade is involved:

- *Equity and Derivative Trading.* E*Trade provides discount trading to both individual and institutional traders.
- *Online Information.* It provides headline and financial news, commentary, and market analysis to its users. Most of the information is free to its members. For a fee, users can also get access to professional reports and analysis.
- *Bond Trading.* E*Trade is one of the few brokerage firms that offer fixed-income trading to individual investors. Customers can trade U.S. Treasury securities and corporate and municipal bonds. This was, in effect, the first time individual investors could trade fixed-income securities online.
- *Internet IPO or E*Offering.* E*Trade users have access to initial public offerings (IPO). Part of E*Trade's strategy is to become a full-service Internet investment bank that will underwrite IPOs and make them available directly to online traders.

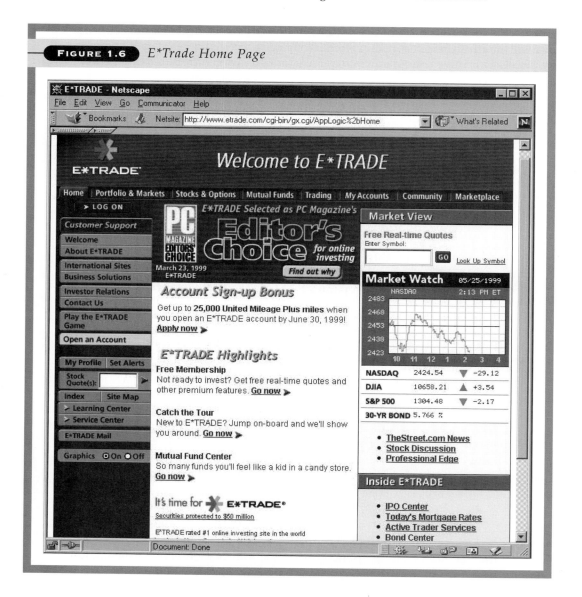

FIGURE 1.6   *E*Trade Home Page*

- *Online Exchange.* E*Trade is a partner in the recently forged International Securities Exchange, the first fully electronic options exchange combining electronic trading with an auction mechanism. It has also acquired a 25 percent voting interest in Archipelago, an electronic communication network (ECN) for Nasdaq stocks.

- *Online Mortgage.* E*Trade owns part of E*Loan, through which it offers online mortgage services.
- *Insurance.* Through InsWeb, E*Trade offers auto, life, and home insurance to its members.
- *Mutual Funds.* E*Trade is also entering the asset management business with plans to launch a series of no-load mutual funds, including Standard and Poor (S&P) 500 Index Fund and money market funds.
- *Online Banking.* E*Trade has acquired TeleBanc, an electronic banking pioneer. The deal was the first combination of an e-broker with an Internet bank.

In a short period, E*Trade has successfully become a major player in online financial services and no longer likes to be categorized as a brokerage firm. It aims to become a financial portal where consumers can execute any kind of financial transaction. Other online brokerage firms are hesitantly pushing in the same direction. Charles Schwab, the largest online brokerage firm, views its business as an online trading and information provider. Unlike E*Trade and other online brokers, Schwab does not accept online advertisement from other parties. Although online advertisement has become a new trend for almost all the online brokerage firms, E*Trade is more revolutionary in adopting innovative strategies to become a true leader in online finance. E*Trade's strategy has been rooted in the following two fundamental principles of critical mass and expansion of scale and scope.

Critical Mass Is Crucial

Right after E*Trade announced that it had more than 1 million account holders in April 1999, its stock soared almost $16 in one day. The online brokerage firm actually spends three times more on marketing than on technology to attract new customers. Executives at E*Trade are fully aware of the importance of building a brand name in cyberspace and reaching a critical mass. It has alliance programs with United Airlines that offer up to 25,000 miles for opening a new account. It also provides free accounts to Internet users and lets them "test drive" the trading system and E*Trade's trading game. To increase its visibility on the net and attract more online users, E*Trade has joined forces with Yahoo!, which has agreed to provide extensive advertising, sponsorship, and promotional programs throughout Yahoo! Finance and other related Yahoo! sites. On the Internet, a brand name and a large number of customers are critical, providing an economy of scale and helping to reduce the average operating cost. More importantly, it has a positive network externality, a critical factor in the success of liquidity-sensitive businesses such as exchange services. E*Trade hopes that its marketing strategy will pay off handsomely in the future.

Expanding Business in Every Dimension

E*Trade is taking full advantage of the economies of scale and scope and is expanding its business in all directions. Horizontally, it has quickly expanded its business beyond the original online trading to areas such as online information, mutual funds, IPOs, and exchange services. It provides high value-added products and services to online investors. Geographically, it is bolstering its presence on several continents, becoming a truly global player. Currently, E*Trade maintains services in Canada, Australia, New Zealand, and France. It also plans to launch investment sites in Japan and Korea. Vertically, E*Trade is entering the asset management and exchange businesses. Traditionally, there has always been some integration of brokerage business with asset management. Full-service brokerage firms such as Merrill Lynch and Morgan Stanley provide both brokerage services and mutual funds. However, exchanges have typically been run independently. E*Trade will not only launch new mutual funds but is also forging new ground by actively creating its own exchange market. Instead of sending its orders to exchanges such as Nasdaq and NYSE, orders can be directly matched at exchanges run by E*Trade.

Does scale really matter? On one hand, the Internet and e-commerce have greatly reduced entry costs. That is why startup companies such as E*Trade have been able to grow. On the other hand, the window of opportunities for companies is very narrow. If a small company does not become a dominant player quickly, it will lose its opportunity forever. With a global brand name and businesses spanning the entire financial services sector, E*Trade has solidified its position in the marketplace. A smaller player can try to develop its niche market, but it is becoming increasingly difficult to compete with E*Trade globally. Eventually, with much deeper pockets and a more efficient cost structure, large digital firms will become even more formidable competitors for smaller players.

However, that does not mean success is given. Entering 2000, many pure Internet firms saw their stock prices plummet. Many investors are getting increasingly worried about the profitability of the Internet firms. Even though marginal cost for e-commerce firms could be low eventually, initial business expansion requires a large amount of upfront investment, which could drain the company's cash flow quickly. Flawless execution of a sound business strategy is more important than ever at the time with escalating competition and uncertainties.

1.6.2 Citigroup

Since the merger of Citicorp and Travelers Group, Citigroup has become the largest financial service company in the world today, with assets of $700 billion and yearly revenues of more than $70 billion. It has 100 million customers in 100 countries. Citigroup provides a full line of financial services to its global customers (Figure 1.7), including individual consumers, small businesses, and the global corporate world. Citibank is the leading global retail bank, with more than 23 million accounts in the world. Travelers Property Casualty Insurance offers

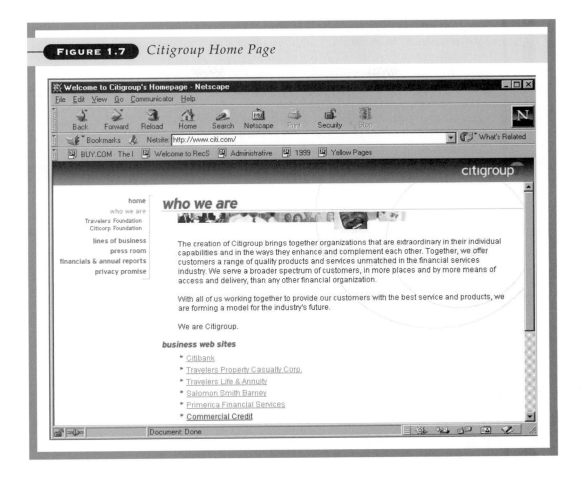

FIGURE 1.7 *Citigroup Home Page*

various insurance services, including automobile, homeowner, boat, and flood coverage. Travelers Life and Annuity provides universal and term life insurance, annuities, and retirement fund management. Salomon Smith Barney is a leading investment bank and asset management firm. The list goes on and on. Clearly, Citigroup has the potential to be the foremost financial supermarket in the Internet.

The company's Internet strategy is absolutely vital to the long-term success of Citigroup. In a business world full of rampant change, if Citigroup does not have a clear online strategy, online financial companies such as E*Trade and Netbank could soon threaten the existing company's core business. The competition between Amazon.com and book giant Barnes & Noble is a good example.

Over time, the Internet can help Citigroup reduce the company's operating costs, making it more efficient. Instead of building branches and expanding physically, the company can use the Internet as a low-cost means of reaching millions of customers using different languages at anytime in any place. For users who seek convenience, Internet banking and investment services have become essential to retain these customers. More importantly, Citigroup could use the Internet to grow and expand its businesses around the world, which is what the merger of Citicorp and Travelers Group is all about. The merger was meant to create synergies between multiple business units, to provide one-stop financial services to individuals, small companies, and large corporations, and to become a true global financial supermarket. The Internet is a key tool to achieving this objective.

Citibank's Internet banking service (Figure 1.8) is already successful. Customers can check the status of their bank account from anywhere via the Internet.

FIGURE 1.8 *Citibank Internet Banking Application*

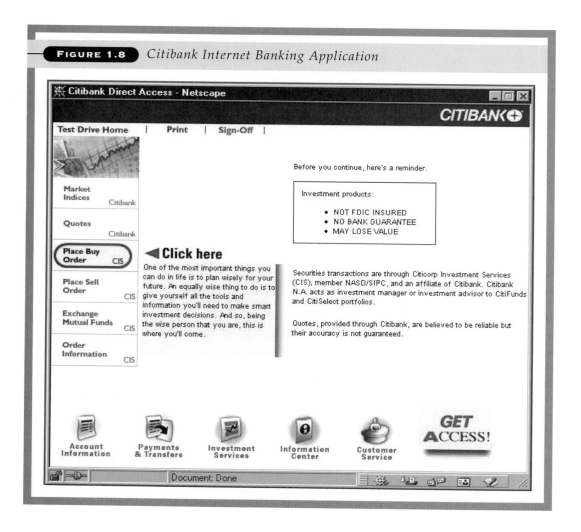

They can check account balances and recent transaction details, transfer funds, and pay bills. With Internet access, customers can also manage their investments by trading stocks and mutual funds. To many of Citibank's customers, the bank's global physical presence complements its net strategy, giving it a current competitive advantage over many of its competitors. First, Citibank can convert its current customers to the Internet. This not only produces cost savings but also provides convenience and more values to its current customers. At the current stage of e-commerce, with many infrastructure standards still under development, a physical presence will provide the necessary services that customers are as of yet unable to get through the network. For example, a business traveler can get his travelers checks and foreign currencies in Hong Kong's Citibank branch. Such services would be difficult for a purely online bank today.

As successful as they are in their own right, do E*Trade and Citibank measure up against each other? Despite its online success, Citigroup has not executed its strategy to its full potential. At this point, it is merely converting its current businesses online. As we discussed earlier, an Internet strategy requires a totally new thought paradigm and the redevelopment of the company's value web. Citigroup's current Internet services have not provided a one-stop center for all the services a customer will demand and that Citigroup can offer. The integration of Internet banking with investment services, insurance, loan, and foreign currency management is one of the areas into which Citigroup has some room to expand. With its full line of products and services, Citigroup already has the resources that new startups such as E*Trade have to form virtual alliances to expand their markets. However, dissolving current divisional boundaries and creating new Internet business cultures could be more difficult for established companies such as Citigroup.

1.7 THREATS TO ORGANIZED EXCHANGES

With online financial firms aggressively expanding their businesses, organized exchanges are facing fierce competition down the road. Financial information providers, full-service brokerage firms, and insurance companies will all have to change the way they do business to compete in the online world. Here, we focus our discussion on the profound changes that are happening in the nation's stock markets.

In the past two decades, financial exchanges have greatly expanded, replacing some financial intermediaries as the institutional structure for performing certain functions. For example, the development of liquid markets for money instruments, such as commercial paper, allowed the money market mutual fund to make major inroads as a substitute for bank deposits. The recent introduction of exchange traded index (e.g., SPDRS [S&P's depositary receipts] and DIA-

MONDS^{SM} [Dow Jones Industrials]) is an efficient alternative to index mutual funds. One of the most important roles provided by organized exchanges is to provide liquidity to the market. As discussed earlier, market liquidity is related to the issue of network externality. The benefit of trading in a particular exchange increases with the number of others trading in the same exchange. The larger the number of traders, the greater the liquidity and the better the market because traders tend to run away from a less liquid market to join a more liquid market.

With the emerging electronic communications networks (ECN) cutting into the market share of existing organized exchanges, the competition in the financial exchanges market has become fiercer than ever. The Securities and Exchange Commission and the Nasdaq market system use the term *ECN* to describe broker-dealer firms that have been authorized to offer automated trading facilities. Although quite new, ECNs already account for 30 percent of Nasdaq's trading volume. The impacts of ECNs and online trading on big boards are tremendous. Recently, we also see record merger and alliance activities of organized exchanges in both the U.S. and overseas markets. In fact, organized exchanges have already started to position themselves in the coming competition. AMEX has already merged with Nasdaq. The market structure in Europe has become almost unrecognizable with many new entry firms and record merger activities. The dramatic shakeup in the securities markets, in our opinion, represents only the beginning or, in the words of NYSE Chairman Richard Grasso, the "dawning moment," of the ongoing revolution in financial markets.

Size DOES matter in financial exchanges, as network externality plays an important role in the market structure. The nature of the business suggests that there will not be a lot of winners and that consolidation at a global level is inevitable. Technology today makes it possible for a handful of exchanges to perform all the trading activities in the world. Linked with high-speed communication networks and supercomputers, these exchanges can have multiple mirror sites all over the world operating 24 hours a day. Traders can trade global stocks and will not notice where the orders are being executed. More efficient matching, execution, and clearing mechanisms will create a more transparent and efficient market. It is too early to tell who the winners will be in this fierce competition. But it is clear that if existing organized exchanges do not innovate and act quickly, their future will not be very bright.

1.8 SUMMARY

In this chapter, we have outlined the future competitive picture of the financial services industry, including capital markets and financial intermediaries. In the future, the functions of the financial system will remain stable while the institutional structure of the global financial system will experience major changes. The Internet and e-commerce will fundamentally change the way existing financial firms do business. The process will continue to reduce transaction costs and move the current system toward a more efficient financial marketplace.

We have discussed the issues of dis-intermediation and re-intermediation. In the new marketplace, new types of financial intermediaries will emerge and perform better intermediary functions. We used the value chain as a tool to analyze the future competitive picture of the financial services industry. In the age of e-commerce, financial services companies have to reinvent their value chains or value web by using digital technology. This is not merely a digitization process of the current business model. Rather, this represents a fundamental rethinking of their business model and competitive strategies. We have outlined the different dimensions in which firms can compete in the digital age. We have also discussed the future of organized exchanges in the global financial markets. Throughout this book, we take a more detailed look at the various financial intermediaries and the organization and function of organized exchanges.

2

ONLINE

REVOLUTION

If you were to prepare a list of industries that have been influenced most by the advent of electronic commerce, financial services would be right at the top. And within the financial sector, trading services such as brokerages and financial information provision have been affected the most by today's pioneers in online services.

As the title states, this book is about the changes that financial markets are undergoing. These changes are twofold: those that affect the surface of the industry and those that affect the underlying structure of the entire business. A close examination of the ongoing developments reveals a much deeper influence than most of us might presume: We are in the middle of a profound transformation of attitudes toward investment. New technologies could potentially change the basic way that we handle our finances and, in the process, cause a fundamental transformation of our markets. By transformation, we do not necessarily mean that we are expecting a complete dis-intermediation of markets. Households and firms will continue doing business with middlemen. It is likely that sometime in the not-too-distant future, we might still be using the same bundle of services that we have been buying for the past eight to 10 decades. But we will most assuredly have to change our definitions of financial service providers, stock brokers, mutual funds, bankers, and stock markets, to name a few, to categorize the nature of services we access online.

As a society of consumers, we have just begun scratching the surface of possibilities generated by the Internet. Later chapters illustrate some of the ultimate possibilities. Some are just around the corner; others, a bit farther away. But in today's "Wild West" of the online world, financial service firms have already been aggressive in exploiting the Internet, with its browser-based user interface, to offer new services to individual investors. This chapter describes today's early efforts in areas such as online trading, online brokerage firms, and online information providers.

2.1 ONLINE BROKERS AND ONLINE TRADING

In an ideal world, we should be able to buy stocks directly from companies and trade these stocks directly with other investors. Ideally, individuals could send their orders to a central location, where all incoming buy and sell orders would automatically be matched. Direct trading between investors as theory suggests can work if the corollary services are in place to support such trading. At a minimum, these "behind-the-scenes" services should include mechanisms in place to take care of credit and collection problems. There has to be a secure way of identifying the person with whom one is dealing, verifying that the sellers really do own the securities being offered, and ensuring that the buyers have sufficient unencumbered funds to pay for the stocks being bought. The technologies to handle these tasks without human intervention are not yet available. The Internet does, however, provide an ideal platform for the automation of this service, as illustrated in the next chapter. Today, we have moved only slightly beyond the traditional friendly neighborhood broker model of yore described below.

2.1.1 The Traditional Stock Broker

Brokerage firms have always done far more than just trade stocks. Ever since individuals first started trading stocks, brokerage firms have handled the task of verifying the creditworthiness of the parties in a transaction. To protect their reputation, they also took on the responsibility of ensuring that any transaction executed through them was settled to the satisfaction of the parties involved. But they didn't stop there. They realized that there was money to be made in making themselves available to the customer, answering his or her questions, and making suggestions for which stocks to buy and which to sell. To perform this task, they employed scores of individuals to answer the phones, do background research, and speak to the investors personally.

To be able to give quality advice (or at least to convince the client that the broker's advice is backed by some superior knowledge), firms have traditionally hired analysts to study company performance and to track various investment opportunities. In exchange for this advice and for ensuring that the order to buy or sell was executed properly and in a timely fashion, brokers have typically considered themselves entitled to fees that could run as high as $500 per trade. The minimum rate at full-service brokers once started at $100 per trade, a figure that rose with the number of shares traded. Dominant firms in the financial sector such as Morgan Stanley Dean Witter, Smith Barney, and Merrill Lynch offer other financial services including investment banking, asset management, and trading foreign exchange.

It is true that since fixed-commissions were done away with in the mid-1970s, discount brokers such as Charles Schwab have been willing to handle customer orders for lower fees, but it was the invention of electronic commerce that precipitated a revolutionary change in the brokerage business.

2.1.2 Internet Technology and Brokerage Services

By empowering the individual, the Internet has changed the dynamics of the relationship between brokerage firms and their clients. In just a short time, there has been a remarkable market change in attitudes. As consumers of technology, we have almost become dependent on e-mail. As Web surfers, we have steadily become more and more comfortable shopping over the Internet. Now, we are beginning to accept the prospect of managing our own stocks over the Internet.

The attractiveness of the Internet as a communication device has led to an unexpected phenomenon. In evaluating their relationships with their brokers, investors appear to have limited their use almost exclusively to the execution service, implying that large numbers of individuals have not cared much for the advice they had been receiving from their brokers. Customers' expectations of their brokers have changed. The friendly neighborhood broker, if such a creature ever existed, is no longer considered indispensable. At most, investors are willing to use brokers to execute trades in various markets, and it seems that certain groups of investors are willing to forsake their brokers' investment advice and trading tips altogether.

There has been a change in the mindset of individual investors. Encouraged by a long bull market, where picking stocks by throwing darts might yield the same results as buying advice from a broker, a new breed of investor has been drawn to the markets. A change in their expectations of brokers has been accompanied by a confidence built up by the ability to trade in a relatively seamless manner. Placing an order has become as easy as clicking a few buttons on a Web browser. In addition, as discussed in later sections, new sources of information have evolved on the Internet, information that is not necessarily of a very high quality but that is surely much better than what was freely available before the advent of the Internet.

2.1.3 Real-Time Access and Lower Fees

Before the advent of browser-based technologies, an investor who wanted to place an order with a broker was forced to either walk to the local office of the broker or call by phone. Then, some time later, a second call was necessary to get a confirmation of the transaction. In addition, the broker would mail a piece of paper with information confirming the transaction. At the end of the month, the investor would receive a statement of his or her account, listing all the securities held, as well as a consolidated statement of all trades and the commissions and fees incurred during that period.

Today, a growing number of brokerage firms are offering Internet-based services that contrast sharply with the traditional scenario. Investors who have

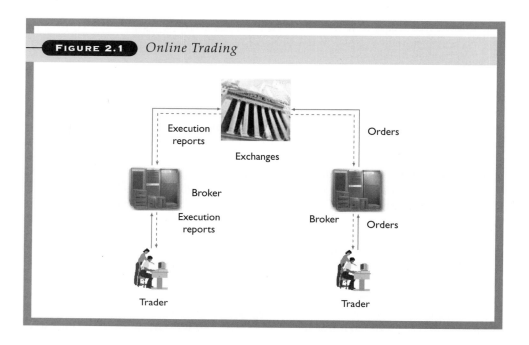

FIGURE 2.1   *Online Trading*

accounts with one of these firms can log onto the Web site of the brokerage firm by using a Web browser (Figure 2.1). Using the typical online broker, investors can

- place buy and sell orders (and receive electronic confirmations as soon as the order is executed),
- check their account balances,
- receive real-time price updates, and
- track the performance of their portfolios on a real-time basis.

Brokerage firms offering Internet-based services can be broken down into two categories:

- Online discount brokers such as Charles Schwab and E*Trade that simply execute orders and settle transactions.
- Full-service firms such as Merrill Lynch and Morgan Stanley Dean Witter that bundle the execution service along with more planning, advice, and personal attention.

Online discount brokers are able to charge lower fees because they offer execution-only service. In addition, they no longer have to employ a large staff to field phone calls from customers. The savings in overhead costs from replacing human brokers with Internet-based communication systems are passed on to investors in the form of lower fees.

As you can expect, full-service brokers, however, charge higher commissions to execute trades. The difference can be substantial. According to an article in *The Wall Street Journal*,[1] an online purchase of 100 or even 1,000 shares of International Business Machines (IBM) would cost just $7.95 at Suretrade Inc., a unit of Fleet Financial Group Inc., and $29.95 at the leading online discount broker Charles Schwab. At Merrill, buying 100 shares would cost about $100, and 1,000 shares, more than $1,000. However, most firms offer discounts to customers who trade frequently and/or carry large asset balances.

The main elements of the order execution, settlement and account maintenance services, remain constant from one brokerage firm to another. With standardization in electronic commerce technologies, it has become apparent that the online brokerage business is basically a commodity-type business. Everything else being the same, the only way an investor could differentiate between firms is with respect to the commissions charged by each, a self-defeating prospect. So, to compete successfully and in the process gain significant market share, firms need to differentiate themselves from their competitors. As in all other early markets, online brokerages have been adopting marketing strategies focused on building brand awareness among the investing community and, in the process, have expanded the size of the overall investing community. They have done this by attracting thousands of individuals and households who otherwise would not have considered buying stock from the stock market. In 1995, online brokers spent about $1 million on advertising. In 1999, they spent about $500 million!

2.1.4 Convergence of the Traditional and the New

In the face of this competition, a serious struggle for market share has ensued between traditional brokers, such as Merrill Lynch and Prudential Securities, and online brokers such as Charles Schwab and E*Trade. The traditional firms have been having a tough time protecting their turf. By the first quarter of 1999, anywhere between 25 and 30 percent of New York Stock Exchange (NYSE) and Nasdaq trading volume combined was initiated over the Internet.

In the process, the strategies to deal with this threat have themselves undergone rapid transformation. Some firms, such as Merrill Lynch, first tried to "talk down" the growth of online brokerages by criticizing[2] them as a danger to the efficiency of the markets in general and to the welfare of the small investor in particular. Unfortunately, this strategy has not bought them any additional market share. Attracted by the low fees charged by the online brokers—$15.00 to $30.00 per trade on average—small investors have continued to sign up in large numbers and, more importantly, have been trading actively. The traditional brokerage firms' hope is that faced with huge losses, investors will somehow realize the "folly" of trading without the hand-holding of brokers. This hope emphasizes a belief that markets are inherently risky and that the self-help policies that have led to the growth of online brokers will result in significant losses to small, ignorant investors.

To compete on price, full-service brokerage firms such as Merrill Lynch and Paine Webber would have to change the way they do their business. It is decidedly expensive to employ thousands of brokers who are paid commissions based on the orders they bring in. Changes in the business model that would make it possible for these firms to reduce their commissions to the $20–$30 per trade range would require a massive layoff of the sales force.[3] Instead, they have decided to join the competition. The five leading traditional brokerages—Merrill, Paine Webber, Salomon Smith Barney, and Prudential—had all announced plans to establish some form of online brokerage service by Fall 1999. Merrill Lynch, for one, has decided to shed its initial inhibitions and embrace the online broker model, taking on Charles Schwab in a head-to-head fight over market share.

Merrill versus Schwab

Merrill Lynch has realized that it cannot afford to ignore the new kids on the block. At the same time, it seems reluctant to desert a business model that has served it well all these years. Instead, the firm has decided to split its customer base. On June 1, 1999, Merrill Lynch announced that it had finally decided to offer a low-price, low-frills online brokerage service. Instead of offering a single type of brokerage account to all clients, it decided to offer a premium level of service to high net worth clients and a cheaper, $29.95 per trade service to others. This price is comparable with that charged by its archrival Charles Schwab.

To take advantage of the no-frills service, a client is required to maintain assets worth at least $20,000 in his or her account with Merrill. The customer is able to buy mutual funds and bonds, as well as get access to investment research from Merrill. The premium service does not charge a per-trade fee. Rather, customers who sign onto this service pay a minimum fee of $1,500 per year and are eligible to make an unlimited number of trades, either over the Internet or by calling a broker. Any fees over the minimum are assessed as a percentage of assets maintained in the Merrill account. By creating a low-cost product, Merrill has effectively created a business that competes head-on with the likes of Schwab, E*Trade, and all the other online brokers. It is tempting to speculate on why the firm did not simply set up a new subsidiary to handle this service. The answer is simple: By offering a low-cost service alongside a premium one, the firm would run the risk of cannibalizing customers from the latter.

It is interesting to note how the stock market reacted to this news. On June 1, 1999, investors sold the Merrill stock, resulting in a 10 percent drop in its price. The concern seems to have been that, assuming Merrill does not change its labor-intensive production process, the cut in prices would lead to lower margins and thus a substantial drop in profitability. In 1998, Schwab moved ahead of Merrill to become the largest brokerage firm in terms of market capitalization. Schwab is a relatively pure intermediary. For example, it does not offer the hugely profitable underwriting service in which Merrill is a leader. The simple fact that a firm such as Charles Schwab, that is basically a straightforward broker offering a basket of transaction services and does not risk its capital in areas such as underwriting, is valued higher must cause considerable heartburn to the management at Merrill.

Schwab, once again, has not been treading water. While Merrill Lynch is entering the low-end online trading and brokerage market, Schwab is moving to the high-end segment. In January 2000, Schwab announced an agreement to acquire U.S. Trust, one of the nation's leading wealth management firms. The deal will enable Schwab to become a full-service brokerage firm that can cater to both wealthy clientele and low-maintenance online investors. Clearly, the Internet has redefined the competitive picture of the brokerage industry. There appears to be a convergence of brokerage firms that were previously focusing on different market segments to a common marketplace, competing head-to-head for both low-end and high-end customers. The glue holding the market together as well as the dynamite ripping it apart is information.

2.2 ONLINE FINANCIAL INFORMATION

The online trading fever would have been impossible without the unprecedented amount of financial information being disseminated through the Internet. Information is wealth, an adage that is never truer than in the financial world. The Internet has put into motion a veritable revolution: Information that previously was not available at all to the individual investor is now readily accessible, either totally free or for a fee. This section examines different aspects of the changing business model for providing financial information and research.

2.2.1 The Race to e-Inform

In the days before the Internet was harnessed as a mass communication environment, when a firm presented a report to the financial markets only those with access to expensive proprietary news sources such as Reuters or Bloomberg could take advantage of the information. In the financial markets, timely and accurate information acquired first can easily be transformed into profit. Individual investors could always get the same information from the next day's *New York Times* or *Wall Street Journal*. But by then the institutional investors would have completely digested the news and even taken steps to profit from it. Thus, individual investors could never compete with a professional investor who has access to real-time information except, of course, if they opened an account with a full-service broker and had them call whenever any new information became available. But that service would not necessarily be free.

The Internet is in the process of altering this. A substantial amount of financial information is available at almost the same time as it is broadcast over Reuters, Bloomberg, and other proprietary information networks. An average investor today has access to much more information than a decade ago was available only to traders at some of the leading investment firms.

And It's All Free

Another fascinating aspect of the development of a financial superhighway over the Internet is not just that a lot of this information is available—it's available for free! Web sites such as quote.Yahoo.com, CNNfn.com, MSNBC.com (along with msn.com or Microsoft's Money Central), and CBS.MarketWatch.com fund their operations by selling space for banner advertisements. Some of these sites are very popular with Internet users and manage to consistently rank among the top few highly trafficked sites on the Internet. More "eyeballs" translates into more ad revenues, and the prospect of higher revenues in turn translates into higher stock prices, which reduces the cost of capital for these businesses and allows them to buy even more information and publish it for free on their sites.

None of the sites mentioned above belongs to a large traditional financial intermediary such as a bank or a brokerage firm who has traditionally made money by rationing out information to customers who are willing to pay heavy commissions. Firms such as Yahoo!, which have had little to lose and a lot to gain in terms of advertising revenues, have made this information freely available on the Internet. By doing so they have forced the information services provided by brokerage firms into redundancy. Why call the Merrill Lynch broker when the same information can be obtained through a few clicks at Yahoo! (Figure 2.2)

It Can Be in Real Time

Although stock quotes provided by Yahoo! and Excite generally have a delay of 20 minutes or more, online brokerage firms offer real-time stock price information to their online account holders. The online brokerage firm E*Trade has gone even further and, in exchange for a small amount of personal information, provides free real-time stock quote information to all—even to those who are not customers of E*Trade (Figure 2.3). Although a mere real-time stock quote does not mean retail investors can access the same amount of real-time information as institutional investors can see, the Internet will soon change this as well.

2.2.2 Information and Market Democracy

Online information, taking advantage of technology-driven lower costs, has actualized a new reality of the financial marketplace. The use of electronic systems to execute trades has reduced the cost of trading stocks in U.S. equity markets. For a long time now, economists have predicted that holding everything else constant, lower transaction costs alone will in time result in higher trading volumes.

FIGURE 2.2   *Quote Information from Quote.Yahoo.com*

Symbol	Ask	Day's Range	Bid	Last Trade		Change		Volume	P/E	52-week Range
^DJI	N/A	10199.98 - 10517.75	N/A	Feb 18	**10219.52**	-295.05	-2.81%	N/A	N/A	9190.94 - 11750.28
^IXIC	N/A	4404.61 - 4564.45	N/A	Feb 18	**4411.74**	-137.18	-3.02%	N/A	N/A	2235.19 - 4564.45
^NYA	N/A	585.44 - 601.26	N/A	Feb 18	**586.67**	-14.59	-2.43%	N/A	N/A	572.38 - 663.50
^SPC	N/A	1345.29 - 1388.26	N/A	Feb 18	**1346.09**	-42.17	-3.04%	N/A	N/A	1216.03 - 1478.38
ARBA	229	221 - 236 $^1/_2$	224	Feb 18	**229**	+2 $^{13}/_{16}$	+1.24%	1,958,700	N/A	30 $^1/_2$ - 236 $^1/_2$
AZX	N/A	7 $^3/_4$ - 8 $^1/_8$	N/A	Feb 18	**8 $^1/_{16}$**	$-^1/_8$	-1.53%	187,800	19.97	6 $^9/_{16}$ - 24 $^1/_4$
BVSN	180 $^1/_4$	179 $^1/_4$ - 187	180	Feb 18	**179 $^1/_2$**	-3 $^1/_4$	-1.78%	1,817,600	830.68	13 - 193
CMRC	180 $^1/_8$	176 $^7/_8$ - 187 $^7/_8$	177 $^3/_8$	Feb 18	**179**	-10 $^1/_4$	-5.42%	1,946,400	N/A	8 $^{13}/_{16}$ - 331
CPQ	N/A	25 $^1/_{16}$ - 26 $^5/_{16}$	N/A	Feb 18	**25 $^1/_4$**	-1 $^{13}/_{256}$	-4.00%	11,357,500	77.36	18 $^1/_4$ - 44 $^7/_{16}$
DELL	40	39 $^{11}/_{16}$ - 40 $^1/_2$	39 $^{15}/_{16}$	Feb 18	**40 $^1/_{16}$**	$-^5/_8$	-1.54%	28,484,200	66.70	31 $^3/_8$ - 53 $^{15}/_{16}$
ITWO	146 $^3/_4$	137 $^1/_8$ - 157 $^1/_2$	145	Feb 18	**145 $^1/_2$**	+4	+2.83%	2,589,300	1010.71	8 $^7/_8$ - 157 $^1/_2$

Accordingly, the evolution of online brokerages offering low-cost execution compounded by the availability of a large amount of financial information has seen the rapid development of a new class of traders, the active individual investor. This increase in market democracy has spawned immense changes already.

E*Trade and other firms have responded with new products and services. In most online brokerage firms, if a customer makes at least 75 trades a quarter, he

FIGURE 2.3   *Free Real-Time Stock Quotes from E*Trade*

FIGURE 2.4 *More Free Services for the Active Trader*

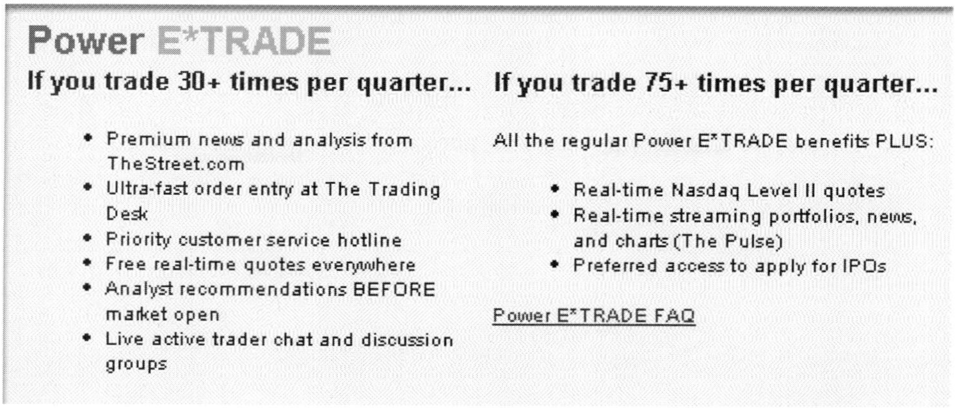

Power E*TRADE

If you trade 30+ times per quarter...

- Premium news and analysis from TheStreet.com
- Ultra-fast order entry at The Trading Desk
- Priority customer service hotline
- Free real-time quotes everywhere
- Analyst recommendations BEFORE market open
- Live active trader chat and discussion groups

If you trade 75+ times per quarter...

All the regular Power E*TRADE benefits PLUS:

- Real-time Nasdaq Level II quotes
- Real-time streaming portfolios, news, and charts (The Pulse)
- Preferred access to apply for IPOs

Power E*TRADE FAQ

or she can get free access to trading tools that have traditionally been available only to large institutional investors and those working at the offices of registered brokerage firms. E*Trade, for instance, has a product called Power E*Trade that is made available to customers who trade actively (Figure 2.4). The Power E*Trade product described in the picture allows active traders to access Nasdaq level II quotes on a real-time basis.

What is so great about Nasdaq's level II service? Well, it includes real-time information about the highest (lowest) price at which someone is willing to buy (sell) every stock traded in the Nasdaq market. These prices are determined either by quotes from market makers or by actual orders from other investors in the marketplace. In addition, the system provides quote information from every market maker who has agreed (with the Nasdaq) to provide such quotes. The level II service provides traders with information about the depth of interest among other traders in every stock traded in this market. In a sense, it depicts a snapshot of the demand and supply schedules for any given stock. Before developments such as this, the individual investor was rather powerless. The lack of access to real-time quote information placed the investor at a disadvantage vis a vis larger institutional traders. But new products from virtual intermediaries such as E*Trade has empowered the small, but active trader and equalized the playing field.

Why is it so difficult to get access to real-time stock price information? Why do we not see the NYSE, Nasdaq, and other markets simply publishing this information over the Internet for all to see? One compelling reason is the value of this asset—these market institutions make millions of dollars a year selling quote and transaction price information to the investment community. If they gave it away for free, they would have to find a different revenue source to make up for the loss. A second, and slightly weaker, reason is that professional brokers and large institutional investors might not be too happy sharing this information with the small individual investor. If everyone has equal access to quote information and every investor can observe changes in buying and selling interest in one or more stocks, this will make it more difficult for any single group of traders to profit from it.

At the time of writing this chapter, most securities exchanges in the United States are still nonprofit entities owned by their members (i.e., broker dealers and large institutional investors). It is difficult to expect these guys to vote in favor of any move to distribute stock price information freely over the Internet. Nevertheless, a fundamental change is in the offing. Exchanges around the world, including the NYSE, Nasdaq, and various commodity and financial derivatives exchanges in Chicago, are seriously considering changing their governance structure to for-profit status. This means they too will issue stock that can be traded in the open market. A change in their governance structure is bound to change the business objectives and strategies of these institutions. It is conceivable that one fine day, someone will conjure a business model that will make it profitable for the exchanges to distribute real-time data freely. The profits themselves will come from some other product or service linked directly or indirectly to access to the free real-time quote and transaction information.

An analogy with the personal computer industry is relevant here. A few years back, no one would have dreamt that we would see a day when firms would give away PCs. Well, such a day is already upon us. Someone found out that there was more money to be made giving away the machine for free as long as the customer also buys one or more telecommunication or computing services—or at the least puts up with a scrolling banner carrying advertisements at the bottom of the PC monitor. The firms following this model—not Dell, IBM, Compaq, or any of the large computer manufacturers but new entrants—might prefer the label of an information technology service provider over that of PC manufacturer. They have redefined the personal computer business. Maybe it's time the exchanges did the same. And if they don't, someone else will.

2.2.3 Methods for Sharing Financial Information

Finance theory teaches that financial securities prices reflect the investors' expectations regarding future earnings from that instrument. When there is uncertainty about, say, how well the economy is doing, investors talk to economists and other experts (especially those whose specialty is reading the mind of the chairman of the Board of Governors of the Federal Reserve Bank of the United States) to improve their forecasts. Large investment banks construct huge dealing rooms where dealers trading a wide array of securities can communicate easily with one another.

Using this theory as justification, the century-old, labor-intensive methods of trading on the floors of the NYSE, the Chicago Mercantile Exchange, and others are claimed to be efficient, as traders get to observe the behavior of one another as well as communicate changes in their expectations via rapid changes in their price quotes. By contrast, individual investors are locked out of the trading floors of various exchanges. They are physically separated by distance and thus cannot share their information with other investors, limiting their sources of information to family, friends, and co-workers.

The Internet changes the dynamics of communication: It enables relatively inexpensive and rapid one-to-one communication, as well as one-to-many and many-to-many. Newsgroups and chat rooms where individuals with similar interests can post messages on nearly every conceivable topic are popular among Internet users. Among the most recognized chat sites are Silicon Investor, Raging Bull, and Yahoo! Raging Bull, a Massachusetts-based company, has more than 300,000 registered users and provides stock analysis and free real-time quotes (Figure 2.5). According to the company, it hosts more than 10,000 discussion boards and its members post an average of 12,000 new messages every trading day, contributing up-to-the-minute stock analysis and creating a live online investment community.

Online communities related to finance and investment topics such as Raging Bull have begun to play a significant role in the financial community. Although these online financial information communities are popular, there is some evidence indicating that a lot of the information that circulates there is of questionable quality. A common criticism of various discussion groups on the Internet is that they are not moderated. As no one checks the truth-value of statements made in the messages posted on these sites, individuals with vested interests can easily distribute misleading information. As discussed above, online brokerages are in the process of implementing features on their Web sites that would attract individual investors. Firms such as E*Trade host chat rooms and message boards. As they have an obvious interest in making sure that discussions that occur on their sites are of a good quality, the firms monitor the messages posted on the sites. If they find out that one or more individuals are consistently posting fraudulent information, these individuals will be denied access to the site.

2.2.4 Buying and Selling Financial Information Online

Real-life business success stories give varying examples of new and traditional financial information services earning money by selling information over the Internet. TheStreet.com, for example, is an online financial information service offering news and commentary on stocks, funds, and market trends, both domestic and international. As of May 1998, it had about 14,500 paid subscribers and was adding new customers at a rate of about 20 percent per month—at a price of $100 per year. The story of TheStreet.com is interpreted as an indication of the willingness of Internet users to pay for investment information and advice. In another example, even as TheStreet.com was celebrating its 14,500

FIGURE 2.5   *Raging Bull Creates an Online Investment Community*

subscribers, *The Wall Street Journal*'s Interactive Web site had recorded 200,000 paying subscribers, a third of whom also subscribed to its printed edition. A subscription to their online edition costs $49 per year for those who do not subscribe to the printed edition and $29 per year for those who do. The *Journal* views the Web edition as a tool to widen its readership, both in the United States and overseas.

Stories such as these are significant because making money by selling information over the Internet is a notoriously difficult task. Internet users are used to getting information for free from multiple online sources. Many reputable sites such as MSNBC.com, CNNfn.com, and CBS.MarketWatch.com are affiliated with businesses that boast a profitable presence in the offline world. Some, such as CBS.MarketWatch, have gone public to raise money. These and other online sources, especially the portals described earlier, fund their news gathering and dissemination services primarily by selling space for advertisements on their sites. Even so, providing information on the Internet runs up against the problems of easy replication and hidden costs.

The Hidden Cost of Information Products

Information displayed on any Web site can easily be duplicated. In an example from outside the financial world, when the U.S. Congress released Independent Counsel Kenneth Starr's report on President Clinton on September 11, 1998, it was immediately *mirrored* on scores of nongovernment sites around the world. And given the widespread interest in the contents of the report, there was an incredible rush to download it. This situation reflects the Internet's incredible reach. The WWW has quickly become the primary information resource for millions of users around the world. The situation with the Starr report also indicates the relative ease with which information on any site can quickly be duplicated. In addition to the numerous security issues regarding the conducting of transactions over the Internet, the relevant question here is how one can make money selling something that can be effortlessly duplicated by someone else.

Compounding this challenge is the fact that it also costs money to acquire information in the first place. News agencies employ reporters and analysts to go out and get the news. Financial institutions such as Merrill Lynch pay their star analysts millions of dollars to produce research on various companies. If financial institutions cannot prevent others from accessing their information once it is posted on the Web, they will keep the information away from their Web servers. The implication is that quality information, information that institutions wish to sell at a price, might stop being available over the Internet. Hence, any information that is available for free on the Web would tend to be of little value and would therefore be useless.

The Travails of TheStreet.com

At the current stage of the electronic markets revolution, it is still not clear whether there is a straightforward way to make money by selling information, especially that of the premium variety. One can only look for signals. One such indication is the view investors have taken about the prospects of TheStreet.com. When the firm went public in May 1999 with about 51,000 subscribers and $2 million in revenue in the first quarter of that year, investors bid up the price of the stock. Within a few days of the initial public offering (IPO), the market value of the company's stock had shot up to $1.7 billion. One of the reasons for this increase could have been the popularity of its co-founder James Cramer, a cult figure among online traders, as well as a general premium for stocks issued by companies with ".com" in their name. Simply discounting the James Cramer factor, one could interpret the high valuation in the post-IPO phase as a belief (by market participants in general) that this company could make money selling financial information over the Internet.

By early 2000, the stock was languishing way below the initial post-IPO valuation. TheStreet.com had failed to produce any positive indications that justified the market's faith in its business model: paid subscriptions for financial information over the Internet. And by February 2000, the company announced that it was in the market for a potential buyout. For practical purposes, this news was interpreted as an acknowledgment by the management of the failure of its business plan. Interestingly, to an informed observer, it is still not clear why anyone would want to buy such a business. If TheStreet.com had failed, there is no clear indication that anyone else would succeed in it.

Ubiquitous Information

So why did TheStreet.com struggle to make money? The answer seems simple: Information is cheap. Information is everywhere. There is a stock price ticker on Times Square. Information about stock prices, interest rates, and various indices such as the Dow Jones Industrial Average, the Standard and Poor's (S&P) 500, are presented on every Web site with all the pretensions of a serious news service. Market analysis is available for free at CBS.MarketWatch.com and Yahoo!

But as argued elsewhere, this explanation has an obvious shortcoming: Free information, without being processed, is not very useful. What investors need is interpretation and analysis. Free information can also be dubious information. If someone willingly supplies information about a stock that he or she claims will multiply in value overnight, then one ought to immediately question the source's motive. Investors have begun relying on the Internet as a critical source for timely information about various investment opportunities. But they are also rather wary about the suspect quality of a lot of matter floating around in cyberspace. Even if the source is reliable, the sheer volumes are so staggering that many individuals might prefer to simply ignore most of it. The press reports frequently about information overload. Investors will eventually seek help finding some method in the madness. The future lies not in supplying basic information over the Web, or for that matter through any other media. The key to success lies in being able to sell tools that will help investors manipulate the data. The challenge lies in being able to customize information services to reflect the needs of each individual.

Customized Information and Research

The secret of success is to offer a service that is otherwise not available in the marketplace for free. Information on the Internet is cheap—even free. Unfortunately, there is so much of it going around that it is impossible for any individual to digest all of it or trust it. And investors are not just any individual; they have unique needs. They differ in their attitudes toward risk; some think investing is fun, others are simply scared by investment jargon and prefer to keep all their money in bank savings accounts. Various financial institutions try to cater to the needs of all these different types of individuals. But they have been restricted by the difficulty of simultaneously communicating with millions of individuals. The Internet has made such communication feasible. To convince customers to pay for services, they have to be convinced that they are getting valuable information. If an appropriate product were priced sensibly, any rational investor would be willing to buy it. One obvious strategy that might be considered appropriate and useful would be one that is both customized to the individuals' needs and impartial.

The information gap has been reduced, but institutional investors have superior access to sophisticated tools that they use to analyze all types of data and to make better investment and trading decisions. It seems obvious that it is time these firms shifted their focus toward helping their customers make better use of the glut of information that is available. Large investment banks such as Goldman Sachs and Merrill Lynch already employ "rocket scientists" to mine huge amounts of data and to hunt down profitable trading opportunities. Mutual funds such as Fidelity and Vanguard use sophisticated portfolio analysis and asset allocation tools to manage billions of dollars worth of funds.

The tools large investors use might not necessarily be appropriate for the small investor looking to invest a few hundred dollars a month or a couple of thousand dollars a year. Their needs are simple, their investment goals are rather straightforward, and the amount of time they are willing to invest in exploring various opportunities is limited. This is not their nine-to-five job. So what these investors need are simpler tools that require neither a degree in financial economics nor a deep knowledge of various exotic derivative securities. A few such tools are already available today; most of them are free. Nearly all brokerage firms with an Internet presence, many large mutual funds, and scores of other financial portals provide portfolio management tools. But generic services offer limited flexibility. In addition, many of them are designed to help individuals plan for their retirement savings and, accordingly, are focused on helping them select the appropriate mutual fund. The challenge for the new class of virtual intermediaries lies in being able to supply tools that will allow individuals to select from a wide range of asset classes, e.g., stocks, bonds, derivative securities such as straightforward put and call options, index-linked instruments such as Diamonds [these track the Dow Jones Industrial Average] and Spiders [that track the S&P 500 Index], and mutual funds of every conceivable flavor.

2.2.5 Demystifying Finance

FinancialEngines.com

Financial Engines is a pioneer in the effort to deliver powerful analytical tools via the Internet. The company claims that it provides individual investors access to the same techniques used by large institutional investors. Although the focus remains on helping investors pick appropriate mutual funds (Figure 2.6), its business model can be extended to helping investors allocate their investments over a

FIGURE 2.6   *Financial Engines*

much broader category of assets. It is important to note that in the United States, the number of registered mutual funds is greater than the number of stocks listed on the NYSE and, surely, larger than the number traded actively on the NYSE and Nasdaq markets.

The fact that the firm is associated with a Nobel prize–winning financial economist draws attention to the importance of basing the design of tools for individual investors on sound finance theory. Over the past 50 odd years, economists have spent considerable effort in designing techniques to help create optimal portfolios for investors, most of which have simply languished in textbooks and academic research journals. It is time someone took the effort to implement some of these findings; and as illustrated by Financial Engines, the Internet is an ideal environment to deploy these tools.

Next-Generation Stock Selection Tools

Numerous online services offer free tools that investors could use to research individual as well as groups of stocks. Tools are also available that will help the individual keep track of portfolios of stocks (Figure 2.7). These applications are not necessarily intended to be used to design portfolios that reflect the income, financial needs, and risk-return preferences of the individual. In addition, over time, even if the individual does not make any trades, the composition of the portfolio will change. Prices of some stocks will have risen, others dropped. Such changes can move the overall characteristics of the portfolio away from the original design. Investors need tools that will help them make adjustments so that the original structure of the portfolio stays constant.

Next-generation stock selection tools will require the providers to move beyond business models that involve aggregation and presentation of tons of

FIGURE 2.7(A) *Stock Selection Tools from Quicken.com*

FIGURE 2.7(B) *(Continued)*

data. Investors do not want to spend all their leisure time figuring out the price/earning ratio, market capitalization, price/sales ratios, and other statistics related to any single company's stock. Instead, firms will have to design tools that reflect the design philosophy of automobiles. A person driving a car does not have to know much about the internal combustion engine. A car owner knows that to maintain the car in good running condition, he or she has to change the engine oil regularly and take the car to a garage for all scheduled maintenance. In fact, most modern cars come with their own intelligence in the form of tiny computers that keep track of different aspects of its performance.

The investment business should move in a similar direction. We should use new technologies to design investment planning and trade execution systems that take the chore out of the financial management process. The way to get to this ideal is not by pushing more information toward the individual investor. Rather, the strategy should be to design systems that ascertain the needs of the individual and come up with solutions that can be implemented in a relatively straightforward manner. In a sense, it is time we demystify (and in the process also de-glorify) investing by improving access to financial intelligence. And the best way to do this is to use new technologies to create smart tools that can be used by the average investor.

One such smart tool would offer "interactive services" using intelligent software agents. The interactive part describes the process of encouraging customers to share their information such as investment objectives, timeline, and risk level. And because no firm would ever be able to assemble enough manpower to analyze all this information, software agents would collect the data, process it, and produce a customized service package for each client, ranging from portfolio composition and stock selections to detailed company research reports.

2.3 THE CHANGING BUSINESS MODEL

Online brokerage and market information provision are clearly among the most popular Internet-based businesses today. In 1997, there were only 3.7 million online brokerage accounts in the United States. This number rose to 7.3 million in 1998. By the end of 2000, there were about 13 million online-accounts.[4] Jupiter Communications estimates that by 2003, 20.3 million households in the United States will trade online.[5] As the market grows rapidly and investors become more mature, online financial firms are also expanding their businesses and improving their services—providing chat rooms, free real-time stock quotes, e-mail accounts, investment research and financial news, and portfolio analysis tools.

2.3.1 From Trading to Full Services

As full-service and online brokerage firms converge to the same marketplace, these firms are offering different service levels to customers. As the basic brokerage business is rather straightforward, pure online trading firms are finding it difficult to make a profit by operating on razor-thin margins. In addition, as there are so many new entrants, online brokerages are investing considerable sums of money in creating a brand image, attracting new accounts, and making sure that the new money stays with the firm. Looking to other ways of making money, brokers have become much like bankers. They have found that a customer who might not trade too often but who carries a large balance can be more profitable than a customer who keeps the bare minimum balance but trades regularly.

So, to encourage wealthy clients and also those who trade actively, brokerage firms are beginning to offer premium services. For instance, such clients will be allowed to participate in an IPO that the Internet broker underwrites,[6] just like the traditional broker-underwriters. In addition, investors will have access to extensive research and analytical tools to help them manage their trading and investment strategies. Forrester Research Inc. estimated that the average net worth of an investor who traded online was close to $235,000, and such a person had at least $90,000 in a brokerage (obviously online) account. Firms such as National Discount Brokers start discriminating at the $70,000 level; Fidelity Investments allows those with $500,000 in the account to participate in the IPOs that it distributes. At Charles Schwab, a $1 million balance can even buy you access to conference calls with executives of various companies.

2.3.2 From Broker to Personal Intelligent Agent

As much as brokerages have been transformed in the past three to four years, the changes are just now starting to speed up. New tools are being developed that will allow individuals to access the Internet by using wireless devices. Firms are experimenting with pager-type devices that will alert an individual to any breaking news concerning a select group of stocks that he or she would like to monitor at all times. As wireless modems and hand-held devices improve in bandwidth and functionality, firms can offer a wider array of services that today can be accessed only by using a standard desktop connected to the Internet via high-speed lines. Brokerage firms such as Charles Schwab run television ads that show a person who is stuck in a traffic jam on a highway, contacting a broker by phone to track the market and to execute a trade. The broker represented in the ad is needed today because firms do not yet have a reliable way to push all the required information to the customer sitting in a car, driving down a road, and monitoring the traffic. The challenge for brokerage firms lies in being able to exploit new technologies in a creative manner. The key is to be able to identify investors' needs in an automated way and to provide customized service to each individual customer smoothly.

The Internet has incredible potential to eradicate a large amount of friction in transactions systems and to enable firms to deliver seamless trading experiences to their clients. Over time, individuals are bound to get used to the novelty of automated trading and execution systems. At that point, investors will start focusing on services that will help them manage their finances better. Instead of simply offering fast, efficient execution, firms have to provide tools that will help customers make good decisions in financial management and allow them to access customized information and services from any place at any time. Competitive success will then depend on the firm's ability to help customers access and make sense of relevant information about various investment opportunities.

Several brokerage firms have started to personalize access by creating dynamically generated content relevant to each user. Schwab, collaborating with Excite, allows investors to view the content tailored to their preferences. Firms are beginning to use data-mining techniques to create a profile for each customer so that online firms can develop targeted products and services. There are many potential benefits—increased revenues from crossing selling, higher customer loyalty, and lower management costs. Charles Schwab and Waterhouse Securities have been the forerunners in understanding their customers through data-mining technology. E*Trade, Ameritrade, Fidelity, National Discount Brokers, and DLJ Direct are quickly following suit and adding data-mining capabilities.[7]

2.3.3 Search for Other Income Sources

As more firms enter the online discount brokerage business, commissions have fallen, and it has become increasingly difficult for a firm to differentiate itself from others in the commodity-type business of executing buy and sell orders. Faced with shrinking brokerage commissions, a firm seeking to increase its income can follow the obvious strategy of adding new income-generating services. Given the current state of development of Internet-based businesses, a second option for firms such as E*Trade and Charles Schwab is to attract more traffic to their sites and in turn to sell space on these sites to online advertisers.

This strategy has proved to be incredibly profitable for firms such as Yahoo! and America Online, Inc. (AOL). Their Web sites attract a large percentage of Internet traffic, and this in turn allows them to profit by selling space to online advertisers. These firms, also called portals, are basically Web sites that serve as one-stop directories for users seeking news and services. Their personal finance sites are also popular. Alone they do not offer any trade execution or any other financial service to Internet users. Instead, they offer an assembled mix of news, search engines, chat rooms, and various financial and nonfinancial tools that make it attractive for millions of users to stop at these sites in their search for information. In addition, they allow their users access to various financial service providers (the latter surely have to pay large amounts of money to be on the list of preferred providers).

The success of these firms as gateways, or portals, for financial information is reflected in a study[8] released in July 1998 by Cyber Dialogue Inc., a market research firm. In a survey among respondents who use the Internet to manage their finances, almost 60 percent reported that they most frequently use AOL, Yahoo!, or Intuit Inc.'s Quicken.com. The study estimated that 32.5 percent of the respondents used AOL Personal Finance—five times[9] the number (6.1 percent) that used the largest online discount broker, Charles Schwab. In the same study, respondents indicated that a top criterion in choosing a site is a trusted brand name. Half of the respondents indicated that they referred to more than one site for stock quotes, and almost one-fifth said that they used multiple Internet brokerages for trades. E*Trade for one is surely attempting to garner a higher market share by capitalizing on this trend.

In September 1998, E*Trade launched a financial portal called "Destination E*Trade." Nearly all online discount brokerages such as Charles Schwab and Fidelity offer a wide array of tools and investment information—including real-time quotes, analyst research, charts, and financial news. However, except for E*Trade, these other firms offer their complete menu of services only to those who have accounts with them. Opening an account typically involves placing some cash or financial securities with the brokerage firm. In the quest to become a leading financial gateway, E*Trade has made about 90 to 95 percent of its services available[10] even to those who do not have an account with it. If the site develops a reputation as an excellent source of financial information, it should be able to encourage more surfers to open trading accounts with it rather than with one of its competitors.

Besides spending millions of dollars on advertisements in various media, E*Trade is throwing out freebies to anyone who is willing to register with it and share some personal information. The freebie comes in the form of a highly valued service: real-time stock quotes. Who might be interested in this information?

Well, anyone who is actively considering either buying or selling a stock. Many online brokerage firms provide free real-time quotes to their customers, but some of them restrict the number of quotes a client can access for free. For instance, Norwest Investment Services provides 100 free real-time quotes to its new clients but starts billing[11] the investor for the information after that.

In the financial markets, information is wealth. Portals such as Yahoo! have become successful by providing investors access to information. The quoted information at Yahoo! and various other sites typically has a delay of about 15 to 20 minutes. As the information becomes stale—something akin to reading the previous day's newspaper—these agencies give it away for free. Nevertheless, to be able to make some money, one needs, among other things, access to real-time information. By making this information available for free,[12] E*Trade is once again pushing the envelope. If it manages to steal sizeable numbers of customers from other brokerage firms that are more tight-fisted with sharing information, the latter will soon be forced to offer free real-time quote and price information to all customers. All this will lead to the further empowerment of the individual.

2.3.4 Intermediaries as Facilitators

As online financial services firms such as E*Trade and Charles Schwab quickly expand their businesses, trying to create financial supermarkets, they are increasingly facing the threat of a new type of business model—intermediaries as facilitators. As we have seen, the Internet has already affected the financial markets in important ways: (1) The cost of conducting transactions, whether it is trading stocks or paying bills, is steadily shrinking; (2) the individual investor today has access to an incredible amount of information, much of which has historically been restricted to a select segment of the investment community; and (3) one-to-many and many-to-many communications that were impossible earlier have now become commonplace. Nowhere in this book do we claim that businesses and households will stop demanding financial intermediation services. The implication of all these changes is, however, that businesses and households might no longer demand the traditional kinds of intermediation services from banks, brokerage firms, mutual funds, and others. Instead, convenience-focused customers may choose an online company that offers a full spectrum of services for a one-stop solution to their financial needs including banking, insurance, and retirement planning. Those who do not mind doing research and refuse to be spoon-fed by these service providers will prefer having the option of choosing which services to buy from. Thanks to the Internet, new options have opened up that make it easier for businesses and households to mix intermediation products to create a unique basket of services that better fit their needs. At the heart of their ability to create this unique degree of customized products is the easy access to online research through the Internet.

Businesses and households will shop for services that will help them take better decisions; help them design appropriate investment strategies; enable them to construct portfolios that will better fit their evolving needs; and aid them in handling risks from uncertainties in different aspects of their economic life. Firms that step in to provide these services will find themselves operating more as facilitators. In the new marketplace, the agenda of a virtual intermediary will be simple: Act as a catalyst in the customers' efforts to achieve their financial goals. These firms not only have to provide financial information as do Yahoo! and CNNfn, but they also need to actively compare and rate the available services from different financial firms.

It is not clear that firms that dominate the financial intermediation business today will be able to succeed in the transformed marketplace—unless they change their traditional mindsets and established ways to re-define their markets and their customers' needs. Large institutions such as Merrill Lynch and the NYSE have traditionally operated under a philosophy that they knew what was good for their customers. Right through 1997–1998, senior management at Merrill openly criticized the phenomenon of online trading. They were of the opinion that the increased freedom to trade would extract a huge price of individual investors. They expected the audience to react by flocking back to full-service brokerage firms. They expected them to turn away from online brokers who charged anywhere from $7.99 to $27.99 per trade to traditional Merrill-type brokers who charged from $75 to $200 per trade. Instead, individual investors rejected the traditional view that they like to be spoon-fed by signing up in hordes with various online brokers. Similarly, for the past few decades the NYSE has been trying to convince the world that its human-based trading system is the only efficient way to trade. But, as pointed out in a later chapter, faced with a situation in which its largest customers, large investment institutions, have been routing orders to electronic trading systems, the exchange has itself begun exploring the possibility of offering similar services.

2.4 ONLINE BANKING AND OTHER ONLINE SERVICES

Even a casual perusal of this book reveals a clear bias toward the discussion of the securities markets and the investment process of all the possible financial services. Whole chapters are dedicated to discussions about trading systems and the impact of new technologies on the NYSE and the Nasdaq market. Our reason is that although a lot of work is being done to develop electronic banking and digital payment systems such as electronic money and digital cash, few banks and even fewer insurance companies have taken advantage of the Internet to offer radically new services. Most of the action has been in the securities markets—especially online brokers. This does not mean that the banking and insurance businesses will not be affected by developments in electronic commerce.

Our interest in these services is restricted to the role they play in improving the efficiency of our markets. However, some of the following developments in banking and payment systems are bound to have a wider impact beyond the securities markets.

2.4.1 Banking and Payment Services

A quantum growth in Internet-based transactions can occur only when secure banking and payment services are in place. Today, when you buy a book from Amazon.com or a CD from CDNow.com, you pay for it by using your credit card. The initial evidence is that most Internet users are comfortable using credit cards for making payments over the Web. But this observation ignores the fact that this community is a small fraction of the total number of non-Internet users. Ignoring reasons such as lack of access to the Internet or not owning a computer, it is conceivable that many potential users are not comfortable using their credit cards for online payments. Their reluctance is not weakened by recent reports of the evidence of an active electronic market for stolen credit card numbers. To make things worse, the continued success of hackers in breaking into what were recognized as very secure Web sites might encourage marginal Internet users to rely more on traditional payment devices.

Safer systems involving the use of digital wallets or electronic money (i.e., money stored on a chip connected to your PC) are still in the experimental stage. The next chapter discusses in more detail the role of electronic payment systems in evolving trading mechanisms. The bottom line, however, is that the trend is toward real-time settlement of transactions. Today, if you buy shares of a company listed on the NYSE, you have to send in your payment within three days of the date of the purchase. You can either send a check by express mail or make a bank transfer. Both options are relatively expensive. Many brokers require that you maintain sufficient funds with them to cover the cost of any such purchase, but there can be situations when you would prefer not to leave money sitting idle in your brokerage account.

Payment systems that allow the investor to make payments directly out of his or her "bank account" would be far superior in a number of ways. For starters, it would not be necessary to maintain multiple accounts, and the individual would have better control over the movement of cash in and out of his or her account. Today's check-based systems are also considerably more expensive than most electronic payment systems under development. Although many banks do not directly charge us for use of checks, they do recover it in other ways, typically by paying low (and in many cases zero) interest rates on checking accounts. Finally, electronic payment systems being designed for the Internet will allow transactions to be settled on a real-time basis—as soon as the transaction is executed—or at least on the same day. Faster settlement will lower the possibility of default by the counterparty. Chapter 3 discusses "smart" trading systems that can be implemented only if such payment systems are available.

2.4.2 Asset Management: Everyone's Business

Throughout the financial services sector, we are moving away from business models that use familiar labels such as savings banks, insurance companies, commercial banks, thrifts, savings and loan associations, mutual funds, pension funds, and brokerage firms. As pointed out in Chapter 1, these are terms that describe the functions of financial institutions. It is high time that we stopped confusing functions with category names. Any firm that offers a service even remotely connected to our finances can be called an *asset management company.*

Everyone is in the business of managing financial assets. Banks manage our regular savings; insurance companies do the same. Banks combine checking and other payment services with savings and checking account management. Insurance companies add a risk management component to a long-term savings scheme. The often-confusing array of financial institutions in the United States is largely due to banking and securities regulations dating back to the years of the Great Depression. Some even predate the Depression years. Congress has been rather lethargic in throwing out many of these outdated regulations.[13] However, the regulators, especially the Federal Reserve and the U.S. Treasury, have been relatively flexible in interpreting these laws. A symptom of this is the recent move by Citicorp, a banking institution, and Travelers Group, an insurance and investment banking conglomerate, to merge their operations. For the first time, financial services of every type will be offered under a single roof—in fact, the Travelers Group uses a red umbrella as its official emblem.

2.4.3 Competing Online for Assets

It was argued earlier that online brokerages have taken the lead in delivering new financial services. Nonbanking firms such as Merrill Lynch, Fidelity Investments, and Charles Schwab have begun providing individual investors access to banking-type services such as interest-bearing checking accounts, debit cards, and bill payment. You can even ask your employer to directly transfer your salary to your account with one of these firms. The only reason why you might want to have an account with a traditional bank would be for easy access to ATM machines. Nonbanking firms do not own ATM networks. New firms such as E*Trade do not even have physical branches.

As argued in the beginning of this section, it is only a matter of time before Internet-based payment systems become as widely prevalent as online brokerages. In the battle for our assets, traditional banks face the risk of losing out to more experienced online firms such as brokerage houses. The latter already have a lead in this race. Studies presented by Jupiter Research, a market research firm, predict that online discount brokerages will dominate Internet-based financial activity over the next few years. Reflecting the earlier argument about the convergence of all types of financial services, Jupiter expects that existing banking institutions will play only a minor role in the delivery of online financial services. In addition, online banking will form a small fraction (18 percent by

2002) of total banking activities, much smaller than the 30-odd percent of investment transactions in the form of online trading. E*Trade is leading the convergence pack; it is in the process of implementing facilities that would allow customers to use electronic money to settle transactions. It has even gone ahead and purchased a bank, Telebanc Financial.[14]

2.4.4 Online Insurance

Banking, payment services, and trade execution are increasingly becoming commodity-type businesses. Developments in new technologies make it easier for other firms to replicate a new feature offered by any firm. In a competitive marketplace, firms offering these services will have to focus on consistently differentiating their product offerings from that of their competitors.

The insurance industry has been lagging behind the banking sector in deploying the latest technologies. This could have been due to the lack of competitive pressures within the industry, but this is changing and the Internet is clearly to blame. Insurance companies have traditionally relied on insurance brokers and agents to sell various products, but several transaction-based services are already offering consumers a *comparison shopping capability.* In a fragmented market with low competition, it is difficult for consumers to compare prices charged by different suppliers of the same product. In a non-Internet world, a person trying to buy whole-life insurance, for example, would have to call every insurance company individually. To quote a price, the insurance companies will ask him or her a series of questions about age, income, wealth, physical fitness, and so on. The whole process can be taxing and confusing for the individual. In an electronic environment, however, the individual can simply fill out an online form at a comparison shopping site. The firm offering this service will handle the problem of procuring quotes from various insurance providers. In the context of the insurance sector, the increasing use of such services by consumers is in the process of breaking the chain linking the insurance company, the agent or broker, and the consumer.

The availability of more information once again empowers the consumer. This can potentially hurt insurance firms, especially those with weak and, worse yet, expensive offerings. Most insurance policies are standard contracts. Thanks to the Internet, consumers will be free to choose policies from a larger selection of insurance providers, even without the help of the friendly neighborhood insurance agent. The key to success will be to offer a tool that will help the individual cut through the clutter in a relatively straightforward and meaningful manner.

A consumer survey by Jupiter Research found that 89 percent of Internet users (or what they call online households) already use the Internet to research insurance product offerings. Quicken's InsureMarket (on AOL) and Yahoo!'s Insweb are viewed as serious threats to the insurance industry and its traditional ways of selling its policies.

Some insurance policies are more complex than others. Automobile insurance, term life insurance, homeowners' insurance, and others are products that have relatively simple features and can easily be sold over the Internet. More compli-cated products such as annuities, universal life, and other advanced underwrit-ten policies inevitably require some level of human interaction in the sale process. The challenge for insurance companies is to modify the distribution of such products into forms that can use the Internet to minimize the role of the insurance agent or broker. To the extent that insurance companies rely on insur-ance agents and brokers to sell their policies, they are in a predicament similar to that of the full-service brokerage houses such as Merrill Lynch and Morgan Stan-ley. Information technology firms are busy experimenting with concepts of artifi-cial intelligence to develop intelligent agents. The deployment of such agents over the Internet could finally eliminate the need for brokers and agents selling insurance policies.

2.5 SUMMARY

It is critical to understand the distinction between the discussion in this chapter and that in the following one. The focus has been on examining how the Internet is currently being used to improve communications between brokers and investors, banks and their checking and savings account holders, insurance companies and their policy holders, and mutual funds and their customers. The Internet provides the perfect medium for one-to-many and many-to-many communications. The following chapter looks at ways by which we can harness the computing power that supports modern electronic networks. Specifically, in a trading environment, if investors use the Internet to communicate their buy and sell orders, we could use computerized mathematical algorithms to process these orders. The use of such methods to match buyers and sellers has opened up a total revolution in the securities markets.

It is not sufficient simply to design smart trading systems to support these markets. They call for completely redesigned institutions. The following chapter illustrates what are to be the nuts and bolts of a virtual trading market. There will be payment service providers, settlement systems, a smart market, and most importantly, new tools that will help the individual manage his or her finances in a more efficient manner. Will we see such a system being implemented in the next year or two? Not likely. Change takes place in increments. The goal is to demonstrate the possibilities offered by the new technologies. The challenge is to change our attitudes in such a way that we no longer treat existing markets as sacrosanct institutions. The idea is to focus on the needs of individuals and households rather than on the brokerage firms, banks, and securities exchanges. The latter are all dispensable; the needs of individuals are not.

3

TOWARD A DIGITAL MARKETPLACE

In Chapter 2, we tried to understand the use of the Internet as a communication tool for various financial service firms to deliver trading and other types of services. We looked at how brokerage firms have been aggressive in embracing the new technology. These efforts are significant in that they have made it easier for individuals to trade in stocks and other financial instruments and have brought many new investors to the market. Furthermore, these efforts are crucial in that they are providing households and businesses initial exposure to an environment where transactions take place through electronic networks. However, it is also important to recognize that the online brokers and other firms described in Chapter 2 have not necessarily changed the fundamental structure of the markets. These enterprises are typically based on a business model that uses the Internet as a mere communication tool. They have simply discovered that it is cheaper, and in some cases more effective, to communicate with customers over the Internet than over the telephone. Firms such as E*Trade and Charles Schwab have substantially reduced the cost of trading stocks, but they have not altered the traditional relationship between investors and brokers. If an investor wants to buy stocks, he or she still has to have an account with a brokerage firm and pay the firm a fee to route the order to stock exchanges.

We are nowhere close to seeing the demise of brokerage firms, as some doomsayers have predicted. Given the high valuations of the stocks issued by these firms, it seems as if the markets believe that brokerage firms will continue to survive and prosper in the future. We firmly believe that the functions of financial intermediaries will always be in demand. It is our conviction that investors will continue to demand transaction, payment, and information services—although not necessarily from the same service providers as they do today. In fact, the goal of this chapter is to convince ourselves that the distinctions between brokerage firms, stock exchanges, mutual funds, banks, and other service providers can soon be rendered obsolete. The following pages demonstrate the need to focus more on the efficient delivery of *functions* than on the form of institutions that can deliver the required *services.* In short, it is time we stopped worrying about the survival prospects of traditional intermediaries such as banks, brokerage firms, stock exchanges, and mutual funds. Instead, we should be more interested in figuring out how to use new technologies to design and deliver services that reflect the true needs of households and businesses.

The following pages present a framework of just such a digital financial market environment. The discussion about the functions of financial intermediaries is made in the context of this framework. As we discuss the weaknesses of current institutions in the investment world and their various functions in Section 3.2, it will become evident that such a marketplace may well be composed of radically new institutions. This chapter addresses the first three issues identified in Section 3.2 in more detail—namely, initial public offering (IPO), order routing, and the clearing and settlement process. The other issues are discussed in later chapters. Section 3.3 talks about how the Internet will potentially change the IPO process, making it more efficient and fair to both investors and issuing companies. Finally, Section 3.4 offers a vision of a direct trading and global real-time settlement system for the future. The argument here is that the world will eventually be populated by new types of intermediaries that use technology to act as facilitators.

3.1 INVESTMENT STYLES

The investment process has already weathered an extended period of a radical change. Over the past five decades, there has been a move away from direct investing by individuals in stocks and bonds to indirect investing through various asset management firms such as mutual funds, pension funds, and insurance companies. Once again, change is looming in both the direct and indirect investment processes—this time because of the Internet.

3.1.1 Direct Investing in Stocks

The traditional direct investing process, as shown in Figure 3.1, is characterized by two types of investors: those who prefer to do their own research and use brokers mainly to execute orders and settle the transaction, and others who look to the broker to provide investment advice as well as transaction services.

Already, the Internet is changing investors' attitudes toward their brokers. As discussed in Chapter 2, the advent of online brokers has resulted in a substantial drop in the cost of trading. Various online brokerage firms are attempting to rise to the challenge by exploiting the Internet to package research (or information) services along with standard transaction services. At the same time, traditional

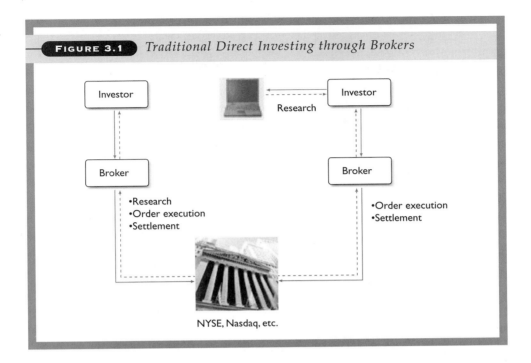

FIGURE 3.1 *Traditional Direct Investing through Brokers*

full-service brokers such as Merrill Lynch are in the process of implementing service offerings that will de-link information services from basic execution and settlement services.

3.1.2 Indirect Investing in Mutual Funds

When individuals invest indirectly through mutual funds, pension funds, and insurance companies, the savings of millions of investors are pooled, and the money is invested in stocks and bonds issued by various companies and government organizations (Figure 3.2). Over the past years, these funds have been so popular with individual investors that the total number of mutual funds available in the United States is now greater than the total number of stocks listed on the New York Stock Exchange (NYSE).

The widespread popularity of mutual funds bears witness to the widely accepted maxim that investors prefer to hold diversified portfolios of assets. However, investing in a large combination of stocks and bonds is a costly process involving research on a wide variety of investment opportunities. The first question the investor must decide is the asset allocation strategy: What percentage of assets should be invested in equity, debt, and cash, respectively? Once the asset allocation decision has been made, the investor has to select the specific stocks,

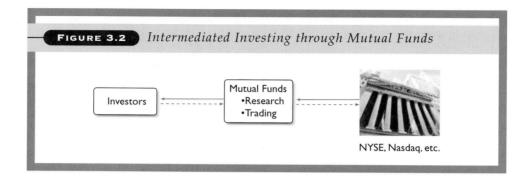

FIGURE 3.2 *Intermediated Investing through Mutual Funds*

bonds, and money market instruments to buy. This could involve analyzing the risk-return patterns of hundreds of instruments. In addition, the investor must form reasonable expectations of the future returns from these instruments.

Having done his or her research and analysis, the investor can go to a broker with a list of stocks and bonds to be purchased. It is here, at the moment of investment, that the lack of true electronic markets will hurt the individual investor.

Markets such as the NYSE and Nasdaq restrict trades to a multiple of minimum order quantities. This means that attractive prices are available only if the order is in multiples of the minimum quantity. This typically is for 100 shares of any given stock. If the investor wants to invest in, say, 20 different stocks, he or she would need sufficient money to buy at least 2,000 shares (20×100). Supposing that the average stock trades for $40 per share, he or she is looking at a minimum[1] investment of $80,000. That's a lot of money for any single investor. In addition, the average household does not have the resources to research hundreds of different stocks and bonds. It surely can be done by subscribing to multiple research reports from firms such as Value Line; but this itself would cost a great deal of money. Clearly, the best option for most investors today is to buy into a mutual fund. These intermediaries pool billions of dollars from millions of investors. Given the large amount of money invested, a mutual fund does not have to worry about the minimum order-size restriction, and the cost of researching various investment opportunities can be spread over all these customers. It does, however, have to cope with the imperfections of the exchange itself, which are discussed in the next section.

3.2 MARKET IMPERFECTIONS

Although mutual funds have been able to provide investors—small and large alike—with a means to diversify their portfolio at an affordable cost, they have not been able to correct for the imperfections of the stock exchange that are inherent in the current systems. A continued reliance on human traders, an inflexible accounting system, and asset-by-asset clearing all perpetuate traditional imperfections that could be alleviated through the adoption of improved technology by the exchanges.

3.2.1 Traditional Initial Public Offering Process

A very special type of trading occurs when a firm first decides to raise money by selling its stock to the public, known as an initial public offering (IPO). The traditional practice for a company contemplating an IPO has been to approach investment banks that offer underwriting services. Those investment banks include national full-line firms, such as Merrill Lynch and Morgan Stanley Dean Witter, and firms that are more specialized in corporate finance such as Goldman Sachs, Salomon Brothers/Smith Barney, and J.P. Morgan. In return for a fee determined as a percentage of the amount being raised, the investment bank will manage the sale of the stock. The services of the underwriting firm typically include helping the client plan the timing of the issue, determining the price at which the shares should be sold, and once the date and price have been fixed, helping to market the shares through its distribution networks. More importantly, in most cases when an investment bank underwrites a stock issue in a firm commitment offering, it is in effect selling an insurance policy to the company: The underwriter purchases all the shares from the issuing firm and then re-offers them to the public, hopefully at a higher price.

The traditional approach to pricing and distributing an IPO, which continues to be followed today, involves something along the following lines. The firm and the underwriter together decide on a tentative offer price. The underwriter then lines up the issuers and takes them on what are called *road shows,* visiting institutional investors to get indications of interest. In addition to these meetings with prospective investors, the underwriter relies on its own brokers to solicit indications of interest from various target investors. Based on this feedback as well as current market conditions, the underwriter fixes the offer price. On the appointed day, the brokers call their favored customers and sell the shares at the offer price. Most brokerage firms restrict IPO offerings to investors who carry large asset balances with the firm and/or to those who trade actively through them. Thus, the shares of hot deals go to Wall Street's favorite customers, most commonly institutions and not individuals.

This traditional approach has come under fire in recent years. A recurrent complaint has been that hot IPOs are priced well below where they end up trading. In 1999, the average first-day IPO stocks had a gain of 68% compared with the average rise of 23% in 1998. This means that companies get less money than they could have from an IPO, and it also means that some of the initial IPO investors potentially make out very well. Anyone who has even casually followed the markets during the past few years would have noticed that the price at which a stock gets traded in the open market after the IPO can be much higher than the offering price. In fact, since early 1997, 90 IPOs have risen more than 50% in the first trading day! There are numerous explanations for this behavior, the most interesting one from the perspective of this chapter being that prices get bid upward by investors who are not on their brokers' most favored customers list.

3.2.2 Order Routing

Although online trading is at the forefront of this Internet revolution, online brokerage firms have yet to fundamentally change the way financial securities are traded. Today, investors still have to submit orders to brokerage firms as they did before. Brokerage firms then route individual investors' orders to the respective exchanges where those stocks are traded. Internet technology has only replaced the human broker or telephone. Why then do we still have to rely on brokerage firms to take our orders to the markets? Currently, brokers still serve the functions of verifying that the sellers really own the securities and that the buyers have sufficient funds to purchase the stocks. To improve the efficiency of the investment process, the next generation of online trading software will have to allow investors direct access to exchanges while providing identities and assurance of the orders submitted by different individuals.

3.2.3 Clearing and Settlement

The next step in the investment process after trading is the clearing and settlement functions that finalize the entire transaction. Clearing refers to the processing of payment instructions, and settlement is the process of delivering securities to the buyer and transferring funds from the buyers to the seller. Let us assume that an investor wants to buy 100 shares of Microsoft (which is trading at approximately $175 per share) and to sell 100 shares of IBM (trading at $150) and would like to complete the whole transaction with a net payment of $2,500 or less. The investor will use some form of electronic payment service to confirm that he or she has enough money to pay for the deal—$2,500 of unencumbered funds—as well as to deliver the 100 shares of IBM once the order is executed. In today's environment, the brokerage firms are responsible for collecting payments from their clients. Banks and other financial intermediaries that offer checking facilities to individual investors simply process the payment when the investor writes a check to the brokerage firm. When an investor opens an account with a brokerage firm, he or she is asked to deposit some money in the account. This money is used to cover any payments that might arise from purchase transactions, interest payments, or margin calls that the brokerage firm settles on behalf of the customer. If the customer does not have sufficient funds in his or her account with the brokerage firm to cover a potential payment against a new order, the broker refuses to process the order unless the customer transfers an appropriate amount of money into his or her account.

Markets in most developed economies today work on a $T + 3$ settlement basis: Securities have to be delivered to the buyers and payments made to the seller within three business days from the date of the transaction. As both volumes and volatility increase in the financial markets, a shorter settlement cycle is crucial to reduce risks to parties involved in a transaction.

3.2.4 Trading on the Exchange Floor

The leading stock exchanges in the world are using what can be considered to be primitive trading systems. Despite the substantial amounts of money they have invested in fancy computer systems, these institutions did not even start to fundamentally change the way they serve their customers until about a couple of years ago, specifically around 1996 or 1997.

A common feature of all the markets remains the need to use the services of a member of the exchange to act as an intermediary who will execute the trade. The NYSE, for example, still conducts all trading on the floor of the exchange. Entry into this hallowed spot is restricted solely to those who are members of the exchange. Some exchanges outside the United States such as the London Stock Exchange and the Paris Bourse did scrap their trading floors some time back (London way back in the late 1980s). But at these exchanges, along with the Nasdaq market, it is still only members who can communicate with each other over screen-based systems. Instead of shouting out prices, they use screens to display the prices at which they are willing to trade different securities. Once a transaction has been completed, they take care of settling the trade—handling the payments and dealing with transfer of ownership of the securities from the seller to the buyer.

Trading on the floor of the NYSE is conducted by a relatively small group of professional brokers. Although the exchange has seen quantum growth in its trading volume, the exchange has not increased the number of brokers[2] on the exchange floor. Given the dynamics of the growth in trading volume and the limited number of brokers on its floor, the exchange has now reached a point at which it cannot do a good job serving the interests of large investors, such as those who place orders for thousands of shares.[3] It has invested hundreds of millions of dollars in technology to support rapid communication of order and trade information between the offices of large brokers (and large investors) and the exchange floor. Although these systems would also be able to quickly transmit small orders from millions of individual investors, the exchange is not equipped to handle orders for small numbers of shares of stocks. This is in part because once the order reaches the floor of the exchange, it still needs a human being such as a specialist or a floor trader to manually process the order. Clearly, it would be humanly impossible to process small orders for millions of individual investors by using this process.

As anyone who watches the financial news on television knows, trading floors are crowded places; and shouting out prices and trading interests can be a noisy process. So traders use hand signals to communicate with others on the floor of the exchange. A whole range of predefined signals are used to indicate whether one is buying or selling, as well to specify quantities, prices, and the instrument

FIGURE 3.3   *The Floor of the Chicago Mercantile Exchange*

being traded (Figure 3.3). It is practically impossible to have signals to indicate every possible order size that investors might be interested in. So these exchanges restrict orders to those quantities that they can "handle."

3.2.5 Outdated Accounting Conventions

The basic design of the accounting systems in the NYSE and the Nasdaq markets dates back to the 17th and 18th centuries. Before the advent of computers, records were maintained in the form of manual entries in huge ledgers. When such systems are used, it is convenient to restrict both prices and quantities to integral amounts. In addition, in earlier periods when stock certificates were actually printed on paper, it was simply easier to issue stocks in round integers— 100's, 500's, 1,000's, and so on.

Fortunately, the financial markets have invested large sums of money in settlement systems that do away with stock certificates. This process of substituting stock certificates with entries in electronic databases is called *dematerialization.*

Records of ownership are now kept in the form of digital entries in computerized databases. In fact, if you want a piece of paper certifying that you own a particular stock, the issuing company will charge you a fee to cover the cost of printing the certificate.

Order Size Restrictions

Restricting trades to minimum quantities makes sense when relying on human intermediaries to execute orders and settle transactions. But they appear incongruous in a world where orders can be executed by using programs running on supercomputers, ownership records are maintained as digital entries in electronic databases, and transactions are processed electronically. By raising the minimum initial investment required to acquire a diversified portfolio to a level beyond the reach of the average household, minimum order size rules raise the cost of trading financial assets. This, in turn, hurts the small investor.

Trading in Integer Quantities

Earlier, this chapter argued that mutual funds are popular among investors as they allow the latter to acquire diversified portfolios of assets for nominal amounts of money. Basically, they provide a service that allows investors to break up indivisible quantities of stocks. However, existing trading and transaction settlement systems still do not permit trades in fractional quantities. These restrictions may be viewed as legacies of ledger-based accounting systems and the practice of issuing certificates of title on pieces of paper.

Electronic order execution and transaction settlement systems can be programmed to handle fractional quantities. Human intermediaries—market makers, accountants, and so on—cannot be reprogrammed to handle fractional trades from millions of investors on a real-time basis. However, when electronic trading systems are implemented, the investor will be able to submit orders to buy fractional numbers of shares. The investor will be able to buy a desired combination containing a large number of stocks for his or her target amount—a true democratization of the financial markets.

3.2.6 Asset-by-Asset Trading and Execution

Over and above the issues of human traders and outdated accounting conventions, the markets' antiquated system of asset-by-asset clearing also hinders investors in achieving their investment goals. For example, if you were an investor looking to build a diversified portfolio, you would target a specific combination of stocks issued by different firms. An investor might, for instance, place the following orders with his or her broker as shown in Table 3.1. (Please note that although the stocks are real, the prices are fictional.) The broker will communicate the orders to the exchange where the stocks are traded. Let us assume that at the end of the day, the investor receives the confirmations from his or her broker

TABLE 3.1	An Investor's Limit Orders		
Stock	Price Quote	Order Quantity	Buy/Sell
IBM	$10	1,000	Buy
CISCO	$50	100	Buy
FORD	$15	100	Sell
GM	$20	400	Sell

as displayed in Table 3.2. The buy order for CISCO and the sell order for GM were successfully executed. However, the investor was willing to pay only up to $10 for each share of IBM and the lowest price at which IBM traded that day was $11 per share. Similarly, he or she expected at least $15 for FORD shares, but the highest price at which FORD shares traded was $14 per share. So these two orders could not be executed.

The investor's aim is to hold a well-balanced portfolio. He or she was planning to move out of the automobile sector and increase his or her exposure to the technology sector. Instead, the investor is left with both technology and automobile stocks. This happens because in traditional markets, each stock is traded separately. However, just as we prefer to hold portfolios of stocks and bonds, would it not make sense to have the option of placing orders for portfolios or, in other words, combinations of such instruments? And in addition, why not allow investors to buy and sell different sets of stocks in the same order? Given the large number of stocks traded in our markets, it is, of course, humanly impossible for a broker to keep track of every stock the investor wishes to trade. A bro-

TABLE 3.2	Order Execution Report				
Stock	Price Quote	Order Qty	Buy/Sell	Transaction Price	Transaction Qty
IBM	$10	1,000	Buy	$11	0
CISCO	$50	100	Buy	$49.50	100
FORD	$15	100	Sell	$14	0
GM	$20	400	Sell	$21	400

ker is also not able to ensure that all the orders in the list above are executed. Clearly, a totally new computerized trading system must be invented that is programmed to handle orders to trade *combinations* of stocks. Before focusing too far ahead of ourselves in the future, however, we explore another financial market innovation already addressing the market imperfections surrounding IPOs—Internet IPOs.

3.3 INTERNET IPOS

As more firms become familiar with the process of pricing and marketing public offerings of stock, some have started questioning the value of paying a broker to distribute the shares. The urge to reach the investor directly has grown stronger in the past few years because of the Internet. The lure of the Internet as a means of reaching a large number of investors is irresistible. Why not offer these shares directly to investors over public networks? As with any other online auction, a firm can set up a site where the issue prospectus can be presented. Investors can ask the firm's senior management questions about their plans; they can access research reports from various online information vendors; if they like what they see, they can submit a bid for as many shares as they wish. As attractive as this may sound, at this stage of the evolution of the markets, not many firms appear keen on following only this direct sale approach. Instead, the pioneers who are willing to test new strategies still incorporate traditional IPO sales practices.

3.3.1 Pricing and Distributing an IPO

A new strategy to counteract the pricing and distribution weaknesses of the traditional IPO approach is to use the Internet to allow individual investors to buy shares of IPOs over the Internet through a process that makes these shares more accessible to them. It is not the case that there has been a change of heart among the investment bankers of the world. The pursuit of this new strategy aimed at the small investors is not due to any altruistic concern for their welfare. Rather, the "new kids on the block"—firms such as E*Offering and Wit Capital—are relying on the Internet to develop a niche in one of the most profitable segments of the investment banking business. The bottom line is this: Underpricing an IPO is not in the interest of the issuing firm. Rather, it is in the interest of the issuing company for the shares to be sold to investors who are willing to pay the highest price rather than to those who have million-dollar accounts with the brokerage firms. The goal of the new approach is simple: Establish an IPO that is as close as possible to the price at which they trade when they get listed on the stock market.

To achieve this goal, the new online investment bankers appear to be moving toward establishing the Internet as a reliable distribution channel for firms seeking to raise funds directly from investors. In fact, in the period from February 1997 to August 1998, 102 IPOs were sold to customers of online brokerages such as E*Trade, Charles Schwab, and Wit Capital. The timing of this trend could not have been more propitious. In May 1999, the U.S. Justice Department announced that it was investigating large investment banks for possible collusion on IPO fees.

What is the evidence of such anticompetitive behavior? Except for very large and very small offerings, the leading underwriters charge a standard fee of 7 percent of the money raised. Jay Ritter, a leading financial economist, has done extensive research on this matter. He has found that in the past four years more than 90 percent of mid-sized IPOs—those that raised between $20 million and $80 million—were charged a 7 percent fee. Interestingly, it was always exactly 7 percent, never even 7.1 or 6.9 percent.[4] Regardless of the outcome of the investigation, by the time regulators complete their work and negotiate settlements with these large institutions, it is likely that the IPO market will have been completely overhauled by the new kids on the IPO block, who promise lower costs and greater efficiency through the Internet.

3.3.2 New Kids on the IPO Block

A handful of path-breaking new firms have set up shop fronts along the information highway, shouting out to all those who care to listen that investment banking on the Web will be at least as attractive as the online brokerage business. Driving these efforts are both those who have hit it big in cyberspace and by the increasing numbers of those who have made fortunes in traditional-style investment banking. E-Offering, an affiliate of E*Trade Group, is one such new online investment bank. It is backed not only by E*Trade, the online brokerage firm, but also by Sandy Robertson, founder and former CEO of Robertson Stephens, a leading investment bank. Another newcomer who is attempting to add a totally new dimension to the whole business of selling stocks through public offerings is San Francisco–based W.R. Hambrecht & Co. Founded in 1998, it intends to conduct IPOs by using the concept of Dutch auctions, as we see below, conducted over the Internet.

The new kids on the block have a relatively straightforward plan to change the IPO in a two-step process. First, use the Internet to reduce costs for their customers—companies issuing stock. Second, use the Internet to expand the base of investors who invest in IPOs, and in the process, expand the market and make it more efficient. Firms can reduce their costs by automating the whole preissue process. Road shows can be held on the electronic superhighway via the Web. This will save time and money for the issuing company as the executives can interact with the investment community from their own offices. Investors can submit their orders either by e-mail or through secure Web transaction systems, reducing the cost of collecting sale proceeds from investors.

The traditional investment banking and technology powerhouses are beginning to get into the act. Goldman Sachs, one of the leading underwriters, has taken an equity stake in Wit Capital, an online investment banker founded in 1996. If Wit's business model comes anywhere close to becoming a success, Goldman has enough resources simply to railroad the whole company. Technology firms too are beginning to see the light. Software maker Novell, Inc., for example, has already invested in Hambrecht.

As promising as these first successes are, these are early days in the world of online IPOs. It is difficult to predict the long-term success or failure of any given business model, be it traditional distribution (brokers selling to their favored clients), online sales on a random or first-come/first-served basis, or distribution by an online auction, possibly the most innovative of all new online approaches.

3.3.3 IPOs and the Dutch Auction Process

W.R. Hambrecht & Co. wants to challenge the normal way of doing business on Wall Street by using the OpenIPO system based on the *Dutch auction process* to set prices and allocate shares for IPOs, leveling the playing field for individual investors. The basic idea is that a potential investor bids for a certain number of shares and specifies a price. The underwriters will accept the highest bid prices that it takes to sell all the shares in the offering. In a traditional Dutch auction, the auctioneer calls for an initial high price and successively lowers the price until there is a bidder who accepts the price. The OpenIPO system works as follows:

- All bidders, whether institutional or individuals, place bids by specifying the number of desired shares and the price they are willing to pay.
- All bids are sealed.
- When the auction closes, the system calculates the lowest price at which all shares can be sold. That price becomes the clearing price for the IPO, and every winning bidder pays the same price.
- Investors who bid exactly at the clearing price will receive a fixed percentage of the shares they bid based on the number of remaining shares.

Dutch auctions have been used in the equities business in the past but mostly with corporate stock buybacks. The same principle applies: A company wants to buy back a certain number of shares and asks holders to tender stock at a price they choose. The company will buy back shares at the lowest price it has to pay. If one specifies too high a price, one gets shut out.

A Level Playing Field?

Will this auction process make it easier for individuals (especially those who do not make it onto any broker's most favored customer list) to participate in IPOs? Absolutely. In an open auction, individuals are able to compete with the large institutional investors. As long as the bids are competitive, the large and small investors should be able to compete on a relatively level playing field. In stock markets, some exchanges impose rules that give priority first to price, then to the size of the order. OpenIPO does not give priority to bid size, and IPO shares are distributed evenly based solely on bidding price. Institutional investors with large capital are not treated preferentially.

Or Money in the Pocket

The small investors would surely be better off in an open auction process as they would have a relatively fair chance of buying stocks at the IPO price. But the real winners would be the firms selling stock to raise money. The competitive auction would in most cases result in higher prices for the stock. This, then, would leave less cash in the pockets of institutions that have traditionally been granted entry into IPOs simply because of a special relationship with the underwriter and would instead leave it with the firm selling stock. The hope is that any increase in prices due to open competition will happen as part of the IPO auction and not after the stock has been sold, so that the company would benefit from the higher price.

The ramifications of this can be mind-boggling. For example, assume that a company sold a million shares of its stock at an IPO price of $20 per share. This IPO was done the old-fashioned way. When the stock opened for trading in the stock markets, the first trade took place at $55, and by the end of the day the price rose all the way to $80. The hope behind the proponents of the online auction method is that the Dutch auction (or any other auction technique) will see the stocks being sold at an IPO price closer to $55, maybe even higher. So, instead of raising only $20 million, the firm would be able to raise a lot more (an additional $35 million if the IPO is priced at $55 per share); money that could be invested profitably in the struggling business.

Dealing with Lower Trading

Why do we see innumerable instances when, after an IPO, investors bid up a stock, at times high enough for the stock to end the day at double the IPO price? In the discussion above, we hinted that as underwriters restrict investors' access to an IPO, there is considerable pent-up demand for the stock. Those who wanted to buy the stock and were willing to pay close to twice the actual IPO price were kept out of the distribution. The moment the stock became available in the open market, interested buyers jumped in to buy it. Higher demand will typically result in higher prices (supply, after all, is limited[5] in the after-the-IPO period). So if the IPO auction process does its job and allocates shares to those who put the highest value on them, then by definition there should be little trading when the stock gets listed in the stock market. All those who wanted the stock and are willing to pay a competitive price will receive a fair share. If they want more shares, they might jump in and buy more, but this might not have too strong an impact on the stock price.

3.3.4 The Case of Ravenswood Winery

Ravenswood Winery, a tiny Sonoma, California-based outfit that specializes in somewhat expensive zinfandel and other reds, was the first company to be taken public by Hambrecht's OpenIPO using the Dutch auction process. The debut was on April 9, 1999, when Ravenswood sold 1 million shares at $10.50 each. Investors with accounts at certain brokerage firms, including W.R. Hambrecht and E*Trade Group Inc., were given an opportunity to place bids for the number of shares they wanted. According to W.R. Hambrecht, 3,000 persons placed bids and about 75 percent of those bidders got some stock. If this had been an offering from a company in the Internet business, the participation rate could potentially have been much greater. Why? Simply because of the craze for technology stocks. Interestingly, numerous investment bankers who traditionally serve large investors thought[6] that the stock should fetch $13.50 a share. One reason for this response could be a belief in their ability to reach a much wider group, consisting of large investors. A higher demand would translate into a better IPO price. This response leads us to a more important question, one for which we do not have an answer: Why did Ravenswood decide to follow the OpenIPO approach? Was it because the larger investment banks were not interested in taking it public?

3.3.5 Potential Problems

The idea behind Internet-based auctions is fundamentally sound, but this new mechanism is in its infancy and problems are sure to arise as the mechanism spreads. At least one potential problem exists because of the large difference between the financial clout of institutional investors and that of individual investors. What's to stop an institution or two from making a big, aggressive bid for a large number of shares at a high price, effectively shutting out retail investors? As the IPO process will involve regular publications of highest bids, a single investor could effectively bid nominally more for a million shares. The obvious solution would be to have well-publicized rules in place that prescribe the maximum number of shares any single investor can buy in the IPO process. A second problem would be the reluctance among large institutions to participate in a process in which their bids would be displayed over the Internet. These guys would surely prefer the traditional arrangement where only the underwriter has access to bid information.

Another potential concern with online IPOs is that if individuals find it easier to participate, there is a risk of them going crazy over the next IPO from any company with the suffix ".com" in its name. Some individuals might be willing to pay any price whatsoever to get hold of what they perceive to be a hot deal despite having done absolutely no research on the prospects of the issue. Trying his hand at participating in an online Dutch auction, Josh Friedman, a reporter for *The Los Angeles Times*, found[7] that the actual process for placing bids for the Ravenswood stock was rather straightforward, so he concluded that the technology to host these auctions over the Internet had arrived. But he did have to contend with a problem that seems to be less a technological issue than a case of not having the necessary infrastructure in place. Friedman had problems getting information about Ravenswood Winery as most chat rooms today focus on technology firms. There were few avenues through which he could get information and discuss prospects with other investors apart from a rather small number of postings on message boards for other publicly traded competitors such as Mondavi and Beringer. In the end, Friedman had to rely on reviews of the wines sold by Ravenswood: If the product tastes good, the chances of the company doing well ought to be higher!

3.3.6 Will Online IPOs Do Away with Underwriters?

The previous section touched on the anticipated impact online IPOs will have on the companies and the individual investors—but what about today's middleman? Will online IPOs do away with underwriters? At this time, the efforts to develop online IPO systems do not seem to indicate any attempt to do away with traditional investment bankers. The use of new technologies seems to be aimed at reforming current processes and making the overall market more efficient. Firms who hire large banks to underwrite their public offerings acknowledge that any large differences between the IPO price and the price at which the stock trades when listed on an exchange goes straight into the pockets of those banks' most preferred customers.[8] The firms would prefer to share in these gains, if possible. But if this is so, why do companies keep returning to large investment banks? Why are we witnessing reluctance among issuers to hire the services of online investment bankers? We propose that a company may have a number of incentives to stay with the traditional underwriter approach, despite the clear financial cost to them, including reputation, expertise, and insurance.

The Reputation Effect

When a relatively new firm enters the market to raise money, there is bound to be considerable asymmetry in information between the owners and the investing public about the company and its business prospects. The investing public might only be willing to pay a much lower price for the company's stock than what its managers would deem fit. How does one resolve the problem of differences in information and a lack of trust? The classic argument is that if a large, reputable bank such as Goldman Sachs or Merrill Lynch agrees to underwrite the stock offering, investors will be more willing to bid for these stocks. So by hiring an underwriter, the issuing firm is relying on the reputation of the bank or brokerage firm to improve the level of trust as perceived by investors.

Need for Expert Advice

By definition, an IPO is a company's initial foray into the stock market, a situation that often holds true for the company's executives as well. Most entrepreneurs tend to be more knowledgeable about their business than about the health of the stock market at any given moment. They prefer to pay a fee and hire the services of an expert—an underwriter such as Merrill Lynch or Goldman Sachs. In return they receive help on various aspects of a public offering, including regulatory approvals, introductions to large investment institutions, pricing of the issue, and equally important, timing of the offering. The last particularly proves critical when the overall market is highly volatile.

There are two other aspects of the relationship between the underwriter and the issuing firm that tend to be ignored in the popular press. First, firms keep returning to the capital markets at regular intervals to raise additional funds to finance the continued growth of their businesses. If an underwriter managed the IPO well, the firm will hire the investment bank to manage the new offerings (of stocks and/or bonds). Second, an issue we will return to in the paragraphs below, is that underwriters such as Merrill Lynch and Goldman Sachs employ highly paid analysts to research firms in various industries. Some analysts end up being considered as experts in specific business segments. A positive buy recommendation from one such star analyst can result in a major boost to the price of any stock. Investment banks use these employees as baits to rope in underwriting businesses. The in-house expert will rarely ever criticize a firm whose stock has been underwritten by the employer. Firms raising money know they cannot lose by having a popular expert on their side. Although it helps in the IPO, the relationship in many cases turns out to be more important for post-IPO stock and bond issues.

The Insurance Element

Finally, underwriting can also be perceived as a form of insurance in the eyes of the company issuing stock. When a large brokerage firm underwrites a stock offering, it basically buys the stock at an agreed-on price—the IPO price—and then turns around and sells it to its customers, who are then free to trade it in the open market. As the size of the offering increases, the issuing firm understandably becomes more concerned about the solvency of the underwriter. Large investment banks tend to be well capitalized and manage to attract scores of firms seeking to raise money by selling stock to the public.

The 7 Percent Issue

Traditional underwriters defend their 7 percent commission by arguing that they spend significant amounts of money on research before the IPO and on trading to support stocks after the IPO. For many stocks, especially those on the Nasdaq market, the main market maker will be the firm that underwrote the IPOs. In a move that reflects the validity and seriousness of this claim, Wit Capital has been hiring stock analysts, including a high-profile analyst from Merrill Lynch, Jonathan H. Cohen, an expert in Internet businesses. It is also in the process of building a trading desk. As Wit adds more and more services, it will soon find itself a mirror image of traditional brokerage firms, albeit a digital one. However, added services will also lead to an increase in Wit's cost of doing business, impairing its ability to charge lower fees.

IPOs and Target Marketing

As a distribution channel, the Internet attracts a particular type of business that would like to have a particular type of investor buying its stocks and bonds. The Web is an excellent medium to reach such a target audience. When the Cleveland Indians Baseball Company decided to go public, Wit Capital advertised the issue by using banner ads on various sports-related sites on the Internet—CBS SportsLine, Yahoo!, One-on-One Sports Radio Network, and so on. The ads contained links to a page containing basic information on the offering. Investors maintaining trading accounts with Wit could invest in the stock. As would be apparent, the firm was using Internet pages selectively to target baseball fans in general and the Cleveland Indians fans in particular. The issue was obviously a success.

3.3.7 Future Prospects for Online IPOs

If a major motivation for the transition to Internet-based IPOs is to allow small investors to participate in the market, the question cries out: What if issuers do not really care for the little guy? In many situations, issuing companies, in fact, prefer institutional investors. One reason involves *flipping*.[9] When issuers can pick their shareholders, most want institutions who have a reputation for flipping stocks less often than individuals. Their fear is that it will be difficult to stop thousands of individual investors from selling stocks they have bought at the IPO price the very first day of trading.

However, this argument is weakened if we assume that auctions will result in stock prices that approximate the true market value. The current volatility in post-IPO prices is partly a function of the restricted manner in which the stocks are distributed. Brokers at underwriting firms sell stocks at IPO prices as a favor to their customers. They want to make their clients happy when they are presented with the opportunity to make a quick killing by selling the stock at a high price on the first day of trading. Brokerage firms have systems and rules in place to monitor and discourage flipping, but the fact that some trading takes place on the very first day after the IPO indicates that one or more investors who bought the stock at the IPO price are selling it. If flipping rules were strictly imposed, then it is highly likely that the craze for IPOs will not be this strong. What's the point in buying a stock that cannot be traded for a month or more?

Managers of a firm that issues stocks do prefer institutional investors for reasons of convenience. They would much rather address questions from one large investor than answer e-mail messages from thousands of individual investors, each of whom might be holding only a few hundred shares of stock. Large institutional investors surely would like to see the current system continue into the indefinite future. They like having direct access to the CEOs and CFOs. Information is wealth. Managers of mutual funds and pension funds, analysts at large brokerage firms, and others would not necessarily be inclined to share their privileged access with "lowly" individual investors. It is conceivable, then, that stock issuing firms and large institutional investors might join in collusion to preserve the current system.

But as stated at the beginning of this discussion, the concept of Internet IPOs is new. And although the currently proposed methods for selling stock over the Internet might not prove to be the best strategies, many view it as an interesting novelty. Firms rushing to the markets to raise money by issuing stock speak in support of the concept, but they seem reluctant to try it out for their own offerings. There is an obvious reluctance to step up and play the guinea pig.[10] As of May 1999, Hambrecht's three-month-old firm had led the way in only one deal, Ravenswood Winery, Inc. Wit Capital, the other promised contender, has participated in 41 IPOs but has co-managed only four. And E*Offering has yet to lead a deal. Maybe what we need is a leader, in other words, a firm that is otherwise held in high esteem by the investment community, to give a jump-start to the process of raising capital over the Internet. One such example took place in the corporate bond market, which is closed to the individual investor.

Dell's Electronic Road Show

In an April 27, 1998, article titled "Dell markets $500 million deal on the Internet," the *Investment Dealers' Digest* reports on how Dell Computer Corp. used the Internet to conduct its *road show* for a bond issue. In the case of bond issues by reputable borrowers such as Dell, investors—mainly of the institutional type—will participate in conference calls over telephone lines with company representatives. To market this particular bond issue, Dell decided to follow a different approach. It decided to take advantage of the multimedia features offered by the Internet. As per regulations, it set up a temporary Web site hosting an audio-visual presentation of the bond issue. Interested investors were given a password to access the site. If they had any questions, they could e-mail them to the investment bank managing the issue.

Private firms issuing stocks and local governments selling municipal bonds have already used the flexibility afforded by the Internet to save the considerable expense involved in marketing their issues. This was the first instance when a highly rated borrower decided to exploit the Internet for this purpose. The firm did this fully aware that there was no shortage of buyers for its highly rated bonds. In addition, the size of the issue was so small, Dell need not have bothered going through the pains of putting up online road shows. Investors would have bought its bonds anyway.

3.4 DIRECT TRADING AND REAL-TIME SETTLEMENT SYSTEM

Once the investor completes his or her research and has decided which stocks to buy and which ones to sell and at what prices, he or she is now ready to trade. In today's markets, the investor has to hire the services of a broker to execute the trade. In the future, the investor will be able to access the markets directly. Large investors have steadily reduced their reliance on brokers to execute their trades. Given our emphasis on using new technologies to empower the individual, it seems as if we should be freeing the individual investor from the clutches of the brokerage business. Chapter 2 looked at some of the services provided by a brokerage firm. The following sections examine the use of new information technologies to dis-intermediate the broker. In place of the traditional brokerage firm, we will see the growth of new intermediaries such as certification authorities and electronic payment providers. It is highly likely that these distinct services will be subsumed within a single entity, the *virtual transaction processor*, another glorified name for the lowly brokerage firm.

3.4.1 Digital Identification

Exchanges surely acknowledge the need to allow direct access to the small investor, but they are cognizant of the obstacles as well. Exchanges do not want to deal with the problem of identifying each investor—making sure that he or she has the money to pay for a trade or is the owner of the securities that are being sold and, more important, that the exchange of money for stocks will take place in a seamless manner. Exchanges have historically stayed away from this business of pre- and postexecution transaction processing. Brokerage firms along with various clearance and settlement institutions, the latter typically being subsidiaries of leading exchanges, have taken on this task.

Today, however, individuals can place direct bids for IPOs. The U.S. Treasury is considering plans to allow direct purchase of bonds issued by the federal government. It appears as if it is only a matter of time before individual investors will be allowed to place orders directly with a securities exchange.

If small investors are to be able to access markets directly, new institutions in the form of virtual intermediaries will have to step in to facilitate the seamless settlement of transactions. Let us start with considering the problems of authenticating the identity and creditworthiness of the investor.

User IDs and Passwords

When an investor wishes to place an order through an online broker, he or she logs on to the broker's Web site where the investor is required to type in his or her name and password. These are supposed to be known only to the broker and the investor. The security of this identification arrangement is based on a trust that the brokerage firm will not reveal it to anyone else and a belief that the investor him- or herself will take care not to share it with anyone whom the investor does not trust. In addition, over the past few years both brokerage firms and their customers have gained a sense of faith in the inherent safety of browser-based security systems; in other words, they believe the claims of various technology vendors that the encryption code used to transmit confidential messages between the investor and the broker will not be visible to any third party trying to "listen in."

However, there are many limitations of the user ID and password approach. Every time an online user accesses a different merchant, he or she has to fill out a new registration form and obtain a new ID and password. A user can try to obtain the same user ID. But it is not guaranteed he or she will be able to get it. This is essentially inconvenient for an investor who uses a couple of online services and has to use a different combination of ID and password to access each service. In addition, the current practice of using user IDs and passwords is static in nature. As we move toward real-time transaction processing systems, we will need applications that can carry a variety of information with the user identification.

If individual investors are to have direct access to exchanges, then the latter will have to take on the user identification tasks now delegated to brokerage firms. Stock exchanges might, however, be reluctant to deal with the chore of recording, storing, and verifying the identification information of millions of investors. In addition, computer systems at a single large exchange such as the NYSE might get overwhelmed with the countless numbers of messages that would have to be dealt with in the process of communicating with such large numbers of investors. New technology in the form of digital certificates is being designed to resolve this problem and aid electronic commerce in all types of markets, both financial and nonfinancial. Cryptographic techniques including encryption and digital signature are fundamental building blocks of the infrastructure for digital financial markets. The cryptographic techniques discussed here include private-key and public-key encryption and digital signature.

Public-Key Encryption

Private-key encryption, also known as symmetric encryption, is the simplest form of encryption. In private-key encryption, the same key is used in the encryption and decryption process. It works as follows:

- Alice and Bob agree on a key as well as the encryption algorithm.
- Alice takes her message and encrypts it using the key.
- Alice sends the encrypted message to Bob.
- Bob decrypts the encrypted message with the private key and reads it.

Key management is critical in secret key encryption because if the key is intercepted during its transmission, then all the messages transmitted between Alice and Bob can be decrypted. This greatly limits the usefulness of secret key encryption for secure transaction, because secure key distribution in a public network is difficult. It also becomes impractical to distribute secret keys to a large number of users with whom the company has never done business before.

For these reasons, Whitfield Diffie and Martin Hellman of Stanford University introduced public-key encryption technology in 1976. In contrast to symmetric encryption, which uses only one key, a public-key encryption uses a pair of related keys—a private key and a public key. The private key is kept secret by the owner whereas the public key is made known to the public. Although the two keys are related, it is hard to infer the private key from the public key. A message encrypted with one key cannot be decrypted by itself and rather has to be decrypted by using the other key. Therefore, anyone with the public key can encrypt a message but not decrypt. Only the owner with the private key can decrypt the message encrypted by using the public key. Public key technology is how Alice is going to communicate securely with Bob:

- Alice gets Bob's public key from a trusted public database.
- Alice encrypts her message using Bob's public key and sends the message to Bob.
- Bob decrypts the encrypted message with his private key.

Even if some other individuals intercept Alice's message, they will not be able to read the message without the private key. In the meantime, public-key encryption has successfully solved the key management problem. Without prior arrangement, a user can send secure transaction information to an online broker just by using the broker's public key.

Digital Certificates

Digital certificates are versatile, secure tools that can potentially replicate the identification services provided by brokerage firms as part of the trading process. A digital certificate is basically a digital attachment added to an electronic message for security purposes. It is typically used to verify that an individual sending a message is who he or she claims to be and to make sure that the message has not been modified by a third party.

Already available, digital certificates are issued by *certificate authorities* (CA) (e.g., VeriSign) and *encrypted* with the CA's private key. Investors can apply to a digital certificate from a CA. The CA, in turn, will issue a certificate containing the applicant's public key and a variety of other identification information. The CA makes its own public key readily available through print publicity or perhaps on the Internet. Suppose Alice sends an order to an exchange. The following is how it works for the exchange to verify both the authentication and integrity of the order using the digital certificate:

- Alice applies a hashing algorithm[11] to her order to produce a message digest; then encrypts the digest with her private key. The encrypted message digest serves as the digital signature for the order.

- Alice sends the order and the digital signature along with her digital certificate to the exchange by using a secure communication protocol (e.g., using symmetric session key).

- On receiving the order, the exchange will get the digital certificate attached to the order, verifies it as issued by the CA, and then obtains Alice's public key and identification information held within the certificate.

- The exchange uses Alice's public key to decrypt the digital signature and reveals the message digest.

- To verify the integrity of the order, the exchange hashes the received order to create a message digest and compares it with the earlier message digest. If the two message digests match, the exchange can be confident that the order has not changed since Alice signed it.

The encryption technology that underlies digital certificates has been around for some time now. The certificates can be transmitted and recognized worldwide. In Washington, Utah, and other states, digital certificates are considered legally binding.

If an exchange relies on user codes and passwords, it will have to store all this information in its database. Such databases will surely be one of the most popular targets for hackers around the world. Use of digital certificates will obviate the need to maintain a database of user information.

Digital Identification

At present, if an individual wants to trade in the markets, he or she has to open an account with a brokerage firm. Among other things, the registration process involves convincing the broker that you are who you claim to be. Once the identity has been established, the investor can communicate orders to the broker through a variety of channels: by phone, in person, or over the Internet. Under a traditional scenario, communication between brokerage firms and exchanges take place over secure, proprietary lines where confirming identities is relatively straightforward.

In a virtual trading environment, the investor will submit a digital certificate identifying him or her to the exchange. These certificates could be designed with a variety of features. For instance, an exchange could impose a rule that all those who trade, say, options, futures, and other derivative contracts on the exchange undergo some formal training. Once the investor completes a training program, this fact can be added to the certificate. So every time an investor submits an order to trade any specific security, the exchange's computer will check the certificate to verify if the individual is eligible to trade it. With digital certificates there is no need to store all this information within the exchange's computers, relieving the exchange itself of an immense data management burden and liability.

Real-Time Credit Verification

Financial service firms today typically use a different form of user authentication. When a credit card company receives an application for a credit line increase, for example, it submits a request to a credit information provider for the credit history of the applicant. Information providers such as Equifax process 2,000 credit information requests a minute. The systems they have in place could easily deliver crucial information about consumers of financial services. Equifax has decided to leverage this strength by offering identity authentication services over the Internet. It has signed an agreement with IBM to jointly develop and market digital certificate services. Firms or exchanges could outsource their identification requirements (certificate issuance, renewal, and revocation) to Equifax.

Banks and Brokers as CAs

In July 1997, the online brokerage firm E*Trade announced that it planned to issue digital certificates from VeriSign to its customers. The firm's plan was to replace the existing system in which users type in their user codes and passwords with digital certificates. The firm planned to enter into agreements with other Internet-based merchants to accept these certificates from E*Trade customers. Losses up to $1,000 from theft, impersonation, or corruption of the digital certificate would be covered by VeriSign's Netsure plan. This will be underwritten by an insurance company, United States Fidelity & Guaranty.

In July 1998, Financial NetNews reported that NationsBank was planning to issue digital certificates to retail and corporate clients. The certificates would allow these customers to access their accounts over the Internet. The bank also planned to allow its employees to use the certificates to log on to the firm's Intranet. Technology vendors IBM and VeriSign were working with NationsBank on this initiative.

Other banks that have offered digital certificates include Credit Suisse First Boston, Zions Bank, and Liberty Financial. The last mentioned was one of the first banks to issue digital certificates. In 1997, it adopted technology from BBN Corp. but faced with customer complaints, it decided to return to the user code/password-based identification system. Liberty's customers had problems downloading and using the certificates. The company had hoped that 25 to 50 percent of its customers would use the certificates, but less than 10 percent actually signed up for the service.

Chicken-and-Egg Syndrome

Despite all the advantages of digital certificates, Internet users have been reluctant to acquire them. The low usage of digital certificates could be a symptom of the classic chicken-and-egg syndrome. As few sites require the use of digital certificates, relying instead on user codes and passwords, investors might not consider it worthwhile to acquire digital certificates. And as few Internet users are willing to download these certificates, merchants are reluctant to invest in digital certificate-based transaction processing systems. Another concern is that businesses and households buy financial services from more than one intermediary. There could be a genuine concern that different online services would require their own unique digital certificates. This would imply that the investor download more than one certificate onto his or her machine. Having multiple certificates on the machine would only complicate matters further.

Carrot and Stick Approach

From the perspective of this chapter, it is possible that consumers are reluctant to take the trouble to learn to use a new technology simply to access their account information with a bank or a brokerage firm. The perception of lower security from using user codes and passwords could be offset by the simplicity of the service offered by these institutions.

It is possible that if there were to be a serious hack of the computer database of a major financial institution, then a larger fraction of Internet users would be willing to switch to digital certificates. It is also conceivable that if appropriate incentives were provided, they might be willing to download these certificates. For example, many investors use online brokers to execute their trades. If they are allowed direct access to the Nasdaq trading system and other exchanges by using the same certificate, it is conceivable that they might be willing to go through the hassle of learning to use digital certificates. The carrot—in the form of an opportunity to save on brokerage fees—would be too hard to resist.

3.4.2 Electronic Payment System

The basic requirement we are looking for in an electronic payment system is that it will allow individual investors to *make* and *receive* payments directly on a real-time basis. Given the increasing need to reduce the number of messages floating around cyberspace, instantaneous payment systems might, however, operate more efficiently on an indirect basis through a virtual bank routing payments on behalf of an exchange. Variations of both are under development. One downfall of most of the following Internet-related payment systems under development today is that they are designed to support secure *one-way* flows between a customer and a merchant, not *two-way* payment flows of the sort between an exchange and an investor.

Secure Electronic Transaction and Credit Card Payments

At present, most payments for purchases over the Internet are made by using credit cards. Most companies use a combination of secure sockets layer (SSL)[12] and transaction processing services for accepting credit card payments. When a person buys a book from Amazon.com, for example, the security of the transaction is governed simply by the SSL technology embedded in popular Web browsers from Netscape and Microsoft. An alternative technology known as secure electronic transaction (SET) has been developed to permit more secure credit card payments over the Internet. SET involves the usage of digital certificates. Merchants can use digital certificates to verify that buyers are who they claim to be, and buyers can make sure that the merchant is who it claims to be. Although buyers will be able to make payments by using their credit cards, merchants will not be able to see the card numbers. Instead, to protect buyers, the SET protocol provides a mechanism for the credit card number to be transferred directly to the card issuer for verification and billing.

Electronic Checks

Modern commerce makes extensive use of paper checks. In the United States, one can even go to a grocery store and write a check for amounts less than $1. So when dreaming up payment systems to be used over the Internet, it is not surprising that someone decided to replicate the paper check. One such someone, the Financial Technology Services Consortium (FTSC), is in the process of developing an electronic check: an enhanced replacement to the paper check. The e-check is similar to paper checks in the sense that it represents what is called a self-contained *information object*—it has all the information necessary to complete a payment. Electronic checkbooks replace paper checkbooks; digital signatures replace handwritten signatures, and the Web browser and e-mail replace stamps and paper envelopes. Like SET, the e-check will revolve around the banking system as it exists today. A common criticism of both these systems is that they are designed to protect the interests of the traditional banking system. Instead of taking advantage of the increased possibilities afforded by the Internet, these consortia of banks and technology firms are simply attempting to replicate aspects of an existing payment system.

Electronic Cash

In addition to the individual payment method described above, numerous efforts are also under way to develop payment systems that will support direct, anonymous, and small denomination payments over electronic networks. Direct payments will obviate the need to hire the services of intermediaries such as savings and commercial banks. Such payments will be in the form of encoded messages representing the encrypted equivalent of digitized money. By definition, e-cash or e-money is intended for settling small value transactions of $20 or less. So, it might not be suitable for settling transactions in financial securities, which typically tend to be for larger amounts.

3.4.3 Digital Transaction System

Trading Directly at Exchanges

The next generation of online trading applications will allow investors to send orders directly to exchanges, bypassing brokerage firms (Figure 3.4). In a future scenario, the traditional broker's task of order verification and rerouting the orders to exchanges can be replaced by new technology using digital certificates. Under this new setup, brokerage firms could continue to conduct the tasks of checking the credit of investors and the validity of orders but in a more efficient way. Every time an investor wants to trade, he or she will open the trading application, which can be a Java applet. The application will have the digital certificate for the investor and the latest account status information including current positions and cash balance. As discussed earlier, the digital certificate is issued by the brokerage firm and carries various information about the investor such as the name of the broker and the type of trading (stocks, options, futures, and so on) for which the investor is authorized.

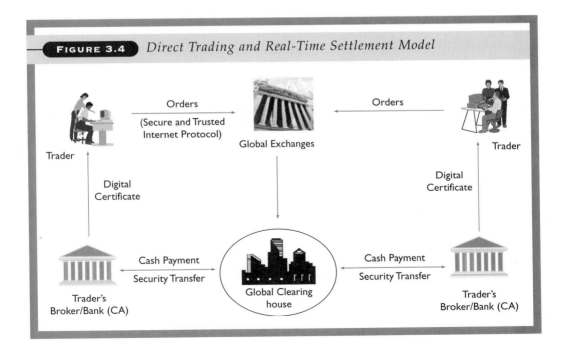

FIGURE 3.4 *Direct Trading and Real-Time Settlement Model*

Virtual Custodian

Another task that the broker of the future may retain is that of custodian. Today, when an individual investor buys a stock, the identity of the buyer might not be recorded in the books of the firm that issued the stock. Instead, the name of the broker through whom the stock was purchased is recorded. The broker, in turn, maintains a separate set of records showing the investor's ownership of the stock. When the firm pays out a dividend, the payment is made to the brokerage firm; the latter credits the dividend amount to the investor's account. If the investor decides to sell the stock, the brokerage firm is responsible for transferring the ownership to the brokerage firm whose customer has made the purchase. In this process, the brokerage firm is a *custodian* of shares owned by its customers. This custody service can be classified as another payment and settlement service provided by an intermediary.

As we move toward a world where orders need not be routed through a brokerage firm, the custody service provided by brokers is still required. Additionally, the brokerage firm serves as a CA for its customers, who can trade in any markets where the brokerage firm is accepted. Essentially, the future brokerage firms will play less of a role in trading but will operate more like a bank, which serves as a CA for its clients and is a custodian of the clients' accounts.

Real-Time Global Settlement

The final task associated with trading is that of settlement. The primary goals of a clearing and settlement system are efficiency and risk reduction. Today, we are witnessing record-breaking volumes and volatility in markets. Various bodies regulating the securities industry are considering moving to T + 1 settlement. It is expected that some markets will even move toward real-time settlement. But given the pace of technological advance and, more important, the rapid rate at which new trading systems are evolving, it should not be surprising if real-time settlement systems are implemented quickly. A shorter clearing and settlement cycle will significantly reduce transaction risks.

In addition, investors are increasingly seeking the best investment opportunities in international markets. Cross-border trading requires the establishment of cross-border, global clearing and settlement services. We foresee in the near future that the trading of non-U.S. securities will be as easy as trading Microsoft and Intel in the United States.

3.5 SUMMARY

The Internet will not make intermediation extinct. Rather, it is in the process of enabling a complete overhaul of financial intermediation as we know it. This is the basic message of the chapter. Investors still need someone to handle their payments, and they still would prefer to pay a firm a fee to take care of various transaction services; as there is too much information floating around in cyber-space, they would even be happy if—in return for a fee—a financial analyst would help them find the method in the madness.

It is not the case that investors have suddenly developed an aversion to traditional banks and large brokerage houses. It is simply that as needs change, investors would like to see their service-providers adapt and take advantage of new technologies to offer improved services. If Merrill Lynch continues to insist on charging hundreds of dollars simply to exercise an order (plus some trading tips that might be of questionable value), then investors will simply move their business to a firm that charges less than $30 per trade.

Clearly, the financial intermediation business is in for a substantial overhaul, but where do we go from here? We have painted a snapshot of a world where investors can trade directly in different markets. At the time of writing this book, it is not clear if we will ever get there in the near future. The idea is not to predict the specific direction in which we are headed. Rather, we have attempted to focus on specific aspects of the financial needs of households and then tried to assemble a framework that we believe will serve these needs. The specific target is not important here; what counts is the motivation, its focus on exploiting technology to get closer to the true needs of our customers.

The past two chapters have focused on the impact of the Internet on traditional financial services. The rest of the book narrows the focus toward the impact of the Internet on the financial markets, in particular on exchanges where various financial instruments such as stocks, bonds, and numerous derivative securities are traded. The Internet is still in its nascent stages; as the cliché goes, it is not yet ready for mission critical tasks. Hence, we are yet to see any pure Internet-based markets. Nonetheless, the evolution of electronic commerce has had significant influence on the various securities markets of the world.

4

FINANCIAL MARKETS

IN A NUTSHELL

The next few chapters focus on descriptions of different trading systems. The emphasis is largely on markets where stocks are traded. This chapter begins by specifying a generic trading structure that will include the key components of any such systems. If one looks at the numerous securities exchanges around the world today, one will find a mind-boggling array of structures. The goal here is to illustrate that all markets are basically variations of the simple market described below. We start with the generic market and then go on, in the next few chapters, to describe some of the premier exchanges of the world and some recent innovations. Along the way, we point out the manner in which these institutions use information technology to develop mechanisms targeted at specific segments of the marketplace.

Readers in Asia, Europe, and other parts of the world may have noticed a marked bias of the book toward developments in the U.S. markets. This focus is unfortunate in that the markets on these continents have taken a lead in adopting electronic trading technologies. The equity culture as experienced in the United States is relatively new to most nations around the world. Wherever the shift toward the new technology has taken place, experience shows that the whole process has been relatively smooth. As a result, many emerging markets have not had to deal with the legacy—and restrictions—of centuries-old floor trading systems and have installed electronic trading systems in their exchanges.

In contrast to the rest of the world, the trading industry in the United States has been "blessed" with a lengthy past and the fact that the U.S. equity markets are the biggest in the world. The leading stock market in the world, the New York Stock Exchange (NYSE) has been using the same floor-based auction system for over 200 years. And although the investment world has undergone substantial changes in the past few years, the exchange has not seen the need to adopt drastically new technologies to improve its trading process.

The next few chapters are dedicated to understanding the functioning of the NYSE and the Nasdaq market. Consequently, the nitty-gritty of how trading takes place in these markets is left to these chapters. This chapter tries to develop an appreciation of the key elements of the overall business of markets including the organization of financial markets, transaction costs, and liquidity.

4.1 AUCTION MARKETS

When an investor decides to trade, he or she routes an order to buy or sell a stock to an order-matching system or a securities exchange market where buy and sell orders from different investors are matched (Figure 4.1). Generally, stock markets can be classified as two types: auction markets and dealer markets. Auction markets are discussed in this section.

4.1.1 Double Auction

Securities exchanges have traditionally been organized as double auctions in which a large number of buyers and sellers trade a common object, in this case, a particular stock in a competitive market. Whenever we think of auctions, we conjure images of Christie's or Sotheby's auctioning off some famous art object or the possessions of a celebrated (or notorious) personality. In these auctions, there is a single seller and a large number of bidders or buyers trying to buy the objects being sold. The seller clearly has a monopoly over the supply of the item.

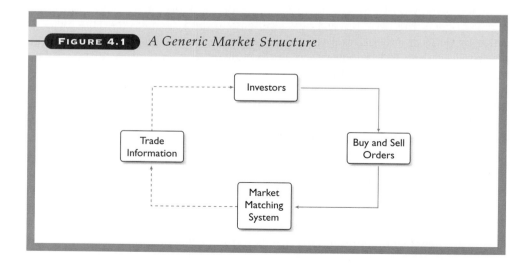

FIGURE 4.1 *A Generic Market Structure*

For example, if the Mona Lisa ever goes on the auction block, there will be a single seller—the museum that owns it—and a large number of prospective buyers. On the flip side, there are other auctions where there is a single buyer and a large number of individuals trying to sell. When a government authority invites bids for the construction of an airport, for example, there is just one item (the airport construction contract) with a single buyer (the government authority) and a large number of sellers (construction firms bidding for the contract). Those auctions, with either one seller and many buyers or one buyer and many sellers, are usually called one-sided auctions.

By contrast, securities markets are usually organized as double auctions, in which both buyers and sellers can submit bids (buy orders) and asks (sell orders) for any given stock simultaneously. Double auctions can have different variations, for example, open-outcry markets and computer-automated markets. In terms of the frequency of trade, double auctions can be classified as continuous markets and periodic (call) markets. For more than 100 years, double auction has been a predominant trading mechanism for most of the financial exchanges in the world. Despite the vital importance of the double-auction mechanism, we still do not understand solely the mechanism of double auction. Much of what we know about double auction today is not due to theory but due to an accumulated body of experimental research dating back to the early 1960s by Veron Smith, Charles Plott, and others.[1] Their laboratory experiments demonstrate that even with rather small numbers of traders who have imperfect information on supply and demand, the double auction has been consistently efficient. Veron Smith calls this finding a "scientific mystery."

The Order Book

Trading in auction markets is organized around the order book. There will typically be multiple order books, each for a security. In a double-auction market, numerous buyers and sellers submit their respective orders. In a generic marketplace, all orders submitted by traders enter an order book arranged in a particular manner. The list of buy orders is descending in price, and that of sell orders is ascending in price (Figure 4.2). Basically, the more aggressively priced orders will be placed at the top of the order book. If a new order is priced at the same level as an existing order (also called a standing order), the latter order will have higher priority.

The order book may have multiple components; parts of the book are open, other parts closed or hidden. Orders submitted for inclusion in the open part are exposed to the rest of the market. Order book information for any given stock includes the limit price, time entered, and order quantity. The identity of the trader may or may not be revealed.

An investor can instruct that the whole order, or a specific part of it, be included in the hidden or closed order book. This would not prevent orders in this portion of the book from being considered for a match. All else being the same, however, orders in the open book have priority over those in the closed book.

FIGURE 4.2 *Limit Order Book of Cisco at Island ECN*

ⓘ CSCO

GET STOCK

CSCO go

LAST MATCH		TODAY'S ACTIVITY	
Price	75 1/16	Orders	20,546
Time	19:53:34	Volume	3,076,425

BUY ORDERS		SELL ORDERS	
SHARES	PRICE	SHARES	PRICE
160	74 3/4	22	75
271	74 11/16	27	75 1/16
56	74 5/8	200	75 1/16
300	74 9/16	250	75 1/8
630	74 7/16	18	75 1/8
100	74 3/8	100	75 1/4
100	74 3/8	200	75 1/4
760	74 3/8	25	75 3/8
310	74 1/4	75	75 3/8
83	74	157	75 3/8
100	74	100	75 7/16
100	74	100	75 15/32
200	74	62	75 1/2
14	74	35	75 1/2
274	74	210	75 1/2
(574 more)		(644 more)	

All markets have some types of formal priority rules. For instance, highest priority can be given to price, then to the time an order has been placed, the size of the order, and so on. As the number of restrictions placed on an order increases, it gets pushed farther down the line in the order book. If an investor indicates that he or she does not want his or her order to be exposed to the market, all else being the same, an equivalent but open order will receive higher priority. The order from the trader who is willing to publicize his or her trading interest to the rest of the market will be executed first.

The trading system described above falls in the category of order-driven markets—the entire trading process is driven by orders placed by investors. In these markets, trading revolves around the order book. By definition, the contents of the open order book are disseminated to all market participants over secure electronic networks. This would enable investors to respond to the buy and sell orders listed by either "hitting" these orders or by improving on the posted prices. In the order book shown in Figure 4.2, the sell order of 22 shares at the price of $75 can be "hit" by placing a buy order for a price of $75.

Limit and Market Orders

A variety of order types is available in markets. Orders such as "good-till-cancel" and "fill-or-kill" allow traders to control the timing of trades. But the two most common orders in stock markets are *limit* and *market*. A limit order to buy 1,000 shares of a particular stock at $75 per share is basically an indication to other traders in the markets that the investor is willing to pay $75 or less per share for up to 1,000 shares of a stock. A limit sell order of $75 per share indicates that the trader is willing to sell the stock at $75 or higher.

An order to sell 1,000 shares of a particular stock at the prevailing price is a market order. Instead of specifying a limit price—the minimum price at which the investor is willing to sell that stock—the investor simply tells the market to sell the stock at the highest price at which some other trader is willing to buy that stock. Market orders are executed at the best price established at the market. For a market sell order, the best price is the highest bid price available at the time whereas the best price for a market buy order is the lowest ask price of the sell orders. Market orders ensure the immediacy of trading; but the execution price is uncertain. By contrast, limit orders allow a trader to receive a better price if the order is executed; but the trade execution is not guaranteed.

Trading by using market or limit orders is a decision every trader has to face. Harris and Hasbrouck conducted a study on market versus limit orders based on a sample of NYSE SuperDOT orders.[2] Their studies show that limit orders placed at or better than the prevailing quote perform better than market orders, even after imputing a penalty for unexecuted orders and after taking into account market order price improvement. Specifically, in a $1/8 bid-ask market, at-the-quote limit orders achieve better performance than market orders, whereas in a $1/4 bid-ask market, limit orders that better the quote by $1/8 perform well.

Competing to Trade

For the shown order book (Figure 4.2), price improvement takes place when another investor with an interest in buying the stock places a new limit order with a higher bid price of $74.875. In doing so, he or she would hope to attract sell orders from other investors who might not be willing to trade at $74.75 per share but are willing to consider a higher price. In a double-auction market with an open limit order book, investors on both sides of the market, the buy side and the sell side, will compete to trade by placing appropriate offers. Buyers will compete to buy by increasing their bids, and sellers will compete to sell by decreasing their asks.

Anonymity and Publicity

As discussed in considerable detail in the following chapters, investors constantly make a tradeoff between publicizing their trading interests to the other traders in the market and protecting their privacy. Generally, when an investor has spent considerable resources researching an investment opportunity, he or she will prefer to keep that knowledge to him- or herself. The investor would like to make his or her trades in that particular stock before letting the world in on his or her "secret." So when an investor trades, he or she will prefer to do so in an anonymous manner. Let us assume that in the market where that stock is traded, the investor is allowed to submit the order to a closed order book. Suppose that the investor has placed a buy order at a price higher than the prevailing price. In selecting a closed order book, the investor runs the risk of not attracting suitable orders from other traders. It is possible that there are investors in the market who are holding that stock but are not interested in selling it at the prevailing price. Maybe if they learned about a buying interest at a higher price, they might be willing to submit their sell orders so as to trade at that price; by choosing to remain anonymous, the investor has lost the opportunity to trade.

In the real world, small investors, typically those who trade 100 to 1,000 shares of a stock, are comfortable exposing their order to the rest of the market. But large institutions that spend millions of dollars in research, and given their size, trade tens of thousands of shares of a stock at any given time, would prefer to trade in markets that preserve their privacy. Once a match takes place, the system sends immediate confirmations to the parties involved in the transaction. Information about the transaction—price, quantity, time—is disseminated immediately to the whole market. However, the identity of the investors is not revealed.

4.1.2 Continuous and Periodic Trading

The order-matching system of a double auction can be programmed to process orders continuously. In this case, the moment an order is submitted to the system, it attempts to match it with other orders in the book. The system can also be set up as a periodic or call auction. Under this scenario, orders submitted to the system will be accumulated in the order book and processed simultaneously at periodic intervals.

Continuous Markets

A continuous market is one where traders submit orders to the order-matching mechanism for immediate execution. Assume an investor submits an order to buy 100 shares of IBM at the best market price. When the order reaches the market, the lowest price at which any other trader is willing to sell these shares is, say, $175 per share. The market order is executed at this price. In markets with continuous trading, a transaction occurs whenever any two orders are matched. Accordingly, it is possible to observe continuous trading and frequent price changes when the market is open for trading. Trading in most markets around the world takes place on a continuous basis. This is particularly suitable for frequently traded securities for which orders to buy and sell are submitted at a relatively continuous rate during trading hours. A few markets do, however, operate on a periodic or call market basis, especially for stocks that see low trading interests.

Call Markets

In a call market, also known as the *clearing house,* orders are collected over a period of time and executed at a single market clearing price. The orders are accumulated over prespecified intervals in the order book and matched in batches. This feature allows liquidity to be built-up over a period of time. For this reason, call auctions are considered suitable for less frequently traded securities. In addition, the feature of single-price execution makes it suitable during periods when there is a high degree of uncertainty in the markets.

Call auctions tend to be single-price or uniform-price auctions. This means that all orders in the system are processed at the same time and trades in a particular stock executed at a single price, one that maximizes the volume of trade between buyers and sellers. The NYSE initially operated as a call market. Today, the NYSE still opens using a call market mechanism but switches to continuous trading right after the opening.

There are clear tradeoffs between continuous and call auction markets. Compared with continuous auction markets, trading prices at call markets is less volatile. This is because accumulation of orders over time and setting price at a point to clear the market can reduce information asymmetry. However, investors who seek immediacy of trading will find continuous markets more appealing. From the perspective of exchanges, continuous markets consistently generate higher trading volumes.[3]

Price Swings and Market Design

Some economists argue that continuous trading tends to aggravate potentially adverse price movements in stocks. For instance, there are times when markets record panic behavior by traders. A classic instance would be the steep loss in stock prices recorded on October 19, 1987, when the Dow Jones Industrial Average lost about 500 odd points, or nearly 20 percent of its value. On days such as this, investors tend to be so keen to sell their holdings that they do not really care about the actual price at which their orders are executed. To restore a degree of calm in such desperate trading conditions, exchanges halt trading for a brief period of time. The idea is that the break in trading will allow investors to reconsider their positions and realign their expectations with reality, and this will hopefully result in more considered trading.

In recent years, these trading halts have been widely criticized by various members of the investment community. The complaint is that trading halts, which vary from half an hour to two hours in the United States, tend to aggravate steep price movements. If traders expect the market to close in 15 minutes, they would like to get in or out of their positions before the halt is enforced. This phenomenon is similar to that in a crowded movie theater that has caught fire, and everyone is trying to get out of the hall through a small opening.

So how do periodic markets help in these situations? As trading does not take place continuously, there is no question of trying to shed one's positions without care for the cost. To illustrate, let us assume that the market receives information that indicates an extreme change in valuations of stocks. In continuous markets, traders would immediately submit market orders to reduce their losses or to increase their gains before stock prices adjust fully to the new information. In periodic markets, orders from all traders would be accepted over a period of time and then processed at a single point in time. So there is no possibility of trade until the specified point in time. At most, the traders can submit their orders as quickly as possible and then hope that their order will receive preferential treatment based on the time it was submitted.

4.2 DEALER MARKETS

Whereas an auction market maintains a public limit order book and public orders are traded against each other, in a dealer market public orders are traded with dealers at their quoted bid and ask prices. Well-known examples of dealer markets are Nasdaq and London International Stock Exchange. Dealer markets function differently from auction markets. Advocates of dealer markets argue that dealers provide liquidity to markets. Even the most liquid markets may have imbalance of buyers and sellers and, thus, require dealers or market makers to provide liquidity. For example, the specialists at the NYSE are required to maintain a fair and orderly market by taking their own positions in the market when there is a temporary market imbalance.

4.2.1 Bid-Ask Spread and Dealer Cost

Assume that you make a "round-trip" transaction for a stock in a dealer market and there is no new information regarding a stock. The stock will be purchased at the dealer quoted ask price and be sold at the bid price. The gap between the bid and ask prices is called bid-ask spread and constitutes the cost of trading. In a dealer market, investors have to trade with dealers and pay the bid-ask spread even if a matching public order is available. But dealers provide a service to the market. By setting quotes in advance, dealers insulate traders from adverse price movement due to market imbalances.

The bid-ask spread is essentially the dealers' compensation for providing liquidity in the market. Researchers have found that there exists an inverse relationship between bid-ask spread and the amount of trading activity of the stock. The more often the stock is traded, the less the spread. The smaller amount of trading, the higher the spread because dealers could possibly face a higher risk by taking a position in the stock.

By taking positions in the market to provide liquidity, dealers are subject to market risks. Consider a market with two types of traders: informed traders and liquidity traders. The former have superior information and know the intrinsic value of a stock. They buy when they know the stock is undervalued and sell when the stock is overvalued. The latter trade for the liquidity purpose. Trading with a liquidity trader in an equity market is desirable for dealers because transaction price changes due to the arrival of a liquidity trader are temporary and reversible. By contrast, trading against informed traders is undesirable for dealers because transaction price changes due to the arrival of an informed trader are irreversible.[4]

4.2.2 Dealer versus Auction Markets

The difference between dealer and auction markets can be categorized as that the former is quote driven while the latter is order driven. In dealer markets, investors can obtain quotes from dealers before submitting orders. In auction markets, traders submit their orders to the market for execution and the market does the price discovery based on supply and demand. As discussed earlier, auction markets can be implemented as continuous or periodic markets. Generally, dealer markets are continuous because traders can always trade at dealers' quoted prices. In the real world, trading mechanisms at exchanges are often the hybrid of dealer and auction markets. Market efficiency is largely affected by the way trading is organized. Therefore, understanding the tradeoff of dealer and auction markets is crucial.

Auction markets are inherently more transparent than dealer markets because more market information can be made available to all market participants.[5] Particularly, auction markets enhance both pretrade and post-trade transparency. Pretrade transparency (i.e., the visibility of the best price an incoming order can be executed at) is better in an auction market. In auction markets, market makers can view the entire limit order book and see exactly at what price an order would be executed. By contrast, the quotes in dealer markets only give a vague indication of the real transaction prices. Post-transparency (i.e., the visibility of recent trading history) tends to be lower in dealer markets as well. Technically, orders that have been executed by dealers in a distributed manner take longer to be reported to the exchange and to be published. Additionally, stock exchange authorities tend to grant long publication delays to large transactions. Consequently, dealers may have to set spreads that are wider on average than in auction markets because there is less information available in dealer markets.

Other things equal, price at an auction market is more efficient because investors do not have to trade with dealers and public orders can be crossed with each other. At dealer markets, dealers ensure traders against execution risk by quoting bid and ask prices. In general, trading prices are better on average at auction markets but more risky. In practice, dealer markets appeal more to large institution investors whereas auction markets favor retail investors.

4.3 TRANSACTION COSTS

The organization of financial markets affects the transaction costs of securities trading. Transaction costs consist of both explicit costs and execution costs.[6] The explicit costs are direct and easy to observe. They involve commissions and taxes. Execution costs are indirect and difficult to measure. They include bid-ask spread, market impact costs, and opportunity costs.

- *The Bid-Ask Spread.* As discussed earlier, the bid-ask spread is the execution cost of a "round-trip" transaction, in which a stock is bought and then sold during a period with no new information about the stock. The stock is bought at the ask price and can only be sold at the bid price, which is lower.
- *Market Impact.* Market impact costs are those related to the buying or selling of large number of shares, which will adversely affect the price of the security. Market impact costs could be significant for institutional investors buying and selling large numbers of shares of the same security.
- *Opportunity Costs.* Opportunity costs refer to the costs incurred due to a delay in executing a transaction. In a market with rapid price movement, any delays in order routing and execution could be costly.

The paramount goal of an exchange is to provide an efficient marketplace that reduces transaction costs. However, transactions cost is not an isolated issue. Transaction costs, especially the bid-ask spread and market impact costs, are closely linked with market liquidity.

4.4 MARKET LIQUIDITY

Why is the NYSE the premier stock exchange in the world? Why do most technology start-ups prefer listing their stocks on the Nasdaq market? Do these two markets have the best systems for matching buyers and sellers of stocks? Or is there another reason for this historical success?

The NYSE has been around for more than 200 years, the Nasdaq market for about 30. The management teams of these markets have not simply been sitting idle all these years. They have been continually fine-tuning their systems and responding to the changing needs of their customers—the investment community—at times whether they liked it or not. Both these markets have also been investing huge sums of money on new information technologies and modern telecommunication systems.

Still, these are not the main factors that allow them to dominate the marketplace. In fact, we have already emphasized that the NYSE and Nasdaq do not have superior trading technology compared with various equity markets around the world. If anything, the NYSE has long been technologically backward. Simply put, investors flock to the NYSE and Nasdaq because as markets, they promise and deliver liquidity. New technology start-ups know that stock issued by most other technology firms, and especially market leaders such as Intel and Microsoft, are traded on the Nasdaq market. Accordingly, investors who are interested in and familiar with such stocks follow the Nasdaq market closely. Market makers who trade in more than one technology stock are familiar with the dynamics of making markets in such stocks. This enables the Nasdaq market to provide a liquid marketplace for technology stocks. It also helps that the listing requirements on the Nasdaq market are less stringent than on the NYSE. This allows smaller and newer firms to seek a listing on Nasdaq. As most of these start-ups tend to be technology-driven businesses, it is not surprising that they flock to the Nasdaq.

Nasdaq's influence extends well beyond the United States. For instance, about 96 Israeli stocks were listed on Nasdaq in 2000. Israel has more companies listed on Nasdaq than any other country outside North America. Nasdaq's overwhelming popularity has actually affected the liquidity of the Tel Aviv Stock Exchange (TASE), a fully automated exchange. The fact that TASE has a superior technology does not make any difference to Israeli companies; they list their stocks on Nasdaq to take advantage of that market's liquidity. In response, TASE has been in talks with Nasdaq to link the two markets so that Israeli investors can easily trade these stocks that are listed on Nasdaq. A classic case of "if you can't beat them, join them."

Although we have talked about the international drawing power of liquidity, we have not yet answered the larger question: Why is liquidity so important?

4.4.1 The Importance of Liquidity

The success of any stock exchange depends on its ability to match the buy and sell orders from investors in the form of order flows. But orders flow into a market in a discontinuous manner. Liquidity refers to the ability of investors to trade quickly at a price that is similar to the price of the previous trade. One approach to measure liquidity involves assessing the depth and breadth of the market for an asset. A market is said to have depth if there exists orders both above and below the price at which a security is currently trading. When a security trades in a deep market, temporary imbalances of buy or sell orders encounter offsetting and hence stabilizing market price. A market is said to have breadth if the orders above and below the current price have substantial volume. The broader the market, the greater the potential for stabilization of transitory price changes, which arise out of temporary order imbalances.[7]

When an order reaches the NYSE or Nasdaq, there might not be an appropriate contra order due to market thinness. This is the specific purpose for which the NYSE has specialists and the Nasdaq has market makers. These individuals trade off their own account, filling in the gaps in the flow of buy and sell orders in the following way. Assume an investor submits an order to sell 1,000 shares of XYZ stock at the best market price. The stock was last traded at $175 per share. When the order reaches the specialist on the floor of the NYSE, there are no bids for XYZ, meaning no other investor has expressed (to the specialist) an interest in buying the stock at a price close to the last traded price. The specialist will announce to the floor traders that he or she has an interest in selling 1,000 shares of XYZ at the best possible price. In that way, the specialist is acting as an agent of the investor here. If no one is willing to quote him or her a buying price, the specialist might execute the trade by buying the stock for his or her own account. The specialist then will hold the position in his or her book till a buy order is submitted by a different investor. By agreeing to buy the stock even though he or she did not have a contra buy order, the specialist has taken a *risk*. But in the process, he or she has supplied liquidity to the market. Whether or not the specialist makes money would depend on the price at which the next buy order flows to him or her.

Liquidity begets liquidity. As investors are well aware of the role played by the specialist, they send orders to the NYSE without worrying about the contra orders. As more orders are routed to the exchange, the risk of not finding an appropriate counterparty or contra order to trade is minimized. This in turn attracts more orders to the exchange, a symptom of what is called the *network effect*. Quite simply, liquidity attracts liquidity. In the case of the NYSE and the Nasdaq markets, the presence of the specialist and market maker, respectively, forms the core of the liquidity generation process.

4.4.2 Risk and Return in Providing Liquidity

What keeps the trading process well oiled is the presence of *liquidity* providers, or to be more precise, *immediacy* providers. No rational trader will be willing to risk capital when that trader knows that he or she will not be able to square-off his or her position within a reasonable period of time. In many markets, dealers who provide immediacy or *short-term liquidity* prefer to go home at the end of the day with a zero-position: neither short nor long. To conclude, the presence of specialists and market makers provides some sort of safety net to the underlying market. But discussed below, this safety net has its limitations. The biggest concern is that it might not be around when one needs it the most.

It should be pointed out that specialists on the NYSE floor as well as many market makers on the Nasdaq market tend be well compensated for the risk they absorb. Specialists on the NYSE, for instance, earn around 50 to 55 percent return on capital in a year. These rates of return are somewhat lower on the Nasdaq market for a simple reason. Specialists on the NYSE floor have a monopoly on the stocks in which they make a market. They are part of a dedicated-specialist system: one specialist per stock. By contrast, there are on average about 15 market makers dealing in any given stock on the Nasdaq market. In this competitive market, rates of return tend to be lower.

A natural question in this discussion of the profitability of the market-making business is whether market makers will continue to earn what one can call supernormal profits in electronic trading environments. The answer is not so easy. One reason for today's superior returns is the privileged access to critical information about trading interests of large customers. The specialist, for example, has access to the order book that he or she might not necessarily have to share with others on the exchange floor. This information allows the specialist to adjust his or her quotes appropriately.

This access to information in a sense reduces the risk inherent in providing immediacy to the marketplace. In electronic markets, this advantage will disappear if the order book is published for all to view, as is the case in some systems. Take away the access to privileged information and you increase the risk of providing short-term liquidity. One can already see this happening. Various new rules introduced in the Nasdaq market have shrunk the quoted spreads and, in turn, have resulted in fewer market makers dealing in any given stock.

Regardless of their access to information, specialists still run a very real risk. The longer the specialist has to wait for the next buy order, the greater the risk of losing money from the trade. Traders have limited financial resources, which limits their ability to supply liquidity. If a large order to sell 50,000 shares is routed to a market maker on the Nasdaq market, the latter will be reluctant to take the position on his or her books. At, say, an average price of $40 per share, one is talking about an exposure of $2,000,000. That's a lot of money to bet on a single trade! Because of this, it is more likely that the market maker will quote too low a price for the sell order. The lower price would allow the specialist to hedge against the risk of any loss that he or she would incur if not able to square off his or her position quickly. In the example above, if the order had been to sell 50,000 shares of XYZ, the specialist could execute a trade at $174.25, a price much lower than the last traded price of $175. The investor thus pays a higher price for the liquidity provided by the specialist.

4.4.3 Trends among Liquidity Providers

This business of liquidity provision is quickly changing. In November 1999, the NYSE announced plans to increase the capital requirements for its specialists. The goal is to improve the ability of a specialist to support the stocks he or she handles in times of increased market volatility. For instance, when The Dow Jones Industrial Average (DJIA) dropped by more than 500 points in August 1998, at least two specialist units were on the verge of becoming bankrupt. The NYSE management would like to avoid a repeat of such an occurrence. This is not necessarily because they are expecting more frequent 500-point drops in the entire exchange. Rather, recent developments in trading strategies followed by large sections of the investment community have caused an increase in volatility, not necessarily in the market as a whole but at least in specific groups of stocks. For instance, one witnesses dramatic fluctuations in prices of stocks when they are just first traded in the market (initial public offering [IPO]). Similar volatility is also observed whenever a stock is either added to or removed from a popular index such as the DJIA or the Standard and Poor (S&P) 500. Inclusion results in a rush by scores of traders who follow index-linked trading strategies to buy that stock. On the flip-side, these same traders will quickly dump the excluded stock that has been removed from an index.

Over the years, the business of NYSE specialists has been undergoing considerable consolidation. The number of firms owning a specialist license has shrunk from around 54 in 1986 to about 27 in 1999. This halving has taken place even as the number of stocks handled by specialists as a group has increased from about 1,550 to 2,875. In effect, this consolidation has seen an increase in the average number of stocks that are handled by any single specialist. As a result of this consolidation, three firms, Spear, Leeds and Kellogg, LP., Fleet Specialists (a unit of Fleet Boston Financial Corporation), and LaBrance and Company, currently account for more than 40 percent of the NYSE trading volume. According to the new plan, any firm that is responsible for more than 5 percent of the NYSE volume will have to have $4 million in capital for each stock contained in the DJIA; $2 million for each stock in the S&P 100 Index that is not included in the DJIA; and so on. This latest act by the NYSE will increase the cost of being a specialist. As a result, smaller firms might be forced to sell their seats to larger, well-funded firms, contributing to further consolidation of the specialist business.

Other trends are also contributing to changes in liquidity supplying services. Over the past few decades, there has been a fundamental change in the structure of the investment community. Individual investors have largely stayed out of the trading process and have instead hired the services of intermediaries such as mutual funds. These funds manage assets totaling billions of dollars. Given the large amounts to be invested, the managers of these funds prefer to trade in larger-than-average order sizes. But as seen in the example above, the NYSE and Nasdaq markets are not designed to supply liquidity at a low cost to such large order sizes. Given a scarcity of capital, most specialists and market makers would be reluctant to quote a competitive price for an order to trade a large number of shares.

To address this problem, new intermediaries have evolved to supply liquidity to such orders away from the confines of the NYSE and Nasdaq markets. The generic term to describe these trades is the phrase *upstairs block trading desk.* These trading desks are basically a group of traders working for large, well-capitalized investment banks with deep pockets that would be willing to quote a price for large blocks of stocks. The term *upstairs market* alludes to the fact that these traders do not work on the floor of an exchange. In practice they work in the offices of their employers, away from the hurly-burly of an exchange floor or a market maker's dealing rooms.

4.5 THE NEEDS OF INSTITUTIONAL INVESTORS

In the above section, we discussed the superior availability of liquidity as the major reason for the success of the NYSE and Nasdaq. Although this remains true to this very day, we can also say that the lack of liquidity is the key problem that faces these same markets. Despite appearances, there is no contradiction in these two statements, which we can illustrate by examining the case of institutional investors where information leaks and lack of capital and liquidity all affect the market.

4.5.1 Agency Problems

As the investor's agent, the broker is expected to procure the best possible deal for his or her client. Despite frequent complaints about brokers trying to scam uninformed investors, orders tend to be processed and executed efficiently. Regulations are in place to ensure that the broker provides the best possible execution for his or her client.

Most individuals trade in relatively small order sizes—a few hundred shares in each trade, small enough for the broker to ignore the reason why the investor is buying or selling a particular stock. But if a large investor, say, a mutual fund with a few billion dollars in assets, places an order to buy a particular stock, the broker will surely be interested in learning more about the motivation for this trade. As institutional investors have access to large amounts of research information, they are viewed as being better informed than the typical individual investor. So when a fund manager sends an order to buy a large quantity of shares in a particular stock, the broker will assume that his or her client has some positive news about that particular stock. Being human, the broker would be reluctant to let go of this opportunity to make some money for him- or herself. Academic economists base their theories on an assumption that all investors are rational. We can explain a related concept of "rational expectation" with the help of this fable:

An economist and a stock broker are walking along a street, let's call it Wall Street, when they come across a $100 bill. The economist, who subscribes to the rational expectations school of thought, asks his friend to ignore the currency note. He explains that the note is counterfeit. If it were real, then someone else would have already picked it up. But does the broker take the economist's advice? No, as he relies on his wits to make a living, the broker cannot afford to go along with the rational expectations theory. He simply picks up the note and pockets it without any hesitation. If it turns out to be counterfeit, he won't have lost anything by picking up the note. Similarly, when a broker learns about a fund manager's trading interest, he or she will promptly execute the order. But at the same time, the broker may be inclined to buy a sufficiently small number of shares in that stock for his or her own account. The broker might even make a few discreet calls to friends working in other brokerage firms (and maybe even some of his or her clients) and pass on the information to them. Hollywood too appreciates this behavior pattern of brokers. An excellent example is the movie "Wall Street," in which a junior broker tells all his friends at neighboring tables to buy or sell a stock that he is trading on behalf of a big speculator.

Like Hollywood, Wall Street also reacts appropriately to the broker's behavior. If everyone acts on the broker's information by buying the stock, the demand pressure for the stock will increase. This will push up its price. Sellers will notice the increase in buying interest and raise the prices at which they are willing to sell the stock. This will lead to an additional increase in the price of the stock. Any increase caused by such leakage of information is termed the market impact effect.

The next time around, the fund manager would consider it wiser to break up his or her large trading interest into multiple orders of much smaller sizes. Instead of a single order to buy 25,000 shares, he or she might break it up into 10 orders of 2,500 shares each. But brokers have a way of catching up with such tactics. If they notice a stream of orders flowing in from a particular client for a specific stock, they will simply add up the trades and reach the same conclusion as earlier: that the fund manager has some positive information about the stock, information that is not widely available to the market. So after the first few trades have been executed, the fund manager might notice the stock price creeping up at a rate higher than he or she would be comfortable with. His or her trading interest has been exposed and buying pressure from other traders has pushed up the price. The fund manager will now have to pay more for additional quantities of the stock.

Given the higher costs of trading through human intermediaries, institutional investors have increasingly preferred alternative venues in which they can trade in relative anonymity; meaning, without having to identify themselves as well as their trading interests.

4.5.2 Illiquid Markets

As intimated earlier, the basic problem here is a lack of adequate liquidity in the NYSE and Nasdaq markets. This is a controversial statement. These two markets dominate trading in stocks in the largest equity markets in the world. The number of shares traded in the NYSE and Nasdaq is much larger than the total number of shares traded in all other markets in the world. So how can one accuse these markets of being illiquid?

We can start with a classic definition of a liquid market. A truly liquid market is one in which an order of any size can be traded with *zero market impact* on the price of the stock concerned. In this sense of the word, the NYSE and Nasdaq markets are clearly not liquid. Orders to trade small numbers of shares in any stock will certainly be executed with hardly any impact on market price. These markets are liquid enough to efficiently handle the trading interests of small investors. But not for institutions seeking to trade stocks worth millions of dollars in a single trade.

A second reason why large investors consider the NYSE and Nasdaq markets to be illiquid is the lack of adequate capital. To illustrate, let's assume a fund manager sends an order to a specialist on the floor of the NYSE to sell 1,000,000 shares of a stock. (This is an extreme example; in today's market, no sensible trader will request a quote for such a large trade size.) Instead of specifying whether he or she wants to buy or sell this stock, the manager will simply ask for a quote.

Let us assume that the spread between the bid and ask quotes is $0.25 per share of stock. Faced with such a large potential trade, the specialist will prefer to cover his or her risk by quoting a wide spread. Instead of the regular 25 cents per share, he or she might even widen the spread to 75 cents or even a dollar per share. The specialist would argue that the low $0.25 spread is for small quantities of shares, say, 1,000 shares or 10,000 shares, whatever is the standard lot in which most trades take place for this particular stock. The specialist is not playing a guessing game; he or she simply wants to quote a wide enough spread so that if a trade takes place, he or she will have sufficient margin to cover his or her position quickly, without having to take a loss.

The specialist does this for a couple of reasons. One, he or she might not necessarily be interested in trading a million shares of the stock. Ideally, he or she would prefer to trade small numbers of shares and turn them over several times a day. The best way to discourage the fund manager from trading the million shares would be to quote an unattractive price, one with a wide spread. Second, given that the average price of a share on the NYSE is approximately $40 per share, a trade involving a million shares will amount to an exposure of at least $40 million. As argued earlier, most specialists on the NYSE (and market makers on the Nasdaq market) will either not have capital sufficient to cover the risks involved in $40-million-dollar trades or they might not be willing to risk such a large amount on a single trade. In such circumstances, a large spread would provide sufficient margin, or compensation, for the additional risk involved in a million-share trade. It might also act as a deterrent to the trader who might not be willing to trade at the quoted prices.

Let's assume the fund manager accepts the quote—with a $1 spread—and decides to trade with the specialist. The quote for a small order would be $40.50 (being the bid)–$40.75 (the offer price); for the million share order, the spread has widened to $1 per share: $40.125 (bid)–$41.125 (ask). If the order had been for say 1,000 stocks, the transaction price would have been $40.50. Assuming the million-share sell order had been executed at this higher price, the market would have lived up to its promise of providing superior liquidity.

But in this case, the market price has moved to $40.125; the trade has adversely affected the market price for the fund manager and thus contradicted the NYSE's claim of being a truly liquid market. In addition, even before quoting a price, the specialist will have communicated with the floor traders to solicit any trading interest in that particular stock. Under certain circumstances, the specialist might even be forced to reveal to these traders the fact that he or she has received a request for a quote for a million shares. This information will cause other traders to react by changing their own quotes and/or leading them to take bets on whether there is a large buying interest or a selling one. Either way, this might cause the quoted spread to widen beyond the $1.00 level indicated above.

So what do investors do? How do they execute trades in large quantities of stocks? The following section will describe an informal network of traders, called a upstairs market, which has evolved over the years. This market specializes in supplying liquidity—and hence a liquid marketplace—to large investors. Later sections and following chapters describe in considerable detail the various new electronic trading systems that have been developed to provide large investors with environments where they can trade directly with each other in a relatively anonymous manner. The goal as always is to reduce the market impact of any trade.

Another factor in the complaint of large institutional investors against the NYSE and Nasdaq markets is the difficulty of trading packages or bundles of stocks. Granted, package trading is not a service that either the NYSE or Nasdaq market is capable of delivering under their existing trading systems. Trading on the NYSE floor as well as the Nasdaq dealer network is organized around individual stocks. Every stock has its own demand and supply schedule. These schedules might be interdependent, but the stocks themselves are traded separately. For instance, if the semiconductor firm Intel announces negative results, this fact might be interpreted as indicative of lower profits for other semiconductor firms as well as various computer manufacturers such as Dell, Compaq, and Gateway. Along with Intel stock, the stock prices of all these stocks might fall. But a trader cannot send an order to sell a combination of technology stocks on an "all-or-none" basis (i.e., either executing the complete combination of stocks or none at all).

Institutional investors pursue asset allocation (reallocation) strategies that involve the simultaneous purchase and sale of packages or baskets of stocks. Each such basket will be made up of a large number of different stocks. The interesting feature of such transactions is that the investor is interested more in the price of the complete trade, or the net price, rather than the prices at which each individual stock is traded. Speed is of the essence, and traders do not want to go through the process of trading each stock in the basket separately. Such orders as well as trading interests involving large blocks of stocks are sent not to the NYSE or Nasdaq but to what is called the *upstairs market.*

4.5.3 The Upstairs Market

Solutions to the liquidity and package trading problems faced by institutional investors have evolved in the shape of two distinct systems. Although it has not fully solved them, the upstairs market is an example of a nonelectronic trading system that has been created in direct response to these problems. Several electronic trading systems, which are discussed in the next chapter, also address these same problems.

Instead of sending large orders down either to brokers on the trading floor of the NYSE or to Nasdaq market makers, institutional investors increasingly rely on specialized intermediation services. Certain brokerage houses, especially those affiliated with large investment banks such as Goldman Sachs and Merrill Lynch, have trading desks, distinct from the NYSE floor and the Nasdaq market makers, that match buyers and sellers of large blocks of stocks. How are these brokers different from the specialist on the NYSE floor or the market maker on the Nasdaq market? Most specialists and market makers are employees of large investment banks and brokerage firms such as Merrill Lynch and Goldman Sachs. The key difference between them and the upstairs trading desks is that the latter specialize in large trades and, hence, are treated as distinct from traditional brokerage activities of a firm. In addition, they do not work on the exchange floor, nor do they work within the confines of the Nasdaq market system.

As explained in an earlier section, brokers need large amounts of capital to execute large trades. Upstairs trading desks have access to much more risk capital than any traditional broker. Traders at these desks are unencumbered by exchange rules. They are free to trade across various exchange markets. They also have access to a wide range of securities that they can use to hedge the risks involved in million-dollar positions. Better access to capital, greater flexibility, and superior risk management capabilities together allow the upstairs trading desk to offer services that no traditional specialist could ever provide. The difference becomes clear as we walk through a typical example found in the upstairs market.

Let us assume that an asset management company such as Fidelity Investments has decided to change the manager of a specific equity fund. The new manager believes in following an asset allocation strategy different from that of the previous manager. When he takes over the new fund, he decides to change the portfolio allocation. This would involve selling a specific basket of stocks and adding exposure to a different combination of stocks. The example here discusses the execution of this basket of different stocks, a growing, but still small portion of the total number of trades executed in the upstairs market. A majority of trades involve large numbers of shares of a single stock. Although transactions can be initiated and structured in different ways, we will look at one specific case that illustrates key aspects of the dynamics of trading in this market.

The fund manager in our example issues the necessary instructions to his trading team, which then contacts a select group of brokers in the upstairs market. The communication provides aggregate information of the bundle of assets to be bought and sold. Information about every stock in the bundles is not included. As described elsewhere, large traders prefer to disclose as little of their trading interest as possible. In the present example, when the investor solicits quotes from brokers, he has to provide them with sufficient—but not necessarily complete information—about his trading interest.[8] Instead, the risk, return, correlation, sectoral composition, and other features of the bundles are released. The idea is to provide the brokers with sufficient information to price the trading interest and provide a quote for the deal.

The actual trades are executed on an agency or a principal basis. A broker working on a commission basis, for example, would agree to find a counterparty for the deal. If acting as a principal, he or she could agree to be the counterparty to the whole transaction, buying the assets being sold and selling the desired combination of stocks to the mutual fund. In either case, the broker has to find either a single investor, typically another fund manager, who might be interested in the whole transaction, or if the broker is unable to find a counterparty quickly, he or she must use his or her execution skills along with a network of salesmen and brokers on the trading floor to break up the bundle into smaller components and trade them individually.

The upstairs market is characterized by strict monitoring of all parties to a transaction. Fund managers have to be careful to describe the pertinent characteristics of their portfolios. If not, brokers might either refuse to make quotes or quote prices with a higher premium to cover the increased risk involved in dealing with a fund manager who does not provide adequate information. Investors, in turn, spend considerable resources in monitoring the performance of brokers. They would like to make sure that the information shared with brokers in the upstairs market is not leaked to other traders in the market; that the broker stuck to his or her side of the deal; and that the transaction was completed at the targeted price and within the specified time frame.

For all its obvious advantages to institutional investors in providing increased liquidity and package trading, the upstairs market has two major shortcomings. First, it relies on the search skills of human traders and on the risk-bearing ability of brokerage firms. Both these services come at a high cost. Second, the system can never be free of information leakage. Consequently, fund managers have to expend considerable resources in monitoring brokers and in evaluating their performance. As seen in Chapter 8, new forms of electronic trading systems are being designed that would overcome these disadvantages by both automating the trading process and allowing investors to pursue complex trading strategies.

4.6 LIQUIDITY SUPPLIERS IN A DIGITAL MARKETPLACE

Markets today are moving away from systems in which buy and sell orders are matched by brokers, away from systems in which trading revolves around the broker-dealer network, away from markets in which primarily professional traders are in the business of risking their capital to make money by supplying short-term liquidity (or immediacy) to the market. Markets are moving more toward the situation in which buyers and sellers can interact directly with each other. The basic issue to be addressed is this: Who will supply liquidity? In the current market structure, intermediaries such as brokers, specialists, and market makers are all important for a liquid marketplace. Can we do away with their services completely? Can markets function efficiently without these middlemen?

Economists have known for a long time now that intermediaries such as banks, mutual funds, and insurance companies have a natural role to play in any competitive market. These institutions have evolved in response to the needs of households and businesses struggling to manage their finances. We will not get any deeper into theories of financial intermediation. It will suffice to state that in the presence of costly information that is surely not evenly distributed—a classic example of this phenomenon being a borrower typically knows more about the state of his or her finances than the lender—banks, insurance companies, and other "brokers" will *always* have a role to play in ensuring the smooth functioning of financial markets. Recently, we have also witnessed a growing role played by direct competitive markets, rather than by brokers and dealers, to supply the functions of risk sharing and resource allocation. For example, derivative securities have been used widely to provide insurance that was previously covered only under policies underwritten by insurance companies.

In the traditional marketplace, brokers and dealers are the main liquidity providers. But customers pay a high price. Brokers and specialists are exposed to certain risks in supplying liquidity to the marketplace. Seeking to mitigate these risks, they have historically managed to lobby successfully for access to superior information. The specialist on the floor of the NYSE has a strategic advantage over all other traders in the market. Brokers and dealers on the Nasdaq market maintain order books, and the contents of these books need not be made public. A limit order placed with a broker has to be revealed only if it is better than the broker's own quote. Orders with limit prices a point—say, a cent—below the best buying price need not be exposed to other traders. The dealer is privy to this information. He or she now has better information about the demand and/or supply for a stock than many large investors. A specialist on the floor of the NYSE, for instance, will argue that access to information in the order book allows him or her to perform his or her job (i.e., supply liquidity, smooth movements in stock prices, and so on) more efficiently.

That will not be the case in the new electronic marketplace. As has been pointed out before, trading in the equity markets today is increasingly dominated by large institutions such as mutual and pension funds. The trading needs of these investors are such that traditional brokers and dealers are of marginal importance to them. Given that a large number of investors find themselves in the same boat, it is a matter of time before someone puts together a device such as electronic communications network (ECN) for these traders to talk to each other and execute trades. The key feature of all these systems is that they are exclusionary in nature—they exclude brokers and dealers from the trading system. Technically, all registered brokers are free to use these new systems. They can submit orders on behalf of their customers. They can also submit orders for their own trading account. But unlike traditional markets, brokers do not receive any special privileges. All traders are treated alike. Information is shared equally among all participants. Bargains are settled largely on the basis of the time an order is submitted and the price at which a participant is willing to trade.

New electronic trading systems are built around a philosophy that treats large institutional traders and brokers as equals. In addition, ECNs do not expose information about orders submitted to the network for execution. Despite the unsuccessful trial, the OptiMark system was able to ensure complete nondisclosure of information in the order book. It hired the services of the accounting firm Deloitte and Touche to certify that there has been no leakage of information from the system.

In the past few years, anyone taking active interest in trading stocks would have observed a steady shrinkage in quoted spreads. This has been especially true in the Nasdaq market. Several factors have contributed to this development. We will look at the impact of new electronic trading systems on quoted spreads. The spread between the buying and selling prices compensates the dealer for the risk he or she takes in supplying liquidity to the market. Given a certain spread, the dealer's revenue depends on his trading volumes: the number of shares that are bought and sold through him or her. As trading volumes increase, total revenue increases proportionately. As trading volume grows exponentially in the past 20 years, investors demand a share in this spread. In a competitive market, wide spread attracts new entrants to the market, and increases in supply of liquidity will, in turn, lead to a shrinking of spreads. On the Nasdaq market, the pressure to reduce spreads has come from regulators. Setting aside the regulatory concerns, the desire to maintain wide spreads by colluding seemed to have backfired. Some clients decided to stay away from the broker-dealer network. Large investors simply set up their own markets, private ECNs. Some of the new trading systems have been designed specifically with the idea of allowing investors to trade at the mid-point of the bid-offer spread quoted by market makers on the Nasdaq market. These systems also offer lower commissions and greater privacy to large investors. Initially, small investors did not have any access to these new electronic trading systems. But this too is changing now.

Soon, small investors will be able to access these new electronic trading systems. Like the ECNs designed for large investors, the new networks will accept orders from smaller investors and attempt to match them with other orders in the system. But any individual who decides to route orders to such systems will have to deal with a basic problem in all markets: Orders to buy and sell shares of any given stock do not flow in continuously. It has been precisely this intermittent flow that has provided brokers with a profitable niche: make money by filling gaps in the order flow. In other words, supplying immediacy. At this stage of development of electronic trading systems, it is still not clear if nonintermediated systems—those that purport to survive without the help of professional liquidity suppliers—can function efficiently. It is more likely that these systems will eventually invite brokers and market makers into the system. But they might not be willing to provide the latter with privileged access to the order book. They will have to compete with the rest of the market. At best, they might be compensated by means to warrants or stock options in the firms that set up these electronic trading systems. In fact, we have already seen this trend but more on that in the later chapters.

A more vicious development—from the perspective of market makers on the Nasdaq market—has been the recent popularity of the phenomenon of day trading. As explained elsewhere, in recent years large numbers of individuals have quit their regular jobs and taken to full-time trading. They "rent" trading desks in brokerage firms around the country. In the early days, these systems were linked to the small order execution system (SOES). But these days, such trading activity uses the SelectNet system to pursue momentum trading strategies. In essence, these day traders also supply liquidity to the marketplace.

Another possible solution is to introduce call auctions that can coexist with the current continuous markets. As discussed earlier, in a call market orders are accumulated over prespecified intervals in the order book and matched in batches. This feature allows liquidity to be built up over a period of time. Traders who want to have anonymity and trade a large volume can wait for the periodic auction instead of trading in the continuous market.

4.7 TECHNOLOGY AND THE EVOLUTION OF MARKETS

At present, investors use various broker-based systems to route orders to the market. Larger investors, however, have access to proprietary systems offered by firms such as Reuters and Bloomberg, to place their orders and to access the contents of order books in various markets. These communication systems are also used to receive quick reports about the status of one's orders. In most markets, the contents of the order book are never really exposed completely. In fact, none of the trading institutions, whether in the United States or in various European nations, publish their order book information in public forums. Instead, parts of the order book are published for selective viewing over proprietary networks, either private ones such as Reuters and Bloomberg or those owned by the exchanges themselves.

But as in so many other areas, the Internet is forcing the pace of change. A few online businesses such as Island and the Arizona Stock Exchange have taken the initial steps to publish limited order book information over the Internet. In addition, the Internet and new computer technology will profoundly change the competitive picture of financial exchanges as well as financial exchanges themselves. This rapidly changing environment presents significant challenges to the financial markets. Traditionally, the markets have taken their time to slowly evolve from a dependence on rather labor-intensive processes to taking advantage of the latest computing technologies.

Over the years, traditional markets with human-centered processes have served us well. But our needs are changing continuously. Over the past three to four decades, the investment community has witnessed a dramatic transformation in the manner in which we manage our finances. We have been helped along by new theories and models developed in leading universities—the portfolio diversification theory and the Black-Scholes option pricing model come to mind here. Even though their customers have become sophisticated in their attitudes and needs, the exchanges have been stuck in decades old business models. Chapters 5 and 6 illustrate the mismatch between the needs of the marketplace and the outdated structures of markets such as the NYSE and Nasdaq.

Fortunately for us, the business of markets is so competitive that new trading systems are being developed, ones that attempt to address the evolving needs of the investment community. The remainder of this book describes the ongoing development of automated systems of varying degrees of sophistication.

4.8 SUMMARY

This chapter discussed the basic organization of financial markets. Depending on how orders are traded, markets can simply be categorized as auction markets and dealer markets. The former can be operated as either continuous or call markets. Different market institutional structure certainly affects the performance of markets, particularly the price discovery, market transparency, and liquidity. Those markets have tradeoffs, and most financial exchanges in the world are the hybrid forms of these market types.

The issue of market liquidity was also addressed. Although important, liquidity cannot be viewed as an isolated issue. In fact, market liquidity relates closely with market efficiency and transparency. A market with high operation and price efficiency and great transparency will attract more traders and thus enhance market liquidity. At this stage, it is still unclear whether electronic trading systems can function smoothly without the help of professional liquidity suppliers. Without access to privileged information, are dealers, professional or nonprofessional, still willing to take positions to provide liquidity?

The next few chapters look at the structures of the world's leading exchanges and examine how technology has affected the way financial instruments are traded at those markets.

5

NEW YORK

STOCK EXCHANGE

Over the past hundred years, the New York Stock Exchange (NYSE) has been without question the dominant stock exchange in the world. In April 2000, NYSE daily trading volume surpassed 1.5 billion shares, compared with the volume of 100 million about two decades ago. Some of the largest U.S. companies are traded on the NYSE. Daily movements in the Dow Jones Industrial Average (DJIA)[1] typically set the tone for trading activity in financial markets around the world. The special place it holds in financial markets warrants a closer look at the logistics and technology encountered in the process of trading on the NYSE. The structure of the marketplace has evolved over the past few years. So, one gets to see an interesting mix of technologies and trading rules in use on the exchange floor.

Given the main thrust of this book and its focus on sophisticated electronic trading technologies, it is tempting to write about the oncoming demise of the NYSE's apparently antiquated network of traders—its specialists and floor traders. In fact, numerous market observers did write them off around the late 1990s. But these intermediaries are still around and, most important, are thriving. The exchange has been willing to experiment with new technologies but has been resolute in its commitment to the labor-intensive floor-based trading system. The mix of 19th- and 21st-century technologies can cause obvious tensions. The unique dynamics of the exchange floor brings into focus critical aspects of the NYSE trading system. The focus here is less on describing in any great detail the trading process within the NYSE than on the competitive pressures it is facing and its evolving responses.

5.1 MARKET ORGANIZATION

The NYSE, to give a "bottom-line" description, can be characterized as essentially an order-driven double-auction market. Under this arrangement, investors route their orders either directly or through their broker to the exchange floor for execution (Figure 5.1). Trading on the floor of the exchange is organized around specialists and floor brokers or traders. Floor brokers act primarily as agents for public customers, delivering orders for a stock to the trading crowd. They operate from booths along the outside walls of the trading floor. This section takes a detailed look at the NYSE, its institutional structure, and its trading process.

5.1.1 NYSE Membership

Members of the NYSE are either individuals who own or lease a membership (called a "seat") or nominees (partners or employees) of member firms that own seats. The number of seats has been fixed at 1,366 since 1953. Seats can be bought, sold, or leased, and their price, as set by buyers and sellers, reflects the demand to hold a seat. In addition to the regular NYSE members, 60 individuals have obtained either physical or electronic access to the trading floor by an annual membership fee. Unlike regular members, electronic or physical access

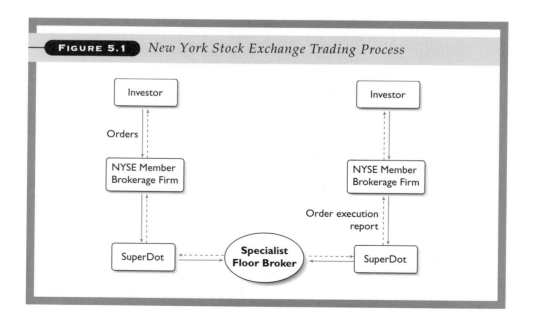

FIGURE 5.1 *New York Stock Exchange Trading Process*

members have no rights to distributive assets of the NYSE. Because NYSE members are also members of the National Association of Security Dealers (NASD; the self-regulatory organization of brokers/dealers that regulates the over-the-counter [OTC] market), many broker-dealer firms are simultaneously members of the NYSE, customers of the NYSE, and competitors of the NYSE. Of the 1,444 members, the 1,366 who hold "seats," are entitled to a proportional share of the exchange's assets (technically, its goodwill, real estate, and physical equipment).

NYSE members who operate on the trading floor include specialists, commission-house brokers, floor brokers, and floor traders. Each is discussed in the following sections.

Specialists

Specialists at NYSE manage the auction process. As agents (broker's brokers), specialists handle limit orders for stocks assigned to their trading posts and execute orders for floor traders. They also electronically quote and record current bid and ask prices for the stocks that are assigned to them. As dealers, they will buy or sell for their own account to supply immediacy to the market in the absence of buyers and sellers and other trading interest.

Each stock listed on the NYSE is allocated to a specialist. Interested specialist firms may apply for the allocation of newly listed securities. The Stock Allocation Committee allocates the securities to a specialist unit that then becomes responsible for making a market in that stock. The committee's allocation procedure takes into account the specialist firm's prior performance record, the firm's score on the Specialist Performance Evaluation Questionnaire (SPEQ), which is filled out quarterly by floor brokers, and the characteristics (such as industry type) of the issues currently assigned to the specialist firm. The allocation committee also considers requests made by the newly listed companies.

There are about 440 individual specialists on the NYSE representing 49 *specialist units*. Specialist units have traditionally been private corporations or partnerships. However, several are subsidiaries of publicly held corporations or brokerage houses. Individual specialists are employed by specialist firms (or units). Many hail from powerful Wall Street institutions such as Merrill Lynch, Bear Stearns, La Branche & Co., and Spear, Leeds & Kellogg (which is now a part of Goldman Sachs, another large Wall Street firm). La Branche sold stock via an IPO in the late 1990s and is now a publicly traded company.

NYSE specialists have an extraordinarily lucrative franchise. In 1995, specialist firms netted $162 million, an after-tax annualized return of 16.3 percent. Reflecting the growth in trading volumes, in the fourth quarter of 2000, the pickings had gotten even juicier. Specialists made $153 million in just this quarter, a 31 percent increase over the same quarter of 1999. Just to give a sense of the money involved in this business, their gross revenue for the year 2000 was $2.14 billion, a 36 percent increase over the 1999 full-year revenue of $1.57 billion.

Commission-House Brokers

Employed by the brokerage houses, commission-house or floor brokers link the brokerage houses with the specialist posts. The commission-house brokers operate from booths along the outside walls of the trading floor where they receive orders from their firms' clients and either execute them with the specialist, with each other, or cross the trades. A cross-trade occurs when the broker has both a buy and a sell order of the same size and completes the trade. All floor trades must be reported to and approved by the specialist. Floor brokers act primarily as agents for public customers, delivering orders for a stock to the trading crowd, whereas the specialist acts as the "broker's broker," providing both dealership and brokerage services.

Floor Brokers

Also called *two-dollar brokers,* a term coined back in the days when they received $2 for every 100 shares they traded, these brokers perform the same functions as the commission-house brokers but are not employed by a brokerage house. Rather, for a commission, they execute orders for commission-house brokers who are not able to handle all of the orders that have been transmitted to their firms. Firms might use floor brokers to disguise the trading interest in a particular stock. Sometimes, both floor brokers and commission-house brokers are together called floor brokers.

Floor Traders

They trade solely for themselves and are prohibited by exchange rules from handling public orders.

5.1.2 Trading Process

The process of trading itself can occur in one of two ways. Buy and sell orders for a particular stock can be matched by the concerned specialist who handles the stock by crossing them with other orders in his or her order book. A cross-trade occurs when the specialist has both a buy and a sell order of the same limit price and order size and matches them with each other. Trading can also take place by open outcry bargains among floor traders and a specialist. Figure 5.1 illustrates this basic market process. We later also examine the process from the perspective of one of the most important elements in the trading process—the order book. Figure 5.2 illustrates the flow of orders between the exchange and investors. A quick comparison of Figures 5.1 and 5.2 shows that the NYSE is not a pure double-auction market where buyers and sellers interact with each other to strike deals. In textbook models of such auctions, all market participants have equal access to trading information.

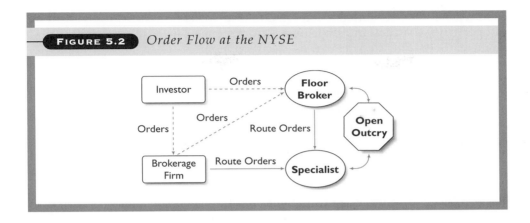

FIGURE 5.2 *Order Flow at the NYSE*

In the NYSE's diversion from the standard scenario, specialists play a unique role in the trading process. They are awarded an exclusive franchise to act as a dealer and auctioneer in each stock. Their primary task is to maintain the order books for stocks assigned to them. This places the specialist at a distinct advantage over the other traders in the market. In return, specialists are expected to maintain orderly trading in the assigned stocks, often acting as a temporary risk absorber in the market. This responsibility might require specialists to buy and sell stocks for their own accounts as temporary imbalances in demand and supply can cause short-term fluctuations in prices.

Let us assume that due to a temporary shortfall in demand, the price of a particular stock has fallen by, say, 5 percent. Also, the specialist is of the opinion that the price will move back to its original level once new buy orders come in. Instead of waiting for investors to place new orders, the specialist will enter appropriate buy orders to offset the higher selling pressure in that stock. Later, when new buy orders from other traders are submitted the specialist will place corresponding sell orders and restore his or her holdings to their previous position. In this manner, the specialist risks his or her own capital to smooth any fluctuations in prices.

A specialist cannot obviously deal with all fluctuations in price movements. If any change in price is caused by new information about the issuing company, specialists will not try to prevent it. In short, the focus of specialists is more on fluctuations in prices due to short-term mismatches in demand and supply. Nevertheless, his or her mere presence assuages the concerns of other traders and results in improved trading conditions.

So how do specialists make money? First, they get commissions as specialists serve as auctioneers and handle public orders. However, this revenue source is shrinking. The NYSE board has approved a major pricing initiative that will eliminate specialist commissions on orders delivered through SuperDOT and executed within five minutes. SuperDOT (also spelled SuperDot) is part of an electronic network that transmits orders from member firms to a specialist's post on the NYSE trading floor as well as execution reports back to member firms.

The primary source of profit for specialists is trading gains. As a dealer, the specialist can trade from his or her own account (or for the firm that employs him or her). Because of the specialists' unique access to the limit-order book, they possess a tremendous advantage in terms of market information for trading. For example, if the specialist sees a lot more buy orders than sell orders on the order book, he or she can sense the market sentiment and can add his or her own positions before the price starts to soar.

Although the NYSE specialists are often referred to as monopolistic dealers, they participate in only about 10 percent of all shares traded. In addition, as illustrated below, they have to compete with floor traders and "outside" investors to participate in trades executed on the exchange floor.

5.1.3 Order Book

As in all exchanges, the order book is the central element of the trading at the NYSE. As described in Chapter 4, the presence of such a book allows all trading interests to interact with each other for the best possible set of matches. Unfortunately, the NYSE does not have a consolidated order book for each stock listed on the exchange. The NYSE is in good company here as its largest competitor, the Nasdaq market, measures up a lot more poorly on this issue.

As Figure 5.2 illustrates, investors can route their orders directly to the NYSE floor or indirectly through brokerage firms. When a specialist receives an order, he or she lists it in his or her limit-order book similar to that described in the generic market in Chapter 4. The order book displays limit orders for each stock handled by the specialist. Similarly, floor brokers enter the orders routed to them in their own order books. The latter enter the specialist's book only when the floor broker chooses to expose it to the rest of the market.

The orders routed to specialists tend to be simple limit orders with prices close to current transaction prices as well as large market orders. Floor brokers, however, receive limit orders, especially larger ones, that are more difficult to execute. The reason for this is that a client seeking to trade a larger than normal quantity of shares of a particular stock might be reluctant to fully expose his or her trading interests to the market. In such instances, he or she might prefer to route orders to a floor broker, who takes the responsibility for efficient execution of the investor's order. The floor broker is required to use his or her judgment and expose a client's interests selectively.

The ability of a trader to thus conceal portions of one's trading interest is functionally equivalent to the hidden order book in the sense of the generic market above. The major difference is that selective or, in other words, *discretionary* disclosure can result in considerable gaming among various traders on the exchange floor, as well as between floor brokers and their clients. A trader does not want to reveal his or her hand completely; but at the same time, the trader knows that some disclosure is necessary to elicit appropriate responses from prospective counterparties.

5.1.4 Competing to Trade

Trading activity in any given stock on the NYSE floor is concentrated around what is called the specialist's post. An incoming order to buy or sell may be executed against the specialist's quotes, against an existing offer to sell or buy that is already in the order book, or in a transaction with a floor trader. The bid and ask quotes at which a trade is executed may be from the order book, or they may be quotes by floor brokers or floor traders if these quotes are better than the quotes in the book.

Although specialists have an exclusive franchise in their stocks, they face *competition* for order flow from floor brokers and traders on the exchange, from other exchanges, and from public limit orders. Limit-order prices are part of the spread displayed to the market and take precedence over specialists' trades for their own account. When a specialist receives a limit order priced outside the bid and ask prices currently being quoted, he or she automatically lists it in his or her order book. An example would be an order to buy 1,000 shares of IBM at $115.65 or better per share, when the highest bid in the book is at $115.75. A floor broker, however, can either hold it in his or her own book or pass it on to the specialist to be included in the latter's order book.

If the broker selects the first approach, he or she can exercise judgment to announce his or her client's trading interests to the other traders assembled around the specific post based on the trading activity and expressions of interests from other brokers. The broker will do this by shouting out—hence the *open outcry* process to describe trading of this type—the number of shares and the price at which he or she is willing to trade a particular stock. If a broker's order has a better price than the one quoted by the specialist, traders in the crowd are more willing to trade with the broker.

The specialist may execute a market order (or a limit order priced inside the existing best bid and offer) against another order in his or her book or against an order represented by a floor trader. Unlike the automated matching system described earlier, most market orders are not executed the moment they reach the trading floor. To attract better bids or offer quotes and in the process try to get price improvement, the specialist or floor trader will expose the order to other traders in the market. If there is no improvement on the price, the order will be executed at the best available limit order exposed to the market. It is in this sense that one sees competition among various players on the exchange floor.

5.1.5 Continuous Trading and Call Auctions

Trading in the NYSE is a combination of two auction mechanisms: The market opens with a call auction and then switches to continuous order-driven trading until closing.

Call Auctions

At the beginning of any trading day, the specialist and floor traders have a number of orders in their respective order books. Each member will announce his or her trading interests in the form of quotes. The specialist then has to determine the price at which the exposed orders will be cleared. If there is an imbalance between the buy and sell orders, he or she may solicit additional orders from floor traders as well as from other exchanges through the InterMarket Trading System (ITS). The specialist will typically announce trial clearing prices (also called "indications") to traders crowded around his or her post and wait for their reactions before settling on an opening price. This process can take place over multiple rounds. The specialist will attempt to ensure that all trades in a particular stock are executed at the same price. If he or she is not successful in attracting additional orders, the specialist will buy for, or sell from, his or her own inventory to resolve the imbalance.

Let's assume that the highest bidding interest expressed to a specialist for stock XYZ is $75.45 for 100,000 shares. The offer size at this price is 75,000. The order imbalance is 25,000. If the imbalance is bigger at all other prices, the specialist will take appropriate steps to attract additional order flow to reduce this imbalance. If he or she does not succeed in this, the specialist will simply step in and sell 25,000 shares out of his or her own account and open trading at the price of $75.45 per share.

It is normally the case that the number of shares changing hands at the market-opening price exceeds the number that is traded in the next several transactions. A similar procedure call auction is also used whenever trading stops during the day. This could happen when the firm that has issued the stock has released some new information and the specialist is unable to facilitate a smooth movement to a new price level. This can also happen when there is extreme imbalance in the order flow, and the specialist needs additional time to rectify the situation by attracting additional orders.

Continuous Trading

In the continuous trading market that follows the initial call auction of the day, investors can place orders with NYSE specialists and floor brokers for execution. The two generic types of orders are market orders and limit orders.

By definition, market orders are eligible for immediate execution. However, there is no guarantee that it will be executed the moment it reaches the trading floor. A simple explanation for this is that although the system can match buy and sell orders continuously, orders do not flow in continuously. One can also come up with extreme scenarios in which even market orders will not be executed. This can happen if investors are reluctant to submit limit orders on the opposite side to trade a particular stock. Consider the case of a stock LF (short for Long Forgotten, Inc.), which is not very actively traded. Mr. Small Guy happens to be doing research on a particular industry and comes across LF. He learns that this firm is on the verge of returning to profitability. Mr. Small Guy logs on to his online broker and types in the stock symbol LF. The last trade in that stock took place at $10.95 per share. He quickly places a market buy order for 500 shares of LF. The broker routes the order to various markets and finds out that there are no selling interests in that stock. The market maker who used to quote prices in it closed shop a couple of years ago. Unable to find "any" sell offers, the broker e-mails Mr. Small Guy that he cannot execute[2] his market order.

To provide immediate execution to those who seek it (and who are willing to pay for the convenience), the exchange permits the specialist to place limit orders on his or her own account. As explained earlier, if the order book is incomplete, the specialist will quote his or her bid or ask price to the incoming order.

5.2 TECHNOLOGY AND THE NYSE MARKET STRUCTURE

Although the NYSE has used various forms of technology for more than a quarter of a century, it seems to have no plans to replace its human specialists and brokers with computers. Faced with the threat of competition from various new electronic trading systems, the NYSE management started voicing ideas in the middle of 1999 about seriously considering the electronic route. But a closer look at the "fine print" indicates plans far removed from doing away with its famed trading floors. The exchange was considering the possibility of buying one of the new electronic trading firms that had been started in the past couple of years. And instead of allowing investors to trade NYSE-listed stocks on the new system, the exchange indicated that its plan was to introduce trading in archrival Nasdaq market stocks.

This scenario was in keeping with the NYSE's classic approach to technology, which has simply been to automate its status quo. It has rarely spoken about adopting computerized trading to trade NYSE-listed stocks, in the process removing its specialists and floor brokers from the loop. For instance, to improve the productivity of its floor community, the NYSE has handed out personal digital assistants (PDA) and cell phones in the hope that wireless gadgetry will help to reduce the costs of executing orders on its trading floor.

As a group, the NYSE members make close to 90 percent of their money from proprietary trading rather than from commissions. Any transaction on the floor of the exchange must involve either a specialist or a floor broker. Individual specialists can easily earn $1 million a year. With so much at stake, they understandably do not want to be replaced by technology.

Setting all this aside, it would not be correct to accuse the NYSE of completely shunning new technologies. Indeed, over the years the exchange has invested hundreds of millions of dollars in introducing new technologies into its operations. But as indicated above, these technologies have been used to improve the efficiency and processing capacity of the exchange and its members. On the communication front, the technological focus has been on increasing the speed at which orders are routed to the floor and trade confirmations communicated back to the investor. But illustrated in Section 4, things are changing. The NYSE is gradually expressing a willingness to experiment and change.

5.2.1 Pre- and Post-Trade Technology

One of the major technological innovations in communications at the NYSE was the introduction in 1984 of the SuperDOT system. The SuperDOT system is part of an electronic network that transmits orders from member firms to a specialist's post on the NYSE trading floor as well as execution reports back to member firms. These orders travel over data communication lines from member firms to the appropriate special post. Execution reports follow the same path in the opposite direction.

The SuperDOT network went through a major overhaul in 1996, when its capacity increased from an average of 340 million shares a day in 1995 to about 2 billion a day. Today, by some measures, slightly more than half the investors who participate in NYSE trading on any given day route their orders through SuperDOT. Still, this network accounts for only 30 percent of the buy and sell volume. Interestingly, a majority of the orders routed through this system are straight market orders. The reason for this is that investors would be reluctant to send large orders electronically to the exchange floor. A market order, as we know, is an expression of willingness to trade at the prevailing best bid or offer. No trader would be willing to buy or sell a large number of shares of stock without negotiating the price.

Investors who do not use the SuperDOT system to electronically communicate their orders to a specialist can use a phone to reach a floor broker. Floor brokers typically receive orders as follows. A member firm's trading desk will telephone large orders (both for their own account as well as on behalf of large institutional clients) to the firm's floor booth.[3] Personnel at the booth page the floor broker, who will respond by using one of the many yellow telephones on the floor to contact the booth. The floor broker will then walk across with the order to the post where the stock is traded. Once at the post, the floor broker will either leave the order with the specialist or join the trading crowd and bid for (or offer) the stock on behalf of his or her customer.

The message that an order has been executed, in part or in whole,[4] is called a report. The report goes from the specialist via the SuperDOT system to the exchange members who entered the orders involved in the trade. Even though the report is a formal notice that a trade has occurred, it is not publicly available. The ultimate destination of the execution report is the investor who placed the order and the path taken by the report is, in most cases, the reverse of the path that brought the order to the post in the first place.

Orders transmitted to the specialist via SuperDOT appear on the specialist's display book screen. The book is an electronic application that keeps track of all limit orders and incoming market orders. The display book screen typically shows the near-the-market portion of the limit-order book for each issue handled by the specialist. Various window-like applications allow the specialist to view one or more stocks at a time at various levels of detail. Incoming Super-DOT limit orders automatically enter the display book. The display book sorts the limit orders and displays them in price-time priority. Similarly, when a floor broker gives the specialist a limit order, the specialist's clerk (specialist trading assistant) can enter the order into the display book by using the keyboard. SuperDOT market orders are displayed at the terminal and await further action. The specialist may execute a market order against another order in the book, against his or her own inventory, or against an order represented by a floor broker in the crowd.[5]

5.2.2 SuperDOT and the Specialist

SuperDOT provides the specialist with detailed real-time order flow information. Aside from the obvious features necessary to execute the order properly—ticker symbol, buy or sell, market or limit, size, and so on—SuperDOT orders also contain other identifying fields that the specialist may view on the display book. The specialist may, for example, view the entering firm's mnemonic, branch number, and sequence number. The exchange also requires member firms to specify account types with their SuperDOT orders (program trading, index arbitrage, principal, agency, and so on). Although this account type information is not available to the specialist in real time, it is present in the SuperDOT order record after hours. Thus, the specialist has unique access to vital information that reveals other traders' interests in specific stocks. This information is power, and the specialist makes full use of it to maximize his or her earnings.[6]

This access though comes with strings attached to it. As explained above, the exchange rules require the specialist to play an active role in maintaining continuous and orderly trading in the stocks assigned to him or her. The specialist is also expected to risk his or her own capital by being willing to step in to cover any gaps in the order flow. The NYSE also has rules that prohibit specialists from disclosing to any person, other than exchange officials, any information with regard to the orders entrusted to them.

There is, however, one exception to this. The specialist is authorized to provide inquiring members with information about a buying or selling interest in the market at or near the prevailing quote. The same rules also require that any such information be made available in an equitable manner to all inquiring members. Despite this ruling, at present, there is no direct way for off-floor market participants to obtain this information. Investors can always call their brokers on the exchange floor and obtain this information, although with some delay. And in a fast-moving market, delays in transmission can turn out to be especially expensive.

There is an even greater asymmetry in information availability that skews the relationship between the exchange members and their clients. Although the information flow from the floor to the clients commonly experiences delays, the exchange provides its floor community with access to all information media, including cable TV and data and news feeds from various information vendors. Skewing the picture even more is the fact that specialists and other member broker-dealers also receive a complete SuperDOT activity log each night. This log contains information on the orders handled by the specialist or member broker-dealer on a given day, all unavailable to nonmembers. By slowing down the exchange of information between the exchange floor and the outside world, the NYSE system ensures that the services of its members are always in demand.

5.3 STRUCTURAL WEAKNESS

The NYSE has been dominating trading in U.S. equities for the past century. Some of the largest corporations in the world list their stocks on this exchange. Over the years, it has faced barely any competition; we haven't yet seen a single firm moving out of NYSE and listing on a different market. It is not clear that a single alternative exchange—electronic or otherwise—that we are describing in this book will be able to successfully steal significant market share from the NYSE. In short, it enjoys absolute leadership in its market. If this is the reality, the perception in the marketplace is starkly different. Pick up any business magazine or trade journal, and one will find scores of articles speculating on the threats facing the NYSE and its shaky future. Reading these reports, a newcomer to this market might presume that the exchange is close to imminent demise. The truth is somewhere in between. As per the underlying theme of this book, the financial markets are undergoing a structural change. In the transformed marketplace, it is highly likely that the NYSE will have to contend with severe competition from a strong competitor. Although it is not clear who this might be, the trends indicate such a possibility.

The NYSE is acting as if it has sensed this change. It is empowered the management to transform the corporate structure to that of a for-profit company, exploring all possible strategies to preserve its inherent competitive advantage. For example, at some point in the year 2000 there were even rumors that the NYSE leadership had held talks with Nasdaq about a merger, something unimaginable just a few years ago.

The question to be answered is this: Why this change of heart? One can present a long list of candidate responses. The sections below consider a handful of them: outdated technologies, resistance to change, and failure in regulating its membership. The focus is on pointing out certain structural weaknesses that could potentially make it difficult for the NYSE to respond to new challenges in the marketplace.

5.3.1 A Labor-Intensive Process

Trading on the NYSE floor is strictly manual. Every trade in that venue requires human intervention. This contrasts starkly with the automated nature of the investment analyses and order-routing processes used by the investment community as a whole. Investors, both big and small, expect their orders to be executed in a matter of seconds. What they find at the NYSE is an arduous and labor-intensive system.

Here is how a non-SuperDOT deal works: A customer or a member firm phones in an order to a clerk in a brokerage booth located on the perimeter of the approximately 40,000-square-foot exchange floor. The clerk completes an order form and summons a "squad" or floor runner to "walk" the order out to the broker on the floor. Once the broker executes the order, he or she writes the details on a scrap of paper and hails a squad. The squad then walks the paper back to the booth and gives it to a clerk; the clerk, in turn, calls the customer to confirm the transaction. The first two steps of this process can be speeded up through the use of SuperDOT technology in what are known as "program trades."

Program Trades

Program trades are trades that are based on signals from computer programs, usually entered directly from the trader's computer to the market's computer system; in the case of the NYSE, these orders are routed to the specialist through the SuperDOT. Such trades are part of index arbitrage trading strategies in which big investors buy or sell baskets of stocks and do the opposite with stock index futures as they seek to profit from price discrepancies between the values of the futures contracts and that of the underlying stocks. Program orders are a classic illustration of the mismatch between the operating styles of investors and the trading floor of the NYSE. Sophisticated technologies are exploited to generate orders and route them to the exchange floor at incredible speeds. But once they reach their destination, they still have to wait for a human agent, the specialist, to manually execute the trades.

New trading systems described later in this book might eventually bridge this gap. Program trades on average account for 15 to 20 percent of the total volume on the NYSE, a potentially attractive market niche for one of the many new electronic trading systems. In a market where time is of the essence to exploit profitable trading opportunities, a few seconds can make an enormous difference. New electronic trading systems being implemented now promise instantaneous execution. The OptiMark trading system discussed in Chapter 8 relies on a sophisticated matching algorithm but manages to execute trades in less than three seconds.

The best efforts toward increasing the speed to execution at NYSE have been focused mainly on supplying wireless devices (PDAs) to the floor-trading community. PDAs are used to receive data feeds (orders, quotes, and news) and allow direct electronic order input. These instruments surely reduce the use of paper to record and report trades; but they do not allow automated execution of trades. This process continues to require human intervention. Any plan to automate any aspect of the trading process has to contend with a highly sensitive issue: complete opposition to any change in balance of power among specialists, floor brokers, and off-exchange investors.

5.3.2 Resistance to Technology

Resistance to technology at NYSE is nothing new. For example, the introduction of wireless technology faced stiff resistance at the NYSE, especially from specialists. The reason: Some of them feared that giving floor brokers faster access to information might diminish their trading edge and affect profits. This harks back to a primary concern among traders: controlling access to information. Historically, floor brokers too have been resistant to the adoption of new technologies designed to automate trading on the exchange floor. The NYSE learned a rude lesson in this subject back in 1971 when it was about to test an automated trading system for 100-share orders. The innovation would have reduced floor broker income by taking business away from them. The weekend before the test, someone took an ax to the wooden supports for the equipment. The culprit was never found. The system was subsequently tested but never adopted.

In the 1990s, telecommunication technology has prevailed to a certain extent. PDAs were handed out to the exchange's approximately 200 floor reporters, whose job is to stand near the specialists' booths and call out the latest trades (Figure 5.3). Now, instead of filling out computer cards and feeding them into a scanner, the reporters record each trade on a hand-held Epson from where it is directly downloaded into the exchange's computers. Seconds later, information about these trades appears overhead on the ticker. Specialists now receive much of their news from data feeds on their own flat-panel screens. They can select a provider of their choice, such as Bloomberg Business News, Dow Jones, or Reuters.

The moral of the PDA story is that the NYSE membership can be coaxed into accepted new technologies as long as these enable them to perform their tasks more efficiently. They tend to be aggressive in preventing any changes that could potentially reduce their role in the trade execution process.

5.3.3 Broker Fraud

This reluctance to accept new technologies that will allow the exchange as a whole to provide superior trade execution service to its customers could in theory prove costly in the long run. A second issue that could hurt the NYSE is its monitoring structure. It has systems in place that are supposed to assure its customers that their orders are handled appropriately. Unfortunately, the labor-intensive process used makes it difficult for the exchange to fulfill this fiduciary responsibility. This structural weakness is of importance as by design, electronic trading systems with automated execution facilities can be audited more efficiently. The NYSE is

currently working on new applications, e-Broker and Broker Booth System (BBSS), that might potentially reduce opportunities for errors entering the system. But given that the underlying matching mechanism will be manually operated, it continues to run the risk of garbage-in/garbage-out.

Self-Regulation Myth

Exchanges such as the NYSE operate under the rubric of self-regulatory organizations. The idea is that these market institutions will regulate the operations of their members and ensure that trading is consistent with securities laws. The securities markets are unique in this respect. The belief is that when confronted with a conflict of interest, say between a gain to its members at a cost to investors (and thus to its reputation and so forth), the exchange will bravely side with the latter group. This is clearly a case of the monitor monitoring him- or herself. But it does contain an element of oversight in the form of policing by the Securities Exchange Commission (SEC). The NYSE has, by and large, been fair in playing the role of a self-regulator. But a single incident that has been playing itself out these past few years has exposed serious flaws in the self-regulation model.

Incident on the Floor

On May 12, 1999, the *Wall Street Journal* reported that federal prosecutors and securities regulators were investigating trading practices of close to 64 brokers who operate on the floor of the NYSE. These investigations were driven by a concern that the brokers had been following illegal practices that involved the sharing of illicit gains with customers. These brokers were suspected of trading out of accounts held jointly with their customers. This allowed them to indulge in trades that they couldn't otherwise have executed for their own account.

Floor brokers on the NYSE (as well as broker-dealers on the Nasdaq market) cannot legally trade ahead of their clients. Agency trades (orders from clients) take priority over principal trades (those for the brokers' personal accounts). This is partly due to the fact that brokers have better access to information, and this rule prevents them from profiting from this advantageous position. Investors, in turn, receive some protection. To get around this restriction, these brokers supposedly opened joint accounts with their clients. Any trades out of those joint accounts were reported to the exchange authorities as client trades. The potential gains from a set-up such as this would be substantial.

Let us assume that a broker comes across a trading interest on the exchange floor: an order to sell 15,000 shares of a stock at $15.00 per share. The broker has two buy orders from clients: one for 10,000 shares at the best market price from XYZ, the second for 5,000 shares also at the best market price from ABC. The broker is of the opinion that this will be a profitable position and would like to buy some stocks at this price for his or her own account. But exchange rules require that the broker execute the two orders from his or her clients before buying some for his or her personal account. If the broker has a joint account with, say, investor XYZ, he or she could add his or her buying interest to this order and report that 15,000 shares have been bought by XYZ. In this scenario, client ABC is left out and might end up buying the 5,000 shares at a price higher than $15.00 per share.

In 1998, eight other NYSE floor brokers were charged with fraud of this type. Prosecutors charged the floor brokers as well as a brokerage firm, Oakford Corp., and two of its principals with participating in an illegal trading scheme on the exchange floor. Oakford Corp is not a member of the NYSE, and hence trades made on its behalf might have been treated as client transactions. Apparently, the group had made more than $11 million from this scheme through transactions that took place over a three-year period from 1993 to 1996. In their suit, the government alleged that the brokers had initiated trades and then falsified trading tickets to make it appear that the orders came from Oakford. The brokers then allegedly split the profits with the firm. These floor brokers were charged with trading in accounts in which they had an interest, falsifying records and "front-running," or trading ahead of their customers' orders. Three of these brokers have already pleaded guilty.[7] In January 1999, one, Mr. Robert Carucci, was sentenced to 15 months in prison.

In what appears to have been an unrelated incident, in February 1999, the NYSE placed a permanent ban on one of its floor brokers, Steven J. Blandi. The crime: taking advantage of customers' orders and trading for his own gain violating NYSE rules and federal securities laws.[8] In the process, this individual demonstrated that a determined individual could bypass NYSE strictures. In our opinion, such problems are endemic to labor-intensive trading arrangements.

Turning a Blind Eye

Interestingly, it seems as if many of the 64 brokers being charged now are reported to have links with Oakford. This then would imply that these brokers were colluding with each other and pursuing a systematic strategy that violated their so-called fiduciary responsibility to their clients. According to regulators at the NYSE, in 1998, they suspected some form of illegal trading by groups of floor brokers. These suspicions arose when it noted that these brokers were executing trades under a single firm. As it did not "dig" any farther, it failed to notice that all these brokers had individual subaccounts with the same firm. The firm's account was being used as a front to cover up the brokers' personal trades.

Brokers are surely aware of the illegal nature of these transactions. Then why would they do such trades? They should have known that the NYSE's self-regulation arm would catch up with them one fine morning. According to lawyers representing some of the accused brokers, the NYSE has traditionally condoned these trades as long as the broker shared any gain from the 5,000 shares (in the example above) with the client (XYZ).[9]

Modernizing the Monitoring Mechanism

As a result of these incidents, the NYSE is now in the process of proposing changes to its rules (including proposing new rules) that would expand the exchange's examination and oversight of the brokers. For instance, it is developing a system to track orders electronically before they are executed; new rules would require floor brokers to keep records of compensation arrangements and would require them to file reports to the NYSE on all accounts in which they have an interest or discretion to make investments.

Account Manipulation in Electronic Systems

The NYSE relies on officials on the floor of the exchange to monitor the behavior of members and to ensure that they play by the rules. This arrangement is one more example of its reliance on antiquated systems that would have been appropriate (and in this instance, adequate) for markets in the early parts of the 20th century. Anyone who has seen television clippings of the NYSE floor would be aware of the hectic trading activity that takes place there. It is inconceivable how the exchange could take comfort in its human monitors to enforce rules in an environment where hundreds of thousands of shares change hands in response to tiny movements in stock prices.

The solution is to deprive the floor trader of the opportunity of defrauding other investors. This can be achieved by putting a system in place that does not rely on information recorded by the brokers. But a system such as this cannot be deployed in an environment where brokers process trades and, hence, are the only ones who can record the transactions. One of the most efficient ways to resolve this would be to introduce electronic trading systems that do not rely on the brokers to process trades. They can be part of the system and submit orders, but the routing of orders from the investor to the trading system would have to be completely electronic. Such a system would go against the grain of the NYSE's current trading arrangement. So as long as the exchange refuses to go electronic, it is highly unlikely that investors can avoid being defrauded by the floor-trading community.

If the NYSE is unable to correct this weakness in its overall trading structure, it might find its customers moving toward alternative venues that promise better fraud-prevention and monitoring mechanisms. In their efforts to grab market share from the leader, the electronic trading systems that are discussed below (and in greater detail elsewhere in the book) could tout the relative superiority of their auditing systems.

5.4 RESPONDING TO COMPETITIVE PRESSURES

As in numerous other industries, the market leader in equity trading in the United States, the NYSE, has had to contend with unprecedented competitive pressure in recent years to change its production process, namely, the manner in which it serves its customers. As argued at various points in this book, the needs of the investment community have been changing over the years. The exchange has invested heavily in technology to speed up the rate at which orders are carried from investors to the floor of the exchange. But it has stopped short of making any radical changes to the basic process by which buyers and sellers of stocks are matched. The main competitive response of the management of the exchange (apart from regular public statements proclaiming the innate superiority of the NYSE trading system) has been *Network NYSE* discussed in detail below.

There is no hiding from the truth that the exchange's leadership position is largely due to its historical dominance of trading in stocks by some of the largest U.S. corporations. In other words, investors and listed companies flock to the NYSE not because they have a strong preference for its trading system. Rather, they are attracted by the superior liquidity provided by the market that meets on the exchange floor. In sum, the NYSE's strength does not lie in its superior market structure. Rather, as argued in the previous section, the current structure of that market has important weaknesses that could potentially cripple its competitive efforts in the near future. The exchange has simply been reaping the benefits of a phenomenon in which liquidity begets more liquidity.

Substantive changes to the NYSE's present structure would imply a significant reduction in the role of its specialists and floor brokers. These intermediaries clearly have an important role to play in the market system. They supply liquidity by taking on risks. This service is vital for every market, financial, or otherwise. The million-dollar question being asked now is this: How do we develop efficient market systems that reflect the needs of the investors and, at the same time, provide a medium that allows risk providers to earn an appropriate return?

The NYSE does appear to be thinking on these lines and has put together a portfolio of proposals under the label of Network NYSE to address some of its apparent weaknesses. Some market observers cannot help pointing out the patchy approach being taken by the NYSE. One can easily criticize the management for taking a Band-Aid approach, trying to come up with quick fixes for various leaks in the system. At some point, it will have to integrate these different applications into a single comprehensive platform. But it has at least made a start to address some of its weaknesses. As argued above, introducing changes to the NYSE floor is not a simple process. There are multiple constituents who have a say in its plans, and theirs are not necessarily aligned in the same direction.

5.4.1 Network NYSE

Network NYSE is advertised as "a growing portfolio of innovative order-execution products and market information services." Its key components, a couple of which have been implemented and others are still in a concept stage, include the following:

- *NYSE Direct+.* An automated execution capability for limit orders (such orders will be labeled auto ex orders) up to 1,099 shares of stock.
- *Institutional XPress.* A suite of three products aimed at large institutions designed to improve their access to floor-trading information, provide more control over the execution of large trades, and route orders anonymously to the exchange floor.
- *MarkeTrac.* A graphical tool that will provide a variety of information on trading floor activity in a three-dimensional format, including a key component, an open electronic order book.
- *Broker Booth System (BBSS).* An order-management service that will support straight-through processing (pre- and post-trade transaction processing within minimal manual intervention) for NYSE member firms.
- *NYSEnet.* Information service targeted at companies whose stocks are listed on the NYSE.

- *NYSE e-Broker.* A hand-held wireless device designed to help floor brokers organize orders, track executions, and improve communications with their clients and with colleagues on the floor.

5.4.2 Institutional Express Order

One area in which the competition has clearly gained on the NYSE over the years is in the market for order flow from large investors, who frequently prefer alternative trading venues. Sometime in mid-1998, the NYSE introduced a proposal designed to attract these trades back to its trading floors. The proposal is labeled Institutional Express (XPress). XPress is a package consisting of three components:

- *XPress Information.* It is basically a set of tools to facilitate information sharing between member firms and their clients launched in June 2000. It delivers information such as preopening InterMarket Trading System indicators (currently available only on the trading floor) directly to member firms, sponsored institutions, and market-data vendors. Large institutional investors can also get instant delivery of information on market-on-close and market-on-open imbalances and trading halts and delays. They can receive these data in three ways: "pushed" directly from the NYSE or obtained through either a password-protected Web site or data vendor.
- *XPress Orders.* Designed to enable speedy execution of large orders.
- *XPress Routing.* An anonymous order-routing mechanism that would allow member firms to entitle or sponsor[10] their institutional customers to route orders to SuperDOT without having their identities revealed, thus satisfying the buy-side's desire for anonymity.

XPress Order is the most interesting of these three products listed above. Accordingly, we describe it in more detail and discuss some of the controversies associated with it.

XPress Orders and Quotes

Institutional XPress would provide for XPress Orders, which are routed through SuperDOT and identified with appropriate tags, to be executed against a displayed XPress Quote without the risk of being broken up by other participants. An XPress Quote is defined as a published bid or offer for at least 25,000 shares that has been displayed (at the same price) for at least 30 seconds.

Once an investor finds one such quote, he or she can route an order via SuperDOT to the specialist, who in turn will fill the investor order for the full 25,000 or more assuming the incoming order matches the bid or offer on the XPress Quote. The specialist will expose the order to the crowd around his or her booth. If someone walks up and is ready to trade at a better price than that of the XPress Quote, the specialist will execute the match at this new improved price.

XPress Orders give a trader complete control over the execution of his or her order, subject to certain caveats listed as amendments to the original proposal. These pertain to circumstances under which an XPress Order might receive a partial execution. Xpress Order also ensures that the trade will take place at the bid/offer of the XPress Quote or better.

XPress Orders are of the fill-or-kill type. If the specialist is unable to execute a trade (for instance, because the XPress Quote has been withdrawn, or another XPress Order is in front of it), then XPress Order is killed. Also, if an XPress Order for 30,000 shares is matched with an XPress Quote for 29,000 shares of the same stock, the balance 1,000 shares of the former will remain unexecuted and automatically cancelled.

A key phrase above is this: *without the risk of being broken up by other participants.* When the specialist exposes the incoming order to the floor crowd, he or she is not allowed to split the order size among multiple contra orders. Meaning, a sell order for 25,000 shares cannot be filled against five traders, each buying 5,000 shares (even if they are willing to pay a higher price than the XPress Quote is).

Thirty-Second Rule

A quote qualifies as an XPress Quote only if it has been on display for at least 30 seconds. The Investment Company Institute, a trade association representing the interests of institutional clients (the group toward whom the XPress Order facility is targeted), has argued for the elimination of this time restriction. The reasoning is that in a fast-moving market, 30 seconds can be too long a time interval. In such conditions, it is highly unlikely that a competitive quote for a large number of shares will remain unexecuted for 30 seconds. The flip side to this argument is that in such market conditions, XPress Orders will get to trade only with non-competitive quotes.

Execution against such quotes could in theory be the price the investor would be paying to use this facility. It is clear why some investors are not too enamoured by XPress Orders. Also by imposing what seems like an arbitrary time condition, the NYSE appears to be biasing its trading rules in favor of smaller orders, those less than or equal to 24,900 shares.

25,000 Shares

The NYSE has defined an XPress Order as one for at least 25,000 shares of any stock. When the XPress proposal was first made public, the minimum size requirement was set at 10,000 shares. But this would have made a considerable dent in the floor-trading community. So the exchange backed off and increased the lower limit to 15,000. Facing continued resistance from its membership, the exchange raised the lower limit farther to 25,000. The standard definition for a block or large trade is not 25,000 shares but 10,000 shares or more.

In fairness to the management of the NYSE, it has to be reported that they have agreed to examine the time and size restrictions and change them as deemed necessary. But this apparent readiness to acquiesce with its membership reveals an important weakness in its ability to introduce reforms that could potentially favor its customers more than the floor-trading community.

Competing with the Upstairs Market

The XPress Order proposal can be viewed as an attempt by the NYSE to attract some of the order flow for large trades that flows to the upstairs market. To the extent these orders do not interact directly with other interests on the exchange floor, they tend to reduce overall liquidity and, hence, the price discovery process. So despite the obvious shortcomings discussed above, if by means of this proposal, the NYSE manages to divert such large orders away from the upstairs market, it would be making a positive contribution toward making the markets more efficient.

5.4.3 NYSE Direct+

If XPress Orders are targeted at large institutional investors, Direct+ is for the small investor. It promises automatic execution of limit orders up to 1,099 shares (and a minimum of 100 shares) against published NYSE quotes. Direct+ orders are to be routed through SuperDOT with the appropriate tag to the display book, the NYSE order book that is available to all floor traders. Once in the book, they will be processed by using a computerized algorithm comparing the bid or offer limit price with the best-displayed quote.

Let's assume that the following Direct+ order has been submitted via Super-DOT: Buy 1,000 shares of XYZ stock at a limit price of $15.00 or less. The lowest offer quote in the display book is at $14.95 for 800 shares. The system will automatically execute a trade for 800 shares at $14.95; the balance of 200 shares will wait in the order book for the next lowest offer.

With numerous ECNs trying to make an entry into trading NYSE-listed stocks, Direct+ can be viewed as an attempt to preempt this competition. We go into further details on ECNs later in the book. At this point, it should suffice to mention that these private, electronic trading systems have been successful in stealing market share from the main Nasdaq market. But they haven't had much success with NYSE stocks. It is possible that the success in trading Nasdaq stocks has been due to the fact that the ECNs have enjoyed the patronage of Nasdaq market makers. There is sufficient anecdotal evidence to support the contention that though ECNs were their competitors, market makers have used them as part of their own trading strategies. With tacit support from market makers, ECNs have been able to build sufficient trading volumes; they now account for more than a third of the trading volume in Nasdaq stocks. But they haven't had similar success with listed stocks. The NYSE floor has been a formidable competitor.

Returning to Direct+, it is evident that the NYSE does take the competitive threat of the ECNs very seriously and has produced Direct+ as part of a strategy to protect its turf. But it is interesting to note that although a leader in terms of market share, it has not necessarily introduced any new innovative ideas in implementing Direct+. It is essentially playing catch-up with the rest of the electronic trading world.

Will the NYSE ever go fully electronic? Let's assume that Direct+ becomes successful. The NYSE could remove all volume restrictions and simply allow all trades to be executed electronically. Well, the exchange is spending close to $60 million on a new exchange floor. So, it appears as if they expect to see floor-based trading continue into the foreseeable future.

Thirty-Second Wait

It is not clear why the NYSE decided to do this, but it has included a restriction on the speed of trading provided by Direct+. An order for the account of any person may only be entered at intervals of no less than 30 seconds. So, let's assume investor Joe Smith is on the phone with his broker who has access to SuperDOT and is giving instructions to buy shares of PQR stock. The first order for 200 shares is sent out at 10:34:10 AM and it gets executed immediately. The company has just announced superlative results, and there is tremendous interest in it. Joe wants to buy some more and is sending rapid-fire instructions to his broker. A second order for another 200 shares is sent out at 10:34:25 (15 seconds after the first one). The system's rules will not accept the second order. It is not clear how the rejection will be implemented as the orders will be identified as coming from the broker. It is likely that the broker will be subject to rules that prohibit such submissions. So the broker will have to wait till 10:34:40 AM before sending the second order. In an active market, the wait for an additional 15 seconds could turn out to be too expensive for the investor.

The example above refers to a typical small investor. But this restriction could have an adverse impact on large institutions trading small-cap stocks. Given the smaller number of outstanding stocks, trading typically will be in smaller lots. By not discriminating between small and large investors, the NYSE has invited approbation from a wide spectrum of interest groups. Worse, the 30-second rule seems to go against the spirit of an automated execution facility. In some sense, waiting 30 seconds for an order to execute is equivalent to waiting 30 seconds before placing a second order. The final risk for the investor is the same: The market can move adversely in that time interval.

No Price-Time Priority

Contrary to standard trading conventions, the NYSE does not extend price-time priority protections to orders submitted to Direct+. Under the proposed rule, if multiple auto ex or Direct+ orders are submitted at a particular limit price, then the first such order will receive time priority at that price. Once that order is executed, the remaining ones will be given the equal time priority, meaning they can receive split executions. For instance, let's assume that the first buy order has been executed at an offer price of $13.15. The other auto ex orders are willing to trade at the next best offer of $13.20 for 1,000 shares. If there are 10 such bids, each for a different amount, they could receive 100 share fills at $13.20 per share.

Summary

To conclude, Direct+ is a useful addition to the NYSE trading platform. It seems to be targeted at the small, active trader (but one who does not choose to trade every 10–15 seconds). Numerous online brokers, especially those that service the active trader with direct access tools, have been building links to SuperDOT so that when a client submits an order over an electronic network, it gets routed direct to the display book on the exchange floor. The NYSE has not pushed the edge of the envelope; there is nothing revolutionary about this facility. Numerous markets already offer automated execution. The NYSE finally decided to join the gang. Will the specialist community get hurt? Not necessarily. On the contrary, to the extent Direct+ steals order flow from the Third Market and, more important, frustrates the aspirations of various ECNs, it might end up strengthening their franchise.

5.4.4 OpenBook

Sometime in the summer of 2001, the NYSE is expected to roll out OpenBook, a transparent book displaying all pending limit orders for any given stock. It is technically an enhancement to MarkeTrac. It will be equivalent to Nasdaq's level II screen. This would indeed be a revolutionary move as to date, this level of information has been available only to the NYSE specialist. As of now, other traders can see only the best bid and offer for every stock traded on the exchange floor.

The question now is this: Why would NYSE open up the order book? We have argued that order flow information is key to survival in these markets. The specialist relies on this special access to hedge some of the risk involved in ensuring a smooth market in any given stock. Market observers reason that the NYSE does not really have a choice. Markets are moving toward greater transparency. Various ECNs have applied for exchange status. This would allow them to trade NYSE-listed stocks. The Nasdaq, too, has applied for exchange status. This latter issue is of greater concern to the NYSE. The threat will be realized in the form of SuperMontage (see Chapter 6 for more on this platform being implemented by Nasdaq).

SuperMontage will be an open electronic order book with the capability to automatically execute trades. ECNs today and Nasdaq in the near future will allow institutional investors to directly interact with each other without having to route their orders through brokers. Private electronic trading systems are primarily designed to allow such investors to interact with other investors by placing orders anonymously in electronic order books. NYSE's OpenBook will simply display bids and offers.

5.4.5 MarkeTrac

A tool in the market information service component of the Network NYSE suite, the web-based MarkeTrac is designed to bring "individual investors closer to the trading floor." Once again, it is an effort to play catch-up with other trading venues including Nasdaq level II screen and various ECNs, which essentially publish their order books for the whole world to see.

Via MarkeTrac (a pilot version was launched on March 21, 2001), the NYSE will publish real-time information from the trading floor. A key component is OpenBook, as discussed earlier. Other components include breaking company news and detailed real-time quote information along with performance graphs and a real-time stock ticker. As anyone who has visited the Web sites of a large online broker, say, E*Trade, would know, these are services that are standard and have been available to the average investor for free for some time now. Interestingly, the Nasdaq market too has been providing some of this information on its Web site.

Using Heat Maps

There is no doubt that the NYSE is committed to its trading floor. A reiteration of this is available in the form of a service that will allow investors to follow trading activity on the exchange floor by means of color-coded activity, or heat maps, with color intensities varying with trading activity on various stocks. Price information for the 30 stocks in the DJIA is listed on the right-hand column (Figure 5.4). Similar heat maps can be found on the Nasdaq market Web site as well as the map of the market at SmartMoney.com. The idea behind heat maps is that they are easier to read than a table of numbers.

Real-Time Ticker

Both the NYSE and Nasdaq are planning to make real-time price information—both quotes as well as transaction prices—available for free. This proposal is already raising interesting questions that will be addressed by the respective agencies. For instance, online brokers (as well as numerous brokerage firms) pay the NYSE and the Nasdaq for their real-time quotes. Now, will the latter continue charging these brokerage firms for the same information?

Fees from selling real-time quote information to brokers and information vendors account for a significant portion of the revenue of both these market institutions. How do they propose to cover the drop in earnings from giving away this information for free?

Market observers propose a couple of arguments to back the free real-time information plan. First, everyone believes that one way or the other, all this information will soon be available for free. Various online brokers are already giving a lot of real-time quote information away. Second, the exchanges are

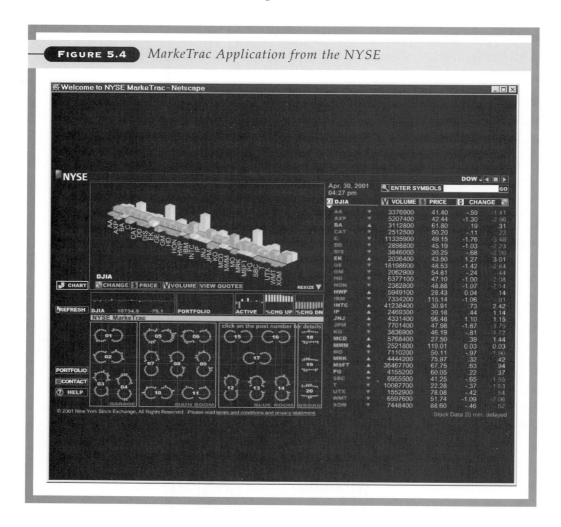

FIGURE 5.4 *MarkeTrac Application from the NYSE*

hoping that access to all this rich information could lead to increases in trading volumes. Incremental fees from these transactions would more than offset the loss in revenue.

5.4.6 A 24-Hour Market

By the summer of 2001, the idea of a 24-hour market was bound to be received with quite a bit of derision. But in the 1998–99 period, everyone was clamoring for it. The NYSE too joined the bandwagon as an attempt to increase its market share in the business of stock trading.

Historically, NYSE has sought to play a role in the international marketplace by targeting non-U.S. corporations. Numerous foreign companies already list their stocks on the NYSE in the form of American depository receipts (ADR). ADRs are secondary listings of a company's ordinary shares based on the performance of the company's underlying shares in its domestic market. Due to time differences, the exchange's share of trading in these stocks is bound to be insignificant. A German company such as Siemens A.G., for example, will inevitably have a larger following among investors in Frankfurt than in New York. As part of its plan for a 24-hour market, the NYSE sought to surmount this problem by opening its trading floors at 4:00 AM New York time. So when trading opens in Europe, the specialists and floor traders at NYSE will be ready to trade too. The plan is to open the market from 4:00 AM to 9:00 AM for European investors, 9:30 AM to 4:00 PM for U.S. investors and 6:00 PM to midnight for Asian stocks. This is obviously not 24 hours; but that is beside the point. Labels given to strategies always have an element of PR (or public relations).

The exchange's management seemed to have immense faith in the superiority of the NYSE trading system. It surely believed that solving the time-difference problem would automatically allow it to increase its market share in various European and Asian stocks. In announcing its plans to have the trading floor open almost round the clock trading stocks of companies from around the world, the NYSE did not bother to explain why a fund manager in Paris would want to call a broker in New York to execute a trade. Given that most French stocks are traded already in Paris, would it not make sense for this investor to call the friendly neighborhood broker? What incentive will the NYSE offer to those traders who might be willing to divert their trades to New York?

Given the higher level of interest in domestic stocks in general, it would be surprising to find higher trading interest and thus risk-taking initiatives from floor traders and specialists for a British stock on the floor of the NYSE than in London. In addition, given the increased competition among various European exchanges, it is not clear that they would sit quietly while the NYSE tries attracting order flows away from them. As most European and Asian exchanges have gone electronic, with their superior technology, they will be able to offer lower fees and commissions than the labor-intensive system of the NYSE. Already competition among various European exchanges, particularly between London, Frankfurt, and Paris, has resulted in lower trading costs for investors. In fact, a recent survey revealed that the Paris exchange has the lowest transaction cost, much lower than the NYSE.

At this stage of the development of this proposal, it is not clear that the NYSE has managed to convince its members to report to work in the middle of the night. An earlier experience will give us some idea of the difficulties facing the management of the NYSE. In 1991, the NYSE proposed starting trading at 9:00 AM instead of 9:30 AM. Its members (floor brokers and specialists) rejected the plan. A typical broker in New York will be willing to work the early morning shift only if he or she expects to earn higher returns from it than from regular 9:30 AM to 4:00 PM NYSE trading hours. This means that the broker would not be willing to compete aggressively with the lower commissions of the European and other electronic markets.

5.4.7 Experimenting with After-Hours Trading

The advent of the Internet has empowered the individual investors by providing them with superior access to the markets. The claim among various market observers is that hundreds of thousands of individual investors are keen on trading actively in the market. Amateur traders would like to take advantage of the new access to improve the returns from their investments. But restricted trading hours are holding them back. When they get back home from their day jobs and are ready to "play" the game of trading, the market is closed.

The NYSE too floated a plan to serve this segment of the investment community. As per the initial plan, the launch of an appropriate service was to take place around mid-2000. By the end of 2000, there was no sign of any such system, and the exchange seemed to have shelved the idea at least for the time being.

Interestingly, the exchange has for many years now had the permission to conduct some form of after-hours trading. Every time the NYSE has attempted to get around its floor traders and specialists, it has faced difficulties. In May 1991, it won approval from the SEC to start an after-hours[11] electronic trading session. There were to be two automated trading sessions after the 4 PM closing bell. In the first session, from 4 PM to 5 PM, firms could place orders for single stocks through the regular SuperDOT electronic order-processing system, in multiples of 100 shares up to 99,900-share lots. At 5 PM, these orders would be matched with the help of a computer at the 4 PM closing price. In the second session, from 5 PM to 5:15 PM, members could trade portfolios of stock made up of at least 15 stocks and worth at least $1 million.

To attract order flow, the exchange decided to relax its reporting requirements. Only the total number of shares and the total value of all basket trades from the second session would be published. As the members of the NYSE felt threatened by the proposed implementation of this plan to extend trading hours on a limited basis, they made sure that the plan did not get too far. It never got implemented. Today, it is private electronic communication networks such as Instinet and Island that dominate after-hours trading. In this market, the name of the NYSE rarely comes up.

5.4.8 Competing with Nasdaq

One competitive pressure that the NYSE faces is that by definition it specializes in trading stocks that are listed on the exchange. The exchange has been able to grow by following two related strategies: attracting more order flow for stocks listed on the exchange, and attracting new listings from companies that have issued stock to the investing public. To attract new listings, however, the NYSE has to go to battle with its greatest competitor—Nasdaq.

Competing with Nasdaq

New listings come in the form of companies that have issued stock for the first time through initial public offerings (IPO). They also come in the form of companies that move their listings from dealer markets such as the Nasdaq market or from auction markets such as the American Stock Exchange (AMEX) to the NYSE. Although there is a steady flow of firms moving from the Nasdaq market to the NYSE, the latter has not been successful in catching some of the big fish, companies such as Microsoft, Intel, and Dell. Firms that have dominated—and largely led—the boom in asset prices in the 1990s have stayed home with Nasdaq. Liquid trading in these stocks has helped the Nasdaq market attract listings by scores of new technology companies.

Hampered by Regulations

Compared with Nasdaq, the NYSE has traditionally had stricter listing requirements. Nasdaq's weaker rules have enabled smaller start-ups with typically shaky finances to list on that market. In the so-called new economy, many of these firms tend to be concentrated in the technology sector. As the NYSE has been reluctant to relax its listing conditions, it has essentially missed the technology "bus." Although traditional technology leaders such as IBM and AT&T and relatively newer ones such as AOL and Lucent Technologies have their stocks listed on the NYSE, the Nasdaq market has managed to participate fully in the ongoing developments in the new sectors of the economy. The NYSE is in danger of losing out on listings from firms that are likely to dominate the U.S. economy in the next few decades.

Competition from the Third Market

Even if it is successful in convincing a company to "jump ship" from Nasdaq, the competition does not end here. Assume a company decides that it wants to have its stocks listed on the NYSE market. If a stock was earlier listed on Nasdaq, for instance, the broker-dealers in that market can, subject to certain restrictions, continue to trade in that stock. Trading of this type can be seen in the third market: the network of Nasdaq dealers who trade stocks listed on other exchanges such as NYSE, AMEX, and other auction markets.

Trading Nasdaq Stocks

Having failed to attract Microsoft, Intel, and other leaders of the computer and information technology fields, the NYSE has decided to copy the strategy of this third market. On February 26, 1999, the exchange announced that it was considering numerous proposals that would allow it to trade Nasdaq stocks, like the Chicago Stock Exchange had done for years. It had finally woken up to the reality that had been staring at it all these years—that there is nothing stopping it too from trading Nasdaq stocks. If the exchange wanted to grow, this was an obvious strategy to follow.

There are a couple of interesting twists to the motivations behind this proposal. Most of the large brokerage firms and investment banks that dominate trading on the NYSE floor also dominate trading on the Nasdaq market. So from the perspective of these firms, it doesn't really matter whether a stock is traded on the NYSE floor or the Nasdaq broker-dealer network. The only reason they will prefer to trade a particular stock on the Nasdaq is that it offers the most liquid market in that stock. A second twist is that it can increase the revenue flow to its floor brokers not necessarily by increasing order floor to the exchange floor. The NYSE can implement an alternative structure specifically for Nasdaq stocks, something similar to an ECN, and pass on the profits from this entity to its members.

Specialists or ECNs

Given that the exchange is run as a membership-based organization, one would expect the NYSE to involve its floor brokers and specialists in any new strategy targeted at Nasdaq stocks. If the floor community does not perceive any direct benefit from the proposal, they would be reluctant to vote to support it. But the plans being espoused seem to indicate otherwise.

The NYSE might be willing to keep trading in these stocks away from the confines of the NYSE floor. Instead, several issues appear to be driving the NYSE toward pursuing a strategy built around alliances with private electronic trading networks or ECNs. The exchange will surely try keeping any electronic trading system distinct from its floor-based systems. Given the incompatibility in design and technologies, any attempt to marry off-exchange trading systems with the exchange floor is likely to be costly and difficult to implement.

Moreover, the Nasdaq market is in many respects an electronic one. It does not even have an exchange floor. These past few years, various private ECNs have gained considerable market share trading Nasdaq stocks over automated, and relatively anonymous, electronic networks. The trend here has been to exploit new technologies to lower trading costs. With its labor-intensive trading process, the NYSE would have a tough time stealing market share from these trading firms if it retained its traditional auction process for Nasdaq stocks as well.

Trading in many technology stocks tends to be volatile. Traditional tech leaders such as Microsoft and Dell (as well as recent Internet darlings such as Yahoo!) have been popular among the day-trading community. This classic hypertrading phenomenon is unique to the Nasdaq market with its large numbers of broker-dealers willing to make market in any given stock. This is in comparison to the NYSE, where a single specialist coordinates trading in and provides liquidity to any given stock.

Given that it is reluctant to alter its time-tested auction process, the NYSE has had to look for alternative trading platforms. Large ECNs that have enjoyed considerable success in capturing market share from the Nasdaq market appear ideal candidates.

CHX, PHLX, BSE, and Nasdaq Stocks

While researching this issue of Nasdaq stocks on NYSE, we came across an interesting bit of information. In May 1987, the Chicago Stock Exchange (CHX) received approval from the SEC to trade about 25 Nasdaq stocks. In later years, the SEC also gave permission to the Boston Stock Exchange (BSE) and the Philadelphia Stock Exchange (PHLX) to trade these stocks. Except for the CHX, the other exchanges never really exploited this opportunity to compete with Nasdaq. And it appears as if the biggest exchange in the world, NYSE, merely sat on the sidelines and let the opportunity pass. The failure of the BSE and the PHLX (and even the CHX) to grab a large market share in this segment of stocks is not too surprising. Over the years, these institutions have instead focused their energies on a near-impossible task: stealing market share from the NYSE.

The 1990s have seen a tremendous change in the level of competition in the equity markets. If it ever makes the appropriate moves, NYSE might have a much tougher time achieving critical mass in trading Nasdaq stocks than it had previously anticipated.

5.5 NYSE AS A FOR-PROFIT COMPANY

In the middle of the summer of 1999, the unthinkable and inconceivable happened. NYSE announced that it was planning to issue its own stock. The exchange wanted to change its governance structure from that of a membership-based, non-profit entity to a full-fledged for-profit corporation. After decades of promising allegiance to the traditional ownership structure, the exchange now seemed to be in a hurry to transform itself. The management of the exchange was planning to issue stock to the public as early as November 1999, barely six months from the date of announcement of the new plan. But November 1999 flew past, and the NYSE hadn't moved any closer to getting all the regulatory approvals toward a public offering. Most important, it was having problems convincing the SEC about its ability to regulate itself in the post-IPO phase.

Although this by itself is an interesting issue, we now move to a relatively more important question: What has led the NYSE to consider subjecting itself to a radical overhaul—and why was it in such a hurry? By the winter of 2000, the NYSE had decided to postpone its IPO plans indefinitely. So given that it is no longer actively considering becoming a for-profit company, the discussions below are largely academic. It is our opinion though that when market conditions improve, maybe after the prolonged fall in stock prices starting March 2000, the NYSE is bound to revisit this question.

5.5.1 Theory of Cashing-in

When the exchange announced the for-profit plan, financial analysts in some of the leading investment banks began speculating on the value of the NYSE. Taking into consideration the revenues and profits of the exchange and borrowing valuation measures from firms of similar size in related industries, a consensus estimate was that the exchange was worth approximately $3 billion dollars.

When the exchange sells its stock, it is by definition selling itself. So the money raised from the sale will go to its owners, the floor brokers and specialists who are its members. Given that there are approximately 1,500 members, one can conservatively assume that each member stands to gain about $2 million. Given that they will be able to continue trading on the exchange floor (they will receive tradable permits for this), the members can simply pocket this gain as pure profit.

The U.S. equity markets had been on a roll all through the 1990s, with investors willing to pay huge premiums over the current earnings of U.S. corporations. Given that the NYSE expected to face increased competition in the future, which in turn might result in lower profits, this would have been an excellent time for it to cash in. Faced with uncertain future returns, it made sense to expropriate the premium investors would be willing to pay for its stocks.

5.5.2 Everyone Else Is Doing It

To be fair to the NYSE, the exchange did not start this trend toward changing into a for-profit corporation, a process also called de-mutualization. Exchanges in Europe (Stockholm and Milan were the early movers), Australia, and other places had already converted their status. Every important equity market in the world—London, Frankfurt, Paris, the Nasdaq market, and even the tradition-bound commodities and financial derivatives exchanges in Chicago—had announced plans to adopt a for-profit status. The NYSE was simply a later entrant to the game. Consistent with complaints that it never does anything innovative, the exchange just joined the herd. The Nasdaq market has already completed its for-profit restructure.

5.5.3 De-Mutualization and Balanced Focus

Various parts of this chapter have attempted to illustrate how the NYSE has consistently taken steps that favor its members. Although investment technology and trading practices in general have undergone fundamental changes in recent decades, the exchange has done little to respond to these changes. Its behavior has been the antithesis of a firm in a competitive marketplace. There is at least one simple explanation for this skewed focus: Members take care of their own interests. If the exchange management proposes an initiative, the Institutional Xpress trading arrangement being a classic example, members will evaluate it from the perspective of its impact on their earnings. If they feel threatened, they will defeat the move when it is put up for a vote.

With de-mutualization, the floor community will have a smaller say in the management of the exchange. In theory, the new owners, the investors who buy stock in the NYSE, will be able to override the objections of floor brokers and specialists. The exchange will now be managed to maximize the return to its new owners. If this means hurting the earnings of its brokers, so be it. The hope is that with de-mutualization, the NYSE will finally start balancing the interests of the different constituents of the investment community. It will stop focusing exclusively on the fears and concerns of the floor community.

So, it is possible that when everybody else was moving to de-mutualize, it was becoming increasingly difficult for the NYSE to justify its membership-based structure. Maybe in announcing plans to go public, the NYSE was simply responding to changes in public opinion?

5.5.4 Money to Buy Others

When asked why it wants to change the corporate structure, the NYSE management explained that it needed to raise money to compete effectively with the Nasdaq market and various other firms that were beginning to dominate the equity trading business. For instance, the exchange wanted to offer an electronic trading system to trade Nasdaq stocks. The NYSE would like to either build its own system or buy one of the many ECNs that trade Nasdaq market stocks.

Did this reasoning make any sense? Let us assume that some of its members decided to leave their capital with the exchange when it went public. The estimates on the amount of money that could be raised ran into hundreds of millions of dollars. Did the exchange need all that money to acquire a standard electronic trading system? Standard systems were, in fact, cheap. The reason we do not see scores of them in use is because firms realize that it is difficult to attract significant amounts of order flow. Building a system is the easiest part of the game. By some estimates, the exchange would not have needed more than $25–30 million to acquire an electronic trading system. This sum was so small that the exchange could dip into its working capital to raise money.

In conclusion, based on the arguments above it is not clear why the exchange planned to change its structure. The reasons put forward by the management reveal an element of contradiction. But irrespective of the true reasons, it appears as if such a move will ultimately benefit the investment community.

5.5.5 A For-Profit Self-Regulating Business

Earlier, we examined some of the risks involved when a firm relies on antiquated systems to monitor the actions of its constituents. This issue will simply get more complicated if the NYSE or any other self-regulating market changes its status by issuing stock, and this raises a number of concerns.

More Concerned about Profits

Markets around the world have traditionally relied on less-stringent regulations (and weak enforcement of them) to attract firms issuing stocks. Regulation has always been a competitive tool to steal market share from an exchange with stronger rules and stricter enforcement. The objective is simply to maximize returns. The concern now is that if the NYSE and other exchanges become more focused on serving the interests of their investors, they might be willing to relax their regulation efforts. These institutions have already demonstrated a willingness to do this to help their owner-members turn a quick profit.

Weaker Management

A related fear is that the management of the exchange will be reluctant to punish a floor trader who happens to be employed by a large shareholder. Punishing the individual will be equivalent to punishing its own investor, who might have an important seat on the board of directors of the NYSE Corporation. The question is whether a salaried employee of the exchange will be willing to risk his or her neck by taking a complaint to the senior management against a powerful shareholder. The concern is that irrespective of the best intentions of the senior management of the exchange, the institution as a whole will not be in a position to enforce its rules in a fair and unbiased manner.

Unaffiliated Regulator

So how do we resolve this conflict of interest? The best response has been in the form of a proposal to shift the regulatory responsibility from all exchanges including the Nasdaq market to an independent body protected by law. An institution of this type would be similar to the SEC. Such an institution would not be directly affiliated to any of the markets and thus would not be subject to the conflicts of interests involved in the self-regulation model.

Of the two biggest markets in the United States, the Nasdaq has expressed a willingness to go along with the idea of an independent regulator. The NYSE has shown absolutely no interest. It has stated that it would like to continue with the current self-regulation arrangement. Unfortunately for the exchange, it does not have complete freedom in this matter. It needs the permission of the SEC to change its status to raise money by selling stock. The SEC, in turn, is responsible for the overall regulation of the market. So, if it believes that the self-regulation model should be scrapped in favor of an independent body, the NYSE will have to accept the decision. Otherwise, it will risk not getting permission to change to a for-profit status. Fortunately for the investors, to date the SEC has made all the right noises that indicate that it shares the concerns of a weakening of the ability of an exchange to monitor itself once it changes its status.

5.6 SUMMARY

The NYSE has historically set the pulse for trading activity in stock markets around the world. As the level of integration among different economies has increased, the NYSE's level of dominance and extent of influence has grown. It remains the most liquid stock market in the world today.

We have argued that the leadership of this exchange is more a function of its historic dominance, in other words, of liquidity attracting more liquidity. The basic structure of its trading system dates back to the 19th century. Over the years, the open outcry system with specialists as market makers of last resort has served well. But in view of broader changes in the financial markets, the labor-intensive system appears increasingly archaic. Although its competitive position appears relatively secure for the present, the exchange is finally seeking to shed its historical reluctance to move to a for-profit status. It is in the process of forming alliances with various markets around the world. It has floated proposals to include certain electronic trading technologies that would automate parts of the market. The problem it is facing is that these efforts appear patchy and not well integrated into a single consistent trading solution. As the membership is firmly against any efforts to weaken its profitable franchise, the exchange today is capable of taking limited steps toward embracing more efficient and fast trading systems.

Some of the new proposals described here should go some way toward improving the transparency of the NYSE floor. A careful reading of these measures indicates that, at least in certain dimensions, the NYSE is moving closer to the structure of an open electronic order book. But it is attempting to modernize itself around the functionality provided by the core group of specialists and floor traders. Maybe the NYSE management believes that it is this rather than the platform itself that should help the exchange dominate trading in the coming years. As in any other market, brokers have knowledge of potential buying and selling interests. As long as they are in a position to access this "latent" order book and bring these interests to the NYSE floor or the new display book, the NYSE members should continue to add value and help the market remain the most liquid in the world.

The NYSE is one of the last few trading institutions that continue to use traditional floor-based trading. The next chapter examines a second dominant market, the Nasdaq market. In comparison with the NYSE, the dynamics of this market are quite different. For starters, the most crucial difference is that the Nasdaq does not operate out of a single physical location. It is a network of broker-dealers and markets.

6

NASDAQ

MARKET

The Nasdaq market is different from the New York Stock Exchange (NYSE). It does not operate from an exchange floor. For that matter, it does not even have a central physical location. It is basically a huge electronic network connecting an incredibly diverse collection of brokers, institutional investors, small investors, and electronic trading systems. Unlike the NYSE, which takes great pains to protect the role of the exchange floor and its members, Nasdaq is in a state of constant evolution. Its loose structure makes it easier for institutions as well as individuals to innovate with different trading systems and strategies. As a result, it has borne the brunt of the changes unleashed by developments in information technologies, including electronic networks—both private as well as of the public variety such as the Internet.

The first few sections of this chapter provide an overview of the Nasdaq market and describe some of the changes to its market structure over the past decade. Whereas the trading system used by the NYSE has evolved over the past 200 years, the Nasdaq has literally grown up overnight. Several changes in the recent past were forced on it by regulators. The market still has considerable scope for reform. Later sections discuss some of the proposals floating around to improve the structure of the marketplace. Unfortunately for Nasdaq, introducing any changes to its structure is not an easy task. As it is primarily a network of a diverse group of players with conflicting interests, every change ends up tearing the market apart.

To the credit of the U.S. investment community, change is never put on hold. The fascinating aspect of the dynamics of the Nasdaq market is that it cannot ignore developments outside the confines of the "exchange floor." If the Nasdaq management and its membership decide to ignore a new need of a segment of users, a new trading entity will crop up overnight to serve the new niche. And this entity will be subsumed within the Nasdaq market. This is possible because it has a flexible structure. This is not possible with the NYSE as the latter has chosen to adopt a tight structure.

Stock markets around the world have rapidly gone electronic. The Nasdaq market is of great interest to us as it is a role model for many of them. Understanding its dynamics will help us develop a deeper appreciation for the numerous new market structures discussed in later chapters. Floor exchanges such as the NYSE are history; electronic markets such as the Nasdaq are the future.

6.1 OVERVIEW

6.1.1 Background Information

Nasdaq falls under the auspices of the Nasdaq Stock Market, Inc, which used to be a wholly owned[1] subsidiary of the National Association of Securities Dealers, Inc. (NASD). The NASD is a national securities association (as opposed to a securities exchange), which operates and regulates the activities of the Nasdaq market and registered brokers. Nasdaq began its existence in 1971 as the National Association of Securities Dealers Automated Quotation System (hence the acronym, Nasdaq). Its main function then was to disseminate quotes from registered brokers for stocks not listed on exchanges such as the NYSE, American Stock Exchange (AMEX), and the different regional exchanges. In other words, it was started mainly as an information service for stocks that traded in the over-the-counter (OTC) market. Over almost three decades, Nasdaq has slowly evolved from an information service to a trading—order routing and execution—institution. On November 9, 2000, Nasdaq filed an application with the Securities and Exchange Commission (SEC) for registration as an exchange.

Nasdaq market is primarily a *quote-driven* market, compared with the NYSE, which is order-driven. It is essentially a telecommunications network linking thousands of traders around the United States. For stocks listed on Nasdaq, dealers or market makers post bid and ask quotes—prices at which they are ready to buy and sell with specified quantities of shares. These prices are then displayed on a nationwide system of computer terminals in brokers' offices.

There are varying levels of information service on the Nasdaq market. Nasdaq workstation level I (NWI) service is distributed by private vendors and includes mainly real-time best bid and best ask quotations for all stocks quoted in the Nasdaq system. Nasdaq workstation level II (NWII; see Figure 6.1) provides real-time access to bid and ask quotes from all market makers active in any given Nasdaq-listed stock. Level III (NWIII) service includes level II plus the ability to enter quotations, direct and execute orders, and communicate with market makers. On NWII, the market makers on the bid side are listed on the left side of the window ordered from best bid (highest bid) descending. The market makers on the ask side are listed on the right side of the window ordered from best ask

FIGURE 6.1 *Nasdaq Workstation Level II*

CSCO

| CSCO | Best Market | P | T | OK |

CSCO + 101   b 100 15/16 a 101   30 x 234   10.9M 12:47

MMID	C.	Bid	BSi...	Time	MMID	C.	Ask	AS...	Time
INCA	+	100 15/16	30	15:47	MASHp	-	101	234	15:47
ISLD	+	100 15/16	4	15:47	MADFp	-	101	104	15:47
MSCOp	+	100 7/8	10	15:47	NITEp	-	101	62	15:47
REDI		100 3/4	11	15:46	ISLD	+	101	50	15:47
SBSHp	+	100 3/4	10	15:46	BRUT	+	101	41	15:47
INTC	+	100 3/4	2	15:46	SBSHp	-	101	34	15:46
DEMPp	+	100 11/16	10	15:47	PERTp	-	101	30	15:12
SHWDp	+	100 11/16	10	15:47	MLCOp	+	101	26	15:42
PRUSp	+	100 11/16	1	15:47	SLKCp	-	101	10	15:42
FBCOp	-	100 11/16	1	15:45	NFSCp	-	101	10	15:33
MONTp	+	100 5/8	10	15:41	PRUSp	-	101	9	15:47
GSCOp	+	100 5/8	10	15:41	OLDEp	+	101	8	15:19
MASHp	+	100 5/8	1	15:47	AGEDp		101	6	15:47
NITEp	-	100 1/2	10	15:47	USCTp	-	101	5	15:47
MLCOp	+	100 1/2	10	15:42	BESTp	+	101	5	15:39
SLKCp	-	100 1/2	10	15:42	JOSEp	+	101	5	15:39
MADFp	+	100 1/2	1	15:47	FCAPp	-	101	1	15:40
CWCOp	-	100 7/16	5	15:46	LEHMp	+	101	1	15:18
SNDVp	+	100 3/8	2	15:36	INCA	+	101 1/16	3	15:47
HRZGp	-	100 1/4	10	15:35	BTRD	+	101 1/8	20	15:47
NFSCp	+	100 1/4	10	15:33	GSCOp	+	101 1/8	10	16:41
OPCOp	+	100 1/4	10	15:11	HRZGp	+	101 1/8	10	15:36
PERTp	+	100 1/4	3	15:12	MWXCp	+	101 1/8	10	15:23
USCTp	+	100 1/4	1	15:47	DLJPp		101 1/8	10	14:57
LEHMp	+	100 1/4	1	15:18	MWQTp		101 1/8	10	14:43
SELZp	+	100 1/4	1	15:08	SELZp	+	101 1/8	1	15:08
WARRp	+	100 3/18	10	15:23	AANAp		101 1/8	1	14:51
DLJPp		100 1/8	10	14:57	SHWDp	+	101 3/16	10	15:47
RSSFp	+	100 1/8	1	15:12	DEANp	-	101 3/16	1	15:44
BESTp	-	100	10	15:39	TWPTp	-	101 3/16	1	15:25
BRUT	+	100	1	15:47	WARRp	+	101 3/16	1	15:23
JOSEp	+	100	1	15:39	COSTp	+	101 1/4	10	15:41
BTRD	-	99 15/16	20	15:47	COWNp	-	101 1/4	10	15:40

Time	Price	Size
12:47	101	200
12:47	100 11/16	700
12:47	101	100
12:47	101	100
12:47	100 13/16	600
12:47	100 13/16	100
12:47	101	100
12:47	101	100
12:47	101	100
12:47	101	1.00K
12:47	101	100
12:47	101	200
12:47	101	100
12:47	101	300
12:47	101	100
12:47	101	100
12:47	101	2.90K
12:47	101	200
12:47	101	400
12:47	101	100
12:47	100 31/32	100
12:47	101	200
12:47	101	100
12:47	101	500
12:47	101	100
12:47	100 7/8	100
12:47	100 15/16	500
12:47	101	200
12:47	100 15/16	200
12:47	100 7/8	100
12:47	100 7/8	200
12:47	100 15/16	100
12:47	100 15/16	100
12:47	100 7/8	100
12:47	100 15/16	500

(lowest ask) ascending. The first five levels of bid-ask prices can be color coded with all market makers bidding or asking the same price having the same color code. Historically, these services were distributed primarily by private vendors such as Reuters and Bloomberg over expensive, dedicated lines. But in recent years, numerous brokerage firms have been providing low-cost (and in some cases, even free) access to NWI and NWII screens over the Internet.

When an individual sends an order to a broker (by phone or over the Internet), the order will be compared with the existing quote. For example, assume a buy order for 10,000 shares of Dell Computer at a limit price of $47 or less per share is sent to a brokerage firm. The broker will check for the best offer; let's assume that the lowest selling price quoted in the market is $46.75. The broker will send a message either by phone or through an electronic link such as SelectNet expressing an interest in buying 10,000 shares at $46.75 or better. The market maker will typically respond with a confirmation of his or her offer (let's assume that the market maker is willing to sell 10,000 shares at his or her quoted price), and the two parties will exchange appropriate messages acknowledging a trade.

The Nasdaq is also interesting in that it has recently become an arena in the United States for increasingly popular electronic trading. The 1990s have seen a small but growing fraction of trades in Nasdaq stocks taking place on alternative order-driven, electronic trading systems. These systems are known as electronic communication networks (ECN), which are discussed in detail in Chapter 7.

6.1.2 Legacy Issue

Later in this chapter we discuss some of the recent proposals from the Nasdaq management to modernize the trading process and make it more efficient. The key aspect of these new ideas is the ability to match buy and sell interests automatically (i.e., without any human intervention). In the current system, the Nasdaq market merely serves as a pass-through communication channel for the quotes of its constituents. As illustrated above, nearly every trade involves a market maker on the opposite side. Some of the future strategies would have the Nasdaq (sans its brokers) involved directly in the process of matching buyers and sellers of stocks. If these proposals ever see the light of the day, investors will be able to trade directly with each other, completely bypassing the broker-dealer network.[2]

Although there is widespread agreement for an improved marketplace, the Nasdaq management has had a tough time getting its constituents—the investors and the broker community—to agree to any of these new ideas. One of the reasons for this reluctance (especially by the broker-dealer community) is the legacy of the original form and purpose of the Nasdaq market. Professional traders would prefer to have the Nasdaq remain basically a telecommunications network, carrying quote information among brokers and broadcasting it to the rest of the marketplace. They would also gladly have the institution play the role of a regulator. But they would surely not want to see the Nasdaq getting into the role of a market mechanism in the sense of actually matching buyers and sellers of stocks. Broker-dealers have traditionally performed this task, and they feel threatened by any move by Nasdaq to encroach on their territory.

6.1.3 Quote-Driven Market

As a quote-driven market, dealers in Nasdaq quote their best bids and offers. Although the Nasdaq market is structured around competing market makers, it does display many features of a double auction. For example, when a market maker quotes his or her bid-offer price, the market maker is in effect placing two limit orders: a limit order to buy a specified number of shares at the bid price, and a limit order to sell at the offer price.

Buy orders from customers are routed to the market maker with the lowest offer and sell orders to the market maker with the highest bid. Market makers are professional investors seeking to profit from the difference between their bid and ask prices. For highly liquid stocks, for example, Microsoft, Intel, and Dell, there could be more than 50 market makers quoting prices for each stock.

Market makers change their limit prices in response to changes in the demand for and supply of a stock. So, to the extent that market makers compete by changing their quotes, this market has the elements of a double auction.

The NYSE operates a double auction in which all orders flow to a common physical location, the exchange floor (although not necessarily to a single consolidated order book). By design, the Nasdaq market does not yet have any mechanism to consolidate order flow to any common point. It is a distributed marketplace where orders are spread out among hundreds of brokers (Figure 6.2).

In typical double-auction markets, orders from buyers and sellers for a particular stock interact directly with each other. This interaction takes place within the confines of an order book for that stock. Investors might hire the services of a broker simply to submit the bid or offer to the order book at the appropriate moment. But historically the Nasdaq market has required that an order to buy or sell a stock be sent directly to a market maker who will execute the trade against his or her quote. The quote published by the market maker need not be related to any orders the market maker might be carrying in his or her book. So, as every trade

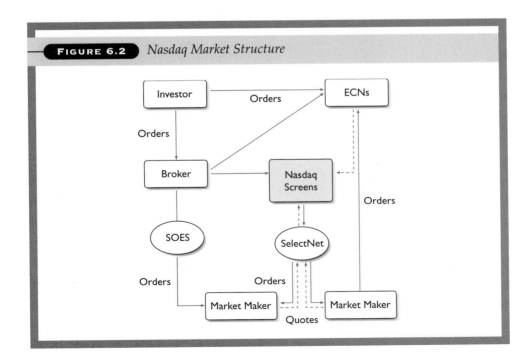

FIGURE 6.2 *Nasdaq Market Structure*

by an investor is against a market maker's quote, there is little direct interaction between any two customers' orders.

In recent years, the Nasdaq authorities have introduced measures designed to allow for more direct interaction between investors' orders. The new rules, which are addressed later in this chapter, require that a market maker's quotes reflect the trading interests submitted by customers. This means that if a customer is willing to buy a stock at a price higher than the broker's bid, then the latter should change his or her quote to the level indicated by the customer. The idea here is to allow investors to submit their trading interests to the market and in the process establish a hopefully more efficient price determination system.

One exception to the normal practice described above is the presence of internalization systems within large brokerage firms such as Merrill Lynch and Knight Trimark (which is more a broker's broker). These firms collect orders from their clients (and also from smaller brokerage firms) and try to find natural matches internally between these orders. So, if there is a buy order at market price for 1,000 shares of MSFT stock and multiple sell orders that add up to 1,100 shares, the system will match the buy and sell orders for up to 1,000 shares within the firm itself. The balance selling interest for 100 shares will be routed outside the firm to a market maker with the highest bid.

A parallel development has been the growth of ECNs, which are primarily private trading facilities connected to the Nasdaq network. They allow large investors to trade directly with each other.

6.1.4 Market Makers

"Business" for broker-dealers in Nasdaq comes in the form of orders from investors. One could crudely classify Nasdaq brokers as retail and wholesale. Retail brokers are ones such as E*Trade, Charles Schwab, and Ameritrade. Small investors send their orders to these brokers for execution. The retail brokers in turn send their orders to wholesale brokers such as Merrill Lynch, Goldman Sachs, and Knight Trimark. The latter also have large retail brokerage operations in which they serve both small individuals as well as large institutional investors. Wholesale brokers compete for business (or order flow) by making aggressive quotes or by promising to match the best quote in the marketplace. This implies that wholesale brokers are "the" market makers we have been talking about all this time.

Given that the securities markets are rather competitive by nature, one would expect brokers to compete aggressively for business from the investment community. Bid and offer quotes are like prices of any good or service. Telephone companies compete for business by cutting prices. Retail brokers compete by reducing their brokerage commissions. Wholesale brokers, or market makers, try to attract order flow by either raising their bid (the price at which they are willing to buy a certain number of shares of a particular stock) or reducing their offer (their selling price for that stock).

In recent years, retail brokers and market makers have moved away from a pure price-based competition model to a practice called *preferencing*. This is basically an arrangement between a broker and a market maker under which the former will agree to route (or *preference*) his or her clients' orders to the latter. The market maker will execute these orders at the best-displayed price in the Nasdaq quote montage; he or she will do this even if the best quote is different from his or her own. In exchange for routing orders, the broker will receive a kickback, also called *payment for order flow* from the market maker.

Here's an example of a preferenced deal. Let's assume a retail broker, Y*Trade.com, receives a sell order for 1,000 shares of LEDD stock at the best market price. The highest bid in the market at that point in time is $75.25. Y*Trade has a preferencing agreement with MightTrident, a market maker who is quoting a bid of $75.20 and an offer of $75.35. The order is electronically routed to MightTrident, which sticks to its promise to match the highest bid and buys the 1,000 shares at $75.25. In return, Y*Trade receives, say, $0.005 per share as payment for order flow.

Y*Trade is expected to deliver the best market price to its client; the order is executed at the highest bid, although not necessarily by the market maker who had posted that quote in the market. Receiving this price satisfies the client. Y*Trade receives $5 from MightTrident. Although this amount looks small, if Y*Trade routes a large number of shares to the latter, say, 1 million shares a day, this amount adds up to $5,000 and over a year (assuming there are 240 trading days in a calendar year) can receive close to $1.2 million as compensation for preferencing.

Now, how does MightTrident gain? Its bid was at $75.20; it ended up buying 1,000 shares at $75.25. Let's assume once again that it has similar preferencing arrangements with numerous other retail brokers (as well as with wholesale brokers with large individual and institutional clients). The market bid is at $75.25, and the offer is at $75.30 (lower than MightTrident's own offer quote). At the same time that it received the 1,000 shares sell order from Y*Trade, it receives two buy orders for 500 shares each of the same stock from two other retail brokers. It matches the existing offer at $75.30 and pays $0.005 a share to each of the two brokers. The total payment for order flow for these three deals is $10 ($5 to Y*Trade.com and $2.50 each to the two retail brokers who routed the buy orders). Its total inflow is the $0.05 per share difference (or spread) between the bid and offer prices. This works out to a net inflow of $40. Assuming 1 million shares a day over 240 trading days, it works out to $9.6 million a year. All this without having to compete for order flow by quoting the best bid and offer!

Not surprisingly, there is a considerable amount of controversy over this practice. Dealers who make such payments are basically sharing a portion of the bid-ask spread with the brokers who are routing orders to them. In a competitive marketplace, dealers will compete for orders by trying to improve on the quotes of other dealers. The complaint is that market makers who pay for order flow are essentially *free riding* on the efforts of other market makers. In other words, they are basically using the quotes placed by other market makers in the Nasdaq system without actually participating actively in the price discovery process. Unfortunately, the evidence on the merits of this practice from the perspective of the overall efficiency of the marketplace is mixed.

6.1.5 Market Opening

Trading on the Nasdaq market takes place continuously during regular business hours. Market makers are required to quote their prices continuously during trading hours, a provision that is designed to ensure a liquid marketplace.

The Nasdaq market formally opens for trading at 9:30 AM Eastern Standard Time. Unlike the NYSE, there is no formal call market to open trading on the Nasdaq. Instead, there is an informal price discovery process starting at 8:15 before the market opens when market makers display nonbinding quotes at exploratory prices that they are not compelled to honor later.

These indicative quotes are advertised over the Nasdaq screens. This process is thus analogous to the calling out of indications by NYSE specialists. The crucial difference though is that at the NYSE the specialist coordinates the price-fixing process in the pre-open phase. As seen earlier, there is no such coordination mechanism among competing market makers in the Nasdaq system.

Ideally, one would have the broker-dealers communicate their trading interests (including that of their clients) to a single entity that would then compute a price at which the largest number of trades could take place. Instead, the distributed nature of the quote generation and display process tends to lead to considerable confusion during the market opening session. For instance, at any given instance, multiple transactions in a single stock can take place at wildly varying prices. Although Nasdaq publishes an official market opening price for every stock, it is typically the case that this price is determined by a single trade that could be for as few as 100 shares.

In theory, what Nasdaq needs is a mechanism that will open trading for any given stock at a single price. The system would take into consideration all the trading interest in every stock at the market opening time and find a single price (per stock) that would maximize the total number of shares traded. Unfortunately for Nasdaq, given its current structure, any such coordinating mechanism might not be acceptable to its constituents. A single price call would require that brokers route their customers' orders to a single "order book" and not to the market maker who has the best bid or offer or with whom they have a preferencing agreement. Market makers worry that they will be deprived of the spread between their bid and offer quote—a primary source of income for them. Retail brokers hate to lose lucrative revenue in the form of payment for order flow.

In January 2001, the Nasdaq market authorities announced that they are actively considering a market opening proposal submitted by James Angel, a professor of finance at Georgetown University. At this time, there is hardly any information on the specifics of this mechanism. But it is highly likely that it will have some of the elements suggested above.

Given previous reluctance of the Nasdaq market to experiment with such an arrangement, some of its members have decided to start their own venture for this purpose (we should point out though that by Spring 2001, there were no indications that this project is anywhere close to a formal launch). A group of large brokerage firms including Goldman Sachs and Morgan Stanley have entered into an agreement with the Arizona Stock Exchange (AZX), which we discuss in a later chapter, to run a single-price market opening procedure on a pilot basis. These firms receive substantial order flows, which they have agreed to route to the AZX. This latest adventure by an important segment of the Nasdaq constituency is a classic example of the innovative forces that drive this market discussed in the introductory section above.

6.2 ROLE OF TECHNOLOGY

The Nasdaq market's advertisements promote it as the largest electronic screen-based equity exchange in the world. They also like to refer to themselves as "the stock market for the next 100 years." Some of us have problems with this statement. For the past few years, markets around the world have been moving toward automated execution. The main Nasdaq market (distinct from the ECNs that are essentially private networks but are connected to the former) offers little in the way of automated execution. The Nasdaq market went into operation in 1971 as an electronic quote dissemination system. Deals were negotiated over the phone, and transaction data were entered into and disseminated over the same network. Except for the SOES (small order execution system), which allows for automated execution of small-sized orders, the main Nasdaq market continues to operate the same way.

A sizeable majority of trades involving Nasdaq stocks are executed outside Nasdaq's order delivery and execution services (meaning SelectNet and SOES, respectively) via direct links among retail and institutional brokers, market makers, ECNs, and other market centers.[3] These participants communicate with each other by using a variety of means including telephone and dedicated links.

Private firms such as Instinet, Island, and Archipelago have taken the lead in introducing new technologies to trade Nasdaq stocks. The main Nasdaq market on its own has only recently taken a substantial step in this direction. Its attitude seems to have been to let its competitors take the risk involved in trying out new innovations in trading systems, letting the benefits flow into the overall market by connecting the new private systems to the Nasdaq network. One bold move from Nasdaq was the introduction of the sophisticated OptiMark Trading System as a facility of the Nasdaq market, which eventually failed. Nasdaq's commitment to OptiMark was limited to allowing the latter to connect to the various communication lines that form the Nasdaq network.

6.2.1 SelectNet

SelectNet is an electronic system operated by Nasdaq that allows brokers and dealers to deliver orders directly to each other. A broker can use this system to either preference an order to a particular market maker or to broadcast it to the entire Nasdaq market.

It is primarily a communication tool that lets Nasdaq brokers and market makers transmit and negotiate buy and sell trading interests with each other. The system is surely not capable of automatically matching buy and sell orders. As a communication device, SelectNet allows brokers to negotiate terms of a deal, especially for large orders in which either broker would have some discretion in price and volume of the trade. Although not an execution facility, it does obligate market makers receiving SelectNet orders at their posted bids or offers to execute them. See the discussion on dual liability in later sections.

After leading a dormant existence for a long time, SelectNet has grown into an important part of the Nasdaq trading system. It now accounts for about two-thirds of all dealer-to-dealer orders placed on Nasdaq and is used by most mid- and large-sized firms. An important reason for this has been the growing popularity of the preferencing approach to trading. Brokers found SelectNet to be an efficient tool to route orders to preferred market makers. A second reason for its increased use was the suite of applications built on top of SelectNet. Once again, the initiative came from the broker-dealer community, not from Nasdaq itself. Market makers have taken the basic features of SelectNet and have integrated it with their own systems, automating their interaction with other traders. The key features of these systems are the ability to enter large orders for multiple stocks, as well as, and maybe more importantly, to respond quickly to incoming orders.

A third important reason for its growing popularity is the fact that the SelectNet system has recently been opened up for traders who are not members of the Nasdaq market, allowing a member broker hooked up to SelectNet to act essentially as a pass-through. Under the new rules, a large mutual fund can establish a special arrangement with its broker (who is a Nasdaq member) to submit orders directly to SelectNet under prearranged conditions. Depending on how this is implemented, a large trader can in certain cases send an order to the market without revealing his or her identity and intentions to his or her own broker, regardless of the fact the order will be displayed as if the broker had submitted it. By means of this device, large investors can trade without having to identify themselves to the whole market, including their own brokers. The only requirement would be to have rules in place that regulate the type and size of orders that can be sent directly through SelectNet. The broker is responsible for ensuring that the client has sufficient capital to cover any liabilities arising from these trades.

6.2.2 SOES

In 1984, Nasdaq implemented a trading facility for another subset of its clientele. The SOES is an electronic system for routing small orders from brokerage firms to Nasdaq market makers. In addition, Nasdaq participants can execute small orders automatically[4] against quotations of market makers at the best bids or offers for different stocks.

It is an automated execution system in the sense that a market maker whose quote is "hit" through SOES cannot back away from it. Orders entered into SOES can be *directed* to a preferred dealer who has agreed in advance to accept such orders from the broker. Orders can also be sent to the market as a whole. Such orders are allocated sequentially to dealers with the highest bid or the lowest offer quotes.

The advantage of this system is that it does not require telephone contact between the broker and the market maker and trades are executed almost instantaneously. Orders entered through SOES are guaranteed execution at the posted price. Today, SOES accounts for about 20 percent of all dealer-to-dealer orders, a popularity that was spurred by a series of changes in Nasdaq's regulations.

System for the Small Investor

SOES has been around since 1984. In the early years, however, market makers could choose whether or not to respond to orders received through SOES, thus limiting its use. Following the 1987 stock market crash, thousands of small investors complained vociferously that they had been unable to reach market makers to execute their trades. Faced with a barrage of complaints, the NASD made SOES participation mandatory for market makers.

The overall objective was to put the individual investor on an equal footing with larger traders. According to the "minimum-size rule" that was passed, dealers were required to accept orders of 1,000 shares or less up to a total exposure of 5,000 shares. These limits were subsequently modified due to an unexpected by-product of SOES popularity—the day trader.

Day Trader Phenomenon

The automated execution feature of SOES resulted in the evolution of a new category of professional traders known as day traders. These traders took advantage of the speed offered by SOES to speculate on intraday price fluctuations in Nasdaq stocks, hence the name.

At the height of the phenomenon in the late 1990s, any one of the estimated hundreds of day traders typically could be found sitting in his or her broker's office, tracking price movements by using sophisticated software. One corner of a typical SOES trader's screen would have quote updates by market makers in many active Nasdaq stocks scrolling across as they occurred. If a day trader spotted a lot of activity in a stock, he or she would type in the stock's ticker symbol (or simply hit a function key) to display the stock's current quotes in another part of the screen. Whenever the day trader wanted to buy or sell a stock, he or she would simply shout out his or her order to the broker's employee, who in turn would enter the order into the SOES system for rapid execution. Many times, day traders were simply taking advantage of a cost-free profit or arbitrage opportunity in the Nasdaq market. Market makers typically quoted prices on close to 200 different stocks. In a volatile market in which prices moved around a lot, they did not have systems in place to quickly change their own quotes. SOES offered smart speculators a tool to quickly punish any market maker that was slow in changing his or her quotes. These traders were given a new name: SOES *bandits.*

By 1997–1998, things had become so bad that market makers started complaining about the abuse of the SOES system, which had been originally designed to protect the interests of small investors. It was always assumed that small investors would not indulge in speculative trading but would buy a stock and hold it for a long period of time. It was never visualized that they would simply turn around and sell it within a few minutes or, worse, taking advantage of any mispriced quotes due to market-maker lethargy!

Discouraging the Bandits

In 1998, the Nasdaq market responded by instituting new rules that made it difficult for day traders to abuse the SOES system. In addition, it took a number of steps to reduce the risk of losses for market makers from participating in SOES. For instance, it removed the minimum-size rule for SOES quotes, allowing market makers the freedom to specify the number of shares they were willing to trade at a particular quote. This change in regulation was accomplished by simply extending the actual-size rule that was in effect for SelectNet users to SOES.

Moving to SelectNet

The extension of the actual-size rule to SOES reduced some of the gain for the SOES bandits. Basically, it reduced the size of their trades; instead of trading 1,000 shares at a time, they now had to trade in smaller blocks as market makers typically committed to a lower number of shares at any one price. Day traders had to literally work 10 times harder just to maintain their previous earnings.

Fortunately for the day-trading community, they had technology-savvy brokers looking after their interests. These brokerage firms figured out ways to execute trades rapidly through SelectNet. They added new features to SelectNet that converted what was basically a simple communications tool into an automated execution mechanism. The most crucial item added to their order routing systems (which were, in turn, connected to SelectNet) was a feature that generates automatic back-away complaints to Nasdaq every time a market maker decided not to honor a quote displayed on SelectNet. In essence, these firms were taking advantage of the fact that if a market maker had accumulated multiple back-away complaints, the NASD regulators would be forced to take disciplinary action against the market maker. Reluctant to face any punitive damages from the regulators, market makers have been coaxed into trading with orders "messaged" to them over SelectNet. By not being able to back away from their quotes, they have essentially converted SelectNet into a SOES-like mechanism but without any of the order-size restrictions imposed on the latter.

6.2.3 SuperSoes

The Nasdaq market is the process of implementing a new system called Super-Soes (or NNMS in official SEC documents) that essentially integrates features from SelectNet and SOES. After numerous delays in testing and implementation, the Nasdaq launched SuperSoes in late July, 2001. This project is designed to divert some of the message traffic off SelectNet (see discussion above and in Section 6.5.2 on recent explosion in SelectNet use). The new system will contain execution capability present in SOES.

Under the new system, it will be more difficult for a broker to back away from a quote. Time priority will be enforced, and faster response hopefully will lead to reduced risk for the brokers and therefore a restoration of the depth of the book to where it was (1,000 shares) rather than the much lower level in the current use of the system. ECNs will be incorporated but will be shut off if they are too slow in responding.

SuperSoes will eliminate the issue of dual liability for market makers by no longer requiring an order to go through SelectNet. Here is a classic example of dual liability under the existing arrangement. Let us assume that a dealer using SelectNet today has just completed a trade, say, bought a large number of shares of INTC. As this has increased his inventory of INTC, he would like to change his displayed quote. Maybe he would like to reduce his holding and accordingly lower his bid as well as his offer. But before he makes the necessary change, an incoming order from SOES hits his old quote. Although this latter trade was perfectly legal and the dealer is bound to honor it, it has resulted in an unnecessary increase in inventory. The "dual" in dual liability refers to the fact that the dealer has to fulfil two trades, the one through SelectNet as well as the SOES hit. SuperSoes mitigates this problem by enabling instantaneous adjustments to displayed quotes.

Moving on to the "Soes" aspect of SuperSoes, the new system allows investors to obtain automated execution of orders of 9,900 shares or less. Investors can trade against both the displayed and reserved volumes of the best bids or offers. For purposes of automated execution, it does not discriminate between a market maker's proprietary and agency quotes.

Interestingly, Nasdaq has maintained a time restriction on the frequency with which a broker can access a particular market maker's quote at the same price via SuperSoes. There is a 17-second delay at present; SuperSoes will reduce this to five seconds.

SuperSoes was considered a crucial step in the evolution toward SuperMontage. As per the original plan, it was expected to go live on January 22, 2001, but has now been postponed until the third quarter of 2001. Issues causing the delay include system failures during testing, questions regarding its operation during market open, and a host of issues related to broker-dealers and their interfacing with the system.

Successful implementation of SuperSoes would result in numerous improvements in the functioning of the Nasdaq market. For starters, it will increase the overall speed of execution. It will allow automatic execution of orders between market markers (a facility that is available right now only via SOES and that too for small-sized orders).

6.2.4 OptiMark Experiment

Another attempted innovation on the Nasdaq was the market's integration with OptiMark, which went live on Nasdaq in October 1999. OptiMark was a computerized trading system developed by OptiMark Technologies, Inc. The system allowed users to specify multiple price-quantity combinations for an order. In addition, the trading using OptiMark was totally anonymous. The trading arrangement with Nasdaq was as follows: At periodic intervals (every two to five minutes depending on the stock), OptiMark would run a call auction to try to find matches among various trading interests in its order book. The components of the order book were those submitted directly by OptiMark users, the national best bid and offer quotes from Nasdaq market makers, ECNs, and unlisted trading privilege exchange specialists. The OptiMark order book was accessed by traders in the Nasdaq market through the Nasdaq network. This was achieved primarily by modifying the existing Nasdaq user interfaces to allow for communication with the OptiMark trading system.

As the OptiMark system was partly designed to automate the price discovery that takes place in the market, market makers were reluctant to allow such orders to interact with their quotes and limit orders from other investors. The reasoning here is that orders submitted through the OptiMark system would be able to absorb liquidity provided by market makers and investors who were not using the OptiMark system.

Anonymity is valued by certain groups of investors. In a free market, if there is demand for a particular service, the marketplace is bound to deliver a solution. The OptiMark system, along with numerous other electronic trading systems, offered anonymity as a service. The Nasdaq's plan to build this feature into the proposed system could be viewed as an attempt by the market authorities to capture some of the orders that otherwise would flow to these alternative systems.

OptiMark executions provided price and time priority protection to all limit orders residing in the Nasdaq limit-order facility. Its algorithm was able to execute trades against multiple price levels. Market makers and ECNs were only guaranteed protection through OptiMark at their displayed price level. The concern among the trading community was that these inconsistencies would further hinder the ability of market makers and broker-dealer firms operating the ECNs to compete with Nasdaq's proposed limit-order book.

The biggest complaint against OptiMark was that it was too difficult to use. Institutional traders who used the system complained that the system was too complicated and took too long to execute orders. In September 2000, OptiMark suspended all its U.S. equities trading[5] due to low trading volumes and heavy losses.

6.3 COLLUSION AMONG MARKET MAKERS

The following sections discuss the continuous evolutionary process of the Nasdaq market. We start by describing the past as well as various pending proposals that might see the light of the day sometime in the near future. A key difference between the NYSE and the Nasdaq is that the former market's basic structure has been frozen in time since the early 1900s. Thanks to a more open design, which means that different trading technologies can be added to its electronic network easily, the Nasdaq market has been continually affected by initiatives focused on serving varying needs of different segments of the investment community. This chapter focuses mainly on changes that have been implemented and are under consideration by the Nasdaq management.

But before we get to a listing of the achievements of the Nasdaq leadership, we should spend some time looking at changes that were forced down their throat by regulators. The changes, which were more in the nature of reforms than competitive responses, were set in motion by a couple of academics. The amazing aspect of their research was that they went looking for explanations of an apparent quirk in the Nasdaq market and ended up opening a big can of worms.

6.3.1 Why No Odd-Eighth Quotes?

In a study published in 1994, William G. Christie and Paul H. Schultz set out to examine why Nasdaq market makers avoid odd-eighth quotes.[6] The concern was that by not using odd-eighth quotes such as 3/8 and 5/8, Nasdaq dealers managed to maintain wide bid-ask spreads. If prices were always quoted in even-eighths, the smallest difference between bid and ask prices would be 2/8, or 25 cents. The use of odd- and even-eighth quotes would result in narrower spreads of 1/8, or 12.5 cents. (As an aside, readers should note that in the past seven to eight years since this study, markets have moved to quoting in increments of first in 16ths and 32nds; by July 2000, numerous trading systems had started accepting bids and offers in one cent increments.)

Interestingly, the wider spreads prevailed in SOES, the computerized execution system targeted at small investors. If a large order came over SelectNet or by phone, a dealer would be willing to use odd-eighths to lower the spread. Christie and Schultz set out to discover whether the lack of odd-eighth quotes was a symptom of tacit collusion among market makers.

6.3.2 Monitoring and Punishing

The screen-based trading system used by Nasdaq traders makes the system highly transparent. A market maker's quotes in a particular spot can be viewed by every trader with access to the Nasdaq screens. So, once a decision was taken to avoid quoting odd-eighth quotes, any dealer who decides to place odd-eighth quotes would be exposed immediately to the whole market. Other traders who preferred to maintain the status quo could easily punish the deserter by selecting from any of the following alternative sanctions.

Don't Give the Offender Any Business

One sanction was to have brokers divert customer orders away from a violator with the best posted but "non-sanctioned" price, thereby depriving the violator of business. As the system allowed traders to preference their orders to favored dealers, the offender would be struck off this list. Instead of sending customer orders to the dealer quoting a lower spread (and thus a better price), other dealers could execute trades at the better price. These orders would never enter the Nasdaq execution systems, and the offending dealer would have no opportunity to receive the trade and profit from the lower spread.

Hit the Offender on the Wrong Side

A second punishment was to hit the violator on the wrong side of his or her quote. Let's assume a dealer used an even-eighth to improve on the existing offer price. Instead of sending him or her buy orders that would benefit from the lower offer, other traders would route their client's sell orders to him or her. Although the size of the preferenced orders would be 1,000 shares or less per trade, the cumulative effect of a large number of such orders from multiple dealers could adversely affect the inventory of this dealer.

Send the Offender the Wrong Orders

A third method for punishing dealers who moved within the accepted spread was to direct customer trades to the offending dealer when the trades were perceived to be motivated by information rather than liquidity needs. An important feature of these sanctions is that they do not impose any costs on the brokers who initiate the preferenced orders.

Dealers expect to lose by trading with a better-informed customer. If an informed trader buys a stock, the dealer would expect the stock price to increase in the future. By selling to the customer at a price lower than the future-high price, the dealer is potentially incurring a loss. The loss will take place when the broker (who has just sold the stock to an informed trader) turns around to "rebuy" the stock from the market to rebalance his or her inventory. Given the nature of the first trade, it is highly likely that other dealers would have raised their offers. This means that the broker will buy the stock at a higher price than that at which he or she had sold to the first trader. Selling low and buying high will surely result in a loss.

Punish the Offender in a Different Stock

Finally, because Nasdaq market makers typically make markets in many stocks, sanctions could be applied in markets for other stocks or by withholding business in other areas (e.g., underwriting).

6.3.3 Wider Spreads and Time Preference

The Nasdaq market does not have a system of centralized order books. As orders for any single stock flow to multiple dealers, the exchange cannot impose a time priority. In other words, it cannot insist that if two similarly priced orders are placed for a given stock, the order that was placed first should be executed first. Similarly, if a dealer improved on an existing quote by, say, using an even-eighth, there are provisions in place to ensure that all new orders are automatically routed to him or her. Other dealers can execute trades at this dealer's better (even-eighth) price.

The securities market is similar to any other market; all else being the same, a trader who lowers his or her selling price expects buyers to come flocking to his or her store. If a market maker cannot expect order flows to increase, he or she will be reluctant to compete on price. In the context of the Nasdaq market, the ability of other dealers to match the better quotes by having orders preferenced to them leaves little incentive for individual dealers to improve their spreads by shrinking it. Doing so would at best have a negligible effect on their ability to attract trades. At its worst, the lack of time preference would make it easier for other market makers to punish dealers who violate their unwritten codes.

6.4 NEW REGULATIONS

In the early 1990s, the Nasdaq faced considerable criticism from academic researchers, various investor groups, and numerous small brokerage firms, compelling the SEC to launch an investigation that lasted close to five years. Based on its findings, which basically confirmed the collusion conjecture made by Christie and Schultz, the SEC ordered the Nasdaq market to clean up its act. In 1997, the Nasdaq management complied with the SEC's directives by implementing two rules that together are referred to as the *order handling rules*.[7] The basic thrust was on two fronts: first, make it difficult for a market maker to maintain too wide a spread; second, prevent market makers from discriminating between investors, quoting narrow spreads for one group and broad spreads for another.

6.4.1 Order Handling Rules

The first component of the order handling rules was called the *order display rule.* Under this rule, when an incoming order from a customer was better than a market maker's quote, the market maker would be required to modify his or her quote to reflect the pricing of the new order. So, if a customer submitted a limit buy order that was $1/8 higher than the market maker's highest bid, the latter should increase his or her bid quote by $1/8. So now, even if market makers were reluctant to make odd-eighth quotes, their customers could send them aggressively priced limit orders that would effectively force them to narrow their spreads.

Another implication of this rule was that for the first time, investors could trade against limit orders that previously would not have been exposed to the market. Before the implementation of this rule, a broker's quote did not need to reflect limit orders from customers. For example, let's say a broker had posted a quote of $15 1/4 bid and $15 1/2 offer for a particular stock. He or she then received a limit order to buy 500 shares of this stock at $15 3/8. Although this price was more aggressive than his or her own bid, the broker was not required to share this information with the rest of the market. The new order display rule forced the broker to change his or her quote to reflect the more aggressive bid. The new quote against the broker's name on the Nasdaq quote montage would be $15 3/8 bid and $15 1/2 offer.

The introduction of alternative electronic trading systems such as ECNs saw many brokers and other professional traders sending their best trades to these new markets. At the time, access to these systems was largely restricted to large institutional traders. (Things have changed since then; these days even large ECNs such as Instinet and Island have started competing aggressively for orders from small investors.) As small investors were left out of this market, the new order handling rules set out to level the playing field. The second component, called the *quote rule,* required that whenever any broker-dealer submitted a better priced trading interest to any ECN, he or she had to modify his or her existing (publicly displayed) quote to reflect this higher bid or lower offer price.

Let's return to the example above, in which the broker had posted a bid at $15 1/4 and an offer at $15 1/2 on the Nasdaq screen. The broker then observed some large trading activity on one of the ECNs and placed a bid at $15 1/4 and offer at $15 3/8. Before the days of the quote rule, a buy order at the market price submitted to the broker via, say, the SOES system, would have been executed at $15 1/2; the lower price of $15 3/8 would be available only to those with access to the ECN. Thanks to the new rules, the broker can no longer discriminate between different investor groups. Once he or she places a lower offer quote in a private trading system, the broker has to change his or her offer on the Nasdaq quote system to $15 3/8.

The main objective of these rules was to reduce the quoted spread for Nasdaq stocks. The limit-order display rule caused a change in the available supply of limit orders. Market participants are no longer at the mercy of professional broker-dealers to set prices. Even individual investors can compete to improve on quoted prices. As the quotes affected by the quote rule were already available outside Nasdaq, the primary effect of this rule has been to increase transparency by bringing them into the main Nasdaq market.

Limit Orders

Why is it important to publicize the limit orders submitted to market makers? Simply stated, these orders are an important source of liquidity to the marketplace. There is considerable evidence that on the NYSE, trading based on limit orders exceeds that driven by market orders.[8] Authors Larry Harris and Joel Hasbrouck report[9] that limit orders account for more than 54 percent of all orders submitted through SuperDOT on the NYSE. This suggests that limit orders have an important role to play in determining the quoted spread.

By widening the range of actual orders that are allowed in the Nasdaq market, the limit-order display rule has brought new competition for existing market makers. So, the purpose of the limit-order display rule has been to ensure that nondealers who are willing to trade at better prices than dealers have their orders publicized to the rest of the market. In a nutshell, the new rules have provided greater visibility to customers' limit orders. Interestingly, in this process, they have gradually pushed the structure of the Nasdaq market toward that of the NYSE.

6.4.2 Lower Liquidity, Improved Transparency

One of the results of regulatory efforts to reduce market-maker spreads has been a drop in profit margins. Accordingly, numerous brokerage firms reacted to the new rules by making markets in fewer stocks. This, in turn, had an adverse effect on market liquidity. Small-cap stocks especially were hurt by this development. These stocks by definition have low liquidity and are more dependent on quotes from broker-dealers. As firms cut back on the number of stocks in which they offer quotes, the market as a whole is pushed toward a liquidity crisis.

By forcing market makers to display orders so the public gets the same picture of the market, the regulations have unquestionably improved the transparency of the marketplace. But at the same time, broker-dealers have been forced to make technological changes to implement the new rules and, as one would expect, have complained of the higher costs that have accompanied the loss of revenue from lower margins. The impact of these rules has been partially offset by the overall increase in trading volumes. Merrill Lynch, one of the large investment banks with huge market-making operations, had reacted to the lower spreads in 1997 by retreating from this business. But in early 2000, the firm announced that it had decided to increase the number of stocks in which it would be making a market from 650 to more than 8,000!

✱

6.5 RECENT DEVELOPMENTS

While the Nasdaq management and the SEC were busy fixing problems and deficiencies in the extant market structure, the world of investment in general and trading technologies in particular have not been sitting quietly. Two large forces have affected the market: Internet-based trading and ECNs.

The development of online brokers has led to a quantum increase in trading activity among small investors. This has resulted in a significant change in the dynamics of the marketplace. The sections below focus on a couple of issues pertinent to the Nasdaq market. We first discuss the technical difficulties of coping with the increase in transaction volumes (not just the total number of shares being traded each day but also the number of transactions executed) and increased volatility in stock prices, especially at the market open. Second, we highlight the ramifications of increasing competition. ECNs and other alternative trading systems now control close to 30 percent of the total trading volume of the Nasdaq market. The traditional broker-dealer network is responsible for the remaining 70 percent. The growth of these trading networks has increased the level of difficulty involved in trading Nasdaq stocks. Investors and brokers have to track stock price movement across multiple trading venues. The typical concern being expressed by numerous market participants is that this market has become highly fragmented. Later sections describe various proposals being considered by the Nasdaq management to address this and other related problems.

6.5.1 Online Investors

Thanks to the phenomenon of the Internet, small investors have more trading resources at their disposal than ever before. And they have been taking advantage of this technology in increasing numbers. A survey released by the Securities Industry Association reported that in 1998, just one in ten investors traded via the Internet; by 1999, this number had increased to nearly one in five.

The new electronic trader has become a powerful force to reckon with, especially in the Nasdaq market. Technology stocks tend to be popular among individual investors trading through various online brokerage services. As most technology stocks are listed on the Nasdaq market, it has taken the brunt of the impact of the surge in trading activity among small investors. This surge in demand is by itself not a bad thing. The problem has been that most brokerage firms and market makers have traditionally handled large orders from a small number of institutional investors. When an institution places a large buy order, its managers take great care to make sure that the execution of the order does not adversely affect the market price of the stock. But when an avalanche of buy orders from a multitude of small online investors hits the market, it can easily lead to skyrocketing prices. On the flip side, massive amounts of sell orders can have a devastating downward impact on prices. More important, from a technology standpoint, this surge in message traffic between investors and their brokers can cause frequent (and unpredictable) breakdowns in overburdened systems.

6.5.2 Breakdowns in SelectNet

A large fraction of the increased trading activity on the Nasdaq is being channeled through SelectNet. Some of this new order flow is from various ECNs that have been connected to the Nasdaq market in recent years. As per its initial design, SelectNet was supposed to facilitate communications mainly among its market makers, not day traders and new electronic trading systems. As it tries to cope with message traffic that it has not been designed to handle, SelectNet has repeatedly slowed and even crashed numerous times. This has led to suspension of trading in substantial sections of the Nasdaq market.

For example, October 17, 1999, saw three ECNs including Instinet, the biggest of them all, locked out of the main Nasdaq quotation system due to a software glitch in the latter. With a relatively significant portion of the market unable to interact with other Nasdaq brokers and market makers, the quality of trading was adversely affected. SelectNet, for instance, was routing orders that were stale in the sense that the investors who had submitted them had withdrawn them 15 to 20 minutes earlier. In addition, as the price broadcast system was badly affected, investors faced the risk of trading at prices that did not accurately reflect current prices. Some corporate issuers reacted by delaying their initial public offerings (IPO) to a later hour when all systems were operating in sync.

In another instance, on November 16, 1999, SelectNet failed for 17 minutes at the end of the trading session and experienced delays for another half an hour at the start of trading the next day. Orders routed through SelectNet did not receive prompt confirmations. Unable to find out if their buy and sell orders had been executed, many investors lost money. Worse, Nasdaq was unable to update stock prices on a real-time basis. This contributed to additional losses for investors.

Interestingly, part of the stated reason for the system breakdown was implementation of new software designed to help Nasdaq's computers cope with the increased volumes, which had increased 35 percent in that month alone, a jump equal to the average annual increase in each of the previous five years. The Nasdaq management is of the view that incremental changes to upgrade existing systems will never be sufficient. They have a proposal in front of the SEC for a system that will replace both SelectNet and SOES. A key feature of the new system would be automated execution of orders. The hope is that this would reduce the message traffic that is routed through SelectNet.

6.5.3 Greater Volatility

In the late 1980s, the Nasdaq composite (an index made up of more than 4,000 stocks that trade in that market) had, on average, about one highly volatile day a month.[10] The definition of a volatile day is one in which the value of the index at close of trading is at least 1 percent above or below the previous day's close. In the first nine months of 1999, this average had increased to three days a week.

Part of the reason for this increase is the growth in the practice of momentum trading. These are trading strategies in which large numbers of investors simultaneously buy or sell a particular stock not because they have a particular viewpoint about the concerned company's profitability. Rather they sense that the stock price will be in an upward or downward trend for a certain period of time. If the expectation is that it will rise, large numbers of them buy the stock, pushing up the stock price farther, and try to sell it before it moves back down. As a classic example of a self-fulfilling prophecy, this strategy pursued by thousands of investors trading actively over the Internet at commissions as low as $5 per trade has surely contributed to increased volatility in the Nasdaq market. Unfortunately for the Nasdaq management, there is hardly anything anyone can do to correct this behavior. Everyone basically had to get used to the volatile market.

6.5.4 IPOs and Market Volatility

The impact of increased trading by thousands of individual investors has been rather drastic on the market for IPOs by firms with the Internet as the primary business and operating environment—Internet IPOs. There have been reports that in numerous instances buy orders for a particular Internet IPO exceeded the entire amount of the issue. This surge in buying interest could potentially lead to unprecedented increases in stock price. For example, when MP3.com, an online music business, started trading in July 1999, it had an offering price of $28 per share. The first trade in the open market (where the seller is typically a trader who bought it from the company) was at $92. Within moments, the stock broke the $100 mark and rose to a high of $105; it ended the day at $68.375.

A second example is one that illustrates some of what (to the uninitiated at least) would seem like perverse motivations of firms in the IPO marketplace. MarketWatch.com was promoted by the television network CBS as an Internet-based financial media business. When its underwriters started accepting bids for the IPO, they received orders for more than 100 million shares, way beyond what MarketWatch.com wanted to issue. It sold 3.1 million shares at the IPO offer price of $17.[11] Given the huge gap between demand and supply, on the first day of trading, the stock price rose to $97.50.

The apparently perverse dynamics of the IPO market have been compounded by the surge in the number of companies going public and choosing to have their stocks traded on the Nasdaq market. In November 1999 alone, such companies raised close to $17 billion. This record was double the amount that had been raised in any earlier month.

Reflecting investor demand for these offerings, the average gain for IPOs in the same month was an unprecedented 102 percent. Such high jumps in stock prices are normally accompanied by a large number of buy and sell trades. Relating this phenomenon to the MarketWatch.com example above, one can argue that the smaller the size of the issue, the greater the number of trades in a single day. This increase in transaction volume has further burdened the already creaky Nasdaq systems.

6.5.5 Inefficient Market Opening Procedures

Earlier, we described some of the shortcomings of the procedures to open trading on the Nasdaq market. The problems caused by the inefficiencies of this process have been magnified by the craze for IPO stocks. A classic example is November 13, 1998, the day TheGlobe.com went public. The IPO was priced the night before at $9 per share. Given the relatively low price, investors rushed to buy the stock when it opened for trading the next day. Because the Nasdaq does not have a coordinating mechanism to ensure that trading in any stock opens at a single price, investors ended up paying a wide range of prices. Some bought it for $96–$97 from one large broker, whereas a second broker was selling the same stock at $90 per share at the same time. To complicate matters further, trades were being executed in alternative electronic trading systems such as Instinet at $87. Some evidently paid too much, others sold at a discount.[12]

A second instance of this phenomenon occurred when DrKoop.com, an online medical operation, announced on June 6, 1999, that it was signing a deal to provide health information services to the 17 million subscribers of America Online (AOL). As expected, a large number of investors placed orders with their brokers to buy DrKoop.com's stocks as soon as the market opened the next day. When the Nasdaq market opened on June 7, a large number of trades in DrKoop.com stock were executed in the $35–$37 ranges.

This acute interest in DrKoop.com stock was accompanied by frenzied trading in AOL stocks. AOL is listed on the NYSE, where every listed stock has a specialist assigned to it who is responsible for orderly trading in that stock. So while DrKoop.com was gyrating at the market open, the NYSE specialist responsible for AOL simply delayed the opening of trading in this stock. He waited till investors had adjusted their expectations and, 10 minutes later, opened trading at $119.9375; close to 1 1/2 million shares traded at this price. Over the next few minutes millions more traded within a 25-cent range from the market opening price.

This is a stark contrast to the DrKoop.com experience on Nasdaq. The first trade in DrKoop was recorded at $35.50, a 50 percent jump from the previous day's close. AOL, in contrast, opened up 4 percent from the previous close. Despite the steep rise, Nasdaq had no mechanism in place to monitor and control the trading. In the next couple of minutes, investors bought and sold DrKoop stock at a wide range of prices. This volatility wasn't helped by the fact that this stock is a relatively illiquid one and hence has a tendency to fluctuate in price a lot more than the more liquid AOL stock.

In summary, the growth of online trading has resulted in systemwide break-downs within the Nasdaq market. This steep increase in trading volumes has combined with developments in corporate America to expose gaping holes in the trading rules that determine the relative efficiency of the market. As would be expected, for the second time in the 1990s, these events have generated pressure on the Nasdaq to improve its market structure.

The markets have taken intermediate steps to reduce the impact of some of the systemic faults in the Nasdaq system. For instance, many retail brokers have implemented policies that do not allow their customers to submit market orders for IPO stocks. This prevents an individual from submitting orders that basically instruct his or her broker to buy a stock at any price. With the new rules, only priced or limit orders will be accepted for such stocks. As customers are forced to specify a price, the hope is that they might be more sensible in making investment decisions. At the time of this writing, it is not clear whether these rules have made any dent on the behavior of the IPO market on the first day of trading. Simultaneously, market makers have been taking steps to reduce their risks from trading volatile Nasdaq stocks. For example, many of them have reduced the number of shares they are willing to trade at their quotes. This helps them avoid running up huge losses by trading with investors who route their orders electronically through SOES or SelectNet in rapidly moving markets.

6.5.6 Nasdaq-AMEX Merger

In November 1998, Nasdaq completed a merger with the American Stock Exchange (AMEX), the second largest floor-based securities exchange in the United States. After the merger, Nasdaq and AMEX continue to operate as separate markets. The two institutions share existing technologies and are planning to jointly develop new ones. At this stage, it is not clear how the present Nasdaq systems will improve the auction structure of AMEX. It is highly likely that the parent organization, the NASD, will use new technologies to move the trading in AMEX off the exchange floor. The evolution from a floor-based auction structure to an electronic off-floor auction format is still an untested one.

As per the initial agreement between the two market institutions, the NASD will invest about $110 million to upgrade the AMEX floor-trading technology over a five-year period. The plan includes an effort to develop a hybrid electronic limit-order book on the AMEX that will provide for automated executions and AMEX specialist "intercession" in resetting quotes. There have been reports in the press[13] that a bulk of the $110 million will be spent on new Internet and network technologies leading to a major online stock exchange. The goal is to enable investors to participate directly in the trading process. The assumption here is that the correct role of a broker is that of an advisor and facilitator and not a bottleneck in the trade execution chain.

6.5.7 Nasdaq's Web-Based Services

The Nasdaq at present has numerous Web sites around the world hosting information about stocks from individual companies trading on it. For instance, it has a Web site dedicated to British investors that publicizes stock prices in British pounds; the stocks themselves are traded in the United States in U.S. dollars.

Another Web-based service the Nasdaq offers is Nasdaqonline.com. This is a service providing real-time stock quotes to chief executive officers and chief financial officers of Nasdaq-listed companies. The quote information is by definition simply an information service, not a transaction service. The service is provided by using secure technologies and can be customized to meet the information needs of individual companies.

Nasdaq is also collaborating with Broadcast.com in broadcasting financial news over the Internet. When firms release their quarterly earning results, they typically hold conference calls with select groups of analysts (working with major banks and brokerage firms) and financial news organizations. Large investors, in turn, learn about any important news through their brokers. A delay in relaying the information can translate into lost trading opportunities. Because of this, there is a movement among regulators and various exchanges to get firms to adopt technologies that will open up these "conference calls" to average investors. Nasdaq has jumped on this bandwagon in cooperation with Broadcast.com.

Broadcast.com is an Internet services company that aggregates information and broadcasts it by using streaming technology. The Nasdaq market has signed an agreement with this company to use its technology to broadcast quarterly earnings conference calls. The program will start with a pilot involving about 100 Nasdaq-listed companies. In the pilot program, each company will be offered up to four live audio broadcasts of quarterly earnings calls per year. Broadcast.com will host the calls on cobranded pages within the Broadcast.com Web site. This will allow Nasdaq and the participating firms to take advantage of the half million daily visitors to the Broadcast.com site. The calls can be viewed either live or can be accessed later on demand. If the experiment is successful, Internet broadcasting might become a standard corporate communications tool for public companies.

6.5.8 Decimalization

Despite calling itself the market for the next 100 years or more, Nasdaq was late to the decimalization party.[14] The securities industry in the United States has been aware of the need to make the switch for the past decade or more. Various committees had been set up in multiple industry associations to steer the decimalization effort. Overseas markets made the transition without much trouble. The NYSE too managed to stick to its schedule. It introduced decimal trading on January 29, 2001. Nasdaq didn't go decimal until April 2001.

The SEC had asked the U.S. markets to go decimal by July 3, 2000. By April 2000, the Nasdaq market had given sufficient signals to indicate that it would not be ready by that date. The key reason for this was simple. It underestimated its trading volumes and did not have adequate systems in place to handle the explosion in traffic over its networks. To give an example of the growth in volumes experienced by Nasdaq, in a period ending March 2000, message traffic[15] increased by a factor of four. Between July 1999 and March 2000, volumes grew two and a half times. So, when the time to go decimal arrived, it was not yet ready to make the required changes.

Apart from the fact that it has had to contend with an incredible surge in trading volumes, Nasdaq's decimalization efforts have been hurt by the use of older technologies powering its networks. Shifting to decimals meant modifying systems used to handle quote feeds. These systems had been programmed to handle fractional prices. The code had to be changed to process decimal values. In addition, and this has been a major cause for delay among various market participants, the move to decimals is expected to result in an increase in trading volumes. Higher volumes mean a surge in message traffic. Telecommunication equipment used to handle this traffic had to be upgraded with more bandwidth.

Some market participants blame[16] the delay on Nasdaq's distraction. It appeared to be more interested in implementing a huge electronic billboard on New York's Times Square. Worse, it was investing a lot of time and effort in its efforts to go global. In the process, it ignored the improvement demanded by domestic investors.

The rush to implement SuperSoes appears to be with a view to reducing the burden on its networks. It is not clear when SuperMontage will actually be launched. As of May 2001, Nasdaq was still having trouble with the SuperSoes implementation. The hope is that SuperSoes will reduce message traffic by at least 25 percent on the network.

Three weeks after going decimal on April 9, 2001, Nasdaq authorities announced that trading spreads for OTC market stocks had shrunk by 51 percent. Decimalization had resulted in the average spread falling from 7.8 cents per share to 3.8 cents per share. Fortunately for Nasdaq, thanks to overall drop in stock prices, trading volumes had stopped growing at the incredible rates previously recorded.

6.5.9 A Nasdaq IPO

Yes, Nasdaq too is considering changing the governance structure of its marketplace. It has joined the NYSE and nearly all the other exchanges, both equity and derivative, in announcing plans to transform themselves from membership-based markets to stock-issuing firms trying to maximize their shareholders' value. The plan that has been laid on the table has an interesting twist. Unlike most companies that go public by selling shares in a single IPO, the Nasdaq authorities plan to pursue their transformation in a two-stage process.

The conversion from member-owned to stock-issuing, for-profit corporation would take place in the first round.[17] Stocks will be sold to a select group of market makers and large banks and institutional investors. The transformation to a publicly owned firm will take place when a second round of stock is made available for sale to the larger investor community in what is known as a seasoned offering.

It is not clear what the Nasdaq authorities hope to achieve by restricting the initial offering to a small group of institutions. But by announcing a decision to do so, it has been successful in attracting criticism from a group of small broker-dealer firms that are part of the Nasdaq membership. Their concern is relatively straightforward: Under the current structure, they have some presence on the Nasdaq board; in the stock-issuing corporation, large shareholders can easily use their votes to overrule their objections. In short, small brokers are of the opinion that their interests will not be protected in the structure that is formed after phase one.

In the case of the NYSE, the plan for going public is to continue to have the regulatory functions performed under the new for-profit publicly traded NYSE Corporation. Unlike the NYSE, the Nasdaq market has expressed a willingness to have a common regulator monitor the applications on various securities trading laws. At present, this function is performed by the NASDR, the regulatory arm of the NASD. In the future, the functions of this institution will be run as a separate entity, distinct from the for-profit Nasdaq market.

6.6 PLANS FOR THE FUTURE—SUPERMONTAGE

The Nasdaq market has recognized the need for change but has been having a tough time to further improve the structure of its markets. The problem has not been a paucity of ideas. Rather, the management has been unable to put together a plan that meets the conflicting interests of all its constituents: investors, broker-dealers, and regulators. Here, we describe two plans that have recently been proposed by Nasdaq. Known simply as "Next Nasdaq" and order display window, both these plans have met with criticism from different constituents. Criticisms of Next Nasdaq were so severe that it was shelved completely in 1998. The second plan includes a bunch of proposals that were included in Next Nasdaq plus some more.

The new thinking within Nasdaq is based around two central components. The first would split the quote and messaging traffic onto a set of scalable computer processing engines. Any unexpected increases in trading volume can be handled by quickly increasing the number of engines. A second component takes the form of a strategy that would consolidate SelectNet and SOES into a single trading system. The basic idea is to centralize trading in a form acceptable to all concerned and, in the process, reduce costs to the investing community.

SuperMontage has been marketed as a "voluntary, open-access integrated quote and order processing system." It is expected to replace the current Nasdaq quotation system and be enhanced with an automated execution capability. The proposed launch date is sometime in 2002. The new proposal, which was approved in January 2001 by the SEC, has three components: (1) a quote/order collection facility, (2) a quote/order display service, and (3) execution capability.

6.6.1 Quotes and Orders

An order is a commitment to trade at a particular price and size. For all practical purposes, a quote too is a firm commitment, except in cases in which the entity submitting does not accept automatic executions. As per Nasdaq and SEC rules, registered market makers must accept automatic executions. This happens today under SOES. Exception from this rule is given to ECNs and unlisted trading participant (UTP) exchanges (the Chicago Stock Exchange is an example of a UTP). These entities may choose to accept automatic executions or request delivery of the order.

In the Nasdaq market, this facility is made available typically to ECNs. Let us assume that the highest bid (size of 2,000 shares) for a stock of company MNP in the Nasdaq quote montage is from an ECN, say, Island. A market order to sell 2,000 shares is sent to the market. Nasdaq will route that order to Island with a request to execute it at the bid. Subject to certain predefined exceptions, Island is obligated to execute the trade within a specified time limit. A common exception would be the case in which the bid has been accessed within Island itself. In such cases, Island will have to change the bid to be displayed in the Nasdaq quote montage.

6.6.2 Collecting Quotes and Orders

SuperMontage will allow traders to submit multiple quotes/orders at the same price or at different prices for any stock. This is an improvement over the current arrangement under which only a single bid and/or a single offer can be submitted for any stock.

A second dimensional improvement will be in the form of a flexibility to reveal or conceal the identity of the firm placing an order. For the first time, the main Nasdaq market will be allowing investors to trade anonymously. Such facility has always been available in the privately operated ECNs. Market makers who are obligated to make two-sided quotes cannot use this feature for such quotes.

Reserve Size

Nasdaq participants will be able to specify reserve volumes for submitted orders. The eligibility condition for this feature is a requirement to display a minimum size of 1,000 shares. Let's assume a large institution wants to buy 5,000 shares of AMTT stock. It can, through its broker, display (anonymously if necessary) 1,000 shares to the rest of the market and specify a reserve size of 1,000 shares with a cap of 5,000 shares. Once the first order for 1,000 shares is executed, the system will refresh the displayed volume by 1,000 shares from reserve. This process will continue until the 5,000 shares have been purchased. Every time the system refreshes the displayed volume, the order/quote will return to the end of the queue (see discussion below on price-time priority rules).

Cancellation Process

SuperMontage will bring a crucial improvement to the manner in which Nasdaq handles order cancellation requests. In the current system, if a broker enters an order into SelectNet, he or she can cancel the order after 10 seconds *regardless* of the status of the order. It doesn't matter that a market maker on the opposite side would have accepted the order and agreed to trade against it. So, the burden of unraveling the cancelled trade falls on the recipient, not the one who cancelled the order.

Under SuperMontage, a directed order (see Section 6.6.4 below for definitions) that is being delivered to an ECN or UTP (these two entities can opt out of automatic execution of their quotes/orders by choosing to have all orders delivered to them) cannot be cancelled. Any such action will be held pending until the system receives a response from the ECN or UTP. If the latter has accepted the order, then the trade goes through and the cancellation is voided. But if the ECN or UTP either rejects the order or fails to respond within the allowable time (typically five seconds), the system will execute the cancel request.

6.6.3 Displaying Quotes

Given that the system will be collecting more quote information than at present, SuperMontage will introduce richer quote display facilities than the existing system.

Three Price Levels

The current quotation system displays just the best bid and offer for any stock. In an effort to improve the overall transparency, SuperMontage will, in addition, display trading interests at up to two price increments from the best bid and offer. For example, assume the best bid and offer on ARBA is $9.75 and $9.80. If the stock trades at five-cent increments, then SuperMontage will display bid volumes at $9.70 and $9.65 and offer volumes at $9.85 and $9.90. But there are no volumes offered at $9.85, so it would instead show the volume at $9.80.[18]

Aggregated Volumes

If a broker submits multiple buy orders at a single price for a stock, the Nasdaq quote display system will aggregate (or add up) the individual order/quote volumes and display the computed value to the rest of the market. If the broker does not request anonymity on any of these orders, then the aggregated volume will be accompanied by his or her identification acronym. If anonymity is requested, then the affected orders will be clubbed with the other such orders at that price and tagged accordingly.

To summarize, under SuperMontage, the following additional quote information for each stock will be available to the market participants:

- The three best bid and offer prices, along with the corresponding volumes through the Nasdaq order display facility, ranked from highest to lowest bid and lowest to highest offer
- For these three price levels (bid and offer), aggregated volumes from all anonymous orders/quotes
- Break up of the aggregated volumes at the best bid and offer, identifying the source (market maker, ECN, or UTP) of the quote/order (anonymous entries will not be included in this list)

Increased Transparency

The belief is that increased transparency will improve the quality of the price discovery process. By displaying trading interests at prices away from the best bid and offer, Nasdaq is supplying information on the *depth* of trading interest in a stock.

It will typically be the case that the demand for a stock (buying interest) will increase as the price decreases (assuming everything else stays the same), and vice versa. This implies that in the example above, bid volumes will be greater at $9.70 and $9.65. So under SuperMontage, an investor with a large selling interest (more than the typical size at the best bid and offer) will be able to get better information on the ability of the market to absorb a big sell order from him or her. Such information will also help some seeking to accumulate a large holding in a particular stock to design an efficient buying strategy.

Investors can implement smarter and more efficient trading strategies only if they have some degree of control over the actual execution of their orders. Existing arrangements are woefully lacking in any such flexibility. SuperMontage will come equipped with rules that should empower the investor. It will allow investors to submit orders anonymously. This, in turn, should reduce the market impact problem discussed in Chapter 4.

In addition, it will allow traders to exercise reserve size options. For example, a person can submit a buy order for 10,000 shares with instructions to display only half the trading interest to the market. So, 5,000 shares will be kept in reserve. This again will help the trader maintain some secrecy. By allowing a trader to hide part of his or her trading interest, it surely reduces market transparency. The expectation is that this loss in market quality will be offset by attracting increased trading volumes from large investors who otherwise might seek the privacy offered by private trading centers such as Instinet and Posit.

Although it is being marketed as a voluntary quote system, there are concerns that SuperMontage will end up becoming a central limit-order book (CLOB). This can happen if it manages to capture a significant share of the order flow that now is sent to various ECNs and market-making firms such as Knight Trimark, Merrill Lynch, and Morgan Stanley.

Since April 9, 2001, all Nasdaq stocks are being traded in increments of as little as one cent (in other words, Nasdaq has finally gone decimal). Decimalization is expected to shrink bid-offer spreads. Lower spreads, in turn, tend to result in increases in trading volumes. This, in turn, will cause more messages to be exchanged between brokers. SuperSoes first and SuperMontage later are expected to handle this additional message traffic. Unfortunately, SuperSoes has been delayed, and at this time, it is not clear if SuperMontage will be launched by the end of 2001.

Reducing Market Fragmentation

At various points in the book, we have mentioned the fragmented nature of the Nasdaq market. Investors who wish to buy or sell any given stock have to choose from an array of different trading points: market makers (some who pay for order flow and others who do not) and a slew of ECNs. As order flow is fragmented, it is difficult for any individual to figure out the trading venue in which he or she will get the best execution at that specific moment. This results in an inefficient trading process and hurts the investment community as a whole. SuperMontage promises to alleviate some of the problems caused by fragmentation. The basic strategy is to provide information on market depth and, more importantly, improve the linkage among various segments of the Nasdaq market.

Interestingly, despite its best intentions, the Nasdaq market continues to lag behind the prevailing conventional wisdom in the marketplace. For example, even before it had finished the process of explaining the benefits of its latest proposal, the equity markets appeared to have moved on to more radical changes. In recent years, the SEC has become vocal in supporting the call for a centralized trading environment. The former chairman of the SEC, Arthur Levitt, has gone one step further. He has been coaxing the various equity markets in the United States to link their trading systems to form a centralized, electronic marketplace. In effect, Mr. Levitt is promoting the idea of having a single market in which NYSE-listed stocks and Nasdaq market stocks will be traded within a common network.

6.6.4 Execution Services

SuperMontage will replace Nasdaq's current SelectNet and SOES services (including SuperSoes discussed earlier) with two new processes: a directed order service and a nondirected order service. Quotes/orders for up to 999,999 shares routed to either of these two facilities will be eligible for automated execution.

Directed Order Process

A directed order by definition is one that is sent to a specific target. It is similar in spirit to SelectNet, which allows a broker to send a message indicating trading interest to a specific broker. Interestingly, Nasdaq has included a provision that allows a trader to elect out of receiving directed orders. This flexibility is designed to help market makers avoid the risk of dual liability.

Assume a broker submits an order to buy 100 shares of TPSG stock, directing it to a displayed offer from a market maker ABCD, 1,000 shares at $56.78. If this happens to be the best offer, the system will automatically match the two and execute a trade for 100 shares at $56.78. ABCD's quote size will be reduced to 900 shares offered at $56.78. This trade will be allowed even if there are other offers for 100 shares or more at $56.78 per share.

Nondirected Order Process

An order not directed at any particular quote/order will be eligible for a match against any other eligible quote/order. A marketable order[19] will be matched with the highest ranked on the opposite side of the market. The execution will typically be automatic unless the opposite side requires that the order be delivered to it. Nondirected orders have to be of the execute-immediately-or-cancel type. So, limit orders that are not within a reasonable limit of the current trading range will be returned to the concerned broker. Market orders obviously will not be subject to this restriction. A nondirected order can be preferenced in the sense that the broker entering it can specify the party on the opposite side against whom the order should be matched. Although the counterparty is designated, such orders are not considered as directed orders.

Sweep Orders

Consider an example of a large order to buy 10,000 shares at the best market price. The offers at the three price increments displayed over the quote montage add up to 10,000 shares (5,000, 4,000, and 1,000, respectively). Assuming that there are no other buy orders in the order book, the system will execute the first trade for 5,000 shares, wait for five seconds, move to the next price level, execute a second trade for 4,000 shares, and wait for another five seconds before moving to the next price increment and executing the last trade for 1,000 shares.

If a trader does not want the system to wait for five seconds after exhausting liquidity at any price level, he or she can designate his or her order as a sweep order. Such orders will trade through all displayed as well as reserve interest at the three price levels without pausing for five seconds between two price increments. In the example above, if the buy order was for 15,000 shares, then a sweep order will be forced to wait for five seconds before moving to the fourth price level.

6.6.5 Price-Time Priority Rules

How will orders be ranked in the Nasdaq quote montage? Orders sent to the nondirected order process[20] will be ranked as per any of the three priority rules:

- price-time
- price-time-size
- price (with ECN access fee)-time

All three priority rules were not present in the initial SuperMontage proposal submitted to the SEC. They were included in response to comments from various market participants. The proposal itself had nine different amendments (eight before receiving SEC approval and the ninth still pending as of Spring 2001), each resulting in a series of modifications to the previous version of the proposal. As we said earlier, introducing changes to the Nasdaq market is never a straightforward process. Given the diversity of interests that dominate this market, every rule and every modification to it gets a mixed reception, with participants changing sides on a regular basis. As the management tries to appease every affected constituency, it ends up producing an incredibly complex proposal. SuperMontage is a classic end-result of one such dramatic process.

Price-Time

Returning to the topic of priority rules, it is easy to argue in favor of a simple price-time priority ranking process. If two orders are submitted with the same bid, the one that comes in early should be eligible for a match first. But if a third bid is submitted but at a higher price, then it should receive priority over the lower bids. So any nondirected order submitted without any qualifications will be processed by using the simple price-time priority rule.

When an order with reserve size is refreshed, the system will reset its time stamp and send it to the end of the queue for orders/quotes at that price increment.

Price-Time-Size

Let's examine the case of the following two offers: (1) 1,000 shares at $12.05 with a time stamp of 10:01 AM, (2) 1,100 shares at the same price but submitted at 10:10 AM. A priority rule that takes price into consideration will rank the second order ahead of the first. It is easy to argue that this rule discriminates against smaller orders. The reasoning used to support its inclusion is that it will encourage the submission of larger orders. The rule protects institutions that tend to trade in bigger volumes and thus bring liquidity to the marketplace.

Let's assume that there are 11 orders at the highest bid, 10 for 1,000 shares each and one for 10,000 shares submitted last. Mutual fund RFM has standing instructions with its broker to specify price-time-size priority while submitting its orders. The broker submits a sell for 10,000 shares at market. Thanks to the choice of priority rule, the system will execute a single trade for 10,000 shares at market, matching the sell order with the largest bid for the same amount.

If the mutual fund had left the default rule to be used, then the system would have executed 10 trades for 1,000 shares each. Given the costs associated with processing trades (these costs tend to be the same irrespective of the number of shares involved), the mutual fund is better off choosing the price-time-size rule.

Price (adjusted for ECN access fees)-Time

This rule is another quirk that reflects the complex structure of the market for Nasdaq stocks. It is also a reminder that SuperMontage will not be the only meeting place for traders. Accordingly, it has been a major point of contention between the Nasdaq and the SEC on one side and the ECNs on the other. The motivation for this rule is the fact that when an order is executed against an ECN quote and that order happens to be from outside that ECN's book, then it charges a fee. The broker handling a customer's order typically pays this fee. Let's look at an example.

Broker X*Trade receives a market order to buy 10,000 shares of stock UVYC. The best offer displayed on the Nasdaq quote montage is at $12.55 for 20,000 shares. Digging farther into the quote display facility, the broker finds out that this amount is supplied by two different entities. Market maker ITNE is offering to sell 10,000 and ECN TRUB 10,000 shares. He also knows that the ECN will charge[21] an access fee of, say, one cent a share for orders received from outside the ECN's network. So if he directs his order to trade against the ECN's quote, he will be paying a net price of $12.56 per share. With a view to save the additional $100 cost, he will route his order to market maker ITNE's quote.

The current market arrangement does not account for this additional fee payable to an ECN. So, to better discriminate between different liquidity pools — those that do not involve access fees, typically market makers and certain ECNs, and those with access fees — Nasdaq has introduced the price (adjusted for ECN access fee)-time priority rule. A trader who wants to access the liquidity offered by ECNs, in other words, who is open to having his or her order automatically executed against a published ECN quote, can now instruct SuperMontage to rank all orders/quotes on the opposite side by using this rule.

We noted earlier that the inclusion of this feature in the SuperMontage proposal has been rather controversial. ECNs think that the system discriminates against their orders/quotes.[22] In addition, they argue that as efficient liquidity centers, they deliver significant price improvement. The efficiency arises from the fact that, among other things, they offer the possibility of trading without the high market impacts involved in routing orders to traditional broker-dealers.

Given the lower cost of trading, investors who send their orders to ECNs might be willing to price their orders more competitively, which means that a non-ECN order that gets matched with an ECN quote/order is participating in the benefits offered by ECNs. In such instance, the ECNs argue, the price improvement more than offsets the access fees charged. Nasdaq has accepted this argument, and amendment number eight to the SuperMontage proposal introduced a complicated formula that will compute the tradeoff between price improvement and access fees in computing the adjustment to an ECN quote. The complication arises from the fact that price improvement tends to be uncertain, whereas the access fee is a certainty.

ECNs that charge access fees have a second option: They can indicate on any individual order/quote that the order/quote would provide price improvement greater than the access fee. In such cases, the affected quotes/orders would be given priority with quotes/orders that did not require payment of a separate fee.

There is absolutely no argument over the claim that price-time priority improves the quality of a marketplace. It surely encourages price competition. Without this rule, traders will not be willing to bid and/or offer better prices to complete a trade. Given the structure of the Nasdaq market with its multiple liquidity pools or trading centers, there is at present no such rule. In approving this rule, the SEC seems to have realized the fact that having multiple ranking options exercisable at the option of the investor is the best solution for the present. It is an improvement over the current free-for-all structure. It acknowledges the fact that multiple market centers will continue to exist and it is next to impossible to have a single rule that appeases every market participant.

On the issue of time priority, the present system has too many loopholes in it to protect an order's time priority. By aggregating multiple orders in a systematic manner and by instituting an automated execution process that cannot be manipulated, SuperMontage will finally bring time priority to the market for Nasdaq stocks. This by itself will be a major achievement for this market that will benefit every investor.

6.6.6 Reactions

Given the past history of proposed changes to the Nasdaq market, market makers and various ECNs have been reluctant to support the SuperMontage proposal. A couple of controversies were discussed above. Here are some more.

SuperMontage has features such as automated execution and elements of a central limit-order book that were criticized when they were proposed as part of Next Nasdaq, one of a series of proposals Nasdaq has been presenting to the market in the past few years, and SuperMontage evolved from comments made on earlier plans. By displaying the relative depth of the marketplace, the order display window is bound to deprive market makers of free-picking opportunities. Right now, market makers are the only ones with access to such information. Large market makers such as Knight Trimark and others buy huge amounts of order flows from various retail and wholesale brokers. Order flows contain information on buying and selling interest at various prices. If a firm has access to a substantially large number of such orders, it is in an excellent position to interpret the numbers and predict the direction of price movements in any stock. They can combine insights into order flows with proprietary trading strategies to earn substantial gains from short-term trading.

The automated execution feature will force various ECNs, all of which offer this feature, to compete directly with Nasdaq. In a sense, SuperMontage is an attempt by Nasdaq to compete with its private competitors by offering better execution services. Such technology-driven initiatives have traditionally been the forte of these private trading services. The Nasdaq market authorities are hoping that the new arrangements will lead to a big growth in trading volume in the market as a whole. Although market makers and ECNs will see a drop in earnings on a per-trade basis, their fervent hope is that they will be able to achieve sufficient increases in order flow and trading volume to offset the drop in per-trade earnings.

Central Limit-Order Book

The order collection and display facilities are part of an obvious attempt by Nasdaq to introduce a common or central limit-order book (CLOB) for the marketplace as a whole. It has been widely recognized that the move by Nasdaq to introduce the limit-order book is part of a broader strategy to compete with alternative trading arrangements such as Instinet and various other ECNs.

From this perspective, the Nasdaq membership should view it as a sound competitive response and welcome it with open hands. Unfortunately, this did not happen. Instead, the broker-dealer community perceived the proposal as a weapon to replace the market-making services[23] that they have traditionally provided. When the idea was released earlier in 1997–98 as part of the Next Nasdaq proposal, it was a much simpler one, without any of the priority rules and other protections included in SuperMontage. The leadership of the market-maker community then complained to the SEC that the Next Nasdaq plan—specifically, the CLOB—would undermine the role of market makers.[24] The opposition was so vociferous that Nasdaq withdrew the proposal.

After adding numerous provisions that addressed some concerns of the market-making community and ECNs, Nasdaq submitted the modified CLOB as part of the SuperMontage proposal. The opposition to SuperMontage has been relatively muted. This could be because Nasdaq is no longer evading the issue of becoming an active market center by itself, matching buyers and sellers. It has been open about its plans to compete with current market centers—market makers and ECNs. Nasdaq wants to use SuperMontage with its enhanced order display and execution capabilities to transform itself into an intermediary (outside of its broker-dealer and ECN network) executing customer limit orders. Nasdaq would then collect execution fees or commissions, similar to Instinet and other electronic trading networks.

SuperMontage as the de Facto Market Center

The controversy over Nasdaq operating a limit-order book is an old one. When the idea was first broached as part of Next Nasdaq, numerous brokerage firms and ECNs pointed out that they too offer limit-order facilities to their customers. SuperMontage would compete directly with these existing services. They feared that as a CLOB, it would basically push the marketplace toward a single execution system, bypassing the existing network of market centers. Their concern was that Nasdaq's limit-order book would gradually reduce competition among existing services and eventually establish itself as a de facto monopoly.

The argument supporting this claim was on the following lines. As the NASD is the default regulator of the market for OTC or Nasdaq stocks, any market maker or ECN that wanted to do business in these stocks would have to make its quotes available through SuperMontage. The rules discussed in Section 6.4 require them to do so. And as SuperMontage is equipped with automated execution capabilities, it would have an enormous advantage over any market maker or ECN. The Nasdaq has responded to this concern by allowing market participants to opt out of the automated execution facility. By choosing this option, they would not be breaking any Nasdaq or SEC rules.

Market observers argue that one advantage the Nasdaq limit-order book would hold over the market makers is that it would be able to accept, display, and execute limit orders at multiple (actually three with SuperMontage) price levels.[25] Under the current system, market makers and ECNs, however, are able to display only one bid and one offer—and have to update their quotation after execution to get to the next level of interest displayed.

In light of this, the trading committee of the Securities Industry Association (SIA) complained to the SEC. Their main contention was that this ability of the Nasdaq limit-order facility to hold and display several levels of interest would almost always result in the Nasdaq book having time priority. This, in turn, could result in poorer executions for customer limit orders held outside the Nasdaq book. Although the NASD characterized the order book as a voluntary option for the display of customer limit orders, the SIA argued that the effect of the proposed book would be to drive all orders toward this one mechanism in which trades would be executed. It would be a case of improving the market by protecting a customer's place in line and, consequently, attracting more order flow. The SIA instead put forward a compromise proposal.

Under this plan, which was to be appended to Next Nasdaq, market makers would be given a chance to either accept or reject limit orders before routing them to the central limit book. This proposed amendment met with little approval as the provision was seen to give too much flexibility to market makers. They would have the freedom to attract trading interests from investors. They would be able to interpret any information that might be imbedded in such messages and then, at their discretion, decide to trade with a particular indication or to reject it. A classic case of having the cake and eating it too! As would be expected, this idea did not find any takers.

Nasdaq seems to have come up with a better idea, one involving multiple priority rules and encouraging market makers and ECNs to submit multiple quotes/orders at a single price for multiple price levels. No wonder the SEC approved this proposal.

Competing with the Regulator

We now examine the conflict of interest raised in the discussion above. Until recently, the Nasdaq marketplace, as a legal entity, has been a fully owned subsidiary of the NASD. The latter also controls and operates NASDR, the entity that regulates the Nasdaq market participants. With the introduction of SuperMontage, the NASD will be playing two roles: a self-regulated organization (SRO), in other words, the entity responsible for monitoring and enforcing rules of an organization that regulates itself; and as Nasdaq, a market operator with exclusive rights to process market information, as well as an operator of trading facilities. In performing the latter function, Nasdaq will, in essence, be competing with traditional market makers and the relatively new ECNs. As the NASD is supposed to be regulating the Nasdaq market and its membership through its regulation arm, NASDR, broker-dealers would find themselves in the decidedly uncomfortable position of competing with their regulators. The argument here is that the NASD is supposed to be looking after the interests of its members, not competing with them.

Once SuperMontage is launched, NASDR will be responsible for regulating Nasdaq's new trading facilities. Market makers and ECNs are not comfortable with this fact. Both entities are owned and controlled by the NASD. The concern is that given common ownership, NASDR might be lax in monitoring and enforcing rules on the Nasdaq trading facility arm. In addition, various observers have expressed a fear that the NASD as SRO will abuse its power over Nasdaq's trading facility competitors.

In its comments as part of the approval notice for SuperMontage, the SEC pointed out that the conflict of responsibilities is inherent to the self-regulation model. Interestingly, it added a comment that it was not planning to rid the SRO model of this conflict. Rather its job was to ensure a fair, functioning market. In addition, it's the SEC's job to monitor the SROs themselves. Which means it will be carefully monitoring the monitor. Anyway, the NASD has been busy reducing its stake in the Nasdaq market.

Should Nasdaq Be Prevented from Setting Up a Market Center?

SuperMontage will convert Nasdaq from a quote collection and dissemination facility to a market center capable of actually matching buyers and sellers. Instead of just providing a telecommunication network linking various marker centers, Nasdaq will now be a market center matching buying and selling interests.

Some market observers have not welcomed this change. Their concern is that by stealing order flows away from market makers—professional traders who have traditionally supported the market in OTC or Nasdaq stocks—SuperMontage will make it difficult for them to compete with Nasdaq's automated execution facility. So, they argue that Nasdaq shouldn't require market makers to accept automated execution. This argument does have some merit in it, but going along with it would mean agreeing with the contention that Nasdaq shouldn't operate an automated execution facility. In a free market with adequate rules and regulations, there is no reason why Nasdaq should be kept out of this business.

SuperMontage will surely strengthen its competitive position. But that alone might not be sufficient to make it a success. Various ECNs and the market makers themselves are free to adopt their own competitive strategies to either profit from the arrangement or exploit SuperMontage's weaknesses and defeat it. Nasdaq by itself will not be able to generate liquidity to the market. It will depend on existing liquidity pools, especially the market makers and ECNs, to build a liquid market center. SuperMontage itself does not impose any new obligations on these participants. As participation is otherwise voluntary, they can form new alliances among themselves and experiment with superior execution technologies—maybe a new and improved OptiMark—to maintain and increase order flows.

6.7 SUMMARY

Nasdaq is indeed in a state of constant evolution. Most recently, it has taken aggressive steps to go global. In May 2000, Nasdaq started a joint program with the Stock Exchange of Hong Kong (SEHK). Seven Nasdaq stocks with strong business interests in Asia, including Amgen, Applied Materials, Cisco, Dell, Intel, Microsoft, and Starbucks, will be traded on the SEHK. A month later, Nasdaq Japan started its first day of trading on June 19, 2000. Nasdaq Japan began operations as part of the Osaka Stock Exchange, the largest Japanese exchange outside Tokyo. It mainly trades high-tech start-up companies and the largest U.S. Nasdaq stocks. In March 2001, Nasdaq acquired a majority stake in Easdaq to create Nasdaq Europe, a pan-European exchange that will trade both U.S. and European blue-chip stocks.

Even with great obstacles, Nasdaq market seems to be moving full speed ahead with changes in every scope of its business. From the very first day of its operation, Nasdaq has been founded on the basis of technology. It is expected that technology—and especially the Internet—will continue to change its market structure extensively in the next few years. The next few chapters examine in more detail the latest changes in the financial markets, including ECNs and computerized automated trading systems such as Primex.

7

ELECTRONIC COMMUNICATIONS NETWORK

This chapter focuses discussion on a particular type of electronic trading systems, electronic communications networks (ECN), which is getting growing importance in our equities markets. An ECN is a broker-dealer firm that matches customer buy and sell orders with direct electronic access. It is different from another type of electronic trading systems—crossing networks, which we talk about in this chapter as well. A crossing network electronically matches buy and sell orders at a derived price such as the market midpoint at discrete times during a trading day.

Electronic trading systems are basically systems with electronic order books that can match buy and sell trading interests with relatively little or no human intervention. It is important to note that the context in which the term *electronic trading* is used in this book could be different from its usage in the popular media. Journalists tend to use it to refer to communications between investors and their brokers over the Internet. Using electronic networks to place orders with one's broker is just an updated form of communication. Instead of picking up the phone, the investor connects with his or her broker by using a computer modem. By contrast, the message of this book is that electronic trading has a much broader connotation; it is more than a mere substitute for the telephone. Our goal in this chapter is to illustrate how electronic trading systems such as ECNs have the potential to completely transform the whole business of investing and, in the process, fundamentally change our financial markets. The details of using automated computer systems to match buy and sell orders are examined in the next chapter.

Markets around the world are undergoing a rapid transformation. This overhaul is obviously due to the introduction of new technologies. The mere growth of online brokerages has pointed out a basic inconsistency in the securities markets: Investors can submit orders electronically, but it takes a human trader to match two or more buying and selling interests. The immense popularity of the Internet has resulted in a fundamental shift in attitudes among individuals, businesses, and regulators. All these entities are actively exploring ways of harnessing the potential of electronic commerce to establish efficient transaction systems. This willingness to "conduct" transactions over the Internet is slowly transforming long-held beliefs that only human agents can efficiently match buyers and sellers of financial securities. In this respect, the financial markets are following the lead of various virtual marketplaces such as Ebay.com, Amazon.com, and Priceline.com and scores of both business-to-business and business-to-consumer electronic auctions.

The belief on human agents has now been irrevocably changed. Innovations in networking technology in general and the phenomenal growth of the Internet in particular have led to a virtual boom in the business of developing electronic trading systems. Slowly but surely, markets around the world are in the process of implementing electronic order books that consolidate orders submitted by all traders in that particular market—both professional traders as well as individual investors. In 2000, ECNs accounted for 30 percent of the total share volume in Nasdaq stocks and around 3 percent of exchange-listed stocks, compared with the figures of 13 percent and 1.4 percent, respectively, in 1993. We examine various aspects of ECNs in this chapter.

7.1 OVERVIEW OF ECNs

Thanks to quirky legalese, the term *ECN* was invented by the Securities and Exchange Commission (SEC) to describe the broker-dealer firms that offered order-matching services outside the confines of Nasdaq market makers and the New York Stock Exchange (NYSE) floor. As indicated earlier, most ECNs concentrate on Nasdaq stocks and those NYSE listed that can be traded away from the floor of the NYSE. Features common to ECNs are

- The trading process is order-driven; buy and sell orders are allowed to directly interact with each other.
- Direct interaction means that there is no need for human intervention to match these orders. Computerized algorithms—and not specialists, floor traders, or market makers—are used to execute trades.
- These systems allow investors to trade anonymously. Orders can be placed directly with the order book where the identity of the investor is not revealed to other traders in the market.
- Some systems allow investors to directly submit their orders to the market; others (and this normally applies to smaller investors) require that orders be routed through brokers.

ECNs are not online brokers. The latter just offer a basket of brokerage services (order submission, access to account information, real-time quotes, and a set of research tools) over the Internet. Brokers, both of the electronic and traditional varieties, route customer orders as well as their own trading interests (i.e., agency and principal) to exchanges, market makers, or various ECNs to execute their orders. Under the SEC's ECN rule, in addition to electronic access, every ECN must also provide telephone access for persons that do not have electronic access capabilities.

Electronic Order Books

ECNs are a relatively new concept. However, the techniques, or *algorithms,* to automatically match buy and sell orders have been around for a long time. Until recently, their implementation has been hampered by the lack of a suitable technology that would allow traders to communicate through an order book, relegating the concept of a consolidated order book to a hypothetical issue to be examined only by the academic world. Figure 7.1 is the electronic order book for Yahoo! at Island ECN. Today, investors can send their buy and sell orders over electronic networks to an order book. These orders are then matched by using mathematical algorithms of varying degrees of sophistication. The greater the degree of sophistication, the more powerful is the computer required to run the algorithm. The algorithm itself is simply a predetermined set of instructions for solving a specific problem in a limited time.

ECNs and Nasdaq

Despite their recent entry, the role of ECNs is already evolving into a more complex one. In particular, the decision by Nasdaq that requires ECNs to publicize their quotes over the Nasdaq quote montage via SelectNet has pushed what was initially a private club into the glare of the broader market. Consequently, many ECNs have a symbiotic relationship with Nasdaq, which both collaborate and compete with each other. The highest bids and offers on every ECN are displayed over Nasdaq level II screens. With SuperMontage, ECNs can choose to send their top three quotes for display.

In 1997, the SEC implemented the order handling rules that require market makers to reflect in the Nasdaq quote the price of any orders they placed in an ECN if that price is better than their public quotation. Previously, market makers could post public quotes in private ECNs that were better than the quotes they posted in Nasdaq. The order handling rules had an immediate impact on the securities markets. The spreads between bids and offers have narrowed significantly.

Access to ECNs

Subscribers of ECNs include institutional investors, retail investors, market makers, and other broker-dealers. All ECNs use similar execution systems that deliver straightforward order matching. The success of any particular ECN depends on its ability to attract a larger share of the order flow. As in any market, the probability of trade is an increasing function of the number of orders flowing into the system.

FIGURE 7.1 *Island ECN Order Book*

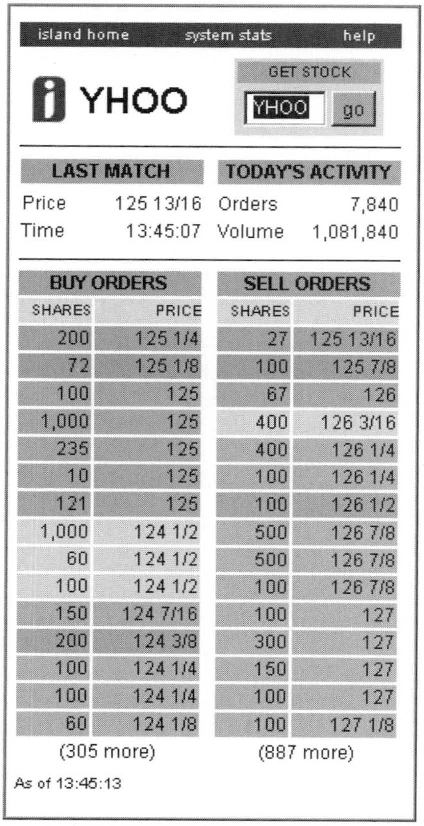

island home	system stats	help

YHOO

GET STOCK
YHOO go

LAST MATCH		TODAY'S ACTIVITY	
Price	125 13/16	Orders	7,840
Time	13:45:07	Volume	1,081,840

BUY ORDERS		SELL ORDERS	
SHARES	PRICE	SHARES	PRICE
200	125 1/4	27	125 13/16
72	125 1/8	100	125 7/8
100	125	67	126
1,000	125	400	126 3/16
235	125	400	126 1/4
10	125	100	126 1/4
121	125	100	126 1/2
1,000	124 1/2	500	126 7/8
60	124 1/2	500	126 7/8
100	124 1/2	100	126 7/8
150	124 7/16	100	127
200	124 3/8	300	127
100	124 1/4	150	127
100	124 1/4	100	127
60	124 1/8	100	127 1/8
(305 more)		(887 more)	

As of 13:45:13

Firms have been adopting different competitive postures. Certain firms charge lower execution and access fees[1] for using their ECN. Bloomberg basically gave away its proprietary screens to a select group of dealers for free.

When a broker-dealer (i.e., a member of NASD) accesses an order on an ECN such as Island, which is displayed in the Nasdaq quote montage using SelectNet, the dealer has to pay a fee to that ECN. Investors use the anonymity of ECNs to indicate their trading interests, which become quotes once they enter an ECN's order book. When a Nasdaq dealer wishes to hit a quote placed in an ECN, he has to pay an access fee, which is basically a charge for withdrawing liquidity from the ECN.

7.2 ECNs' Impact

Given the large volumes of stocks that are being traded through various ECNs, academicians and stock market regulators have taken a more active interest in understanding the impact of these systems on market efficiency. Despite their recent entry onto the scene, ECNs have already affected market operations, lowering the spread and improving the flow of information through open order books. The main concern appears to be the contribution of ECNs to the fragmentation of the Nasdaq market system and the resulting inefficiency of multiple trading systems.

Superior Service?

In a letter to the *New York Times* dated April 11, 1999, the president of the Island ECN claimed that an order submitted to its network is executed the moment a match occurs. By contrast, when a broker submits a customer's order via Select-Net to a market maker, the latter can take anywhere from 30 seconds to three minutes to execute the order. An order routed through NYSE's SuperDOT system can easily take above 20 seconds to execute. It, after all, relies on the specialist to hit a few keys for the execution to happen.

This argument ignores the fact that an order submitted to an ECN might not be able to find a match the instant it hits the order book. Finding an immediate match requires the presence of a "matching" quote on the opposite side. By contrast, the market maker on Nasdaq provides immediacy by executing a trade by risking his or her own capital. So, speed of execution is a function both of design of the system as well as liquidity in the order book, in an ECN as well as with a market maker.[2]

A better argument for superior service could be made by pointing out that ECNs provide impartial treatment to all limit orders. As they are pure agents (without any competing proprietary trading interests), they do not have an incentive to trade ahead of their clients' orders. Numerous market makers, especially large ones such as Knight Trimark and Merrill Lynch, use the information present in their customers' orders to manage their own trading strategies. So, to the extent investors are not satisfied with the way market makers handle their limit orders, they will prefer to route such orders to ECNs.

Increased Market Share

ECNs offer brokers an alternative to market makers and compete mainly on price and the speed of trading execution. Through this process, they have managed to steal substantial business from traditional market-making firms. In 1994, the SEC's division of market regulation reported that ECNs accounted for 13 percent of the volume in Nasdaq securities. By the end of 1997, 20 percent of transactions in Nasdaq securities took place on ECNs. Today, the percentage has increased to 30 percent. The damage incurred may, however, not be as great as one would first expect. As noted elsewhere, online brokers such as E*Trade, market makers such as the Knight/Trimark Group, and securities firms such as Goldman Sachs have invested in firms that operate these new trading networks.

Lower Spreads

After the implementation of order handling rules regarding ECNs, bid-ask spreads have shrunk dramatically.[3] In our discussion of market makers, we described how traders who submitted odd-eighth quotes were identified and punished by their peers. Such action was possible because the Nasdaq system identifies the broker. But ECNs do not. So prima facie, the anonymity offered has encouraged competitive quotes from market makers and, in the process, led to a lowering of spreads.

Improved Information Flow

ECNs operate following the principle of open order books. This means that they provide their users with information on the various buying and selling interests submitted to the order book. But they do not reveal the identity of their users. Investors are thus allowed to trade in relative anonymity. Let us look at Island's order book for Yahoo! stock (Figure 7.1). The information is available over the Internet at the ECN's Web site (http://www.isld.com). As is evident, the identities of investors are not published. In the above example, if an offer for 200 or more shares at $125 1/4 is submitted to Island, the system will automatically match it with the highest bid at that price.

An interesting feature of this presentation is that it provides a trader with information on the depth of Island's order book. By comparison, the electronic order display system proposed by Nasdaq will publish only the three best bids and offers. A trader who wants to sell a large number of shares has access to enough information to price his or her offer so as to clear the appropriate number of bids in the book.

Multiple Trading Systems

The multiplicity of trading systems makes it difficult for traders to work orders in more than a few stocks at any given moment. They tend to restrict their use of these systems to the most liquid of stocks. Despite all the fancy technologies that underlie these systems, traders complain that their job has not become any easier, at least in this phase in which markets are in transition from floor-based systems to order-driven electronic matching systems.

An added complication comes from the fact that there tends to be little standardization[4] among different systems: user interface, messaging protocols, and other features. The typical analogy is that of having to jump from one car to the other while driving on a highway at faster than 70 miles an hour. This is obviously a very inefficient way to trade. And moving from one system to the other can be costly, too. In a rapidly moving market, taking one's eyes away from the screen for even a brief moment can cause traders to miss profitable trading opportunities.

7.3 WHO ARE SOME OF THESE ECNs?

The roster of firms that offer ECN services keeps changing frequently. At the time of writing, the following names were included in that list:

- Reuters' Instinet
- Bloomberg's Tradebook
- Datek Securities' Island
- Brut, owned by SungGard Data Systems, Inc.
- Archipelago
- All-Tech Investment Group's Attain
- NexTrade, operated by PIM Global Equities, Inc.
- REDIBook, backed by Charles Schwab, Donaldson, Lufkin & Jenerette, and others.
- Market XT

The business of ECNs is in a process of continuous transformation and growth. When two ECNs, Brut and Strike, announced a merger in November 1999, within a week three new ECNs were proposed. Along with a group of brokers, Nyfix Inc., a firm that operates the networks that connect trading desks at various brokerage firms and other large institutions with the NYSE floor, wants to launch an ECN labeled Nyfix Millenium LLC. Here, we introduce some of the ECNs with a detailed discussion on Instinet.

7.3.1 Instinet

Instinet, short for Institutional Network, is the oldest electronic trading network operated by Instinet Corporation, a subsidiary of Reuters Group. The firm markets itself as "the world's largest agency brokerage firm." By definition, this implies that it never trades for its own account with a client. So, it is basically a brokerage firm that offers an electronic trading facility. It just happens to be the largest one of its type, enjoying more than a 60 percent share of the ECN market.

The growth of Instinet as an alternative trading mechanism reflects the increasing power of institutional investors. Its popularity is emblematic of a change in institutional trading patterns—the growth in passive money, the increased emphasis on execution costs, and the increased professionalism of buy-side trading desks (or the asset management companies). The 1987 crash helped Instinet because as institutions shifted assets out of equities, they came to put a much greater premium on reducing trading costs. Many money managers found themselves chasing too few pension dollars and focused on the cost of doing business, especially the cost of trading.

From its early days, Instinet has focused mainly on serving the trading needs of the institutional investment community. As discussed in earlier chapters, these investors trade large volumes and have an interest in pursuing strategies that would enable them to complete their transactions without affecting market prices significantly. Instinet provides them with that opportunity. Institutions have been willing to use the order book to publicize their trading interests and the negotiation facility to strike bargains directly and anonymously.

Instinet accounted for close to 14 percent of Nasdaq volume in 2000, or 46.2 billion shares in the first nine months of that year. This compares with 29.8 billion shares in the first nine months of 1999. In 2001, it filed with the SEC for an initial public offering (IPO) to raise close to $450 million. When this happens, it would be the first publicly traded ECN in the United States.

Trading Facility

As part of its electronic trading facility, Instinet (Figure 7.2) offers investors two distinct trading options: a standard crossing arrangement, and a continuous trading system. Investors enter orders into a central limit-order book. The

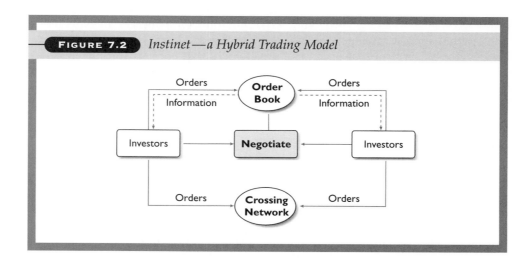

FIGURE 7.2 *Instinet—a Hybrid Trading Model*

contents of this book can be viewed by using Instinet's proprietary terminals, which the firm supplies free of charge to brokers and institutional investors. The trading facility differs from the various other ECNs in that Instinet does not offer an automated matching feature. Instead, it provides an interface that allows its users to view various trading interests and negotiate electronically with specific counterparties.

If a trader scanning the order book takes interest in a particular entry, he or she can either hit the order and strike a deal or, by using a special window on the screen, negotiate anonymously with the counterparty to improve on the posted order. Although the execution mechanism is distinct from the NYSE and Nasdaq markets, the prices quoted in the Instinet order book are related to those quoted in these other markets. By allowing investors to trade anonymously, the system encourages them to expose their true trading interests, which aids in price discovery.

In addition, thanks to Nasdaq's order handling rules described in previous chapters, if a trading interest in Instinet happens to be either the highest bid or lowest offer these prices get posted on the Nasdaq quote montage. Other traders who are not logged on to Instinet can also access these quotes.

Order Monitoring and Routing Services

In addition to its trading facility, Instinet operates a trading desk that keeps track of orders submitted to the order book that would be of interest to its customers. The trading desk can be interpreted as the functional equivalent of a closed order book. Investors can express their trading interests with the desk with instructions that the details not be published in the open order book. Once a suitable order is entered into the system by other traders, the desk will inform the customer. This service is similar to the agency service provided by Investment Technology Group's (ITG) Portfolio System for Institutional Trading (POSIT). These firms claim that their goal is to provide the best execution to their clients, even if this means routing orders to other competing systems.

Membership in all these exchanges allows Instinet's brokerage function to offer superior order routing service. For example, clients can place a single order and rely on Instinet to route it simultaneously to multiple markets for execution. The firm uses this facility to attract more order flow to the trading service. Customers can specify the manner in which they would like Instinet to handle a particular trading interest.

Using Instinet, investors can trade stocks listed on nearly 17 different exchanges on which it is a member—all U.S. regional exchanges, the American Stock Exchange (AMEX), the London, Paris, Toronto, Zurich, Hong Kong, Frankfurt, Stockholm, and Bermuda stock exchanges, the Chicago Board Options Exchange (CBOE), and the European Options Exchange. In November 1999, Instinet purchased Lynch Jones & Ryan, a private New York company that specialized in institutional trading and research. This deal made Instinet a part owner (9.9 percent) in this firm's NYSE floor brokerage unit. Given this worldwide reach, Instinet's "market" is always open. With 5,400 terminals internationally, its terminals are ubiquitous on institutional buy- and sell-side trading desks and is by far the largest ECN with the greatest liquidity.

Instinet and Nasdaq

Due perhaps in part to some of the abuses by Nasdaq market makers, institutional investors have displayed a marked preference for trading Nasdaq-listed stocks on Instinet. In fact, Instinet now accounts for, on average, about 15 to 20 percent of Nasdaq's trading volume. Its volume has grown from less than 10 million shares per day in 1987 to more than 150 million by 1998. Revenues in 1995, for instance, equaled $376 million, up 31 percent from the year before. U.S. revenues accounted for 86.8 percent of the total. Most of this volume again is siphoned off Nasdaq.

By allowing anonymous trading that is well inside the notoriously wide bid-and-ask Nasdaq spread, Instinet has won a huge following among Nasdaq investors and dealers. Many over-the-counter (OTC) market makers prefer Instinet over Nasdaq's more open interdealer trading system, SelectNet, because it offers greater insight into the market for Nasdaq-listed stocks. Also, traders can either negotiate trades directly or use the crossing network to trade between the spreads for these stocks.

The introduction of the order handling rules has changed the dynamics of the interaction between Instinet and the Nasdaq market. We have already pointed out how the rules provide non-Instinet traders information about the best bid or offer available with Instinet. Some traders have tried exploiting this arrangement in an interesting manner that plays one system off the other. Let's assume, for instance, that a large institutional trader such as Goldman Sachs wants to buy, say, 100,000 shares of stock in a particular company. It submits a low bid (lower than the current highest one) to Instinet. At the same time, it improves on the existing lowest offer on Nasdaq for a smaller quantity of shares, say, 5,000. The smaller offer from Goldman is visible to the whole market; the bid within Instinet is not because it is lower than the current highest bid. Other traders in the market will observe Goldman's selling interest on SelectNet. It is possible that a sufficiently large number of these traders will interpret this interest as an indicator of some negative information about that particular stock. They may react by deciding to get out of their positions in that stock. A typical impact would be an aggressive lowering of the offer price. When this price reaches the level of Goldman's bid within Instinet, the firm will quietly clear up the available selling interests up to the specified limit of 100,000 shares.

Instinet and the SEC

Instinet is not registered as a self-regulating exchange, but as a broker-dealer bound by a 1986 no-action letter from the SEC. Because of this, the trading system is vulnerable to regulatory interference. For example, the SEC has introduced legislation requiring traders to quote the same price publicly that they quote privately on ECNs such as Instinet. To an extent, this reduces the "privateness" promised by Instinet.

In addition, the SEC has proposed tighter rules targeted at ECNs with at least 5 percent trading activity in any given stock. Under these rules, the highest bids and lowest offers for these stocks in Instinet will have to be disseminated through Nasdaq's quotation system. If passed, this rule will adversely affect Instinet's ability to protect the anonymity of its order book. This would hurt its relationship with large institutions that flock to it mainly to avoid exposing their trading interests to other investors and broker-dealers in the market. They would only prefer the counterparty with whom they are negotiating to be able to observe their trading interest.

Instinet and Broker-Dealers

Instinet has been steadily stealing business from stock broker-dealers on exchanges. Indeed, it has managed to blur the difference between an exchange and a broker. Of course, the competititors are not taking this lying down. Broker-dealers fight to keep Instinet's terminals out of town. Stock exchanges steer members away from it. Unwilling to part with any piece of their profitable turf, broker-dealers have tried to prevent Instinet from encroaching on their business. In London, for instance, a stock exchange rule that protected its brokers kept Instinet a bit player in the European market for years. But the rule was finally overturned in 1997. In Canada, too, regulators have not been too welcoming of Instinet. For example, in 1989 Instinet Canada was prohibited from offering electronic trading services in Canadian stocks to Canadian clients. This happened after it tried to buy a Toronto Stock Exchange seat and was blocked by member firms that thought networks such as Instinet threatened the exchange's viability. During this period, every major Canadian broker lined up against Instinet's entry into the market. The Toronto Stock Exchange granted it membership, but the company was unable to install terminals at institutions due to broker resistance. The Ontario Securities Commission finally gave Instinet permission in late 1995 to bring terminals into Canada and serve as an international dealer. After a gap of 10 years during which competitive pressures on exchanges changed drastically, the Toronto Stock Exchange finally helped to get the restriction lifted in November 1999.

Competitive Strategies

As pointed out earlier, by early 1999 there were nine ECNs registered with the SEC and Nasdaq. The new entrants managed to give Instinet a run for its money. ECNs such as Island and Archipelago have managed to take advantage of the latest networking technologies to offer efficient execution at low cost and have been particularly aggressive in attracting order flow. Until now, Instinet has made a success out of trading Nasdaq stocks. However, as the competition among ECNs for trading Nasdaq stocks has heated up considerably, Instinet has had to look to other markets for increasing its trading volume, including linking up with exchanges, expanding services, and entering international markets.

In 1998, reports were floating around about Instinet seeking to link up with the Chicago Stock Exchange. Any link-up between the two institutions would be attractive to Instinet as it would gain entry to the intermarket trading system (ITS) that links the nation's exchanges to each other but does not allow direct access to private trading systems or brokers. This would also have provided Instinet with a means to get around Rule 390, which prohibits NYSE member firms from trading most of the exchange's listings off-exchange but does not affect transactions on the regional exchanges. If Instinet gains access to orders flowing through the ITS, it will be able to compete directly with specialists on the floor of the NYSE. But later in 1999, the NYSE finally decided to repeal Rule 390. In December 1999, the SEC voted to open up the ITS to both Nasdaq as well as the ECNs. These measures leveled the playing field for all ECNs, making it much more difficult for Instinet to gain a competitive advantage against other ECNs.

Instinet has also responded to the increased competition by focusing more on client services such as research and analytics. Its managers frequently refer to its business as being that of a "global broker" rather than an ECN. Instinet takes great pains to explain to reporters that the ECN business is a small component of the overall suite of products—upstairs block trading, research and analytics, transaction-cost analysis.

Another strategy that Instinet has been pursuing rather aggressively is to expand its competitive position overseas. On May 6, 1999, Instinet announced that it was taking a stake in the London-based electronic stock exchange Tradepoint Financial Networks (which has since changed its name to virt-x). It is interesting to note that Instinet has invested in Tradepoint as part of a consortium of leading institutions that includes broker-dealer firms such as Morgan Stanley Dean Witter and JP Morgan, fund management companies such as American Century, and the ECN company Archipelago. Unlike Instinet and other U.S.-based electronic trading systems discussed above, Tradepoint is a full-fledged for-profit stock exchange operating an electronic trading system. Established in 1996, Tradepoint uses a transparent, electronic order book for U.K. securities.[5] In April 1999, it obtained permission from the SEC to open up its order book to investors in the United States.

For a long time now, Instinet has been operational even after the regular market hours (which is from 9:30 AM to 4:00 PM EST). But this trading service has been available only for institutional investors. Retail or small individual investors were not registered users of Instinet and hence could not participate in its after-hours trading. In its hunt for increased order flow, Instinet has decided to welcome the latter group of investors. In May 1999, it announced that retail[6] investors would be allowed access during normal trading as well as after hours.

This decision by Instinet reveals an interesting aspect of how brokers handle their customers' orders. As per law, brokers are expected to provide the best execution to their clients. This implies that orders are routed to the market where the best prices are available. If the best price happens to be available in Instinet, the order should be routed to it. But apparently, brokers have traditionally not bothered to route their customers' orders to Instinet. One reason for this could be that until recently, Instinet was not required to publish its best bids and offers on the Nasdaq quote montage.

So, now that these Instinet prices are visible to all market participants—at least to those who have access to Nasdaq level II screens—should it not be the case that orders from individual customers would automatically be routed by brokers to Instinet? Yes, at least in theory. But this reasoning is one-sided. It assumes that the best bids and offers on Instinet are established by the large institutional investors who have traditionally been trading on it. By overtly inviting retail investors to use its system, Instinet is simply reacting to the new reality in the marketplace—at least with regard to Nasdaq stocks. Increasingly, large movements in trading interest in any stock are initiated by individual investors trading small numbers of shares. They might be individuals who have quit their regular jobs and make a living (or hope to make a living) trading in the offices of a day-trading firm or simply individuals who trade individual stocks either from home or work. So, whenever big moves happen in this fashion, it is likely to be the case that the best bid or offer is not established by an order routed to Instinet. If institutional investors find that they can get better prices at ECNs such as Island—which cater to online brokers and day-trading firms—they will start routing their orders to these markets. So, with the objective of maintaining its market share, the logical strategy would obviously be for Instinet to attract orders from the new market participants.

Accordingly, Instinet has signed an agreement with the large online brokerage firm E*Trade, which will route its after-hours order flow to Instinet. It has also set up a new subsidiary, named Instinet.com, which will focus on offering electronic trading services to small, retail investors. Instinet might also prefer to have various brokerage firms routing their orders to it. In this connection, there have also been reports that Instinet is in talks with Yahoo! Inc. to set up a link with the portal so that retail clients can easily route their orders to the electronic trading service. Clearly, Instinet is following a multipronged strategy to compete with its growing competition in the interest of maintaining its market leader position.

7.3.2 Archipelago

Archipelago L.L.C., initially known as Terra Nova Trading L.L.C., is headquartered in Chicago and is one of the first four ECNs approved by the SEC. It was launched in 1997 as a joint venture with a software development firm, Townsend Analytics. It subsequently changed its name in April 1999.

In March 2000, Archipelago acquired the Pacific Exchange and announced a plan to create the first fully electronic national stock exchange. Once this purchase was consummated, Archipelago withdrew its own previous application for exchange status with the SEC.

Trading volumes in Archipelago are much smaller than at Instinet and Island. The numbers fluctuate often, with public announcements proclaiming any milestones achieved. For example, one day in late February 2001, Archipelago issued a press release claiming that it had handled 6.2 percent of the trading in Nasdaq shares that day.

7.3.3 Island

Island and Archipelago have been traditional rivals competing for second place among ECNs. Given its genesis,[7] Island's order flow comes primarily from day traders. As mainstream Wall Street firms have never been comfortable with day trading, Island has had a tough time garnering order flow from large investment houses.

Although it has been on the fringes of Wall Street, that hasn't kept it from being an aggressive innovator. Island was the first ECN to publish real-time information from its order book over the Internet (Figure 7.1). In the fourth quarter of 2000, Island recorded trade volume of close to 17.6 billion shares, more than doubling the 8.32 billion shares in the same quarter in 1999. Part of this volume comes from large investment firms. Island has managed to use its day-trading order flow to attract orders from large firms.

The sections below discuss other aspects of Island. For example, Section 7.4.1 illustrates the interaction between the day-trading business of Datek and Island. Section 7.4.6 discusses some of the problems Island has been having in its efforts to improve its image with mainstream Wall Street.

7.3.4 NexTrade

During 1998, the Nasdaq market was busy approving new ECNs. In November 1998, an ECN named NexTrade received the necessary approvals (Figure 7.3). NexTrade, based in Clearwater, Florida, was started by two brokers who had a few years back quit a traditional discount broker Olde Discount Corp. to start a day-trading firm in Florida. For approximately $4.5 million, they stitched together 10 servers running on the Windows NT operating system. The system is open for trading 24 hours a day and is accessible over the Internet.

NexTrade has developed proprietary software, Pro-Trade, which allows retail clients of sponsoring firms to enter trades for execution on NexTrade ECN. The basic software to connect to NexTrade can be downloaded over the Internet. Some of NexTrade's largest customers are Brown & Co. and Dreyfus Brokerage Services. In 1999, NexTrade developed the world's first Internet-based spot foreign currency trading platform, Matchbook FX, of which it is one-third owner. In January 2000, the firm formerly applied to the SEC for exchange status.

7.3.5 Brut

Brut is a subsidiary of SunGard Data System, which sells order-routing systems to brokerage firms and institutional investors. In early 2000, Brut merged with Strike, another ECN. The new company is named Brut ECN. About 130 brokerage

FIGURE 7.3 *NexTrade ECN*

firms use its services to route orders and settle trades. Offering trading services in the form of Brut is part of the company's strategy to enhance a dominant position in one segment of the trading process. The firm hopes to attract order flows from what it perceives as a captive group of dealers and investors who already use its services. Brut has decided to pay brokers for feeding orders into its system. It pays up to one dollar to any broker-dealer who puts an order into its system that gets executed and charges up to four dollars if the broker takes out liquidity by hitting an order displayed on the ECN. Brut also plans to trade shares listed on the NYSE.

7.3.6 Bloomberg Tradebook

Bloomberg Tradebook (Figure 7.4) is a subsidiary of Bloomberg L.P., one of the best-known financial information, news, and media companies. Bloomberg was started in late 1998. Currently, it is with CLSA Global Emerging Markets to

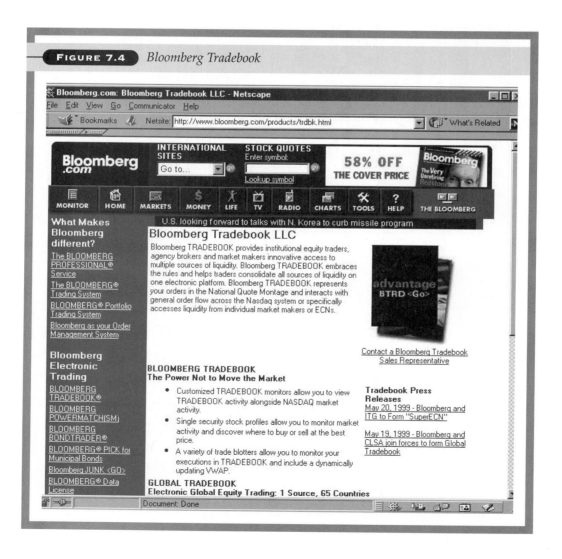

FIGURE 7.4 *Bloomberg Tradebook*

establish a global electronic trading system—Global Tradebook. The new system will allow investors and broker-dealers in about 65 countries to place orders through Bloomberg's electronic terminals. Trades will be processed by CLSA. In keeping with the global nature of the market, Global Tradebook will operate 24 hours a day. The main competitor of this system will be Instinet, which offers execution services in numerous countries.

7.4 CHANGING LANDSCAPE OF EQUITY MARKETS

7.4.1 ECNs and Brokerage Firms

It is just a matter of time before investors start accessing trading systems directly over the Internet. ECNs are aware of this. The networking technologies that they use can be easily connected to the Internet. Island, Archipelago, NexTrade, and others have already made that connection. Their customers no longer require access to proprietary networks. They simply connect via the Internet. Online brokers are also aware of this; their primary goal is to make money by encouraging individual investors to trade over the Internet. In addition to providing investors a seamless trading experience—something that might happen in the near future—these arrangements are driven by a desire by brokerage firms to reduce the cost of execution services. In today's markets, ECNs provide the ideal venue for such savings-motivated strategies.

Buying a Stake in ECNs

So, it is quite natural for an ECN and an online brokerage firm to form an alliance. In January 1999, the online brokerage firm E*Trade announced that it had decided to take an equity stake in Archipelago. Interestingly, as a sign of the old world not wanting to lose out, the Wall Street broker-dealer Goldman Sachs announced that it was also taking an equal stake (25 percent) in Archipelago. In addition to this equity interest, Goldman Sachs has invested in at least two other electronic trading systems: the ECN Brut and the advanced automated trading system OptiMark.

More significantly, Goldman Sachs and others have been making moves that reflect their belief in the enduring quality of traditional floor-based trading. In a classic illustration of this, in 2000, Goldman Sachs paid $6.5 billion for Spear, Leeds & Kellogg, a large specialist firm on the NYSE.

While large brokerage firms have been busy investing in ECNs, the ECNs themselves have been taking an interest in other brokerage firms. For example, in an effort to shore up its execution services, Instinet bought an institutional discount broker, Lynch, Jones, & Ryan, Inc.[8]

Setting Up Their Own ECNs

In some respects, these alliances are similar to the links between Datek Holdings Corp.'s online discount brokerage, Datek Online, and the Island ECN (as we discuss below, both the brokerage firm and the ECN are popular with day traders).

Another recent strategy has been for a group of brokerage firms to join hands and set up their own ECN. This is exactly what happened when Fidelity Investments (affiliated to one of the world's largest mutual fund firms), Charles Schwab, one of the largest online discount brokers, Donaldson, Lufkin & Jenerette, a brokerage firm with an online presence, and Spear, Leeds & Kellogg, a brokerage firm that owns a number of specialists on the NYSE and is also a large player in the options market, announced a plan to set up their own ECN.[9] Spear, Leeds has its own ECN called REDIBook. It is highly likely that the proposed ECN will subsume REDIBook. These partners were not setting out to add one more ECN to what is considered to be an already-too-crowded field. Rather, the firms were attempting to create a marketplace that could potentially survive the competition. The plan is to route their huge order flows to this ECN and in the process generate sufficient critical mass for a profitable existence.

Private, Internal Matching Networks

Fidelity Brokerage is a discount broker under Fidelity Investment. Being the parent company of mutual funds managing billions of dollars worth of assets, Fidelity would be tempting to cross orders internally. This would allow its manager to trade anonymously and, more important, could save its constituents millions of dollars in commissions and other trading-related costs. Fidelity's Investors Liquidity Network (ILN) was established to do precisely this.

Not strictly an ECN, ILN is used to cross orders from individual and corporate investors internally. ILN was initially used as an internal order-routing system and to mop up various sources of liquidity among Fidelity's fund managers and brokerage customers. In May 1997, the firm opened it up to accept orders from select brokers, dealers, and institutional investors. The network is operated by Fidelity's subsidiary National Financial, which also developed the system. When an investor sends an order, ILN allows him or her to choose from a range of execution options from immediate execution to waiting in the crossing network for an appropriate match. If no match takes place within a specified time period, the order can then be routed to an exchange or electronic trading network of choice.

ECNs and Day Trading

Another partner of ECNs is the multitudes of day traders and the brokers that assist them. Day trading has become an increasingly important trading alternative for individual investors. The printed media has been full of stories of individuals making (and also losing) large sums of money during the course of a regular trading day. Day traders generate a lot of order flow for firms such as Datek and All-Tech, which have also discovered ECNs.

The ECN Island is run by Datek Securities, a leading day-trading firm that specializes in assisting individuals to speculate on short-term price movements by using Nasdaq's SOES and SelectNet systems.[10] It is also one of the largest discount brokerages in the country and has been aggressive in adopting the Internet to sell its brokerage services. All-Tech Investment Group is another large day-trading firm that offers its own ECN called Attain. Instead of simply routing customers' order to the Nasdaq market or the NYSE, Datek Brokerage routes them to the Island ECN. Here, these orders can be directly matched with each other. Customers gain from not having to pay the market maker's spread. Instead, any spread between the highest bid and the lowest offer is split between the respective orders.

Once the ECNs have garnered sufficient order flows from its day-trading customers, they use it to attract order flows from scores of other brokerage firms as well as large institutions. They are aided in this by the fact that day traders as a group target technology stocks. These stocks are also popular with individual investors who have been signing up in hordes with online brokers such as E*Trade and Ameritrade. Trading in this sector has been growing at an exponential rate. So, if large numbers of trades in a particular group of stocks is taking place in a particular corner of the market (in this case, the Island ECN), anyone else who wants to trade these stocks will route his or her orders to that corner. It is no wonder that Island trades more than 100 million shares a day.

This has not escaped the attention of other brokers. Like Datek, E*Trade will now route customer orders to Archipelago ECN. Any unmatched orders will be automatically routed to either another ECN or to the Nasdaq market.

7.4.2 Dealer-Friendly ECNs

Are ECNs in the business of driving market makers out of business? From the business models discussed above, it should be plainly evident to readers that ECNs deliver cost savings primarily by splitting the market-maker spread among the buy and sell orders. Given the intense competition among various ECNs, it will not be long before someone designs a business model that would make the ECN more attractive than professional market makers and broker-dealers.

In a fashion symptomatic of how quickly things change in the world of electronic trading, by 1998, Brut had decided that it wanted to take the ECN game more seriously. Instead of a let's-kill-the-dealer strategy, it decided to market itself as a broker-dealer-friendly ECN. In December 1998, it entered into a partnership with four of the largest broker-dealer firms, handling up to 25 percent of Nasdaq's volume: Goldman, Sachs & Co., Knight Securities, Merrill Lynch & Co., and Morgan Stanley, Dean Witter & Co. The relationship is in the form of equity interests in Brut.[11] Broker-dealers are involved in the trading process by a policy that allows a buy-side firm—in other words, a large institutional investor—to access the ECN only through a sponsoring broker-dealer. The marketing of the trading system to such investors is left in the hands of broker-dealers. This strategy contrasts starkly with that followed by other ECNs that market themselves directly to the user community—mainly buy-side firms.

7.4.3 Market Fragmentation

The market share figures show that large investors have been flocking to ECNs in great numbers attracted by their anonymity and lower execution costs. In response, new ECNs have also been cropping up at a rapid pace. It is not surprising that complaints have started pouring in as well. Large institutional traders have already begun complaining about the adverse impact of this proliferation of electronic execution systems. The allure of lower costs is now being offset by the need to monitor trading in multiple trading venues. Many investors are having a tough time tackling the problem of tracking trading activity in the various competing networks.

In addition, the fragmentation of liquidity among the multiple trading systems makes it more difficult for a fund manager to execute trades in large blocks of stocks. Liquidity gets fragmented when orders flow to disparate books such that it becomes difficult for an investor to form an educated judgment of the state of demand and supply for any single stock in the market.

Let's assume an investor wishes to buy, say, a million shares of a particular stock. In a world with a single consolidated order book, as liquidity will be concentrated in this book, the investor will simply send his or her order to this book. Holding everything else constant, as the number of books increases, the liquidity in any single book will shrink, thus forcing the investor to break up the million-shares trade into smaller ones. A trade that could potentially be executed in a single transaction will now have to be broken up into smaller pieces. This surely does not result in any improvement in efficiency and instead increases the cost of trading.

The SuperECN as a Potential Solution

As ECNs proliferate, they end up stealing order flows away from each other. The market gets fragmented, hurting the efficiency of the marketplace. Faced with such a situation, firms in most industries will try to form alliances with one or more competitors. This strategy works in the equities trading business, too. In May 1999, two firms with competing electronic trading systems, ITG and Bloomberg, formed an alliance called Tradebook SuperECN. The name is a direct reference to the Bloomberg ECN, Tradebook. In late 1999, two ECNs, Strike Technologies, LLC, and Brass Utility, LLC (Brut), merged their businesses.[12]

Under the new arrangement, customers of either Tradebook or ITG's POSIT, a crossing system that we discuss later in this chapter, will have the option of routing their orders to both systems. But to make sure that the same order is not executed twice—once in Tradebook, and once in POSIT—the search for a match will take place sequentially. If one system is unable to find a match, the order will be automatically routed to the other. In effect, the alliance is little more than an automated order routing system. It is designed to reduce the effort involved in waiting to see if an order is executed in a particular "market," and if not, routing it to a different "market." Other ECNs have announced similar alliances at various points. There has not been any evidence on whether such linkages actually deliver as promised.

This particular alliance has been made possible because the two firms offer distinct trading systems. Bloomberg's Tradebook is an ECN, where investors can post their trading interests anonymously. ITG's POSIT offers a crossing system, one in which investors submit nonpriced orders that will be matched at the midpoint of quotes established in the primary market where a stock is traded: NYSE, Nasdaq, or one of the regional exchanges.

At the time of writing, the two firms were encouraging other ECNs to join their alliance. Ownership in the alliance—and hence share in profits—is designed to be a function of the transaction flow (distinct from order flow) contributed by each member.

Consolidated Order Book

The Nasdaq market has been aware of the problems caused by fragmentation of the market thanks to the proliferation of ECNs. It is hard to escape the fact that by permitting numerous ECNs to operate, the Nasdaq and the SEC, both of whose permission is mandatory, have played an active role in giving "birth" to this problem.

Stung by growing criticism and concerned by the negative impact of this development on market efficiency, the Nasdaq has put forward proposals[13] for a consolidated order book. But faced with considerable resistance from its members—broker-dealers and market makers—the Nasdaq has not yet been successful in implementing a central limit-order book. The basic complaint it has faced from sell-side firms is that by forcing all orders to flow to a common order book with an automated matching feature, the Nasdaq would be competing directly with its members. Even if the consolidation is on a voluntary basis, from the perspective of a broker-dealer, it does not necessarily matter. If their customers insist, then they will be forced to route their orders to the consolidated book.

Although the proposal was submitted with the best of intentions, the market authorities were unable to sell it to its constituents. The inability of Nasdaq to introduce a consolidated order book is because it is in effect owned by the very individuals who would be thrown out of business in this event. An analogous predicament would be this: Assume Ford Motor is owned solely by its assembly-line workers. Ford's management introduces a proposal to install a fully automated production system and asks its workers to vote for it!

7.4.4 Do ECNs Make Any Money?

Although ECNs are reported to be responsible for a third of the shares traded on Nasdaq, as a group they hardly make any money. Instinet, for example, is the largest of all ECNs, and makes money from other traditional brokerage services.

In the first nine months of 1999, Instinet reported pretax profit margin of 31 percent. At the same time, it declared that its margins were being threatened by other ECNs that were trying to undercut it. It is now trying to market itself as a global agency broker offering sophisticated intermediation services for which it could potentially charge higher fee income.

The second largest ECN, Island, executes on average 100 million shares a day. In the first nine months of 1999, its revenue was about $14 million, which translates to a commission rate of about $1.50 for every 1,000 shares, much smaller than that charged by Instinet. It expects to lose money for the next year and a half. Given the potential competition, the expectation of a profit anytime in the near future might be overly optimistic. Archipelago, the third biggest ECN, barely makes any profit but is valued at close to $400 million. It does about a third of Island's volume.

ECNs are following different strategies to increase profits. Island and Archipelago, for instance, have both filed to become exchanges, as we discuss later. Companies list their stocks on exchanges and pay a fee for this privilege. An ECN, however, is a simple broker-dealer and cannot charge such a fee. Income from this fee is a major source of revenue for the NYSE and the Nasdaq market, a revenue source that some ECNs hope to tap into.

The key to making money[14] is obviously to generate a critical mass of trading volume. In the face of shrinking commissions from increased competition and given the need to invest heavily in technology, the threshold for break-even volume will keep increasing. The obvious prediction from pundits is that we will see considerable consolidation in this business.

This gloomy predicament is not one-sided: Market makers are in no way better off than these ECNs. The overall trend toward electronic trading has gradually shrunk their spreads, the primary source of income for a market maker. The ECNs are seeing downward pressure on their revenue due to the heightened level of competition in that market. The decisive question is, where will all this lead?

7.4.5 Do ECNs Have a Future?

The future of ECNs takes different scenarios according to different experts. Once the fog clears, we may well see just a couple of ECNs in operation. However, these will have to contend with competition from a more competitive NYSE, a sensible Nasdaq market, and automated trading systems such as OptiMark and Primex.

In recognition of the threat posed by ECNs, the NYSE is proposing its own ECN for small-sized orders (less than 1,000 shares). It is also in the process of making substantial cuts in the fees that specialists charge to execute orders. Nasdaq, however, is taking a more direct approach. As described in a previous chapter, subject to permission from the SEC, it would like to build a central limit-order book that would do all that ECNs do today. Some of these actions under the rubric of the Network NYSE are discussed in Chapter 5, Section 5.4.

One incident reveals that certain sections of the investment community hold a different and more optimistic view of the future of ECNs. In November 1999, Track Data Corporation, a firm that specialized in the options market and operated an online brokerage service, announced a plan to set up its own ECN. Its stock jumped 35 percent. When the *Wall Street Journal* queried the CEO of the firm, he was at a loss to explain how the firm would make any money from the ECN.

In conclusion, it seems as if ECNs are a temporary phenomenon and might face extinction soon. As we know, SuperMontage will finally introduce anonymous trading to the Nasdaq market. The venerable NYSE too has announced its intention to implement an ECN-type mechanism for a subset of its stocks. Maybe that's one reason why numerous ECNs, Island and Archipelago in particular, have applied to the SEC for permission to become exchanges.

What's working against these efforts of various ECNs is that various studies regularly confirm the relatively low trading costs on the NYSE floor. An implication of this is that given the low costs, there is no obvious motivation for a trader to move his or her orders to an ECN.

One problem with some of these studies is that they compare the NYSE costs with that of the Nasdaq market as a whole. It would be interesting to compare trading costs on the NYSE floor *vis a vis* the ECNs. But given the low trading volumes of NYSE stocks on ECNs, such a study will not yet be meaningful.

7.4.6 ECNs as Exchanges

ECNs have typically been set up by broker-dealer firms and have fulfilled this function. But recent proposals by the SEC concerning regulating alternative trading systems have encouraged ECNs such as Island, Archipelago, and Nex-Trade to apply for a change of status from an ECN to an exchange. The rules give ECNs and other alternative trading systems the option of either continuing to be regulated as broker-dealers or converting their status to that of an exchange. Instead of being part broker-dealer, part execution-service, the ECNs that have filed for exchange status have indicated that they would prefer to focus on the latter function.

Case of Island

So, Island now wants to become a full-fledged exchange. What would it gain from such a strategy? Simple: This would allow it to trade all stocks listed on the NYSE. By early 1999, Island had about 10 percent of Nasdaq's volume. Island can now use its technology and competitive advantages to compete for a slice of a much larger market. Becoming an exchange would provide numerous advantages to Island and its main customers, who are primarily small investors whose orders are routed to it by various online brokerage firms. The hope is that it can use its existing customer base to attract order flow from larger investors to create a liquid marketplace. In addition, the move is designed to help save the firm some costs. As trades executed over Island are reported through Nasdaq, it has to pay the latter a fee. Island also pays for any quotes that it buys from the NYSE and Nasdaq. As an exchange, it could save on both these costs.

However, the change in status is bound to add other costs to Island. For example, it will burden itself with additional regulatory responsibilities. These issues are now being handled by NASD Regulation (NASDR), the regulatory arm of the Nasdaq market. It is possible that Island will decide to outsource the service to NASD for a fixed fee. But if the additional costs are not offset by cost savings and increased revenue from higher transaction volumes, it might regret the decision to convert to an exchange structure.

Island has been having problems raising money to fund its exchange plans.[15] Early in 1999, Island was planning to sell shares amounting to about 12.5 percent of its equity to Waterhouse Investor Services, Inc. for about $25 million. Waterhouse is a leading discount broker both in the United States and Canada and had the potential to route orders from its clients to Island's electronic trading system. But the deal fell through. A Reuters' report explained that this was due to problems related to the valuation of Island and issues regarding the governance of the firm. Waterhouse instead preferred to go along with REDIBook ECN. This was not the only case of investor pullout. Vulcan Ventures, the venture capital fund of Paul Allen (Microsoft's cofounder), withdrew from a financing agreement with Island in July 1999. Island will still need additional funds to build the infrastructure required to function as a stock exchange once it receives the approval from the SEC.

Some of the problems in obtaining SEC approval stem from regulatory issues related to its parent, Datek Online Brokerage Service, and its day-trading unit. The day-trading division has been accused by its customers of making unauthorized trades or failing to execute orders. In April 1998, the latter was sold to Heartland Securities, a trading firm partly owned by two minority Datek owners. To further improve its reputation, Jeffrey Citron, Datek's founder, stepped down to make way for Ed Nicoll. The latter was the founder of TD Waterhouse.

ECNs and For-Profit Exchanges

Exchanges in the United States have traditionally been organized as nonprofit institutions run collectively by their members. Brokers, dealers, market makers, and specialists who are members of any such exchange are profit motivated; but the exchange itself is a not-for-profit entity. Exchanges around the world—Stockholm, Sydney, Milan, Vienna, and others—have either already converted to for-profit status or are at least seriously considering changing their structure. In the United States, the Nasdaq as well as the NYSE have begun discussing this issue in the open.

ECNs are businesses that operate with the goal of maximizing profits for their owners, who have invested money in the business. When Island and Archipelago become full-fledged exchanges, they will operate as for-profit private enterprises, responding to the needs of their customers. In a competitive market, they will be attempting to snatch market shares from established not-for-profit exchanges such as the NYSE.

In a rapidly evolving market driven by continually changing technologies, firms will have to be flexible to survive. Faced with the possibility of being driven out of business, some of our venerable exchanges might soon decide to change their governance structure and become for-profit entities. This will send a signal to the investment community that these institutions are more interested in serving their customers than in heeding the self-serving interests of their members.

7.5 CROSSING NETWORKS

This section discusses crossing networks (Figure 7.5), which are different from ECNs. Certain electronic trading systems simply match buying and selling interests in any given stock at the midpoint of the best bid and offer quotes established in a parallel market. They are called *crossing networks.* In such networks, orders are accumulated over an interval and executed, or *crossed,* at the midpoint of bid and offer prices established in a different marketplace, say, the NYSE floor or the Nasdaq market-maker network. So, all trades in a stock at any given moment will take place at a single price. ITG's POSIT is a classic example of such a crossing system. Reuters' Instinet offers both the regular ECN as well as a crossing network.

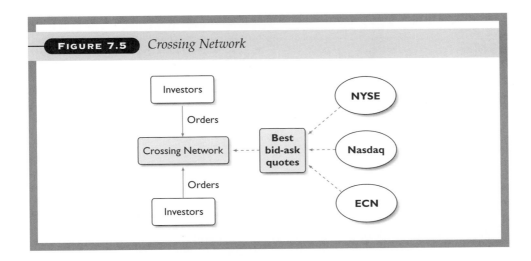

FIGURE 7.5 *Crossing Network*

7.5.1 Crossing Explained

Let us assume that the following orders are submitted to the crossing mechanism:

Stock	Buy	Sell
ABC	100	100
ABC	50	25
ABC		25
XYZ	1000	100
XYZ	2000	200

Let us assume that all the above orders are on an all-or-none (AON) basis, meaning either the order is filled completely or not at all. At the time these orders are processed, the following quotes are available:

Stock	Best Bid	Best Offer
ABC	25.00	25.25
XYZ	102.75	103.00

The crossing system will execute the following trades:

Stock	Transaction Quantity	Price
ABC	150	25.125
XYZ	0	102.875

For stock ABC, the buy order for 100 shares is matched with the sell order for 100 shares, and the buy order for 50 shares is matched with the two sell orders for 25 shares each. As the selling interest in XYZ stock is much lower than the buying interest, no trades will be executed.

7.5.2 POSIT

POSIT is a joint venture between BARRA, a quantitative investment research firm, and Jefferies & Co.'s ITG. When introduced in 1987, it was the first crossing system to be implemented. Five times a day—at approximately 10 AM, 11:30 AM, 12:30 PM, 1:30 PM, and 3:00 PM Eastern time—the main POSIT computer processes and compares all orders in total anonymity. For security reasons, each match is run at a randomly selected time within a seven-minute window immediately following the scheduled match time. Immediately after each crossing session, clients are electronically notified of the status of their orders. Investors with unmatched orders can decide whether to keep these orders in the system for a future match or instruct ITG to execute them through alternative routes.

Competing for Order Flow

POSIT is currently used by more than 400 major institutions and broker-dealers. Interestingly, despite the large number of clients, just 10 percent of orders submitted to POSIT get executed. ITG is resorting to a couple of different strategies to attract more order flow. It is constantly trying to add more buy-side and sell-side firms to the list of clients. It is also adding innovative features to its crossing algorithm. To differentiate itself from ECNs that offer relatively straightforward order-matching services, POSIT markets itself as an execution specialist. The crossing system is just one among a wide array of other agency services it provides its customers—mainly large institutions.

Innovative Order Crossing

In addition to the generic crossing service, POSIT offers additional capabilities: *dynamic substitution* and *enhanced risk control,* terms that POSIT uses to describe what are basically agency-type services it has tacked on as complementary to the electronic matching system. These features have been incorporated into a recent version of the crossing system, called POSIT 4. The strategy is to attract additional order flow by improving traders' control over the trading process.

Previous versions of POSIT had a single objective: to maximize the number of shares matched in each crossing. Investors had to specify the number of shares available for each matching. In addition, they could place a lower bound on the number of shares to be matched or specify a dollar restriction in the form of the total inflow or outflow of cash from a single transaction. POSIT 4 allows traders to substitute orders dynamically in response to the liquidity available within the crossing session. If a particular set of stocks is not available, the system will look for an alternative set that fits previously specified characteristics. So, if a preferred security is not available, it allows investors to substitute a different security. A trader who wants to increase exposure to banking stocks, for example, can submit a preferred list of alternatives along with a dollar limit on the total trade amount.

Traders can also use POSIT 4 to control different dimensions of their portfolios: expected return as well as risk. While processing orders, the crossing algorithm will control the tracking error of a portfolio relative to a benchmark. For example, a fund manager can set parameters that would limit the tracking error of a portfolio to no greater than 1 percent. This particular feature should be of special interest to index fund managers.

Connectivity

ITG has entered into an order routing arrangement with Jack White & Co., a large discount brokerage firm. Jack White runs its own crossing network called InterConnect that focuses on the retail or individual investor market. Investors can place orders via the Internet. Under the arrangement with ITG, any unexecuted orders from InterConnect will be routed to POSIT's five daily matches.

In addition to the Jack White arrangement, Bloomberg L.P. has agreed to add POSIT to its 75,000 terminals. This link opens up a potentially large market; thousands of traders using Bloomberg screens can now access POSIT's order book. POSIT is directly linked with several order proprietary trading systems, including Bridge, BRASS, and others. Like Instinet, POSIT too offers crossing services in international stocks through a companion service, Global POSIT.

7.5.3 Evaluating Crossing Networks

Differences: Crossing Networks and ECNs

An ECN allows some form of price negotiation and thus participates in the price discovery process. They try to match the highest bid with the lowest offer. They expect their users to specify price levels at which they are interested in trading specific numbers of shares of different stocks. Thanks to ever-evolving regulations from the SEC, they also participate in the montage of the Nasdaq quotation system. For instance, if a broker sends a quote to an ECN that is more aggressively priced than that displayed on the Nasdaq market, he or she is required to change his or her published quote on the latter by the more aggressive one. So, in effect, the best bid or offer (or both) used by a crossing network can actually be determined by trading interests submitted to an ECN.

When a trader submits an order to a crossing network such as POSIT, he or she will only indicate the stock and the number of shares he or she wants to buy or sell. However, in an ECN, one will specify a limit price except if one is submitting a market order. In that case, a buy order will be executed at the best offer price and a sell order at the best bid price. In a crossing network, the buy and sell interests will be traded at the midpoint of the best bid and offer. To summarize, crossing networks do not directly participate in the price discovery process.

Price Discovery

What is price discovery? Assume that the last trade in a stock took place at $15.50 per share. An order to buy 1,000 units of the stock at market price is submitted to the system. In a market that accommodates price discovery, this order will be matched against the lowest price at which someone is willing to sell this stock. Assume an investor had previously submitted a limit order expressing a willingness to sell up to 2,000 shares of this stock at a price of at least $15.625 per share. The market order will be executed at $15.625, 12.5 cents higher than the last traded price. Price discovery has taken place!

Crossing networks do not necessarily allow this to happen. They are not in the business of setting new prices. They simply provide an environment in which investors can quietly trade at the midpoint of the bid and offer prices quoted in a market, which allows price discovery to take place. Crossing networks attract investors who are simply content to trade at this midpoint of the current spread. Their goal is mainly to avoid paying the spread to the liquidity supplier in the main market where a stock is otherwise traded.

Free Riding

A common criticism of crossing networks is that they simply free ride on national markets such as the Nasdaq and the NYSE. Trades that take place on these markets determine the price of a given stock at any given moment. As many of us would have learned in Economics 101, prices are determined at the intersection of demand and supply curves.

Whenever an order is routed to a crossing network such as POSIT, information about the trading interest reflected by this order does not get factored into the demand and supply curves for this stock on the main market. For example, if a large order to buy 100,000 shares of Dell Computer stocks is submitted to POSIT, the Nasdaq market is completely in the blind about this trading interest. If the order had been routed to a market maker or ECN, the trader would have had to specify a limit price or request execution at the best market price. Either way, it would have some impact on the market price (even if the trade takes place in complete anonymity). Given the size of the order, it is highly likely that the trade would take place at a price different from the last trade price. Absent this order, when one or more market makers display their quotes on the Nasdaq system, their prices will not reflect the true state of demand and supply for Dell Computer stocks.

A Fragile Existence

What would crossing networks do if all Nasdaq market makers stop quoting prices on Dell Computer stocks? At what price would this order to buy 100,000 shares be executed? In the long run, it is inconceivable that any market can survive without directly affecting prices of items traded in it. Strictly speaking, a crossing network is just that, not a market. A market establishes prices; crossing networks take prices from other markets. The midpoint crossing might be appropriate in the context of specific types of trading strategies. If these strategies go out of fashion, crossing networks will have a tough time attracting significant order flows.

7.6 SUMMARY

This chapter discussed two types of trading systems: ECNs and crossing networks. The latter simply match buyers and sellers of stock at the midpoint of the best bid and offer established in a parallel market. In this context, we described the POSIT system. Such systems have a fundamental drawback: They depend on other markets to establish prices. By definition, POSIT can never be the sole market (or even the dominant one) for any given stock. It seems content to be a niche player.

ECNs evolved in the 1990s. They are simple electronic trading systems that execute trades by matching the highest bid with the lowest offer. As a group, these networks are responsible for close to a third of the total number of shares traded on the Nasdaq market. Thanks to Rule 390 (that prevents NYSE members from trading certain NYSE-listed stocks away from the exchange floor), ECNs have not been able to cause much harm to the latter exchange. But in late 1999, the NYSE relented[16] and repealed this rule. At the end of 1999, there were about nine ECNs in operation. The important ones are Instinet, Island, and Archipelago. The latter two have applied to the SEC for permission to become exchanges. This could potentially help them survive in an increasingly competitive marketplace.

The growth in the number of ECNs has made it difficult for both incumbents and newcomers to gain market share. Their ability to compete on price has shrunk; commissions are already terribly low. Island, for instance, appears to be making about 15 cents a share. These trading systems have basically been exploiting certain shortcomings in the Nasdaq market. In particular, they have been able to provide large investors an anonymous trading environment, in which they can trade directly with each other without having to pay a market maker's spread. ECNs such as Island have grown by intelligently exploiting standard computer systems to develop fast and efficient execution systems. In addition, they have been able to link with online brokers such as E*Trade and Schwab.

Unfortunately for these firms, Nasdaq (in particular), as well as the NYSE, appears to be taking steps toward setting up its own ECN-type trading system. Nasdaq, for instance, has proposed a central limit-order book with automated matching facility. The NYSE is talking about setting up an ECN-type facility, NYSE Direct+, for small order sizes. The story of electronic trading is getting more interesting. The next chapter presents brief snapshots of some of the main automated trading systems.

8

COMPUTERIZED
AUTOMATED
TRADING SYSTEMS

Electronic trading systems are computerized systems with electronic order books that can match buy and sell orders with relatively little or no human intervention. We have examined an emerging electronic trading system—electronic communications network (ECN), its business model, impacts, and challenges. Advances in technology and economic theory on markets have enabled ECNs as well as other types of financial markets to implement trading systems that can better match buyers and sellers than ever before. Although the fundamental principle of markets remains the same, the details of operation in many markets could differ significantly, which have profound economic implications for investors as well as the exchanges themselves. Some systems are rather straightforward in that they simply line up buy and sell orders in the order book by using the price-time priority rule and matching the highest bids with the lowest asks. Others use sophisticated optimization techniques (e.g., OptiMark System) to enable traders to pursue complex trading strategies.

This chapter examines four different trading systems: Arizona Stock Exchange (AZX), the OptiMark system, Primex, and bundle trading. At the time of writing this book, the OptiMark system suspended trading in the United States. It will be fascinating to see why such an interesting system would fail in practice. The common features to all these systems include

- Trading is order driven.
- Contents of the order book can be either closed or open.
- Investors' identity is not revealed to market participants.
- Systems can be operated as either continuous or call auctions.

8.1 ARIZONA STOCK EXCHANGE

Unlike other electronic trading systems such as POSIT and Instinet that are regulated as broker-dealer firms, the AZX is a regular stock exchange although exempt from some of the regulatory burdens imposed on the New York Stock Exchange (NYSE) and the Nasdaq market. Founded in 1990, it is the first exchange in the United States that is owned by a for-profit private company, AZX Inc. It is also the first trading system that publishes its open limit-order books over the Internet. Order and quote information from most other trading firms and exchanges are available only via private information vendors such as Bloomberg and Reuters. AZX offers two distinct trading mechanisms: a single-price call auction and a crossing service.

At the time of writing, AZX holds four call auctions every day: two in the morning and two in the afternoon. The crossing session is held in the evening. The first call auction is at 9:29 AM EST. Orders can be submitted from 9:00 AM onward for all stocks traded on the Nasdaq, NYSE, and American Stock Exchange (AMEX). The second auction is at 10:30 AM EST (orders accepted from 9:45 AM) and is limited to stocks traded on Nasdaq. The two afternoon sessions are at 2:20 PM and 5:00 PM. The order book for the crossing session, which is limited to Nasdaq stocks, takes place at 5:00 PM EST and is open from 4:25 PM.[1] Faced with low trading volumes, the exchange has been experimenting with the schedules for various calls. As might be expected, this can cause the timings listed above to become stale.

8.1.1 Trading Mechanism

Order Book

The AZX accepts limit buy and sell orders. The order book has two components: an open and a closed one. Orders submitted to the open book are anonymously displayed to the whole market (Figure 8.1). The contents of the closed section are, by definition, hidden from the market. However, if any orders from this section of the book are executed, the transaction amount and price are revealed to the market. AZX charges different commissions for each type of orders: 1 cent per share for those not displayed, and 1/2 cent for those displayed.

Competing to Trade

Before the appointed auction/crossing time, investors exchange their buy and sell indications by entering orders in the open order book. To attract trading interests from a large section of the investment community, the exchange publicizes order book contents over the Internet. The hope is that such advertisement will attract orders from multiple sources.

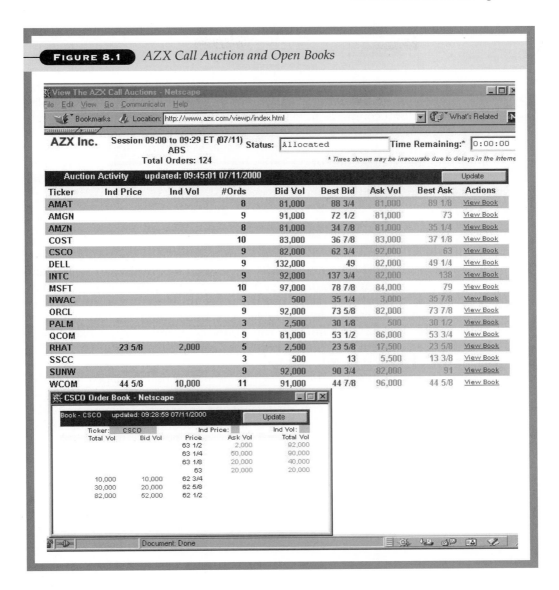

FIGURE 8.1 *AZX Call Auction and Open Books*

Any market with an open order book runs the risk that some traders might place orders that they are not serious about. With a view to either misleading the market or even manipulating it, very high buy orders and/or low sell orders could be placed early and removed just before the auction takes place. To prevent such abuse of the system, AZX imposes a penalty in the form of an order-cancellation fee. This fee does not apply to the closed section of the order book.

Automated Matching

The call auction is conducted by processing the contents of the order book by using an algorithm designed to find a price for each stock that balances demand and supply. This price also maximizes trading volume in that stock. When the system is open for new orders (as well as for order modifications and cancellations), the algorithm computes indicative prices by using orders already submitted to the system. At the appointed time, the final price is determined for each stock. Orders with limit prices better than or equal to this price are ranked. Those submitted to the open section of the order book are executed first. If two orders are priced identically, the order submitted first is given priority. Orders in the closed section are then filled in the same manner.

8.1.2 Competing for Order Flow

In recent years, the AZX was experiencing problems attracting order flow to the evening auction. The AZX was faced with a situation in which the 5 PM auction was drawing little attention from active traders, partly because many of them had been on the job since early in the morning (remember, the after-hours trading phenomenon took off mainly in late 1998, early 1999). Many money managers who did not participate in the intraday calls found it inconvenient to log off their order management systems to gain access to AZX through a dial-up PC connection or even its Windows-based software.

Early in 1998, with the hope of improving this situation, it managed to get the required permissions from the SEC to hold the 9:15 AM auction. In addition, it has negotiated with a variety of order management and order entry systems providers to provide access to its order book. It has also been looking to the growing list of online discount brokers and various ECNs to route their retail order flows to the AZX.

AZX today has about 275 customers, with just 30 to 40 using the system each day to execute a few hundred thousand shares each. The bulk of the orders come from "passive" money managers who run index funds and submit lists of orders in advance rather than interacting with the postings in the 15 minutes or so before the auction.

8.2 OptiMark System

The OptiMark trading system was an automated system that operated as a facility of the Pacific Stock Exchange as well as the Nasdaq market for about a year. Unlike most trading systems, which attempt to simply match the trading interests of their users regarding price and quantity, OptiMark goes further. It attempts to find a set of matches that maximize the mutual satisfaction of the participants. In addition to price and quantity, users can satisfy their trading preferences. The latter can be across a spectrum of prices and quantities, not just for a single price-quantity combination.

In other markets, traders can specify only a single price and quantity. OptiMark allows users to specify multiple price-quantity combinations, with varying levels of satisfaction (in the range of $0-1$) for each such combination. If an order (called a profile in the context of the multidimensional specification) is executed, the trade would be for only one specific price-quantity combination. The matching algorithm was designed to offer price improvement whenever feasible. Such improvement happens when a trade is executed at a price below (above) the stated limit bid (offer). Finally, the system was operated as a closed order book. It follows the principle of zero, pretrade information. The search for matches takes place through a series of multiprice call auctions every few minutes, depending on the level of trading interest in any specific stock.

8.2.1 Multidimensional Trading

A series of vignettes will best illustrate the unique multidimensional trading mechanism of OptiMark.

Simple Limit Orders

Let us assume that a trader is interested in buying a particular stock. He or she can submit a simple limit order. The information is represented graphically in Figure 8.2. The white portion represents 1.0 satisfaction or highest willingness to trade. The dark portion represents the region of zero satisfaction. The grids show volume increments of 1,000 shares each. Basically, the trader has submitted a

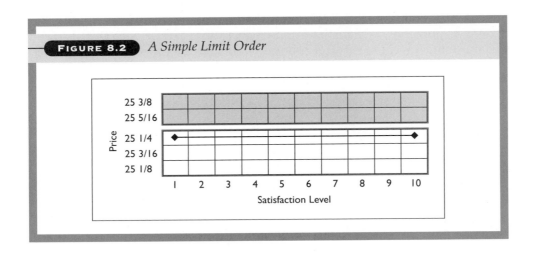

FIGURE 8.2   *A Simple Limit Order*

limit order to buy up to 10,000 shares of stock XYZ at $25 1/4 or better. These price and quantity details are entered into the buy section of the order book. The matching mechanism will use this information and search for an appropriate match for the order.

Complex Orders

There can be instances, however, when a trader is willing to trade different numbers of shares at varying price levels. Let us consider the case of one such person who wants to sell a large number of shares, say, 500,000, in a stock. The prevailing best bid is for 40,000 shares at $64 7/8. How will this trader go about completing his or her transaction?

In the non-OptiMark world, if the stock is listed on the NYSE or on the Nasdaq market, the investor can contact a floor broker or a broker-dealer and indicate to them that he or she has a larger-than-average selling interest in that stock. Unless the broker is an employee of the trader's firm, it is highly likely that the latter will inform the broker that he or she is looking to sell, say, 100,000 shares and would be willing to go as low as, say, $64 3/4, in other words, two ticks below the current best bid (assuming a tick equals $1/16). The broker will shop around for a "good deal." But given that he or she has to spend additional effort to process the information and search for an appropriate counterparty, the broker will also charge a higher than normal commission. Let's assume that by the prescribed time, he or she manages to sell up to 100,000 shares. Thanks to the large size, the best bid is now at $64 5/8. Now, the trader has to decide whether he or she should do another tranche of 100,000 or wait for the price to rise a bit. Irrespective of the decision, once the market learns about his or her selling interest, there will be a downward pressure on the stock price.

If the trader chooses to trade through OptiMark, he or she will only signal that he or she is an aggressive seller and is willing to go as low as $64 per share if someone (or a group of traders) is (are) willing to buy the full 500,000 shares in a single transaction (Figure 8.3). Due to concerns about market impact costs, the trader was unwilling to share this information with a human being. But he or she will not mind specifying it to a computerized matching system such as those used in the upstairs market. But as pointed out earlier, the execution service of the upstairs market comes at a steep price. OptiMark, however, charged the trader a fixed price per share irrespective of the number of shares traded.

Partial Satisfaction

Let us consider what OptiMark offers in a second scenario. A trader wants to buy 10,000 shares of stock. The current bid is at $39 3/4 for 1,000 shares. From his knowledge of the typical buying and selling interest for the stock, he knows that he can get the total order filled at $40 per share. At the same time, he expects some positive news about that stock and would like to complete the purchase quickly—this would require that he be willing to pay more than $40 per share.

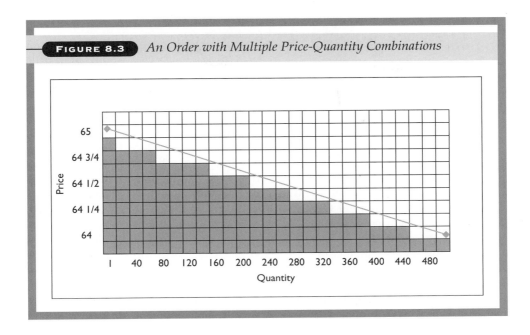

FIGURE 8.3 *An Order with Multiple Price-Quantity Combinations*

With OptiMark, he can specify his price preferences in the following manner: 10,000 (all or none) shares at $39 7/8 with satisfaction level of 1.0; 10,000 (all or none) shares at $40 with satisfaction of 0.90; 10,000 (all or none) shares at $40 1/8 and satisfaction 0.80; and so on (Figure 8.4).

These satisfaction levels indicate that he is willing to pay up to $39 7/8 without any hesitation; that he is willing to pay $40 per share but would do so rather

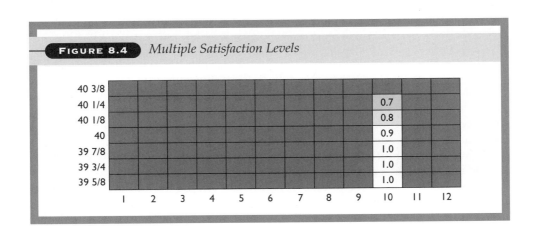

FIGURE 8.4 *Multiple Satisfaction Levels*

reluctantly; and that if absolutely necessary, he is ready to trade at $40 1/8, but he would like the system to know that the satisfaction at this price level is the lowest.

Sophisticated Trading Strategies

The OptiMark system also attempted to provide a solution to the trading problems faced by the most sophisticated traders. Individual investors have limited resources, and so they tend to be satisfied with placing straightforward orders. But institutional investors follow sophisticated investment strategies that in turn require complex trading tactics. Markets such as the NYSE and Nasdaq were not designed with these interests in mind. And as seen elsewhere, institutions are reluctant to expose their full trading interests to brokers and dealers. The Opti-Mark system is an attempt at providing a solution to the trading problems faced by sophisticated traders.

Trading strategies can include, for example, specifying limit prices that are pegged (or linked) to another market variable; for instance, a buyer can submit a bid that is priced at the national best bid plus one price increment ($1/16 or $1/8 as the case may be). At the beginning of every call, the OptiMark system will read in the national best bid and offer for every stock (this is possible as it is linked to the InterMarket Trading System) and price the pegged order appropriately. Such a strategy helps traders save time without having to keep track of every fluctuation in price in the continuous market such as NYSE or Nasdaq. Clearly, OptiMark's matching algorithm is the key to successfully fulfilling sophisticated trading strategies.

8.2.2 Matching Algorithm

In matching the various three-dimensional profiles submitted by its users, Opti-Mark used a patented set of rules—the search for the set of trades that maximize mutual satisfaction takes place in a two-stage process. Stage one is called the aggregation stage.

In the first stage, the algorithm takes into consideration all trading interests with 1.0 satisfaction. This means that if a profile has regions with discretion (or less than 1.0 satisfaction), these price-volume-satisfaction combinations will not be considered in the search for a match. If all trading interests have 1.0 satisfaction, the question of maximizing mutual satisfaction does not arise. A bunch of small trading interests can be aggregated and matched with a single large profile. The second stage, called the negotiation stage, includes any profiles that were not traded in stage one, plus all the profiles with partial satisfactions. Unlike the aggregation stage, mutual satisfaction does come into play here. This measure is defined as the product of the satisfaction of the buyer and seller.

The negotiation here is bilateral (i.e., between one buyer and one seller). The mutual satisfactions for all feasible combinations of buying and selling interests are computed and sorted in descending order. The algorithm will start with the match with the highest mutual satisfaction and go down the list, executing all feasible matches. One implication of this is that in any single call, trades in a single stock can take place at different prices. In traditional call auctions, the market process will search for the single price at which the maximum number of shares can be traded. The difference between traditional call auctions and OptiMark's calls is that the objective of single-price call auctions is to find the single price that maximizes the total number of shares traded whereas the objective of the latter is to find a set of trades that maximize mutual satisfaction. This three-dimensional problem is coded as a polynomial optimization problem and solved by using a computerized algorithm running on a supercomputer.

8.2.3 A Credible Promise

To provide credibility to its promise of anonymous trading, the OptiMark crossing system hired the services of the Computer Assurance Services Group of Deloitte & Touche to attest to the secrecy, security, and optimality of the system. Deloitte was responsible for independently assessing the design of information security and controls within the OptiMark system and was required to examine and report on OptiMark's assertions about related aspects of the system, including optimality. One of the tests performed was whether the system consistently output the same results from the same input information. In addition, the accounting firm reportedly posted a $50 million bond to guarantee no leaks of traders' intentions from OptiMark.

8.2.4 Competing to Trade

When OptiMark was launched as a facility of the Pacific Stock Exchange in January 1999, its goal was to steal market share primarily from the NYSE, the market, as we know, that has dominated trading in listed stocks for over a century. To sustain itself as a profitable market, any trading system must attract significant amounts of order flow from a large number of traders. As described earlier, the ability of any system to succeed depends partly on the particular structure of the trading mechanism.

How well did OptiMark perform? Evidence indicated that the firm was having a rather tough time attracting any meaningful levels of liquidity during its operation.[2] This happened despite the fact that the system was backed by a very sophisticated matching algorithm. This section looks at a couple of issues that could explain the lower-than-expected performance of the system.

Zero Transparency

The OptiMark trading system was the only market during the time of its operation that did not disclose the contents of its order book. The idea obviously was to provide the maximum possible degree of anonymity to its users. But in pursuing this strategy, the firm appeared to have taken on a significant amount of risk. Wall

Street traders place a high value on information about the trading interests of other traders in the market. The structure of the NYSE trading floor is designed to provide privileged access to such information to its floor-trading community. Everything else being the same, the lack of order book information made it difficult for OptiMark to attract orders from other traders in the market. As discussed elsewhere, exchanges prefer to publish some of or all the order book contents as this would enable a single trader to negotiate with a large number of traders simultaneously.

Traders who traded by using OptiMark were completely in the blind about the level of trading interest in any given stock. As they have to choose from among multiple trading systems to execute their trades, the lack of information made it difficult for them to choose OptiMark. The risk they had was that they would send a large order to OptiMark, wait for a couple of calls, and then when the system failed to find a match, withdraw the order and try to execute it in a different market. Most traders might be unwilling to take such a risk.

A related issue is that of price discovery. As traders did not have access to order book information, they found it difficult to form reasonable expectations of the state of demand or supply for any stock. Accordingly, they were unable to improve the pricing of their standing orders. This resulted in lower competition to trade, making the market less efficient.

OptiMark attempted to provide a partial solution to this problem. It signed an agreement with Autex, an information service where traders could indicate their trading interests in any stock. When a large investor sent a sizeable order to OptiMark, he or she could use Autex to signal the market that he or she had placed an order with OptiMark. The investor indicated the name of the stock and was not required to provide information about whether he or she was a buyer or seller; neither did the investor reveal any price information.

It Was Too Complicated

The approach adopted by OptiMark was to use its sophisticated order-matching algorithm to offset the lack of transparency. Its target group was made up largely of institutional investors who value privacy. This section of the trading community had been proactive in using the new electronic crossing networks introduced in the past few years. Compared with the networks, OptiMark offered a much superior matching service. This complexity may, however, prove to be its downfall. Many users complained about the complexity of the OptiMark system. Apparently, the market in general, and the trading community in particular, was not yet ready for this level of sophistication.

One way to resolve this dilemma was to argue that the initial version of the OptiMark trading system was an experiment in designing and implementing an automated process that mimics existing markets and, at the same time, provided some value to the trading community. Given the inevitability of the ongoing move toward electronic trading systems, it is highly likely that future systems will have to adopt a more user-friendly trading philosophy.

✴ 8.3 PRIMEX

The race to set up a potentially dominant electronic trading system grew more heated in early June 1999 when a group of leading brokerage firms, Merrill Lynch, Goldman Sachs, and Bernard L. Madoff, announced a plan to launch Primex. The new system is designed as an electronic auction rather than as a traditional ECN that automatically matches buyers and sellers. Nasdaq was scheduled to begin operation of the Primex auction system on September 10, 2001. At first, the system is trading all Nasdaq 100 Index and Standard and Poor (S&P) 100 Index securities. Later, trading will be expanded to include most U.S. securities.[3]

Initial comments published in the media indicate that the system will be open to broker-dealers, institutions, and individual investors, although only registered broker-dealers will be able to conduct trades. It thus seems as if Primex will focus on serving the broker-to-broker market. As will become clear soon, this appears to be another attempt by firms with a vested interest in existing market structures to prolong the life of their current labor-intensive business models.

8.3.1 Alliance with Nasdaq

To surmount the problem of gaining critical mass, the group hopes to enter into some form of alliance with either the Nasdaq or NYSE. In December 1999, reports started floating around that Primex had reached an initial agreement with Nasdaq. At the time this book was being written, Nasdaq was scheduled to launch Primex auction system on September 10, 2001. The system will run on a separate network and operates as a facility of the Nasdaq. The Primex auction system will be a voluntary service for all NASD member firms and other entities they may sponsor. Non-NASD members will be able to access the system through a participant by becoming a sponsored subscriber of the participant.

8.3.2 Replicating Floor Trading: Price Improvement

The proposed system attempts to electronically replicate certain portions of the bargaining and negotiation process that takes place among market makers on Nasdaq or among floor brokers and specialists on the floor of the NYSE. Primex will maintain an electronic order book; the contents of which will be displayed to all registered brokers who have signed on to use the system.

An interesting difference between Primex and ECNs is that the latter do not allow for price improvement. For instance, if the best bid for a stock at the ECN is $40 (for 1,500 shares), a market sell order will be executed at that price. Price improvement happens when it gets executed at $40.125! Let's assume that a sell order for 1,000 shares of company XYZ stock at the best market price is submitted. The broker could fill the order by matching it against the best bid (at $40). If the order is forwarded to Primex, the system will expose the selling interest to all bidders who are logged on. Any buyer who wishes to trade with the incoming order will be given the opportunity to improve the highest bid of $40. If the highest bidder bids $40.125, he or she will win the order and the seller will sell the order at $40.125, which is $0.125 more than the initial best bid of $40 for a total gain of $125 ($0.125 × 1,000 shares = $125) by using Primex.

The system has the ability to publicize the contents of the order book over a wide network of brokers, one that could be potentially larger than the floor of the NYSE. In addition, it allows brokers to compete for a trade by improving on the best bid or offer (the lowest offer in the example above) existing in the market at that moment. This is the only new feature offered by Primex that is not offered by any other electronic trading system in use today. The exception to this is the OptiMark system. But the process of offering price improvement is different in the latter system because OptiMark's zero transparency fundamentally changes the dynamics of the auction process.

In a sense, Primex is automating the role of the specialist on the floor of the NYSE, merely moving the price improvement process beyond the confines of the exchange floor. For those that trade on Nasdaq, Primex will offer a price improvement process similar to that of the NYSE. Traditionally, this service is rendered by a process of negotiation between a large investor and a broker-dealer. The implementation of the OptiMark system has already brought an element of price improvement to the Nasdaq market.

8.3.3 Challenges

Risk of Advertising

The designers of Primex appear to be focusing mainly on improving the price discovery process on the NYSE floor and the Nasdaq market. But they seem to be ignoring a key aspect of our markets: Large investors do not like to publicize their trading interests. Although investors are interested in price discovery, at the same time, they do not want to pay too high a price for it. Exposing an order over a widely accessed network would surely lead to an increase in market impact.

If an investor places a large buy order, say, for 10,000 shares, at $40.25 or better, one or more brokers could simply log on to a different market (assuming that Primex is not the only trading system where this stock is being traded) and place their own buy orders at slightly higher prices. As described elsewhere, institutional investors are concerned about such reactions from other traders in the marketplace. Hence they prefer systems that reduce the impact of their large trades on market prices. Unless Primex can convince large institutional investors that using its network will reduce overall trading costs, we predict that it will have a tough time capturing critical mass. Having an electronic version of the NYSE specialist might not be sufficient.

Relying on the Broker-Dealer Network

The current design of Primex continues to place brokers in the center of the market. This reliance on professional immediacy suppliers surely ignores the ongoing trend in markets around the world to provide facilities for investors to trade directly with each other. It is possible that by the time the Primex system is implemented, changes will have been introduced to allow investors' orders to interact directly with each other.

Conflict of Interests

Primex's current design also ignores some of the relationships between established players. Merrill Lynch and Goldman Sachs are important players in the equity markets. Bernard Madoff is one of the largest market makers in the third market (the group of broker-dealers who make markets in NYSE-listed stocks away from the floor of that exchange). The media expects these institutions to commit the lion's share of their trades to Primex. What it ignores is that some of these institutions have invested in many other electronic trading systems. Goldman Sachs, in particular, has taken equity stakes in numerous trading ventures: Archipelago, Brut, OptiMark, and Wit Capital. Merrill is an investor in Brut and OptiMark. In addition, Goldman Sachs and Merrill are known to be loyal to the NYSE, routing the lion's share of their orders to the exchange floor.

This leads us to an interesting question. Are the leading trading institutions, who have a lot to lose from the demise of traditional markets, simply hedging their future by betting on as many electronic trading systems as possible? If this is true, and there is no reason for us to think otherwise, then is Primex one more attempted shot in the dark? The lack of conviction in the quality of any single system leads one to discount the commitment of Merrill, Goldman, and Bernard to the success of Primex.

In summary, Primex seems to be an attempt to improve on one aspect of the NYSE. It allows a larger number of traders to trade with an incoming order by improving on the existing bid or offer. But it ignores that traders might be concerned more about reducing market impact than the possibility of getting an improvement of a few cents on the price. It is being founded by an illustrious group of founders. But these firms are simultaneously backing numerous competing electronic trading systems.

8.4 BUNDLE TRADING

The equity markets, including the electronic systems mentioned above, have traditionally followed an asset-by-asset trading and clearing mechanism. For example, if you want to buy a portfolio of stocks you have to buy each individual stock separately. There are no markets available that allow you to purchase a bundle of stocks at a time. We learn from modern portfolio theory that investors prefer to hold a diversified portfolio of financial assets rather than an individual asset. For institutional investors who manage an index fund, they have to maintain a portfolio to match the investment performance of the U.S. equity markets as represented by the S&P 500 stock index. As the composition of the index changes, the fund manager has to rebalance the portfolio by trading a basket of stocks. Using current financial market arrangements, fund managers have to trade stocks individually, a process that not only incurs large transaction costs but also increases the uncertainties of the overall cost of the portfolio. Bundle trading allows market participants to trade assets in bundles or baskets in arbitrary proportions. Therefore, an individual investor or a fund manager can pay more attention to the overall cost of the bundle, which essentially matters to the fund's performance, rather than the cost of individual stocks.

We use a trading example to illustrate the benefits of bundle trading. Assume that a fund manager decides to rebalance her portfolio and wants to execute the following trades: buy 100 shares of IBM, 200 shares of Microsoft, 125 shares of Cisco; sell 200 shares of GM, 150 shares of Ford, and 50 shares of Chrysler (Table 8.1). If she thinks that the previous day's close prices are fair values for all six stocks and places limit orders based on the prices as displayed in column (ii), her buy order for IBM and Cisco and sell order for GM will not be executed according to the next day's trading ranges for these stocks (column [iii]). Instead of having a balanced portfolio, the investor remains overexposed to the auto sector and underexposed to the technology sector. The investor could use bundle trading to avoid such trading risks. She could have specified a limit-order price of $10,675 (line [a]) for the whole basket

TABLE 8.1 *A Bundle Trading Example*

Stock	Shares (i)	Previous Close Price (ii)	Next Day's Trading Range (iii)	Next Day's Worst Price (iv)	Trade Executed? Yes/No
IBM	+100	98	$98^{1/2}-98^{3/4}$	$98^{3/4}$	N
Microsoft	+200	$152^{1/2}$	$150^{1/2}-151^{1/2}$	$151^{1/2}$	Y
Cisco	+125	73	$73^{1/4}-74$	74	N
GM	−200	$81^{1/4}$	$80^{1/4}-81$	$80^{1/4}$	N
Ford	−150	119	$120-120^{1/2}$	120	Y
Chrysler	−50	93	$95-96^{1/2}$	95	Y
(a) = $\Sigma(i)*(ii)$		10675			
(b) = $\Sigma(i)*(iv)$				10625	

of orders as shown in Table 8.1. The order as a bundle would have been executed with certainty, because the highest cost of the bundle, based on the worst prices of the assets during the day (i.e., highest price for buys and lowest price for sells) would have been $10,625 (line [b]), which is still lower than the investor's valuation of $10,675.

There are two major advantages of trading bundle assets. First, investors can trade a bundle of assets simultaneously in a unified market instead of dealing with separate orders. The investor can be certain that he or she will have a balanced portfolio at all times. Second, in real life, an investor may need a bundle of resources that cannot be matched at all by any single seller. The bundle-trading mechanism provides the function of market intermediary, automatically recombining resources from different sellers to satisfy the buyer's request for a specific bundle. By offering traders an additional trading option, the bundle-trading mechanism increases the liquidity of the markets.

The automated bundle-matching program matches orders by solving a mathematical optimization problem. The logic of our bundle matching mechanism can be summarized as follows:

1. *Order Eligibility.* A bundle is matched with one or more other bundles under the following conditions:
   - For each financial instrument in the bundle, a buy order must be matched with a sell order.
   - The buy price is greater or equal to the sell price.
2. *Transaction Price.* The transaction price will be automatically calculated by solving the mathematical problem. Traders will get prices no worse than the price they submit.
3. *Trade Quantity.* If a match is found based on order eligibility, the trade will take place for a quantity that is the maximum number of shares allowed to be traded based on the availability of the matched bundles.
4. *Trade Priority.* For matched bundles, the trading system will give priority to those orders that will maximize the trade surplus. In other words, a higher buy price has higher priority, and a lower sell price has higher priority. For the same price priority level, trade priority is on a first-come first-served basis.

The bundle matching mechanism is able to find one-to-one, one-to-many, or many-to-many matches between offers. This type of match requires sophisticated computation and is too complicated to be handled manually. Computerized automated matching is the ideal solution for this type of problem. The Financial Bundle Trading System (FBTS) was developed as an experimental financial market at the Center for Research in Electronic Commerce, the University of Texas at Austin. The system uses a distributed object architecture. The market houses a Web server and an Internet remote application server. On the trader side, the trading application is implemented by using Java applet. Each time a trader wants to access the market, he or she will go to the market's Web site and dynamically download the trading applet. The applet is used as an interface for an investor to submit orders and view account and market information. There are many advantages in using this approach. First, it guarantees that the trade application can be deployed without additional effort on different computing platforms. Traders can always access the updated software and their account information, which is stored centrally on the server side. Second, the applet is a full-fledged application that can communicate dynamically and interactively with the application server. For example, market price information and open order status will be dynamically updated on the applet.

8.5 SUMMARY

In this chapter, we have discussed different types of computerized automated trading systems. AZX implements a call auction, which executes trading at discrete times, compared with continuous trading in the other three markets. As pointed out earlier, a matching algorithm is critical to an electronic trading system. The matching mechanism at AZX is relatively straightforward compared with sophisticated trading and matching rules implemented at OptiMark, Primex, and FBTS. Optimark allows traders to submit orders with multiple price-quantity combinations and varying levels of satisfaction, whereas Primex attempts to electronically replicate some bargaining and negotiation process that takes place on physical trading floors and provides the function of price improvement for market orders. FBTS allows traders to buy or sell a bundle of securities. All these markets maintain an electronic order book. However, the rules regarding to the access of the book are different. AZX has an open as well as a hidden book. By contrast, the OptiMark system's order book is totally hidden. All those differences have significant impacts on trading costs, trading strategy, overall market performance, and intermarket competition. Although technology provides endless possibility of designing and implementing markets, creating an optimal market is not an easy task because the interests of various market participants are not necessarily in harmony. As we have more competition in the exchange marketplace, the task of designing a fair and efficient market mechanism is more important than ever before.

9

OVERSEAS FINANCIAL

MARKETS

This chapter discusses some of the world's most innovative and fast-changing financial markets. Significant changes are happening in financial exchanges all over the world. Rapid advances of computer and communication technology have revolutionized the way financial instruments are traded. Companies want to be listed in a market that can best serve the firms' interest. Investors want to trade in a market that has a high liquidity and great transparency. As a result, the financial exchanges have taken steps to build on their comparative advantages and improve their competitiveness. A growing number of existing exchanges have formed alliances or merges into a super exchange to be more competitive and become more attractive to investors. Many exchanges in the world also look at computerized trading as a way to improve their trading efficiency and increase market transparency. The exchanges we discuss in this chapter clearly represent these two trends.

In Europe, the financial markets have never been more dynamic. The adoption of the Euro—the common currency of the European Monetary Union (EMU) countries—makes it increasingly feasible to create a pan-European super bourse that crosses borders and geographic boundaries. After an overview of the progress of the development of the pan-European market, we discuss some of the individual stock markets in Europe. We introduce the OM Group, the leading company in the world in building and operating computerized financial markets. Next, we discuss the Swiss Exchange (SWX) and Eurex. The latter is a derivative exchange developed by the SWX and the German Futures and Options Exchange. Furthermore, we describe Easdaq (European Association of Securities Dealers Automated Quotation), the European stock market for high-growth companies. Modeled on the successful Nasdaq in the United States, Easdaq aims to become a common marketplace to all of Europe's high-tech companies. Recently, it has been acquired by Nasdaq and will be renamed Nasdaq Europe. Lastly, we move our discussion away from Europe. Traditionally, financial exchanges have been organized as nonprofit entities. The Australian Stock Exchange (ASX) along with the OM Stockholm is one of the first to be for profit in the world. We discuss the recent demutualization process and subsequent changes at the ASX.

9.1 DEVELOPMENT OF A PAN-EUROPEAN STOCK MARKET

The European financial markets are experiencing a remarkable shake-up that will reshape the financial landscape of Europe in the future. Today's European market has become a fierce battleground of multiple forces. Following EMU's unification of Europe's currency, Europeans are rapidly developing an American-style equity culture. Compared with the U.S. stock market, European financial markets are smaller and more fragmented. For example, current German stock market capitalization is only 38 percent of gross domestic product (GDP) compared with 138 percent in the United States. But the picture will soon change as a growing number of European firms are raising capital in equity markets. Markets across Europe are facing consolidation to bring down transaction costs. But competition is intense. First come the Americans. Facing tough competition within the United States, major exchanges in the United States are aggressively going global. In 1999, Nasdaq formally unveiled its plan to launch a pan-European equity market. Aspired to create the first global stock exchange that does 24-hour continuous trading, Nasdaq plans to link Nasdaq Europe with Nasdaq in the United States and the recently launched Nasdaq Japan. Meanwhile, new beasts are also emerging in Europe. Tradepoint,[1] an electronic trading network based in London, is developing its own online European trading network that vows to provide low-cost trading to investors. Deutsche Boerse, in 1997, created Neuer Market, an equity market that targets growth companies in Europe. Today, Neuer Market has already become a dominant partner of EURO.NM, an alliance of new markets that are dedicated to high-growth companies; it provides a single access of information and trading. Facing all these, established exchanges in Europe such as London Stock Exchange (LSE), Frankfurt Stock Exchange, and Paris Bourse have been desperately searching for a counterstrategy to stay competitive. Numerous deals and alliances were formed and then later abandoned. This section discusses the evolution of the financial markets in Europe.

9.1.1 Euronext

In March 2000, the Paris, Amsterdam, and Brussels stock exchanges announced plans to merge and form an integrated market, named Euronext. However, the story started a few years back.

In July 1998, the LSE and Frankfurt Stock Exchange, the first and third largest equity markets in Europe, announced a strategic alliance. The goal was to create a low-cost and efficient market infrastructure. Under the agreement, the two exchanges would take steps to harmonize trading rules, operation hours, and computer systems. The deal particularly enraged the Paris Stock Exchange, Europe's second largest equity market, which was also in an alliance talk with Frankfurt. The London-Frankfurt alliance made it clear that they would welcome other European exchanges to participate, but other exchanges would have to be junior partners. For example, if Paris joined the alliance it would get only 20 percent stake of the alliance with 40 percent ownership each for London and Frankfurt. To French financiers, it only aggravated the insult. The Paris exchange then quickly started to plan its own alliance with other European markets such as Milan and Madrid.

In November 1998, after exchanges in Madrid, Milan, and Amsterdam all expressed their interest in joining the London-Frankfurt alliance, the Paris exchange finally changed its mind and decided to participate in the Anglo-German alliance. In September 1999, eight European stock exchanges, including London, Frankfurt, Paris, Amsterdam, Brussels, Madrid, Milan, and Zurich, announced their collective desire to develop a pan-European equity market. The deal would require the exchanges to adopt common rules and regulations for stock trading and develop a single platform for trading blue-chip stocks.

Did Paris Bourse really put its national pride and its earlier battle with the London-Frankfurt behind? Although the agreement of the eight exchanges created a great momentum in developing a single European market, the negotiation between them was never smooth. First came the failure of agreeing on plans for a single trading platform. Later, the exchanges instead planned to create a virtual market that would link their trading systems together. But eventually the alliance fell apart. One of the main reasons was that the Frankfurt Deutsche Boerse wanted to push its Xetra trading system to be the future platform that other exchanges would have to converge to. The idea was resisted by other exchanges.

Then finally came the merger of the exchanges of Paris, Amsterdam, and Brussels. The merger created continental Europe's largest stock market, still trailing LSE in market capitalization. According to the merger agreement, Paris will concentrate on blue-chip companies while Amsterdam will trade derivatives and Brussels will become the center for small- and medium-sized company listings. The merger is largely seen as an attempt by the Paris Bourse to act as a counterweight to the London and Frankfurt exchanges. The next move of Euronext is to continue to expand. It had talks with London's Liffe derivative market. Their potential merger targets include Luxembourg, Milan, Madrid, and Zurich.

The merged exchange uses an order-driven trading system based on the French NSC system. At the end of December 2000, 1,653 companies, including 437 from outside Euronext home countries, listed at Euronext, with a total market capitalization of EUR 2,420 billion. The exchange had a good start in 2000. Trades totaled EUR 1,706.67 billion, 59 percent more than the previous year.

9.1.2 Ups and Downs of iX

Less than two months after the forming of Euronext, London and Frankfurt exchanges unveiled their response, which would overshadow the Euronext. They formed an alliance in May 2000 to create a joint financial market named iX (International Exchange), and Milan and Madrid exchanges signed to merger within the future. They would also set up a separate market for technology stocks in a joint venture with Nasdaq. The new technology market, Nasdaq iX, would combine the two exchanges' segments for high-growth companies—London's techMark and Frankfurt's Neuer Market. The merger would create the world's third largest equity market, trailing the New York Stock Exchange (NYSE) and Nasdaq.

However, the newly formed exchange was short-lived. The planned merger between LSE and Deutsche Boerse collapsed in September. The event that helped sink the merger was the surprise takeover bid for LSE from OM Group, a financial technology conglomerate that owns Sweden's Stockholm Stock Exchange (SSE),[2] which we also discuss in this chapter. After LSE quickly rejected the initial bid, OM increased its bid to as much as $1.45 billion. But the new bid was not received well by LSE either. After all these, it seems that LSE is still unsure about the path it will pursue in the future.

9.1.3 Global Equity Market

Nasdaq's expansion in Europe caused serious concerns for its archrival—the NYSE. After the initial iX merger announcement, the NYSE and Euronext were quick to reveal that they got an even bigger deal. In June 2000, 10 of the world's top exchanges, including the NYSE, Tokyo, Toronto, Hong Kong, Australian, Mexico, Sao Paolo, and the bourses of the newly formed Euronext, announced that they were planning to set up a 24-hour, $20 trillion global market controlling 60 percent of the world equity market. The Global Equity Market (GEM) will attempt to link the trading systems of the 10 exchanges and trade global blue-chip companies in an order book passed from one time zone to the next.

9.1.4 "You Ain't Seen Nothing Yet"

According to Howard Davies, chairman of the Financial Services Authority in London, "You ain't seen nothing yet," declared when he was addressing the competition among stock exchanges in Europe. Right now, exchanges in Europe as well as in the United States and other continents are busy positioning themselves for the next round of competition. Following the initial merger and alliance announcement, a lot of details are yet to be worked out. A lot of deals are yet to be started and firmed. Compared with the United States, the clearing and settlement process in Europe is far more complicated. But none of the deals have really addressed that problem.

Politically, competition to become Europe's future financial capital has been heating up in recent years. London has traditionally been the financial center. But it seems London, with its recent technology and management problems, has lost its momentum to its continental competitors Paris and Frankfurt. Technologically, trading on the Internet is a reality. Emerging electronic markets such as Tradepoint and Jiway are offering low-cost trading and winning more businesses from traditional exchanges. To investors, it does not really matter where the market is physically located as long as they can access the market electronically. But investors do want to trade in a liquid market with easy trading and settlement process. Although it is important for exchanges in Europe to realize in this global economy that they can no longer protect their markets with national borders and have to join forces, they have to put politics aside and understand how they can deliver value to investors at the Internet age. In today's global financial market, technology, economy of scale, and liquidity are the most important factors. There is a long way to go for exchanges and the newly formed entities.

9.2 OM GROUP

The hostile bid for LSE has made OM Group and its CEO Per E. Larsson well known in the world's financial world. Relatively a newcomer in the exchange business, OM Group is one of the most innovative financial firms in the world. The OM Group has two major businesses: exchange market and technology. A pioneer in many respects, it operates the world's first for-profit exchange market, OM Stockholm, which is a derivative exchange in Sweden. In 1999, OM Stockholm merged with the the Stockholm Stock Exchange to form OM Stockholm Exchange. The newly formed exchange is a subsidiary of OM Group and aims to become a single marketplace that offers a comprehensive range of products including equities, bonds, commodities, foreign exchange, and derivatives. Besides operating organized exchanges, OM Group has strong expertise in the entire transaction chain, including creating systems that support a new marketplace, clearing, and settlement. In addition to being the vendor of various financial trading systems all over the world, OM Group operates the energy trading system at California Power Exchange (CalPX). It has also assumed responsibility for the operation of the two Nordic electricity exchanges: Nord Pool in Oslo and Finland's EL-EX. Recently, OM and Morgan Stanley Dean Witter (MSDW) have teamed up to establish Jiway,[3] an online cross-border European exchange. This section discusses various activities across the OM Group ranging from stock and bond trading at SSE and OM CLICK Exchange System to Nordic Exchange (NOREX) and Jiway.

9.2.1 Computerized Equity Trading System: SAX

In Sweden, equity is traded at the SSE whereas derivative products are handled at OM Stockholm. The plans are for trading in equities and derivatives to be completely integrated at the OM Stockholm Exchange. We first discuss the trading systems at the SSE.

Since 1990, trading at the SSE has been based on the computerized trading system SAX (Stockholm Automated Exchange). With SAX, trading no longer takes place on the exchange floor. Instead, traders operate from their own offices via PCs connected to the SAX computers at the exchange. The trading system, SAX2000, is an order-driven trading system. Bids and offers are automatically matched to generate deals when price, volume, and other order conditions are met. For large trading lots, deals may be made via telephone, but they still have to be entered manually into the system. The traders can thus enter their orders without having to be in personal contact with the other party. The system continuously broadcasts changes in the market. Information is displayed in real time in the form of order books, market summaries, concluded deals, index information, and other reports. All traders get the information at the same time.

The SAX2000 system consists of three main parts: the central SAX2000 system, a network, and a local trading environment at member firms. The local trading system usually consists of a number of workstations that are connected to the trading network via a server. The member firms can either develop their own local systems to interact with the SAX2000 system or buy a system from a third-party supplier. An alternative is to use the trading software developed by OM Technology—SaxessII. The main principle of the trading system is that orders sent from a workstation are registered and time stamped by the central SAX2000 system. SAX2000 then sends updated order information simultaneously to all authorized traders so that they can follow the market developments on their workstations. An important function in SAX2000 is multicasting. With this function, a transaction from the central system to the communication computer is copied and multicasted to all connected workstations and computers simultaneously. The multicast function is used to give all traders quick and fair information about changes to the order books and executed trades.

Most of the trading in the SSE occurs in the trading lot market, where shares are traded in amounts of trading lots (hundred shares). To maintain an efficient market for small orders, a specific odd-lot market has been developed in SAX2000 system. The two markets are integrated in such a way that the remaining odd-lot portion of a larger order is automatically moved to the odd-lot market if the order's volume falls below that of a trading lot.

Similar to the NYSE, the SSE starts its trading day with an opening call session during which traders can enter limit orders. The order book is not revealed during this opening session. Orders for each security are accumulated and the opening price is determined at the level where most shares can be traded. Once trading for a specific stock opens, continuous trading begins at the SSE. During continuous trading, all order books are open to the traders with the bids recorded on the left side and the offers on the right.

9.2.2 SOX: The Automated Bond Trading System

SOX is the SSE's marketplace for trading bonds. One of the major advantages of SOX is that traders have access to a large number of bonds in one and the same place. Current information regarding trading and the prices of the various bonds is easily available in the daily press or via the Internet.

Bond trading first started in SSE in 1991 and has gained significantly in popularity in Sweden since then. Formerly, the tax system made savings in bonds less attractive than equities. However, since 1991 the same tax rules apply to savings in bonds as to other forms of savings.

Bonds Traded on SOX

Bonds traded on SOX are primarily aimed at smaller and medium-sized investors. The borrowers are banks, home loan institutions, the Swedish State (through the Swedish National Debt Office), and other companies that choose to borrow money by issuing bonds. The different types of bonds traded on SOX include bond loans, subordinated debentures, and indexed loans. The difference between bond loans and subordinated debentures is that bonds usually have a superior right of priority if the borrower is forced to suspend payments, which means that subordinated debentures should provide a higher yield because the risk is greater. There are two special types of bonds traded on SOX: inflation-linked bonds and indexed bonds.

Inflation-Linked Bonds Inflation-linked bonds are issued by the State through the Swedish National Debt Office and are the only type of bond that provides protection against inflation. Inflation-linked bonds guarantee a real rate of interest (i.e., a nominal rate of interest minus inflation) on both the capital investment and the yield. Inflation-linked bonds exist as both coupon bonds and zero-coupon bonds.

Indexed Bonds The yield on an indexed bond is not determined in advance but rather depends on the development of the underlying index to which the bond is connected, usually a share index. If the index for the market in question has fallen during the period, the holder receives no yield on maturity, although the nominal amount is always repaid. If, however, the index has increased, the holder receives a yield calculated on the basis of the increase in the index for the market, in addition to the nominal amount. Indexed bonds thus have the potential to provide a higher yield than customary bonds. At the same time, there is a risk that you will not receive any yield at all.

Trading

An investor can buy or sell bonds on SOX through a bank or a security company. The investor must hold a securities account at the Swedish Central Securities Depository (VPC), which handles the registration of ownership of bonds. Similar to stock trading, the investor gives a buy or sell order to the bank or the broker, who places the order in the SOX system, where a transaction is then carried out against a corresponding order. As the SAX system, SOX is designed to facilitate trading via the Internet. When a transaction is carried out in SOX, information regarding the transaction is sent via the bank to VPC, where the bonds are transferred from the seller's to the buyer's securities account. Simultaneously, payment takes place via the parties' banks. As confirmation of the transaction, the investor will receive a contract note from the bank and a securities notification from the VPC.

In Sweden, many banks have their own bonds, and it is possible to buy or sell those bonds at banks. One of the major advantages of SOX is that investors have access to a large number of bonds in a single marketplace. Investors can easily find out information about the different bonds and choose the one that best suits their investment objectives. Compiled information regarding interest rates and prices for SOX bonds is available on the business pages in the daily press. It is also possible to find current information on text TV and on the SSE's home page, where prices are published continuously, subject to a 15-minute delay.

9.2.3 OM CLICK Exchange System

Although the OM CLICK Exchange System was originally developed to support derivative trading at OM Stockholm, the system has been marketed by OM Technology to support exchanges all over the world. To date, the OM CLICK Exchange System has been implemented at 13 exchanges throughout the world including the American Stock Exchange (AMEX), the derivative market of the ASX, and the Vienna Stock Exchange.

The OM CLICK Exchange System features an integrated order book. It supports different types of orders including fill-or-kill, immediate-or-cancel, good-till-cancel, and rest-of-day orders.[4] One special type of order that the system implements is combination orders. There are many advantages in using combination orders. An investor can use combination orders to take advantage of arbitrage opportunities in the market. The combination order will automatically be executed based on the relative prices for different stocks or derivatives so that the investor does not have to continuously monitor the price movement for different assets. Here, we use an example to illustrate how a combination order is executed in the OM CLICK Exchange System.

Suppose that a combination order has two assets: A1550 and A1552. Figure 9.1 displays the order books for these two assets before and after the combination order CO12101. The combination order indicates a quantity of 10 shares and a limit buy price of 65 with the ratio of A1550 and A1552 being 1:1 for each combination order (Figure 9.1). After the combination order is entered, the system automatically generates two derived orders based on the limit price of the combination order and current market prices for the two assets. For asset A1550, a derived order (buy 10@9) is generated, which means that if the derived order (buy 10@9) can be executed, the other part of the combination order can be executed based on the A1552's market price of 56. Similarly, a derived order (buy 10@54) is created for asset A1552 because the market price for A1550 is 11 (Figure 9.1).

FIGURE 9.1 *Order Book for Combination Orders*

Market Prices:

Asset	Bid Price	Qty	Ask Price	Qty
A1550	8	10	11	10
A1552	54	10	56	10

CO12101 10@65 bid (A1550, A1552; 1:1), market price 67--->

Asset	Bid Price	Qty	Ask Price	Qty
A1550	8, 9	10	11	10
A1552	54, 54	10	56	10
CO12101	65	10		

Derived orders

The derived orders are monitored continuously based on the market prices. When the market prices change, the derived orders are recalculated (see Figure 9.2). For example, if someone submits an order for asset A1550 (sell 10@10) that changes the current market price from 11 to 10, the derived order for asset A1552 will be changed to (buy 10@55) so that the limit price for the combination order remains 65. If somebody submits an order that hits one of the derived orders, that will trigger the combination order to be executed. For example, an order (sell 10@55) for asset A1552 will automatically initiate the combination order. After the execution, the combination order as well as its derived orders will be deleted from the order books.

The OM CLICK Exchange System also has some features that are essential for a computerized trading system:

- *Adaptable.* The system can easily be configured to fit the special needs of different exchanges. For example, the trading time and products in the market can easily be configured to suit the needs of individual exchanges.

- *Scalable.* The architecture of the system allows additional servers to be added to handle more users with high trading volume. Expansion in this form is much more efficient than replacing old servers with completely new machines.

- *Integrated.* The OM CLICK Exchange System can be easily integrated with analytical tools and other office systems such as spreadsheet and word processing. It is easy for both trading members and exchange staff to use the system.

FIGURE 9.2 *Execution of Combination Orders*

Asset	Bid Price	Qty	Ask Price	Qty
A1550	8, **9**	10	10, 11	10
A1552	54, **55**	10	56	10
CO12101	65	10		

When the market price changes, the derived orders are recalculated.

Asset	Bid Price	Qty	Ask Price	Qty
A1550	8, **9**	10	10, 11	10
A1552	54, **55**	10	56	10
CO12101	65	10		

sell 10@55

When somebody hits one of the derived orders, the combination order is automatically executed.

Asset	Bid Price	Qty	Ask Price	Qty
A1550	8	10	11	10
A1552	54	10	56	10

When the combination order is executed, the combination order and the derived orders are automatically deleted from the order book.

- *Fault Tolerant.* Any exchange system should be developed to function properly even with hardware or software faults. OM CLICK Exchange System uses duplication of mission critical transactions at a secondary, geographically separate server so that the duplicated system will operate automatically in case of emergencies.

9.2.4 Trading in Euros

Starting in 1999, a majority of share trading in Europe has been taking place in Euros. Although Sweden is outside the EMU, OM Stockholm Exchange is prepared to offer companies, members, and investors the possibility to trade in Euros in 1999. OM Stockholm Exchange provides three trading alternatives for its listed companies:

- *Trading in Swedish Kronor (SEK).* Trading and settlement will continue as before, and market information will be disseminated in the same manner as previously.

- *Trading in Euros.* In this case, shares can only be bought and sold exclusively in Euros. Companies whose shares are traded in Euros will still be included in the exchange's indices and turnover calculations. The stock exchange's system contains information regarding current price relationships between Euros and SEK, and the system recalculates prices and turnover and includes these in the total figures.

- *Trading in both SEK and Euros.* In this case, an investor has various options to purchase and sell shares. As long as he or she purchases or sells in the same currency, the procedure is identical to trading in SEK. It is only where he or she has purchased in one currency and sold in the other that a difference will be noticed. In such a case, the procedure takes four days instead of three. The first day is, in fact, dedicated to the "exchange" of the shares in two currencies. Thereafter, the traditional three-day settlement cycle occurs.

In the SSE's trading systems, the share has two order books—one for kronor and one for Euros. For the calculation of indices, the exchange will use the order book (the currency) that has the greatest liquidity. Similarly, for derivatives, OM Stockholm will use the order book that has the greatest liquidity.

9.2.5 Nordic Exchange

NOREX (Figure 9.3) is a virtual alliance between OM Stockholm Exchange and the Copenhagen Stock Exchange started in 1998. The vision of the alliance is to create a common Nordic securities market through which exchanges and market participants can offer their services with the fewest possible barriers. Existing members will benefit from the larger market that the alliance brings about. Investors will have the advantage of increased liquidity brought by the common Nordic market. In June 2000, the Iceland Stock Exchange joined the alliance, and in October they started trading shares and bonds in the joint trading system. In October 2000, the Oslo Stock Exchange signed the formal agreement to become the fourth member of the alliance.

Under the alliance, the Copenhagen Stock Exchange and the OM Stockholm Exchange will become a part of a large interrelated stock market, offering a large number of securities traded on the common trading system, SAXESS, developed by the OM Group. In the beginning, the alliance will concentrate on stock markets. In the long run, the alliance will include trading of bonds and derivatives. With few exceptions, the rules for trading are uniform for the two exchanges.

Danish stocks are traded in Danish crowns and are settled via the Danish Securities Center (VP). Swedish stocks are traded in Swedish crowns and settled via the VPC. Final payment transfers for the OM Stockholm Exchange equities are settled in Sveriges Riksbank´s payment transfer system (RIX), and for Copenhagen Stock Exchange equities in the central bank of Denmark, Danmarks Nationalbank´s payment transfer system. In both VPC and VP, trades are settled

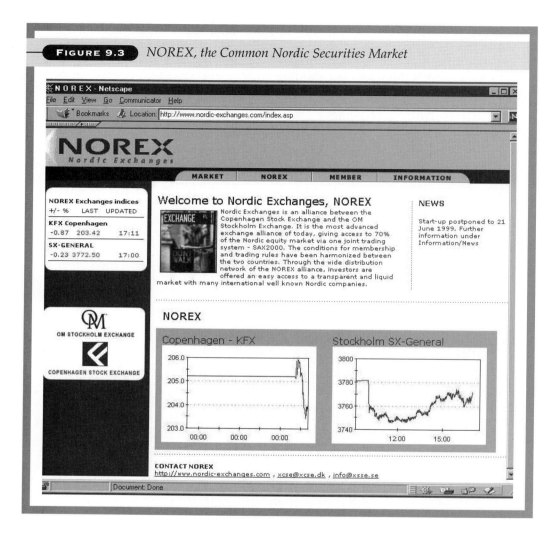

FIGURE 9.3 *NOREX, the Common Nordic Securities Market*

on a delivery versus payment basis (DVP). There are two main ways for an exchange member to settle trades:

- Participating in VPC/VP as a clearing and settlement member.
- Participating indirectly in VPC/VP through a custodian.

In both cases, the clearing participant must have a cash settlement account either with one of the central banks or a clearing bank. In this system, the settlement processes of VPC and VP are not identical, and operations take place according to national rules and regulations.

9.2.6 Jiway

The OM Group and MSDW launched Jiway in November 2000. It is one of the few exchanges in Europe that truly does cross-border trade and settlement. The volume of retail trading through the Internet has grown sharply recently in Europe. But much of this only happens in domestic markets. For a U.K. investor, trading German companies is still costly because markets in Europe are still fragmented despite the recent merger and alliance progress. Jiway is created to target online retail investors who are interested in cross-border trading. Retail investors get access to Jiway through online or traditional brokerage firms. Powered by the trading and clearing system developed by the OM Group, Jiway plans to trade roughly 6,000 European and U.S. stocks and offers a full spectrum of trading-related services including order matching, execution, clearing, settlement, and even custody services. Immediately, Jiway was welcomed by brokerage firms such as E*Trade Europe and Barclays.

According to Per Larsson, president and CEO of OM Group, the current fragmented stock-trading infrastructure has to be rebuilt rather than being modernized. Larsson was invited to attend a summit in Paris in November 1998 to discuss prospective alliances in Europe. He walked out halfway through the meeting, declaring that the idea of taking a number of existing monopolies and trying to create a new one was not the best way forward. Given the difficult and complicated process of merger and alliances of existing exchanges in Europe today, starting a groundbreaking electronic market without the constraints of existing stake holders might be a great solution.

At present, customers can trade in U.K., U.S., German, Swedish, Dutch, and French stocks, with 10 brokers now using the system and 20 more signed up to come online. So far, the trading volume at Jiway is relatively low. Jiway will soon face stiff competition as Knight Trading, the Nasdaq's largest market maker, plans to open its own pan-European market with a consortium of 19 brokers.

9.3 SWISS EXCHANGE

Switzerland is one of the world's most important financial centers. About 40 percent of global cross-border asset management for private clients is carried out there, a fact that has helped the growth and development of the SWX. Today, SWX is the seventh largest stock market in the world, according to the International Federation of Stock Exchanges. It is also a leader in electronic trading and settlement. In 2001, SWX and Tradepoint will jointly launch virt-x, a pan-European blue-chip market. This section discusses the development and innovations of SWX since the early 1990s, including market design and electronic trading. The creation of Eurex (European Exchange), the largest derivatives exchange in Europe, is discussed in the next section.

9.3.1 Innovations in the 1990s

At the end of 1990, there were seven stock exchanges in Switzerland, including SOFFEX (Swiss Options and Financial Futures Exchange). Rapid advances in technology in the 1990s made it possible to create a single integrated national exchange. Other exchange organizations in Switzerland were either dissolved or incorporated into SWX when it was founded in 1993. Over the past decade, SWX has introduced a series of innovations that have fundamentally changed the way it does business.

Electronic Trading

SWX is the world's leader in electronic trading. In August 1996, SWX successfully launched an electronic trading system for stocks, derivatives, and bonds. This was the world's first fully integrated electronic trading system covering the entire spectrum of trading and settlement. Computerized trading has led to increased efficiency and greater market transparency.

SWX electronically links trading with settlement. Transaction information is automatically transmitted to SEGA (the Swiss Securities Clearing Corporation) via the SECOM (SEGA Communication System).[5] This has greatly simplified and speeded up the settlement process.

Market Innovations

SWX has introduced longer trading hours, new types of orders, and electronic order matching. From November 6, 1998, SWX has added a closing auction for its traded equities to improve the price discovery process. SWX has also positioned itself in a more unified European market. In collaboration with Deutsche Boerse it has formed Eurex. The next step for SWX is to create a single pan-European derivative exchange by linking Eurex with French derivative exchanges.

9.3.2 Market Design

SWX supports a wide variety of orders, including market orders, limit orders, stop orders, fill-or-kill orders, and hidden-size orders. With a hidden-size order, a trader can enter an order in the order book in such a way that only part of the volume is revealed. As soon as this part of the order has been executed, a further part of the order is disclosed.

Trading at SWX is divided into the following four periods: preopening, opening, regular trading, and closing auction.

- *Preopening.* Preopening starts at 5:00 PM on the previous business day and lasts until 10:00 PM. It resumes at 6:00 AM on the current business day. During this period, orders may be entered or deleted in the electronic order book , but no actual trades take place. A theoretical opening price is continuously calculated and displayed to guide traders.

- *Opening.* The market opening determines the opening price and executes the orders according to the matching rules. This procedure takes place at 8:30 AM for Swiss government bonds, 9:30 AM for all other bonds, 9:00 AM for stocks, and 9:15 AM for derivatives. In establishing the opening price at the start of trading, the highest execution principle is used; in other words, the price is fixed in such a manner as to achieve the largest possible turnover.

- *Regular Trading.* After the opening, regular trading begins. New orders are continuously matched with existing ones in the electronic order book. All orders are stored in the order book until a match is found.

- *Closing Auction.* On November 6, 1998, the SWX started to introduce a closing auction for all equities traded on SWX. The start of the closing auction differs for Swiss Market Index (SMI) equities and other equities. The start time for the former is at 4:55 PM whereas the start time for the latter is at 4:50 PM. At the start of the closing auction, the status of all equity order books will change from "Trd" (regular trading) to "Auc" (auction). After the start of the closing auction, orders can still be entered in the order books, but they will not trigger a trade. Every new order entry will prompt a recalculation of the theoretical opening price, which is shown on the trading screen. At 5:00 PM, the closing auction enters the run-and-close stage. At this stage, the system operates as it does in the opening phase of the market. The highest execution principle is used. Once the last paid price has been determined, the order book status immediately changes to the preopening status for the following trading day.

The SWX also supports off-exchange trading, which is not matched through the SWX matching algorithm. This is how off-exchange works. During trading hours, a trader can indicate by issuing a nonbinding statement of interest to all other members that he or she would like to trade in a certain security. Other traders may respond to this with a bid addressed to the interested member. An addressed offer of this type is directed to a specific trader and is not revealed to other traders. The offer can be accepted, ignored, or rejected by the other trader. If the offer is accepted, then the trade is automatically registered in the SWX system.

9.3.3 Electronic Trading and Settlement System

Electronic trading at SWX is implemented as a distributed computing system, connected by communication networks. Exchange members can access the SWX through client workstations using a client application, which was developed by the SWX and is available to all exchange members. As Figure 9.4 shows, the gateway serves as a link between the central exchange system and the member's trading workstation. The most important task of the gateway is to ensure equal treatment of all members. Through the gateway, all members receive the same

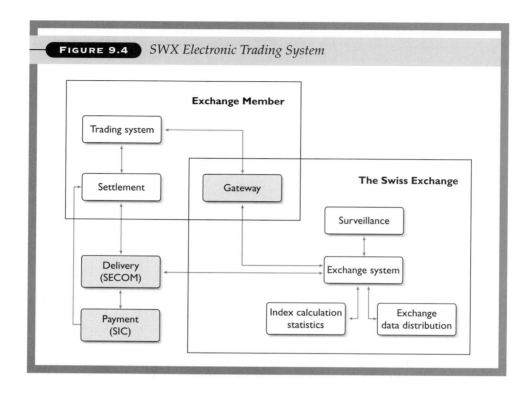

FIGURE 9.4 *SWX Electronic Trading System*

information at the same time and all orders are dealt with in sequence of entry. Another feature of the system is high security. Access to the exchange is secured by a special software system, Kerberos.

SWX's central exchange system comprises several modules ranging from the computerized order book and the matching algorithm to the administration of exchange data and the surveillance program. The modular structure of the trading system provides great scalability. Each module operates as an independent subsystem and can be reconfigured without affecting other subsystems. Modification of the trading system is also easy. After modification, the system can be simulated and analyzed before being put into operation.

The strength of the SWX trading system lies primarily in its fully integrated trading, clearing, and settlement. The SWX trading system is linked electronically with the clearing and settlement system. Buyers and sellers are obliged to settle all completed transactions on the value set at the exchange. The SWX automatically transmits transactions information to SEGA, which then debits the agreed purchase price to the purchaser's account with the Swiss National Bank via Swiss Interbank Clearing (SIC) and credits the seller. In return, the securities are transferred from the seller's SEGA account to the purchaser's.

9.4 EUREX

Eurex is the leading derivatives exchange in Europe, and the second largest worldwide after Chicago Board of Trade (CBOT). Eurex was created in 1998 by the merger of SOFFEX, a wholly owned subsidiary of SWX and the German Futures and Options Exchange. After the merger, SWX and Deutsche Boerse each hold 50 percent of Eurex. A further step toward expansion is already in the planning stage: The amalgamation of Eurex with the French derivative exchanges MATIF and MONEP by around 2002 will create a single pan-European derivative exchange.

9.4.1 Market Organization

Institutions wishing to trade at Eurex must be admitted as Eurex exchange members. Companies must meet the basic requirements set up by Eurex to be admitted as exchange members. Additionally, all exchange members may apply for a market-maker license for one or several products. Market makers are obliged to quote binding bid and offer prices at any time on request. In turn, they enjoy the benefit of reduced transaction fees. Exchange members are either clearing members or nonclearing members. With a clearing-member license, the exchange member is authorized to clear its own transactions as well as those of its customers and of nonclearing members. Clearing members must maintain cash clearing accounts with Deutsche Boerse Clearing AG, the Landeszentralbank Hessen (LZB), and the Schweizerische Nationalbank (SNB), as well as a securities custody account with Deutsche Boerse Clearing AG or SEGA, respectively. Currently, only banks domiciled in Germany or Switzerland are eligible for admission as clearing members.

9.4.2 Products and Trading

The wide range of derivatives traded on Eurex includes equity-based products, index products, and money market and fixed-income products. Equity-based products traded on Eurex include options on 41 blue-chip German equities, as well as options on 17 Swiss equities. Among all its products, the DAX Option is the strongest individual Eurex contract, with an average daily trading volume of about 100,000 contracts. Eurex achieved a breakthrough in capturing market share in BUND Futures (German government 8.5- to 10.5-year bonds). The average daily trading volume grew from 125,854 contracts in 1997 to 358,079 contracts in 1998, and 626,270 in May 1999. Today, about 99.9 percent of BUND Futures trading takes place at Eurex. The gains in market share are mainly due to the efficiency of electronic trading, combined with low transaction costs and a significant increase in membership across Europe and the United States.

Eurex is a fully integrated electronic exchange allowing participants decentralized and standardized market access on a global scale. Trading on the computerized Eurex platform is different from traditional open-outcry systems. It transcends borders and offers members access from any location, creating a global liquidity market. The international access points to Eurex are located in Amsterdam, Chicago, Helsinki, London, Madrid, and Paris. A further access point is planned for New York. This worldwide liquidity network provides market participants with cost-effective, fast, and reliable access to the Eurex trading and clearing platform.

All orders and quotes are entered into the central Eurex order book, where they are automatically sorted by type, price, and entry time. Market orders always have the highest matching priority. Every market provides real-time information on the market. The 10 best bid and ask prices and their respective bid and offer sizes can be called up at any time, allowing members to constantly monitor market depth and to keep abreast of the latest price trends on a real-time basis.

Orders entered with the same price are executed on a first-come, first-served basis. When two orders are matched, the system automatically carries out the transaction. Confirmation of all trades is given immediately. Orders that cannot be executed at once, or only in part, are stored in the order book waiting to be filled.

The opening price of a contract is determined on the basis of both limited orders and market orders and quotes contained in the book order and is set so that the largest possible number of such orders and quotes may be executed. During the trading period, prices will be determined through the matching of orders and quotes at the best respective bid and ask prices. In the event that prices are identical, orders and quotes will be matched in the order in which they were entered into the trading system of the Eurex exchanges. Market orders will be given priority.

9.4.3 Clearing and Settlement

Eurex provides an automated and integrated clearinghouse for all products and participants. The clearinghouse of Eurex is Eurex Clearing AG, a wholly owned subsidiary of Eurex.

- Eurex Clearing AG acts as the central counterparty between the buyer and the seller and guarantees the fulfillment of all obligations received by the clearinghouse. This division into two separate contracts with the central clearinghouse enables the parties on both sides of the transaction to make their decisions independently of each other and to concentrate the respective counterparty risks (default and liquidity risks) in a single party to the contract. Eurex Clearing AG protects itself against the risk of default by individual clearing members through an efficient collateral system.

- Eurex participants have a trading platform and clearing "from a single source." This saves the time and effort that would be needed for additional coordination with an external clearinghouse.

- Cross-border and multicurrency clearing is possible. This offers Eurex participants a broader exchange landscape, independently of their local currencies.

- All the transaction processing and administration is documented clearly and in detail. Data are transmitted to all participants at the same time. Eurex Clearing AG thus gives all participants equal opportunities.

9.5 EASDAQ

Easdaq (Figure 9.5) was established in 1996 and is one of the few cross-border European stock markets today. Modeled on the successful Nasdaq, Easdaq focuses on high-growth companies and offers access to a wide institutional and retail investor base. Europe has more than 26 equity markets that use many different accounting standards and principles. With one market rule book and a single trading platform, Easdaq aims to offer investors and listed companies a single transparent European stock market. The goals in launching Easdaq are twofold. First, the market aims to remove the problems associated with cross-border trades on different national markets in Europe by providing one market common to the whole of Europe. It will also provide a dual-trading mechanism with Nasdaq. Therefore, investors in both Europe and the United States can invest through Easdaq in European companies without having to concern themselves with the extra costs and settlement problems associated with cross-border trades. Second, it is the founders' belief that Europe's economic future lies in the advancement of high-growth, value-added sectors such as biotechnology, pharmaceuticals and health care, telecommunications, and engineering and computer technologies. The new market provides investors access to those high-growth companies.

9.5.1 Market Organization

Although Easdaq is based in Brussels and regulated by the Belgium Commission for Banking and Finance, it is connected to the rest of Europe and the United States electronically. Investors can also be reassured by the fact that the Easdaq systems have been built largely on those used by Nasdaq and those required by the Securities and Exchange Commission in the United States. This will also ensure a much easier transition between Easdaq and Nasdaq for dual listings.

Easdaq's membership is spread widely across Europe and the United States and over a broad professional range, with a combination of brokers, banks, and securities trading houses being the initial members. Easdaq members fall into three categories: sponsors, broker-dealers, and market makers. Sponsors are responsible for preparing companies for admission and ensuring that they meet

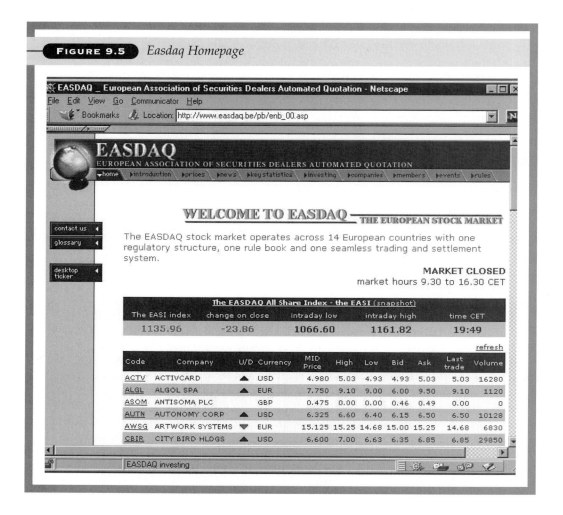

FIGURE 9.5 *Easdaq Homepage*

Easdaq's requirements. Brokers trade in the shares of Easdaq companies on behalf of private and institutional clients. Market makers commit capital to buying and selling shares in certain companies, creating liquidity in the market through their commitment to trade. Some Easdaq members fulfill all three roles. To qualify as members of Easdaq, which can be found around the world, investment companies or credit institutions must meet the following requirements: As a member, the firm must be registered as a business in a European Union member state. It must be authorized to provide investment services in the member state in which its business is established. Finally, this authorization must extend to allowing the firm to conduct investment business throughout the European Union under the terms of the Investment Services Directive.

9.5.2 Trading and Settlement

Easdaq is a screen-based, quote-driven market that uses a multiple market-maker system similar to that used by Nasdaq in the United States. Each company listed on Easdaq must appoint a minimum of two market makers to trade in its securities. Market makers for each company must make firm bid and offer prices in the shares of that company, and these prices are shown on the screens of each member of Easdaq throughout Europe and the United States. The quotes are binding on a market maker for a given size of deal. Market makers must be willing to buy and sell the securities of the company during market business hours. Market makers will compete against each other in the market. It is believed, following the Nasdaq model, that this competition among market makers will give better pricing and greater liquidity in those securities.

Easdaq brokers are connected to the quotation display, which shows all current bid and offer quotes for each listed company. Brokers are engaging trades with the market maker over the telephone. Each telephone trade must then be reported to Easdaq within three minutes by using the "TRAX" communications network. This system is designed to automatically match trades that have been carried out. Those transactions are then automatically published over the screen system both to Easdaq members and through other information display systems to the public. There are real-time feeds of Easdaq prices to a number of information vendors including Reuters, Bloomberg, and Telerate.

The Easdaq settlement system is designed to be highly efficient in that as soon as a bargain has been confirmed and matched on the TRAX system, it is also automatically passed into the Intersettle settlement system. This is a paperless settlement system set up by a number of Swiss banks and based in Zurich. As a result of the direct interface between the two, settlement details are automatically passed from Easdaq to Intersettle, and there is no need for a separate input of settlement details. This direct interface will allow settlement on a $T + 3$ basis initially with the potential to move to $T + 0$. An Easdaq member must either hold an account with Intersettle or must appoint an agent that has an Intersettle account to act on its behalf.

9.5.3 Nasdaq Europe

In March 2001, Nasdaq acquired a majority stake in the struggling Easdaq to create a pan-European exchange that will trade both U.S. and European blue-chip stocks. Easdaq will be renamed Nasdaq Europe. The move represents Nasdaq's third attempt recently to enter the highly competitive European markets. The original Nasdaq Europe plan was rejected by major securities firms. The second plan involving the creation of Nasdaq iX with LSE and Deutsche Boerse collapsed as well.

Nasdaq has decided that the newly created Nasdaq Europe will not be the old Easdaq but will reinvent itself. In 2001, Nasdaq plans to launch the new European trading system, which will be compatible with the Nasdaq system in the

United States. Nasdaq Europe will deploy a hybrid market model that will combine the best features of order-driven and quote-driven markets.

9.6 AUSTRALIAN STOCK EXCHANGE

Thousands of miles away from Europe, stock trading in Australia is also undergoing rapid changes. Stock trading started as early as in 1828 in Australia. In the past dozen years, the ASX has changed dramatically. In 1987, ASX was formed through the merger of the six regional exchanges, including the Stock Exchange of Melbourne and the Stock Exchange of Hobart, to create a single stock market in the country. In the same year, ASX introduced its computerized exchange system, Stock Exchange Automated Trading System (SEATS). Three years later, ASX totally abandoned its floor trading. Since 1990, all trading has been conducted on SEATS. In 1998, ASX became a public company, and its shares were traded on its own board.[6] The now Australian Stock Exchange Ltd. along with the OM Stockholm is one of the few of its kind.

9.6.1 Demutualization

Most stock exchanges around the world operate as a mutual company, a nonprofit organization, run collectively by their members with a single vote for each member. In the 1990s, people began questioning whether there were inefficiencies inherent in this mutual structure that inhibits the exchange's ability to meet current and future challenges. In 1995, ASX started an investigation to review ASX's business strategy and its organizational structure. In 1996, on the recommendation of the board of ASX its members approved the resolution that began the demutualization process. Following the vote, ASX management worked closely with the Australian government and the demutualization bill became effective in December 1997. The legislation approved by the government imposes a 5 percent limit on all investors. Because ASX, as a listed company, could not supervise its own compliance, the Australian Securities and Investments Commission (ASIC) took over the role of compliance supervision. After demutualization, access to the market no longer has membership as a requirement nor a shareholding of ASX. However, requirements still remain. Access is open to any organizations or individuals meeting the existing qualifications.

Demutualization enables ASX management to radically change the organizational structure and improve the efficiencies of the operations of the exchange. Under the previous mutual structure, the objective of the exchange was to serve its members, and efficiency and profits were not considered the primary purpose. With increasing globalization and growing competition among exchange markets, the efficiency of the exchange has become an increasingly critical question.

After demutualization, ASX has looked into many areas that can improve its operation efficiency. It has moved aggressively from traditional paper-based delivery of information to digital processes, eliminating many physical service centers and devoting more resources to online transactions.

9.6.2 Electronic Trading and Settlement

As mentioned earlier, ASX abandoned its physical trading floors in 1990 and switched to fully automated trading using SEATS. SEATS compares buying and selling orders entered into the system and automatically executes trades in strict time-price priority whenever two orders match. Orders, which can be entered on SEATS terminals in stockbrokers' offices anywhere in Australia, are routed to network processors in capital cities. Currently, there are more than 1,200 terminals on the SEATS system. Options and futures are traded in a different computerized system called DTF, which was developed by the OM Group.

Settlement of trades at ASX takes place at the automated Clearing House Electronic Subregister System (CHESS). This system brings equities market settlement processes in Australia up to world standards. It uses electronic data interchange and largely eliminates paper documents in the settlement process. The combination of CHESS and SEATS provides investors with a paperless trading environment.

9.7 **SUMMARY**

This chapter has discussed the development of financial exchanges outside the United States, particularly in Europe. Advances in technology, increasing competition, and the adoption of a common currency for EMU nations have changed the European financial markets beyond recognition. We have discussed market organization and trading and settlement processes for these markets. All the existing exchanges discussed in this chapter have abandoned trading floors and adopted computerized trading and settlement systems to stay competitive. In today's global economy, these exchanges have also recognized that upgrading their own trading systems is not enough. Markets will increasingly be consolidated to provide efficient trading to investors. This is certainly happening in Europe. It is not without possibility that something similar will soon take place in Asia or even in the United States.

10

FIXED-INCOME MARKETS

The significance of today's fixed-income market—commonly referred to as the bond market, which includes U.S. Treasury securities, corporate bonds, and municipal bonds—is demonstrated by its sheer size. In 2000, outstanding U.S. Treasury securities alone amounted to about $3 trillion in value, and there were about $3.4 trillion worth of corporate bonds and $1.5 billion municipal bonds outstanding. In 1999, U.S. Treasury securities accounted for trade of more than $186 billion per day, compared with the daily trading value of $35.5 billion on the New York Stock Exchange (NYSE).

However, fixed-income markets have trailed behind equity markets in the use of technology. It was estimated that only 1 to 3 percent of U.S. Treasury securities were traded electronically in 1999. Unlike stocks, bonds do not have a central exchange. Most deals in the bond market are executed over telephones and fax machines. This "people-intensive" trading is highly inefficient and hinders real-time market information collection and dissemination.

This dichotomy signals a market that is ripe for change, and the current bond market structure is indeed experiencing major changes. There has been, for example, a growing interest in electronic bond trading. According to a 1997 survey conducted by the Bond Market Association, the majority of respondents believed that most dealers would offer electronic trading to institutional customers within two years. In addition, about 75 percent of the respondents also expected institutional investors to demand access to multidealer systems within two years. In 1998, several multidealer bond markets were launched, and the development continues today. These markets are fundamentally different from existing single-dealer systems, in which competition is weak, and will significantly improve market transparency. Market efficiency, however, is an issue that is rarely raised in reference to exchange-market design. Most exchange markets are, in fact, designed by software engineers and traders and are not necessarily based on economic principles. Today's rapid advances in information technology have created a unique opportunity for researchers to design electronic markets based on economic principles.

This chapter first gives an overview of the U.S. fixed-income markets. It then discusses the recent advances in electronic trading and information dissemination in the debt markets, including GovPx, the fixed-income pricing system (FIPS), the single-dealer trading system, multidealer markets, and markets for bond initial public offerings (IPO). We also discuss issues of market transparency, electronic trading, and overall market design.

10.1 U.S. TREASURY SECURITIES MARKET

The underlying objective of the bond market—also known as "fixed income" or "debt market"—is to raise capital for the U.S. government as well as for private corporations. Today's U.S. bond market, with more than $14 trillion in outstanding debt obligations in 2000 (Table 10.1), is the world's largest securities market. About one-third of the total market value belongs to U.S. government debt securities, which include Treasury securities and federal agency securities. This section focuses on U.S. Treasury securities.

With a large outstanding value (more than $3 trillion) and high liquidity, the U.S. Treasury securities market is the world's most important debt market. It

TABLE 10.1 *Size of the U.S. Bond Market in 2000 (in Trillions)*[1]		
		Outstanding Value
Government securities		$4.9
Treasury securities	$3.0	
Agency securities	$1.9	
Municipal bonds		$1.5
Corporate bonds		$3.4
Mortgage and asset-backed securities		$3.3
Money market instruments		$2.7
Total		$15.8

includes discount securities, with initial maturities of three months, six months, and one year, and coupon securities, with initial maturities of two, three, five, 10, and 30 years. The initial issuance of U.S. Treasury securities in what is known as the primary market is conducted through auction. The U.S. Treasury auctions have a regular cycle. The three-month and six-month Treasury bills are auctioned every Monday. The one-year bills and the two- and five-year notes are auctioned monthly. And the three-year, 10-year, and 30-year Treasury securities are auctioned quarterly.

The secondary market for U.S. Treasury securities is largely an over-the-counter (OTC) market. This market is organized through the primary dealers, which are large investment banks and commercial banks with which the Federal Reserve Bank of New York interacts directly. The primary dealer system was established in 1960 and began with 18 primary dealers. Over time, the number of primary dealers grew. In 1988, the number of dealers grew to a peak of 46. From the mid-1990s, the number has declined. As of December 2000, there were 26 primary dealers, including Goldman Sachs, Bear Stearns, and Lehman Brothers. Treasury market is the most liquid security market in the world. According to the Federal Reserve Bank of New York, daily average trading volume for all Treasury securities by primary dealers for the week ended on April 4, 2001, was about $298 billion (Table 10.2).

Unlike the market for stocks, trading in the OTC Treasury market is people-intensive and the market is fragmented. Investors, including institutional investors or individuals, buy and sell bonds through individual dealers without formal consolidation of orders or trading. Although there have been some advances in electronic information dissemination and trading systems such as GovPx, there is no comprehensive electronic network like Nasdaq that displays real-time quotations for all the trading activities and allows dealers to compete for the orders. In terms of order transmission and trade execution, a large number of trades is conducted over telephones and fax machines. When trading with

TABLE 10.2 *Daily Average Trading Value by Primary Dealers in U.S. Treasury Securities for the Week Ended April 4, 2001 (in Billions)[2]*

Treasury bills	$36.299
Coupon securities	
Due in five years or less	$175.345
Due in more than five years	$84.809
Treasury inflation index securities	$1.794
Total	$298.247

each other, the dealers go through intermediaries called brokers. Brokers enable speedier transactions and allow the identities of the dealers involved in trades to remain confidential. There are six interdealer brokers: Cantor Fitzgerald Securities, Garban Ltd., Liberty Brokerage, RMJ Securities, Hilliard Farber, and Tullet and Tokyo Securities. In the interdealer market, dealers can view other dealers' indications of interest for trades on their computers, which are connected to the broker's proprietary system. However, dealers still have to submit orders to brokers through either phone or fax.

10.2 CORPORATE BOND MARKETS

Corporate bonds are by definition issued by corporations. They are similar to other kinds of fixed-income securities in that they promise to make payments at specified times and provide legal remedies in the event of default. We have seen a sharp increase in corporate bonds for more than a decade. Outstanding corporate debt has more than tripled since 1986, from $960 billion in 1986 to $3.4 trillion in 2000.

In contrast to U.S. Treasury securities, which are considered to be default risk-free, corporate bonds are associated with default risk exposure. If a company wants to borrow money from a bank, it is taken for granted that the bank will be able to examine the company's credit in the course of approving or disapproving the loan. If a company wants to borrow money from investors by issuing a bond, most individuals and even institutional investors will not have the ability to conduct research on companies and various bonds issued by them. Instead, they rely primarily on nationally recognized bond ratings. The four commercial companies that produce ratings on all publicly issued debt instruments are Duff and Phelps Credit Rating Co., Fitch Investors Service, Moody's Investors Service, and Standard & Poor's Corporation. Issues in the top ratings of all raters are referred to as investment-grade bonds, whereas those below the top four ratings are called noninvestment-grade bonds or high-yield bonds.

Similar to a stock IPO, most corporate bonds are underwritten by investment or commercial banks on a competitive basis. This guarantees that a bond issuer will receive a certain amount of proceeds from the bond. Merrill Lynch, Morgan Stanley, Goldman Sachs, and Lehman Brothers are the top corporate bond underwriters. The majority of trading happens on the OTC market. Some corporate bonds are listed on the NYSE and the American Stock Exchange. On the NYSE, subscribers to the automated bond system (ABS) can view bond quotation and submit orders through proprietary terminals. The more active issues of bonds listed on the NYSE are directly traded in a "ring" in the bond market.

10.3 MUNICIPAL BOND MARKETS

As with municipal bonds, there has also been a rapid increase in outstanding municipal bonds, growing from $920 million in 1986 to $1.5 billion in 2000. There are two basic municipal securities. Short-term notes are sold in anticipation of the receipt of funds from taxes. The proceeds from the sale of short-term notes permit the state or local government to cover seasonal and temporary imbalances between outlays for expenditure and tax inflows. Long-term bonds, however, are used to finance long-term capital improvement projects such as the construction of roads and airports. The most important advantage of investing in municipal bonds is that the majority are tax-exempt.

When a municipal bond is brought to market, it too is underwritten by either an investment or a commercial bank. Public offerings may be marketed through either competitive bidding or direct negotiations with underwriters. State and local governments usually require a competitive sale to be announced in a recognized financial publication such as *The Bond Buyer*. *The Bond Buyer* also provides information on upcoming competitive sales and most negotiated sales, as well as on the results of previous weeks.

The secondary market for municipal bonds is largely an OTC market supported by municipal bond dealers across the country. Here, too, investors have to buy and sell municipal bonds through dealers, and there are brokers who serve as intermediaries in the sale of large blocks of municipal bonds among dealers and large institutional investors. *The Bond Buyer* has a teletype system that provides dealer quotations. In addition, every weekday Standard & Poor's Corporation publishes a *blue list* that has municipal bond quotations from various dealers.

10.4 ADVANCES IN INFORMATION DISSEMINATION

Albeit later than in other financial markets, in recent years significant progress has been made in using information technology to enhance both transparency and efficiency in all sectors of the U.S. bond market. For example, GovPx was created in 1991 to improve transparency by collecting and disseminating quotes and transaction prices on government securities. In 1995, the Municipal Securities Rulemaking Board started to develop an automated system to report transaction data in the municipal bond market. Although the system currently reports only interdealer transaction data, it will be expanded to include dealer-customer transaction information in the future. And in the corporate bond market, market information for bonds that are traded on exchanges are reported. Subscribers to the ABS at NYSE can view bond quotation and trade information through proprietary terminals. The ABS also allows electronic order entry and automatically executes trades for matching buy and sell orders (SEC, 1998b). In corporate bond markets, FIPS provides quotations and summary transaction information for a group of high-yield bonds but does not yet provide electronic price disclosure for the majority of the bond trading that occurs at the OTC market.

10.4.1 GovPx

Encouraged by the Securities and Exchange Commission (SEC), primary Treasury dealers and interdealer brokers founded GovPx, a system to disseminate real-time prices on U.S. Treasury securities. Prior to GovPx, interdealer market data were only available to dealers, who were reluctant to allow the general public access. GovPx now provides 24-hour, worldwide distribution of securities information as transacted by the primary dealers through five of the six interdealer brokers for all active and off-the-run Treasury securities. The data include the best bids and offers, trade price and size, and aggregate volume traded for all Treasury securities. GovPx currently extends its market coverage to provide worldwide distribution of information regarding the interest rate swaps market. This service, known as SwapPx, provides real-time benchmark rates, data, and analytics for U.S. medium-term swaps, basic swaps, and spot/forward swaps ranging from 90 days to 30 years. Although GovPx represents a big improvement in market transparency, it is believed that significant gaps still exist in the current system. One such gap is the fact that large market dealers can easily hide a trade from the public by dealing directly with one another.

10.4.2 FIPS

FIPS was created in response to the 1980's junk bond market collapse and began operating in April 1994. FIPS is a screen-based system that collects, processes, and displays quotes and summary transaction information for certain high-yield corporate bonds. The system now lists prices on a group of 50 high-yield bonds, reporting the high and low prices and volume every hour during trading. The FIPS 50 list represents some of the most active and liquid issues currently trading. The list is periodically updated to replace called and matured issues and to reflect changes in the market. As a particular issue no longer represents its sector or industry, it is replaced with more representative issues.

Information disseminated through FIPS includes bids and offers communicated by dealers and brokers, as well as a calculation of an inside market that includes the best bid and the best offer for each FIPS security appearing in the system. A trade summary of transaction reports entered into the system during operating hours is disseminated on an hourly basis. This information includes high execution price, low execution price, and accumulated volume in all transactions reported in that hour for FIPS securities. An updated daily summary is also disseminated each hour, listing that day's cumulative high/low volume up to that hour. FIPS provides easy access to market information for the high-yield bond market and enhances market transparency. In the future, the National Association of Securities Dealers plans to enlarge the system beyond the present 50 and to include all corporate and municipal bonds and to provide real-time trade reporting.

10.5 ELECTRONIC BOND MARKETS

As for improving overall market efficiency, electronic trading is clearly the key. The development of single-dealer trading systems started in the early 1990s. Recently, several multidealer markets were launched. The major factor that contributes to the growth of electronic bond markets is the unprecedented development of the Internet, which allows all market participants, institutional or individual, to access the market with a low cost. Here, we review the development of a number of markets.

10.5.1 Single-Dealer Systems

Of the estimated 1 to 3 percent of the bond market that uses electronic trading, most of the trades go through single-dealer systems (SDS). Table 10.3 lists SDSs operated by different brokers and the particular segment of the bond market that they trade in. Through SDSs, customers can view the quotes and enter orders by using computer terminals rather than telephones and fax machines. For example, CS First Boston's GovTrade system started in 1992 and can be accessed through Bloomberg's terminals. To trade, an investor selects from a Bloomberg screen menu an issue that has First Boston's bid and offer quotes. The investor then fills out a "ticket" that pops up on the screen, and the order is transmitted to First Boston's traders. Companies that offer electronic trading to their customers believe that the SDS offers convenience to customers and increases the speed of order execution. Instead of using telephones and fax machines, investors can access price quotes and enter orders from the same computer terminal. Meanwhile, the SDS enables bond traders to focus more on market research, analytics, and trading strategies, rather than just on taking orders. Despite these obvious advantages, the SDS has only changed the order entry process but has not fundamentally improved the way that bonds are traded. As long as investors can interact with only a single dealer through the SDS, they do not have strong incentives to use the system. Instead, investors are still inclined to use telephones to call different dealers and negotiate better prices.

TABLE 10.3	Single-Dealer Trading Systems[3]	
System and Company	**Securities Traded**	**Trading Medium**
Auto Execution Ragen MacKenzie	Treasury, agency	Bloomberg
Autobahn Deutsche Bank	Treasury, mortgage-backed securities (MBS)	Bloomberg, proprietary network
Bear Stearns	Treasury	Bloomberg
Fixed Income Securities	Treasury, agency, MBS, corporate, repos	Internet
Fuji Securities	Treasury	Bloomberg
Goldman Sachs	Treasury, money market	Internet, Bloomberg
GovTrade, ADNTrade, etc. CS First Boston	Treasury, agency, commercial paper, CD, repos	Bloomberg
LMS Merrill Lynch	Treasury, corporate, municipal, MBS	Bloomberg, proprietary network
MSZeros Morgan Stanley Dean Witter	Treasury strip securities	Bloomberg
Spear, Leeds & Kellogg	Treasury, agency, municipal, corporate	Internet, Bloomberg
Winstar Government Securities	Treasury	Internet, proprietary network
Zions GovRate/Odd-Lot Machine Zions Bank Capital Markets	Treasury	Telnet, dial-up, proprietary network

10.5.2 MultiDealer Exchange Markets

Several electronic trading systems with multiple dealers have also been launched recently, with a few more still under development (Table 10.4). The fundamental difference between a multidealer exchange market and a single-dealer system is that the former allows competitive quotes by different dealers. This is the same idea behind Nasdaq, in which multiple dealers can compete with one another, thereby leading to narrow bid-ask spreads and "best" prices for investors. In some markets, investors can trade directly with each other without going through dealers. We give an overview of selected electronic trading systems in each market segment.

TABLE 10.4 *Multidealer/Exchange Markets for Bond Trading*[4]

System	Company	Securities Traded	Trading Medium
Automated Bond System	NYSE	Treasury, agency, municipal, corporate	Proprietary network
BondAgent.com	Monton Clarke Fu & Metcalf	Agency, municipal, corporate	Internet
Bond Connect	State Street	Treasury, agency, MBS, corporate	Bridge telerate
BondDesk.com	BondDesk	Treasury, agency, corporate, MBS, municipal	Internet
BondGlobe	BondGlobe, Inc.	Treasury, agency, corporate, municipal	Internet
BondHub.com	BondHub	Corporate, MBS, municipal	Internet
BondLink	Trading Edge	Corporate	Internet
BondMart	BondMart Technologies	Treasury, agency, MBS	Internet
BondNet	The Bank of New York	Corporate	Proprietary network, Internet (Java applets), Bloomberg
BondTrader	Bloomberg	Treasury	Bloomberg
Cantor Muni	Cantor Fitzgerald	Municipal	Bloomberg, Internet
IBX	Integrated Bond Exchange, Inc.	Treasury, agency, corporate, municipal	Internet, proprietary network
InterVest	InterVest	Treasury, municipal, corporate	Internet, dedicated line
LIMITrader	LIMITrader Securities	Corporate	Internet
MuniAuction	MuniAuction, Inc.	Municipal	Internet
PARITY	Dalcomp-Thomson	Municipal	Proprietary network
TradeWeb	TradeWeb, LLC	Treasury, agency	Internet, proprietary network

TradeWeb

TradeWeb, which started operation in the first quarter of 1998, offers real-time trading, price information, and research for U.S. Treasury securities (Figure 10.1). Initially, five primary government dealers—CS First Boston, Goldman Sachs, Lehman Brothers, Merrill Lynch, and Solomon Smith Barney—participated in the electronic market. Today, TradeWeb has 15 of the largest market makers in U.S. securities, including ABN AMRO, Bear Stearns, Deutsche Bank, Barclays Capital, J.P. Morgan, Chase Securities, Greenwich Capital, Morgan Stanley Dean Witter, Prudential Securities, UBS Warburg, and the original five dealers. TradeWeb users can view the quotes from different dealers and communicate with them simultaneously. The system also provides access to an analytical suite

FIGURE 10.1 *TradeWeb*

of products as well as trade history and real-time pricing information. In its first year of operation, the company already had a transaction volume of $170 billion. TradeWeb currently has a customer base of nearly 600 buy-side institutions and transacts an average of more than $7 billion per day.

BondNet

BondNet started in June 1995 as an electronic trading system for corporate bonds. In 1997, it was acquired by the Bank of New York. Right now, in addition to corporate bonds, the system trades U.S. Treasury bills, notes, bonds, and Eurobonds. BondNet is an interactive and real-time trading system that allows users to submit orders electronically. The system can be accessed through the Internet as well as through other proprietary networks. Orders submitted to BondNet can be entered based on several user-selected criteria. Unrestricted orders are live and firm and can be hit and executed immediately. Traders can also provide indications that orders are subject to negotiation through a private and anonymous messaging system. Besides trading, BondNet also provides analytical tools and access to historical bond trade data.

BondLink

BondLink is a corporate bond-trading system developed by Trading Edge, Inc. The system is available through the Internet and will allow traders to execute transactions in high-yield and distressed corporate debt securities. In 2000, the market started trading emerging market and convertible bonds. Trading over BondLink is anonymous. However, the system provides total price transparency and allows users to see all buy or sell orders, including their prices and quantity information. The system automatically matches orders on a strict price-time priority basis. In addition, BondLink provides real-time detailed financial news regarding the issuers whose securities are available for trading.

LIMITrader

LIMITrader started trading corporate and high-yield bonds in 1999. It operates as an electronic communications network in the corporate bond market. Traders can access the system over the Internet (see Figure 10.2). Once logged in, a user may view current bids and offers, trade or negotiate with participants, or enter his or her own orders. A unique feature of LIMITrader is its negotiating capability. When a customer enters an order that matches an indication or falls within a specified range of a contra order, the system places both parties into direct negotiation. If one of the parties is off-line, the system will phone that customer, announcing that he or she is needed for negotiation.

FIGURE 10.2 *LIMITrader*

MuniAuction

MuniAuction allows municipal securities dealers to submit bids electronically for new issues of municipal securities through its Internet Web site. The system, which started in 1997, allows municipal issuers to offer securities to qualified municipal dealers through a real-time electronic auction. Dealers must register with MuniAuction prior to participating in the auction. Then, underwriters can access the site to submit bids for a specific issue. Bond issuers have the option of allowing bidders to see their status relative to other bidders. MuniAuction also distributes notices of sale and preliminary official statements through its Web site.

Starting in 1999, MuniAuction began hosting auctions for repurchase agreements, agency securities, and commercial papers.

10.5.3 Interdealer Systems

Interdealer systems allow dealers to trade with each other electronically. All the major interdealer brokers in the U.S. Treasury securities market currently offer or expect to offer electronic trading. Soon, these firms plan to extend trading in other bond products.

Here, we briefly introduce two of the systems.

eSpeed

eSpeed was a division of Cantor Fitzgerald Securities, one of the interdealer brokers. The company went public in 1999, and its system currently allows customers to electronically trade U.S. Treasury, non-U.S. G-7 government bonds, Eurobonds, corporate bonds, agency securities, and emerging market securities. It also operates Cantor Exchange, a U.S. Treasury futures exchange market.

eSpeed and Charles Schwab plan to team up and offer individual investors broader access to electronic trading of U.S. Treasury and U.S. agency securities. Through an electronic link to eSpeed, Schwab customers will have the opportunity to buy and sell a broader array of fixed-income products through Schwab. But financials are only part of the picture for eSpeed. The company's strategy is to take advantage of its expertise in creating markets by expanding its business in the B2B marketplace. The company is considering creating exchanges for electricity, communication bandwidth, and so on.

LibertyDirect

LibertyDirect is operated by Liberty Brokerage, another interdealer broker. It provides electronic trading for the U.S. Treasury market. LibertyDirect provides a unique trading system that combines both voice and electronic orders to allow traders to view and execute orders and negotiate prices.

10.5.4 Market Design and Market Success

Even though many believe that electronic bond trading is the future, the success of an individual market relies on a number of factors such as market liquidity and technology. InterVest, an electronic bond market launched in 1996, ran into problems because it was not able to generate much trading volume. Early in 1998, Bloomberg removed InterVest from its terminals. InterVest battled with Bloomberg in court, accusing Bloomberg of reneging on their agreement under pressure from bond dealers who were concerned that an electronic exchange would reduce the profitability of their fixed-income operations. InterVest now is trying to develop an

Internet-based trading system that can reach traders directly and does not rely on any proprietary technologies.

It will be interesting to see how multiple bond markets will coexist and compete with each other in the future. Liquidity is a huge factor in intermarket competition and will be a key factor in determining the success of a market. Liquidity tends to increase with the number of traders in a market. If prices are "better" in more liquid markets, then there should be a natural incentive for traders to converge on one market rather than split their trades across markets. Although some believe that providing liquidity is the primary role of the market maker, it cannot be viewed as an isolated issue. In fact, market liquidity relates closely to market efficiency and transparency. Obviously, a market with high operation and price efficiency and great transparency will attract more traders, thus enhancing market liquidity.

An exchange market is a unique economic institution that matches buyers and sellers and provides liquidity and price discovery mechanisms for the traded assets. Efficiency, transparency, and liquidity are the top priorities of the market. Traditionally, exchange markets have been designed by traders and software engineers. With the rapid advance of computer and communication technology, especially the Internet, the exchange market is increasingly becoming a digital marketplace that has to follow economics and provide efficiencies to both buyers and sellers. We expect to see more electronic markets being designed and implemented based on economic principles that put efficiency and transparency at high priority.

10.6 SUMMARY

We have discussed the present market structure and the advances in electronic trading for fixed-income securities. Computer and information technology, especially the Internet, will transform the overall bond market in the next few years. We have already seen quite a few electronic markets being developed recently to trade a wide range of fixed-income products. Some online brokerage firms begin to offer online bond trading to retail customers as well. Although computerized trading and electronic dissemination of market information will make the market more efficient and transparent, the current marketplace is fragmented. New entries of bond exchanges bring new competition and enable companies to design and operate an efficient marketplace. The market for bonds is so big that it will probably support several electronic exchanges. But the question is, how many markets are too many. Fragmented markets tend to reduce individual market liquidity. In the long run, there will definitely be winners and losers and more consolidation in this highly competitive business.

11

UNCONVENTIONAL

"FINANCIAL" MARKETS

Up to now the discussion has been focused on financial markets. This chapter discusses some new, unconventional markets that borrow their ideas from financial markets and operate like financial markets. However, the instruments traded in these markets are not traditional financial instruments such as stocks, bonds, or derivatives. Rather, the instruments traded range from electricity and insurance risks to movies and political events.

Markets, a fundamental underpinning to modern capitalism, have a long history behind them. In the medieval period in England, for example, fairs and markets were organized by individuals under a franchise from the king. Organizers of these markets not only provided the physical facilities for the markets but were also responsible for security and settlement of disputes in trading.[1] Throughout history, some traditional markets have diminished in importance while new ones have gained in importance. Recently, stock and commodities markets have come to play a vital role in the world economy. However, the fundamental functions of markets remain the same, i.e., to match buyers and sellers, enforce contracts, and provide a price mechanism to guide the trade. Increasingly, individuals are discovering new functions of markets. Traditional studies look at a market as a resource allocation mechanism in the economy. More recent innovations in the electronic marketplace have used the market as a tool for sharing risk and information. This chapter discusses a number of emerging, innovative markets and their functions.

We discuss four specific markets in this chapter: electricity markets, catastrophe insurance markets, the Iowa Electronic Market (IEM), and the Hollywood Stock Exchange (HSX). The first two markets are in the early stage of development. Despite the recent problems in California's electricity market, the experiment to use market mechanisms to provide electricity and other energies will continue as the utility industry is being deregulated in the United States as well as in many other countries. The catastrophe insurance market, however, is a good example of using the market concept to change the way that the traditional reinsurance industry does its business and brings new efficiencies to the industry. The other two markets, the IEM and HSX, are anything but conventional. No goods or services are exchanged in these two markets. Rather, they trade pure digital products—information. In the Iowa Presidential Market, people can bet on the fortunes of potential political candidates, whereas in the HSX movies become MovieStocks and stars become StarBonds, which can be bought and sold. As we move rapidly to a digital society linked with high-speed networks and computers, markets such as those represented by the examples in this chapter will play an even more important role in our everyday lives.

11.1 ELECTRICITY MARKETS

This section, after a brief introduction of the deregulation of the electricity markets, looks at California's electricity market and examines why the market performed poorly. We also describe trading energy futures and options at the Chicago Board of Trade (CBOT).

11.1.1 Deregulation of the Electricity Market

The U.S. electricity market is huge. It is estimated that the total assets are worth approximately $500 billion, with net revenues of more than $200 billion annually. Despite the fact that almost all Americans buy and use electricity, few have a true choice in deciding their provider. Lack of price competition and consumer choices and limited innovation are some of the negative effects of the current regulated monopolistic system.

It is widely believed that deregulation of the electricity market and introduction of competition mechanisms could bring significant benefits to consumers as well as to the electricity industry. Deregulating the electricity market can create a level playing field for future rivalry and competition in the industry, ensuring that all companies have an equal chance to provide service to consumers. No longer will regulators determine which firms are granted exclusive franchising arrangements. Incumbent firms no longer will have their market turf protected through generous returns on their investment guaranteed by the regulatory system. Possibly, consumers will pay lower prices. Such cost savings would come not only from direct competition as new firms enter the market but also from the higher quality of service that this competition will foster. Competition will also provide an incentive for utility firms to be innovative.

Deregulation in the electricity industry is not a phenomenon unique to the United States. The British government, for example, was the first to outline a plan to privatize the electricity industry in 1988. Today, we can find deregulated electricity markets in Britain, Norway, Sweden, New Zealand, Australia, and Argentina. The many different approaches to restructuring the electricity industry have mostly to do with the original utility industry structure, such as the regulatory environment, the level of vertical integration (including generation, transmission, and distribution), and the ownership structure. In Britain, Argentina, and Victoria, Australia, restructuring began with the break-up and privatization of a government-owned, vertically integrated electric system. These markets immediately established power exchanges or pools for trading. In Britain and Victoria, Australia, the restructuring process is based on the notion of a mandatory centralized pool. All buyers and sellers are required to bid their electric supplies through a pool or centralized energy exchange. The California restructuring model, which is discussed later, is different from that of Britain and Australia in that the California Power Exchange (PX) is an optional pool.

In most markets opened so far, retail access has been phased in. Britain, Finland, Argentina, and Australia opened to larger customers first. Norway and Sweden, like California, were opened to all customers on day one. But in most of these countries, large industrial customers switched first and residential and small business users switched more gradually, as we see below.

11.1.2 California Electricity Market Structure

California enacted deregulation legislation in September 1996. The new electricity market opened shortly thereafter in 1998. Figure 11.1 illustrates the traditional organization of the electricity market in California. Electric utility companies such as Pacific Gas & Electric (PG&E), Southern California Edison (SCE), and San

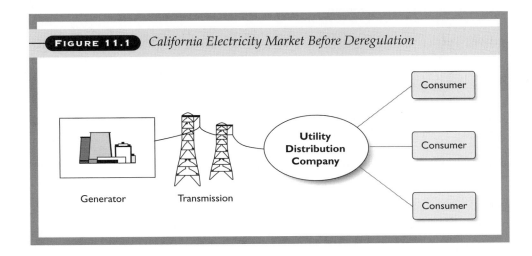

FIGURE 11.1 *California Electricity Market Before Deregulation*

Generator   Transmission   Utility Distribution Company   Consumer

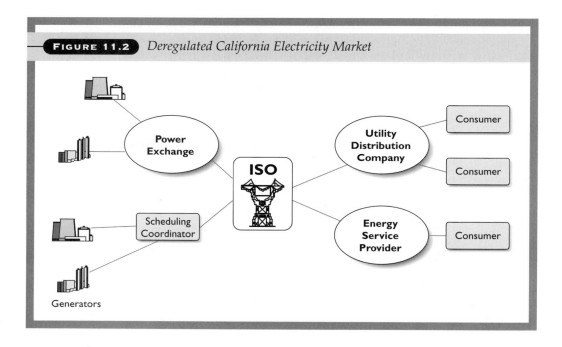

FIGURE 11.2 *Deregulated California Electricity Market*

Diego Gas & Electric (SDG&E) provided bundled service including generation, transmission, and distribution to consumers.[2]

After deregulation, in contrast to most other open markets, the California market is completely open. It is not restricted only to certain customers or electricity providers. As Figure 11.2 shows, the major players in California's deregulated electricity market are as follows:

Independent System Operator The independent system operator (ISO) is a major player in the restructured California power market. Although utility companies such as PG&E, SCE, and SDG&E will continue to own their electric transmission facilities, operational control of these transmission facilities will be turned over to the ISO. The ISO will serve as the control area operator for most of California. The ISO is located in Folsom, California, with back-up facilities in Alhambra, California. The following are the major functions of the ISO:

- Provides open access to the transmission.
- Manages the reliability of the transmission grid.
- Buys and provides ancillary services as required.
- Coordinates day-ahead, hour-ahead schedules and performs real-time balancing of load and generation.

- Settles real-time imbalances and ancillary services sales and purchases.
- Administers congestion management protocols for the transmission grid.

California Power Exchange The California Power Exchange (PX) is another major player in the new power market. Located in Alhambra, California, it is a non-profit corporation established for the primary purpose of providing an efficient, competitive energy auction open to all suppliers and spot market purchasers. The PX is a scheduling coordinator (SC). It submits balanced schedules to the ISO for all its participants. But the PX is not the only mechanism that supplies energy to the ISO. Other SCs provide an optional pool as well. The following are the responsibilities of the PX:

- The PX accepts demand and generation bids from its participants and determines the market clearing price (MCP) at which energy is bought and sold.
- It is an SC and submits balanced demand and supply schedules for successful bidders to the ISO.
- The PX submits ancillary service bids, adjustment bids, and supplemental energy bids to the ISO to maintain the reliable function of the whole system.
- It performs settlement functions with the ISO, PX participants, and other SCs.

Scheduling Coordinator Scheduling Coordinators (SC) submit balanced schedules and provide settlement-ready meter data to the ISO. SCs settle with generators and retailers, the PX, and the ISO. They have to maintain a year-round 24-hour scheduling center and provide some operating instructions to generators and retailers. As discussed earlier, the PX is one such SC.

Utility Distribution Company Utility companies such as PG&E, SCE, and SDG&E are utility distribution companies (UDC), which provide distribution service to all customers within their service territory. These companies also meter the energy delivered and bill for energy and use. They buy bulk power from the PX for their customers and offer optional meter reading and usage measurement services to other market participants.

Retailer or Energy Service Provider Energy service providers (ESP) or retailers are the competitors of UDCs. They buy power for retail customers and serve as demand aggregators for retail loads. They also bill retail customers for energy and contracted services and schedule load and generation through an SC or PX.

Generators Generators are power producers. They may bid power into the PX or schedule power through an SC. They will respond to ISO and SC instructions and may also have contracts directly with retailers.

Customers All customers, either residential or commercial, may choose to receive their power supply via a local UDC or an ESP.

The way that the deregulated California's electricity market works is as follows:

- After deregulation, electric utility companies such as PG&E, SCE, and SDG&E continue to provide regulated service to customers but no longer control their transmission systems. They have also divested much of their generation resources.

- Competition in power generation first began in 1998. Out-of-state utilities and independent energy producers can now compete in the power generation market. The ISO ensures that energy generated by various companies reaches its destination safely and reliably.

- Investor-owned utilities are mandated to sell all their generated power into the newly created PX during a four-year transition period that ends in 2002. The PX schedules its deliveries through the ISO. If a consumer lives in the ISO control area and continues to buy power from the local utility, the PX is where the power will come from.

- UDCs purchase power or generation from the PX. Power delivery is scheduled through the ISO by the PX. UDCs, in turn, deliver power to the customers.

- Metering and billing functions are no longer monopoly services provided only by the UDC. Certified ESPs, meter service providers, and billing agents can now compete with the UDC to provide metering and billing services.

11.1.3 California Power Exchange

Currently, there are two markets managed by the PX, the day-ahead market and the hour-ahead market. Market participants can trade and schedule in the day-ahead power market for next-day delivery. The hour-ahead market provides a means for participants to trade power to adjust their day-ahead commitment based on real-time information.

Day-Ahead Market

Participants in the market have to be validated by the PX. The following scenario illustrates how the day-ahead market works:

- The PX aggregates all the validated orders and constructs a supply/demand curve, the intersection of which will be the market price. A market clearing price is determined for each hour of the 24-hour scheduling day.

- After an initial price is determined, participants can submit additional orders, or bid iterations, to ensure that the market converges to optimal schedules and prices.

- Participants then have to submit generation-unit schedules, adjustment bids for congestion management, and ancillary service bids to the PX.

Hour-Ahead Market

In the hour-ahead market, bids are submitted to the PX at least two hours before the hour of operation. These orders are generation unit-specific bids. The market gives participants an opportunity to make adjustments based on their day-ahead schedules so that they can minimize real-time imbalances. The market clearing price for the hour-ahead market is determined by supply and demand conditions as well. The PX sends price and traded quantities to participants right after the close of the hour-ahead market.

Real-Time Operation

The real-time market is not managed by the PX but by the ISO. The ISO has to deal with real-time imbalances, which are caused by many different factors originating from both the supply and demand sides. The ISO arranges for ancillary service energy and supplemental bids for the real-time supply of energy. The ISO also determines the real-time market price based on actual metered data.

Settlement

The PX also provides settlements for the trading participants in the market. The week for day- and hour-ahead markets is from Sunday midnight to the next Sunday midnight. A preliminary settlement statement is sent to market participants within three days after each trade day. Market participants have five days after each trade day to dispute settlement statements. Invoices are issued seven days after the end of each trading period or calendar month. Invoices include all PX and ISO administrative charges as well as settlements for energy trades. Payments from participants are required 15 days after the end of the trade period. Payments to participants will be made 17 days after the end of the trade period.

11.1.4 What Went Wrong in California?

It is a great idea to introduce market force in the utility industry. However, the electricity market in California failed miserably. In summer 2000, residents in California, especially in the San Diego area, experienced power shortage and soaring electricity prices.[3] The problem worsened in 2001. California experienced four blackouts in early 2001, which cost the state's business more than $1 billion in lost production. On April 6, 2001, PG&E filed Chapter 11 in federal bankruptcy court, saying it could not pay its bills when wholesale electricity prices skyrocketed.[4]

There were two major flaws in California's market design in the deregulation process. First, the three utility companies had to divest their own generation and buy power exclusively through the PX. This prevents the utility companies from hedging their risks by developing their own energy products. Second, California mandates a retail rate cap, reducing the incentives for demand reduction, discouraging entry by competitors for retail sales, and threatening the financial health of the utility companies by delaying or denying their recovery of billions of dollars in costs incurred to provide service to retail customers.[5]

In addition, several other factors also contributed to the energy problem in California. There has not been major investment in power generation in California for a long time, and it takes time to build new power plants. Once the industry is deregulated and supply cannot keep up with demand, price will rise sharply. Meanwhile, natural gas prices increased sharply, which raised the cost of electricity generation.

Californians have indeed learned an expensive lesson on free markets. Other states in the United States that are also interested in deregulating their utility industry are more cautious now. Does California's problem pronounce the failure of market force and competition in the utility industry? To the contrary, it demonstrates the need to embrace competition fully, instead of tentatively. There are successful deregulation cases in the state of Pennsylvania and in other countries. We have recognized that it takes time for the market force to work its way through. Often, the process can be quite painful.

11.1.5 Trading Energy Futures and Options at CBOT

In the future, there are multiple ways a utility company can manage its risks. On September 11, 1998, the CBOT launched new futures and options contracts based on the physical delivery of wholesale power of Commonwealth Edison (ComEd) and Tennessee Valley Authority (TVA) electricity systems.[6] Companies can now use electricity futures and options to reduce their financial risks due to price changes.

The ComEd electricity system has connections to nine utilities located in Illinois, Iowa, Indiana, and Wisconsin. The TVA electricity system has connections to 18 states that contain 47.8 percent of the population of the United States. CBOT electricity futures and options contracts are priced in dollars and cents per megawatt hour (MWh), with the contract trading unit sized at 1,680 MWh. The contract delivery points were chosen based on the development of liquid cash market trading hubs on each respective utility's system.

A hypothetical but realistic example illustrates how electricity futures can be used to hedge risks. Suppose you are an industrial company that buys power. One important feature of the electricity market is that price is more volatile in winter and summer, the peak demand seasons. Your goal is to control the electric power costs for your company. Your company has a base load of 100 MW of power during the 16 on-peak hours (6 AM to 10 PM) of on-peak days. For the 23 on-peak days of August 2001, you will need 36,800 MWh. To avoid rising prices, you can lock in a price by placing a long hedge using CBOT electricity futures. The way to do so is to buy the futures contract at CBOT. When the time comes to buy the actual power, you do so at the one-month forward price and simultaneously sell the futures contract. Because the price of the futures contract will reflect the rising price, your gain in the futures will offset the rise in electricity price.

Let us look at the numbers. By dividing 36,800 MWh by the standardized contract size (1,680 MWh), you get the number of contracts for the hedge. You will need to buy 22 August 2001 TVA Hub futures at a price of $32/MWh, with a total cost of $1,182,720. Suppose the electricity price is $36/MWh on July 28. You can sell August futures with a total price of $1,330,560. The cost of August electricity of 36,800 MWh will be $1,324,800. By hedging, you will actually pay $31.98/MWh [($1,182,720 + $1,324,800 − $1,330,560)/36,800] for electricity in August, rather than the going price of $36/MWh.

11.2 CATASTROPHE INSURANCE MARKETS

Our second example of using electronic market concept is catastrophe insurance market, which is fundamentally changing the way that risk is underwritten and shared.

11.2.1 Insurance and Reinsurance

Risk and insurance have become integral parts of modern-day life. Insurance companies provide protection against loss in value of human capital, physical property, and financial assets. Without insurance, many economic activities would be too risky to function. Reinsurance, however, is the business that insures the insurers. It is perhaps the most critical segment of the insurance market today.

Reinsurance takes two basic forms: quota share and excess of loss. In a quota share contract, the reinsurer simply shares in the profits or losses of the insured on a proportional basis. In an excess of loss reinsurance contract, the reinsurer agrees to indemnify an insurance company for all or part of its losses in excess of a fixed dollar amount called an attachment point. For example, reinsurance company A agrees to indemnify insurance company B for $500 million of losses in excess of $1 billion. In this case, if company B incurs underwriting losses of $1.1 billion, company A would pay B for $100 million.

Reinsurance provides the means for an insurer to assume more original insurance liability than its own resources would permit. In other words, reinsurance improves an insurer's capacity to serve its market. With reinsurance, an insurance company can write policies for monetary amounts substantially greater than those it could afford without reinsurance. Almost any insurer is limited in the amount of insurance it can write on any one risk. The law of averages makes it safer to write a large number of small risks than to write a few large risks. For example, a catastrophe as big as Hurricane Andrew can easily bankrupt an insurance company. Reinsurance can grant additional capacity that enhances its position.

In addition, reinsurance protects the insurer from a catastrophe and provides an element of stabilization to its performance.

11.2.2 Securitizing Insurance Risk

The reinsurance market works similarly as the over-the-counter (OTC) market for stocks. Although some insurers are in direct contact with reinsurance companies, a more typical arrangement is to use a reinsurance broker who charges a hefty commission. The catastrophe insurance market brings new efficiency in this industry by directly trading risks in a market. The process is called securitization, which is the process of removing nontraded assets from a financial intermediary's balance sheet by packaging them in a convenient form and selling the packaged securities in a financial market. Securitizing insurance risk enables institutions and individuals who are not in the insurance business to participate in the insurance market.

One of the advantages of this arrangement is that it provides more resources for the insurance industry to insure large catastrophes. Large catastrophes such as Hurricane Andrew ($16 billion, 1992) and the Northridge earthquake ($12.5 billion, 1994) cost the property insurance industry tens of billions of dollars. Some believe that even larger catastrophes are looming because population and building development continue to increase in highly exposed coastal areas such as California, Florida, and Texas. In addition, it is believed that such catastrophes will occur more frequently and with greater force in the future because of changes that are taking place in the earth's atmosphere. The insurance industry itself does not have enough resources to support major catastrophes. It is estimated that the total capital of the insurance and reinsurance industry has only about $275 billion, compared with the $25–$30 trillion worth of property in the nation. A large catastrophe could easily wipe out a large proportion of the whole insurance industry's assets. One way to introduce more resources in the insurance and reinsurance industry is to securitize insurance risks into tradable securities that can be exchanged in capital markets. After major catastrophes such as Hurricane Andrew, reinsurance rates tripled for almost every region in the world. Allowing investors in financial markets to participate in the reinsurance market will help to reduce premiums and costs of insurance.

But why would investors want to invest in such catastrophe-related securities? One reason is the high return. For example, although U.S. Treasury bonds pay an average 6 percent interest, the average catastrophe (cat) bond pays 10 to 12 percent. Another attraction of cat bonds is that their performance is not linked to the performance of the financial markets. Thus, portfolio managers may look to catastrophe securities as a means for diversification.

11.2.3 Cat Bonds

Cat bonds are financial instruments that turn reinsurance contracts into securities. If a catastrophe does not hit the regions covered by the insurance firm issuing the cat bond covering a particular period, investors will get back all their

FIGURE 11.3   *Securitizing Insurance Risks*[7]

principal plus a big interest payment. If a catastrophe does occur, investors may lose part of or all their principal (Figure 11.3).

One of the difficulties investors face when investing in cat bonds is how to evaluate the risk and pricing of these bonds. In 1997, USAA, a Texas-based insurer, successfully issued a $477 million cat bond. This bond is composed of two types: A-2 notes with a coupon of 5.755 percent plus LIBOR, in which the principal is completely at risk; and A-1 notes with a coupon of 2.82 percent over LIBOR, in which the coupon is at risk but the principal is guaranteed. An important element in the success of the USAA cat bond was the involvement of the rating agencies. The A-1 notes were AAA-rated because it guarantees the full return of principal. The A-2 notes were rated BB. Because a BB corporate bond pays an average of only 2 percent over LIBOR, the cat bond pays a substantial premium to investors. To investors, the rating makes it easier for them to assess their risk and return level and decide what kinds of investment they want.

11.2.4 CBOT Cat Options

On September 29, 1995, the CBOT began trading options contracts based on Property Claims Services' (PCS) indices, which track the aggregate amount of insured losses resulting from catastrophic events that occur in given regions and risk periods. PCS provides each index daily. After a catastrophic event occurs, PCS estimates the insured property damage by surveying a wide range of insurers regarding the dollar amount of claims they expect to receive. In addition, PCS also uses its own information about the value of the property in the affected counties and, in some cases, conducts its own on-the-ground survey of the damage. We next describe how catastrophe insurance options are traded at CBOT.

Market Instruments

At CBOT, option contracts are traded on one national, five regional (Eastern, Northeastern, Southeastern, Midwestern, and Western), and three state (California, Florida, and Texas) indices. Each index tracks PCS estimates for insured industry losses resulting from catastrophic events in the area and loss period covered. Each PCS index represents the sum of the PCS estimates for insured catastrophic losses in the area and loss period covered divided by $100 million. At the beginning of its risk period, each index is zero and increases afterward.

Loss Period and Development Period

The risk period for each index is the time period over which losses must occur for the resulting losses to be included in a particular index. For an index in which catastrophes are seasonal (e.g., hurricanes, tornadoes), the risk period is quarterly and the options trade on a March, June, September, December cycle, with the March contract covering first quarter and so on. For regions in which catastrophes are not seasonal (e.g., earthquakes), the risk period is annual and only a December contract is traded. The national index trades on both a quarterly and annual basis. Following each risk period, there is a loss development period of 12 months. During this time, PCS will update the amount of damage that occurred during the risk period as more information becomes available. Contracts are available for trading throughout the development period. The development period is necessary due to the difficulty in making a timely and accurate assessment of the amount of damage that has occurred after a large catastrophic event.

Small/Large-Cap Options

Each PCS index has both small-cap and large-cap option contracts listed for trading. Small-cap contracts track aggregate estimated catastrophic losses from $0 to $20 billion. Large-cap contracts track aggregate estimated catastrophic losses from $20 billion to $50 billion. These caps limit the amount of losses that are included under each contract and thus turn a buyer of a call into a call spread buyer. For example, a buyer of a December Northeastern 1998 100 call, in essence, is buying a 100/200 call spread. If there is an aggregate amount of insured damage in the Northeastern region totaling $25 billion dollars (250 index points), the owner of a 100 call will only be paid $20,000 [$(200 - 100) \times \$200$] for each call spread purchased and not $30,000 [(250 − 100) × $200]. In theory, these caps play an important role because traders would not want to write out-of-the-money calls for a small premium while bearing the risk of unlimited losses.

Call Spread

In practice, market participants recognize that the small/large caps do not provide enough protection against large losses and have therefore only traded call spreads. A call spread is essentially purchasing a call at one strike value and simultaneously selling another call of the same expiration at a higher strike value, thereby limiting the buyer's potential gain to the difference between the strike prices of the two options. The most commonly traded small- and large-cap call spreads transfer $4,000 (20 index points) and $10,000 (50 index points) of risk per spread, respectively. For example, a National 60/80 call option spread is equivalent to buying a National 60 call option and selling a National 80 call option.

Option Pricing

PCS index options are quoted in five-point increments, and the option prices, or premiums, are quoted in points and tenths of a point, with each point equaling a cash value of $200. Let's assume, for example, that on April 22, 1999, the market on a National Annual 60/80 option spread is 6.0/12.0. This means that the 40/60 strike prices are PCS Index values for industry losses of between $6 billion (60 × $100 million) and $8 billion. The 20-point ($2 billion) width of the spread has a value of $4,000 (20 × $200), and the market price of the spread is $1,200 bid (6.0 × $200) and $2,400 offer (12.0 × $200).

In addition to quoting prices for options and option spreads, CBOT also quotes "combo," which is the price quoted on a series of options (or option spreads). The following is an example of "combo":

- Buy Nat Jun 10/20
- Sell TX Jun 10/20   1.3 2.0
- Sell MDW Jun 10/20

The bid price is 1.3, and the offer price is 2.0.

An Example

Here, we use an example to demonstrate how an insurance company may seek to buy a call spread as an alternative to buying a traditional layer of reinsurance. Suppose a hypothetical insurance company, Newport Mutual, has a high concentration of its exposure in Florida and wants to limit its potential worst-case scenario loss of $120 million to just $80 million. Newport Mutual comprises 1 percent of the industry in Florida but has found that because they are underexposed (relative to the industry) along the coast, they experience losses of 80 percent of their expected market share. Instead of buying a traditional $40 million in excess of $80 million reinsurance layer, they can buy PCS call option spread at CBOT.

First, Newport Mutual has to calculate the appropriate amount of protection by relating its attachment points to the industry's attachment points. By dividing $80 million by the product of 1 percent and 80 percent, the company gets the industry attachment point of $10 billion or 100 index points. Similarly, the industry attachment point for $120 million loss is $15 billion or 150 index points. Therefore, Newport's $40 million in excess of $80 million level of protection is approximated by a 100/150 call spread. This translates to an industry loss range of $10 billion to $5 billion. Second, by dividing the amount of protection needed by amount of protection offered by each spread, we can calculate the number of spreads Newport has to buy. The total number of spreads in this case is 4,000 ($40 m/[(150 − 100) × $200]).

11.2.5 CATEX

The Catastrophe Risk Exchange (CATEX) is a New Jersey–based electronic market that allows property and casualty insurers, reinsurers, and brokers to swap or trade risk exposure to natural disasters (Figure 11.4). Developed in reaction to events such as Hurricane Andrew and the Northridge earthquake, the exchange is designed to allow insurers to protect themselves against severe losses by geographically distributing risk and diversifying across different perils through an electronic marketplace. CATEX was developed by a team led by Samuel Fortunato, former New Jersey Insurance Commissioner and cofounder of the Princeton-based CATEX, which is licensed by the New York Insurance Department as a neutral reinsurance intermediary. Trading operations on CATEX started in 1996. In 1998, CATEX was launched over the Internet. Meanwhile, CATEX is evolving from the initial swap exchange to a more complete insurance market, which supports the reinsurance transactions of marine, energy, political risk, and so on.

To qualify to use the system, a company must be registered with the New York Insurance Department, whose licensed insurers account for approximately 70 percent of all U.S. premiums. The initial cost to subscribe is $75,000 per year, and participating companies pay transaction fees to CATEX of $150 per $1 million of insured property risk traded. CATEX allows market participants to advertise potential trades for other subscribers to view and respond to. The market uses an open bid and ask system to let the market form prices for different transactions. Executives at CATEX hope that the system will improve the efficiency of the reinsurance market by allowing for greater input of potential trades for insurers to evaluate.

The System

The earlier CATEX system was operated via a nationwide computer communications system developed by Sun Microsystems and Science Applications International. Subscribers to the trading system can post catastrophe exposures they wish to exchange and view catastrophe exposures being offered by other risk bearers.

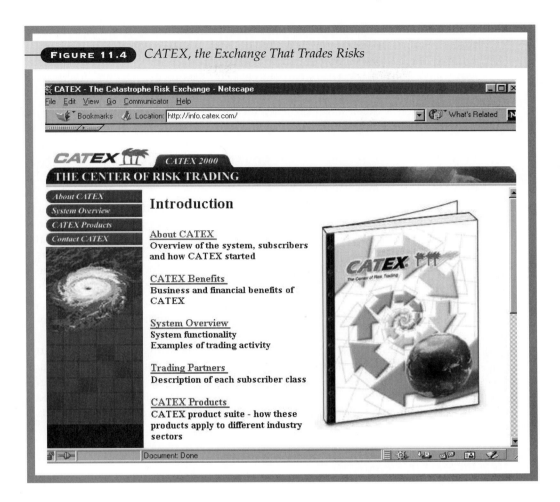

FIGURE 11.4 *CATEX, the Exchange That Trades Risks*

The subscribers would directly negotiate swap transactions, whereby two companies assume partial, reciprocal liability for a defined component of each other's risk, such as $50 million of New York windstorm exposure for $100 million of Midwest tornado exposure. A company can post risks anonymously and defer disclosure of its identity. Parties can negotiate via telephone, fax, mail, or e-mail.

Recently, the CATEX has been made available over the Internet. This Web-based system, which won the 1998 *Computerworld* Smithsonian Award, has the following four modules:

- The Post and Browse Module acts as a smart bulletin board that lets traders post and search offers to distribute and assume risk. The core technology is a relational client-server database. The key innovation is a controlled lexicon.

Listings are given a loose structure through templates. Within the template, the user describes the offer in free form text. To make text searches highly reliable, the system's Complex Instrument Trading Engine (CITX) provides a controlled vocabulary. Users can suggest changes to the lexicon, enabling it to evolve and keep pace with the industry.

- The Research Module uses browser technology to deliver vast amounts of information and help evaluate risk. In a single screen, this module provides a directory to Internet information, CATEX Intranet information, and links to companies that provide risk assessment services. The module flawlessly integrates these information sources behind transparent security firewalls to provide protection while preventing interruptions.

- The Contract Module provides tools for negotiating and signing a contract. Reinsurance contracts are typically complicated, with options on how a catastrophe is defined, how loss is calculated, how losses and premiums are paid, and many other factors. CATEX includes six standard contracts, each with 100 to 250 places to enter information. The contracts are programmed in Visual Basic for Applications (VBA) and run behind a word processor for fast and easy editing.

- The Communications Module is a suite of advanced tools, including off-the-shelf e-mail and fax technology, that traders use to contact one another. The model offers chat rooms with date and time stamping, a white-boarding capability, and application sharing with audio and optional video. Using the application sharing feature, traders can display the draft contract on several screens at once and make final changes to the contract language together. The innovative anonymous mail capability allows traders to send and receive mail through aliases.

How the Market Works

Here, we use an example to show how a company can use such a system. Suppose an insurance company in Iowa primarily writes farm policies, and the number one catastrophe in the state is crop damage. Because the company's exposure to this one kind of disaster is so large, it wants to seek reinsurance. Using CATEX, the company advertises its need to distribute risk and places offers to assume risk in a public "bulletin board"-like area. Responses from potential buyers with reciprocal interests are communicated electronically. If a transaction seems possible, the Iowa insurance company can easily access the information needed to determine if the other company can pay a loss quickly. To help in this assessment, CATEX provides online links to financial and related information about the trading companies. For companies assuming risk, CATEX offers links to risk analysis and information on weather events and forecasts, earthquakes, and other hazards.

Special code developed for CATEX creates the anonymous environment required for placements, research, and initial discussions. When it's time to finalize the transaction, both companies involved in the deal can drop their veil and negotiate a contract online. CATEX provides fill-in-the-blank contracts as a starting point, or negotiators can use their own. When the contract is final, CATEX allows for secure digital signatures.

Industry Response

CATEX has recruited nearly 60 subscribing companies and 200 traders, with more coming on board every week. Measured by assets (a traditional measure of insurance company size), this represents more than 15 percent of the entire U.S. insurance industry. Some insurance companies believe that the market will provide realistic pricing in terms of occurring events and allow for the commoditization of insurance and reinsurance down to a per-risk basis. For a start-up company bringing a completely new idea to a traditionally conservative industry, this is astounding market penetration.

There has, however, been a great deal of skepticism about CATEX. Because CATEX is independent of any insurance company or brokerage house, it did not have the backing of an established name in the business. This barrier was only overcome through persistence—speaking at every possible forum, making repeated visits to potential members of the exchange, and repeatedly demonstrating the technology. Some industry players note that the problem in negotiating reciprocal reinsurance contracts is not technical but rather involves the inability to come to terms on an exchange.

CATEX (Bermuda)

In 1998, the Bermuda Stock Exchange (BSX), an electronic offshore securities market, announced that it will launch, in conjunction with CATEX, an offshore insurance exchange market. The market, called CATEX (Bermuda), will allow participants to trade natural disaster risks that are available on CATEX but will do so in an offshore regulatory environment. This will make it easier for many companies, particularly those in Bermuda and Europe, to participate. Many non-U.S. insurance and reinsurance companies would prefer to participate in an offshore legal environment. The less stringent regulations at Bermuda allow nontraditional risk bearers, such as hedge funds or investment banks, to participate in the market. Whereas only insurance products can be traded on CATEX, CATEX (Bermuda) could be used to trade alternative products such as insurance derivatives.

11.3 IOWA ELECTRONIC MARKET

We now move from buying and selling electricity and catastrophe risks to trading political events. The IEM is a real-money futures market in which the value of the contracts traded depends on the realized value of various political events (Figure 11.5). Previously, the IEM was predominantly a market that traded

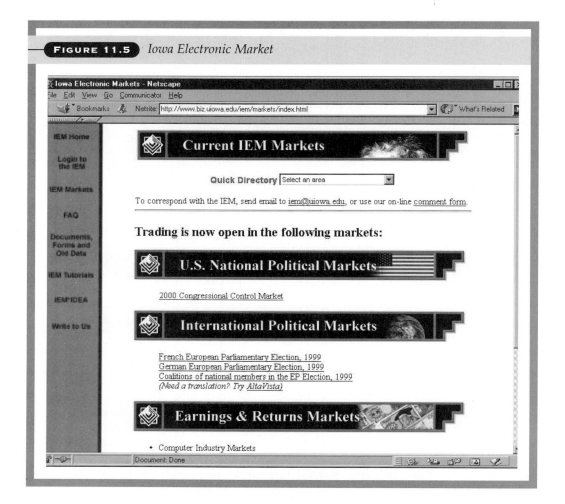

FIGURE 11.5 *Iowa Electronic Market*

contracts for the U.S. political events such as the presidential or congressional elections. Recently, international political markets such as the German parliamentary election and economic returns markets such as the computer industry return market have been added to the IEM.[8]

The goal of the IEM is to predict the outcome of future political or economic events through a market mechanism. The information about a political event such as a presidential election can only be found out through public polls. However, the accuracy of these polls is questionable. The results vary across different polls at the same time and also vary within the same poll over time. As unusual as it may seem to some, using a real-money market to predict the future political or economic outcome has the following advantages:[9]

1. Market participants have a financial stake in the outcome, and they have the incentive to trade based on their knowledge. However, respondents in a poll have no incentive to tell the truth other than their own consciences.

2. Because the goal of each market participant is to make money, he or she will trade according to his or her own beliefs about which candidate will win, whereas a respondent in a poll expresses an opinion about which candidate he or she prefers to win. As a result, the market reduces the bias of the market participants, which may distort the prediction results.

3. The IEM is continuous. The fluctuations of the contract values provide a low-cost way to reveal the collective impression of the effects of the current events on the prospects of each candidate. By contrast, polls lag behind current events and are costly.

11.3.1 Market Instruments and Payoffs

All financial instruments traded in the IEM are called contracts. Each contract has a final liquidation value or payoff determined by the outcome of some future political or economic events such as the final results of the presidential election. To take part in the IEM, a participant has to open an account at IEM by depositing cash. Currently, the minimum investment for an account is $5, the maximum $500. The limit on the maximum investment curtails the possibility of individual players influencing the prices. After opening an account, each participant receives a newly issued bundle of contracts with one share for each contract. In the 1998 Congressional Control Market, for example, the bundle included the following four contracts:

- RhRs: Republican House, Republican Senate
- RhNs: Republican House, Non-Republican Senate
- NhRs: Non-Republican House, Republican Senate
- NhNs: Non-Republican House, Non-Republican Senate

A unit bundle consists of one share of each of these four contracts. Participants can purchase the unit portfolio for $1. The total liquidation value of each unit bundle is also $1 because exactly one of the four contracts will be the result of the congressional election. After acquiring the unit bundle, the participants are allowed to trade the individual contracts within the bundle. There are two types of payoffs for the contracts:

- *Winner-Takes-All Contracts.* Only one contract in a winner-takes-all bundle will have a $1 liquidation value; the others will expire worthless. For example, in the 1998 Congressional Control Market, the contract that denoted the actual election outcome had a liquidation value of $1 and all other contracts had values of $0. Since the 1998 elections resulted in Republicans controlling both the House and the Senate, the contract RhRs had a liquidation value of $1, while the other three contracts had zero values.

■ *Linear Earnings Contracts.* Unlike the winner-takes-all contracts, all contracts in a linear earnings bundle can have a positive liquidation value. The total unit bundle liquidation value will still be $1; but how the $1 is divided between different contracts is determined by the liquidation formulas for the bundle. For example, a presidential election can be designed based on linear earnings contracts. The payoff of a contract can be computed as $1 times the percentage of the popular votes earned by the candidate specified in that contract.

11.3.2 Market Format

The IEM is organized as a continuous double-auction market. Market participants trade with each other in the market. The bids and offers are stored in the market limit-order table. Current market prices can be observed by anyone with Internet access, but only registered participants can actually trade in the market. Trading in the IEM takes place according to the following market format and trading rules.

■ *Limit Order.* To submit a limit order, the trader has to specify the contract name, the price, the number of shares, and the order time limit. For example, a trader can bid $.75 per RhRs contract for a total of four contracts, and the order is good for three days. For a unit portfolio with $1 value, bid and ask prices must fall in the range from zero to $1.

■ *Market Order.* Traders can buy or sell by using market orders. The market order is executed immediately. The price for a market buy order equals the current lowest ask, and the price for a market sell order equals the current highest bid. Using market orders, traders can seek immediate transactions but at an uncertain price.

■ *Order Execution.* An order is executed only if the buy price for a contract is higher or equal to the price of the same contract. If this price condition is not met, the order is placed in the bid or the offer queue waiting for execution. In addition, the IEM has feasibility checks for the submitted order. For a buy order, the total transaction price cannot exceed the cash account balance for the buyer. For a sell order, the seller has to own the underlying contracts.

■ *Cancel an Outstanding Order.* A trader can view his or her outstanding orders and cancel the open orders. To revise an order, the trader has to cancel the existing order first and submit a new one. The order is not eligible for cancellation after it has been executed.

The goal for traders in the IEM is to make as much money as possible. Traders can make money in two ways. First, a trader can buy a contract and sell it at a higher price. The price in the market fluctuates over time as more political or economic events unfold. For example, a trader who bought a contract for $.40 can make $.10 profit per contract by selling the contract if the market price for the contract rises to $.50. Second, a trader can buy a contract and hold it until the expiration of the contract and get paid according to the final liquidation value.

11.3.3 Market Performance

First created in 1988, the IEM has performed well. It has forecasted election results with surprising accuracy. In the 1988 presidential election, Bush won the
election over Dukakis with a margin of about 7.8 percent. The IEM predicted a 7
percent advantage for Bush on October 17, and from then until the election it had
Bush winning by a margin ranging from 5.6 to 8 percent. Over the same period,
the major polls predicted Bush's winning margin to be between 4 and 14 percent.
In 1996, Clinton won the presidential election by a margin of about 10 percent
over Dole, quite close compared with the IEM market prediction of a winning
margin of 9 percent.

The IEM's performance to date has created some interesting results that deserve
more rigorous study in the future:

1. The IEM has achieved highly accurate predictions from the trading of an
   unrepresentative sample of electorate. By contrast, a representative sample
   is critical to the accuracy of an opinion poll.

2. The IEM demonstrates market efficiency. Market price shifts reflect the new
   events and new information that are available to the public.

3. Generally, opinion polls are believed to affect the outcome of the political
   process. In the IEM, the release of the poll results had little impact on market
   prices.

From the IEM, we can see that the market has an enormous ability to aggregate
and process information. Originally, economist F. A. Hayek claimed that markets
could work correctly even if the participants had limited knowledge about their
environment or about other participants. This is the famous Hayek hypothesis.
The IEM provides further evidence that this hypothesis holds. How exactly the
market achieves such remarkable success is not yet fully understood. The most
interesting point is that the market accurately predicted the future events by
aggregating information from an unrepresentative sample of the population.
Although we understand that incentive plays an important part in the success of
the market, the mechanism of the "invisible hand" deserves more research.

11.4 HOLLYWOOD STOCK EXCHANGE

The HSX functions similarly to the IEM (Figure 11.6). Participants can learn about
movies in development, production, and release. They can also buy and sell
shares in MovieStocks and StarBonds. The market was created in late 1996 by
Michael Burns and Max Keiser, two former stock brokers. It is operated much
like a regular financial market, with financial instruments such as stocks, bonds,
options, and mutual funds. Currently, however, trading in HSX uses only token

FIGURE 11.6   *Hollywood Stock Exchange's Home Page*

money. Anybody can open an account with HSX. On opening a new account, a participant is given $2 million token money and some shares of a stock or StarBond. A participant can earn an additional $50,000 in token money by answering a survey about the movies he or she recently watched.[10] Eventually, Burns and Keiser want HSX to be used to finance the production of films as market participants put up their own money to invest in movies.

11.4.1 MovieStocks, StarBonds, and Options

HSX has various financial products that participants can trade, including stocks, bonds, and even options.

MovieStocks MovieStocks are the stocks for movies. The value of a particular stock is based on what a movie will gross at the box office during its first four weekends in its release on 650 screens or more in the United States. After four weekends in release, the HSX will cash in a MovieStock at the price that corresponds exactly with the amount a movie has grossed to that point. At that time, the MovieStock is delisted from the exchange. The delist price is calculated by dividing the four weekends' box office revenue by the outstanding shares for the movie. All the shares for the delisted MovieStock will be converted into cash with no commission charges. Before delisting, the price of a MovieStock is determined by the supply and demand of the market. But on its opening weekend, the price of a MovieStock is adjusted by HSX based on the multiple of 2.9 and the box office gross to bring the price closer to its final delist price.

A MovieStock can be traded in HSX after its initial public offering (IPO). In fact, a MovieStock has its IPO long before the movie is officially released. In fact, a MovieStock's life consists of four stages:

1. *Concept (C).* At this stage, the MovieStock represents a rumored film project. The concept stocks are speculative with high risk. A trader can own up to 12,500 shares in each concept MovieStock.

2. *Development (D).* The development stocks represent projects in the preproduction phase with a writer, director, and possible actors. But the arrangement can still change at any time. A market participant can own up to 25,000 shares in each development stock.

3. *Production (P).* These MovieStocks represent projects that have already started filming. The risk of owning a production MovieStock is significantly lower than that of a concept or development stock. A trader can own up to 37,500 shares in each production MovieStock.

4. *Release (R).* These MovieStocks represent completed movies that are in release or about to be released. A trader can own up to 50,000 shares in a release stock, which typically carries the lowest risk of all.

As a movie progresses through the above stages, HSX will issue additional shares for the movie. As of July 2000, the movies that were in concept stage include *Austin Powers 3* and *The Monica Lewinsky Story.* The development stage movies include *Airframe* and *Cold Mountain.* The production movies include *Atlantis* and *Charlie's Angels.* The movies that were in release include *Perfect Storm* and *X-Men.*

StarBonds Traders can invest in individual actors by using StarBonds, which pay interest depending on a star's rating. A StarBond's rating is determined by a star's average box office gross of the movies that the star has been in during the past three years. That number is called the trailing average gross (TAG). For example, a AAA rating, which pays $60 coupon annually, requires the TAG to be $100 million or more whereas an A rating, which pays $100 coupon, has a TAG between $50 and $74.9 million. Lower-rated StarBonds have higher risks, so the coupon rate for a lower-rated bond is higher than a higher-rated bond to compensate traders for investing in riskier bonds. The price of a StarBond reflects the current and future earnings of the bond plus the value of any ratings changes of the bond.

Options HSX options are different from regular financial markets options. The value of an HSX option depends solely on a MovieStock grosses in its opening weekend, not the full four weeks. For example, if an option has a strike price of $20, it means the MovieStock is expected to earn $20 million at its opening. A call option of the MovieStock allows a trader to speculate that the movie will do better than $20 million, whereas a put allows a trader to speculate that the movie will do worse than $20 million. The payoff of a call option equals to *max {0, option price − strike price}.* For a call option with a strike price of $20, the movie has to make more than $20 million for the investor to have any possibility to make any money. If the movie makes less than $20 million, the option is worth zero. Similarly, for a trader holding a put to make money, the movie has to make less than the expected dollar amount.

Trading in a MovieStock option is halted on the Saturday of the opening weekend of the movie. The option will then be delisted on the Monday following the opening weekend. Owners of the option will be credited with cash if the option makes positive returns. Before delisting, the option price fluctuates depending on traders' expectation and supply and demand.

11.4.2 Market Information

Trading in HSX is complicated because of the enormous amount of information available on the movie industry and the complexity of the instruments traded in the market. Providing up-to-date information is critical to the success of the market. HSX and its fan sites provide rich information to help individuals at all levels become informed traders.

Stock Profile The value of a movie stock depends on many things such as the director, star power, and the producer. Almost all the information can be found on a movie's profile page provided by HSX. The title indicates not only the name and ticker symbol of the movie but also the stage the movie is in. As discussed earlier, (C) and (D) movies are far riskier than (P) and (R) movies. In addition, the profile page tells the genre of the movie—whether it is a drama, a comedy, a thriller, or a science fiction.

Fan sites HSX has several high-profile fan sites, which have played an important role in supporting the HSX. Here we describe some of them:

- The Hollywood Stock Journal offers an up-to-date look at the movie business, with real-time charts of box office performers and scoops of HSX developments. It has columnists who write regularly about the movies and the entertainment industry. Besides the latest box office data, the Journal also maintains movie reviews, staff predictions, an HSX players' guide, and historical box office data.
- The Hollywood Stock Brokerage & Resource is one of the top HSX fan sites that features columns from Curtis Edmonds, Bond King, and so on.

Curtis Edmonds, known as "Blueduck," auctioned off his portfolio on ebay, the Internet auction house, in February 1999. The highest bid for his imaginary portfolio, which is worth $136 million in HSX dollars, was $1,050 in real dollars after a seven-day auction.

■ The Traders is a site for the more advanced HSX trader, or the trader who wants to become more advanced. The site is a virtual HSX community with columnists who write daily articles about the movie industry. It also publishes the latest entertainment news. Its members run several mutual funds that are also traded at HSX.

11.4.3 The Future

It is interesting to speculate how HSX will develop in the future. Possible directions include

1. Becoming a mechanism to finance the future of development of movie and other entertainment programs. Traders can bet by using their own money to finance the next *Titanic* or *Jurassic Park*.

2. Even though traders are not using real dollars, the trading generates valuable information that can be used to help studio executives or independent filmmakers make better decisions as to what films to develop.

3. With a couple of million potential users, HSX and its fan sites could become a virtual entertainment community with a tremendous marketing power. The site could generate enormous advertisement revenue and sell merchandise related to movies such as toys and games to the users.

Whichever direction HSX will go in the future, attracting a large number of users to the site is crucial. Once there is a large number of users, HSX will become a significant player in the entertainment industry. As we are writing this book, HSX has opened a Music Market where people can trade ArtistStocks for musical artists of all types.

11.5 SUMMARY

This chapter has discussed several unconventional "financial" markets. Even though these markets borrow their ideas from the financial markets and use basic operating principles of financial markets, they all function somewhat differently. The focus of the electricity markets and catastrophe insurance markets is to have a price discovery mechanism for the underlying assets and to bring new efficiencies to the traditional industry. In the IEM, HSX, or even the catastrophe insurance markets, although the underlying instruments are based on physical events, there is no physical delivery or settlement using physical products. The trading, information dissemination, and settlement processes are totally digitized. These markets, in addition to the traditional functions of matching buyers and sellers and discovering prices, also serve as mechanisms for risk sharing and information aggregation and processing. With the rapid advances of information technology, particularly the Internet and the WWW, more new innovative markets will be developed to solve traditional problems. It is fair to say that our understanding of markets is still at an early stage. More research, experiments, and innovative applications are expected in this area.

12

EMERGING TECHNOLOGIES FOR ELECTRONIC MARKETS

Rapid advances in computer and communication technologies are revolutionizing the way financial information systems are developed. The Internet and the World Wide Web (WWW) have changed the landscape of computing in a way that no other technologies have done before. Together they provide a universal communication network and standard user interface that unify different computing platforms and allow individuals to access information and execute applications from virtually anywhere. Internet- and Web-based computing have crossed the boundaries of different firms and nations and provide a computing infrastructure for the financial industry to develop integrated trading and financial systems.

Because of the tremendous anticipated advantages of the Internet, many companies jumped to Web-based computing before it was actually ready. Earlier Web-based computing systems used the hypertext markup language (HTML) and common gateway interface (CGI) approach. The focus was on information retrieval and display rather than computing. The Web browser is simply a display tool that provides limited interactivity between the client and the server. Therefore, there is a strong need to integrate Web-based computing with distributed object technology to overcome the limitations of earlier Web-based applications. The integration of the WWW, distributed objects, and Java offers a solid technological infrastructure and a set of tools to develop the next generation of software systems. The infrastructure has the following synergies:

- Applications can be deployed universally over the Internet and the Intranet. Users can access the system from virtually any place at any time by using all kinds of devices, such as laptops, desktops, workstations, phones, or handheld wireless devices.

- Applications implemented in different languages and running from different operating systems and platforms can communicate and share functions with each other through communication protocols such as the Internet inter-ORB protocol (IIOP) or Java remote method invocation (RMI). Data and information flow in a company can be seamlessly integrated. The ability of information sharing and exchange will be further enhanced by the development of extensible markup language (XML), the future of the markup language for Web browsers.

- The system development cycle will be shortened significantly by using the Java computing framework and component-based software engineering approach.

- The resulting systems can be highly customized by using the component approach, assembling individual components that fit the business processes best. Systems can evolve with changing business strategies and processes easily.

From a computing point of view, an electronic market over the Internet is a large-scale distributed computing system. The trading and clearing system consists of a large number of autonomous computers linked together through a communication network. A distributed computing framework has many advantages. Clients can access different investment services throughout the system. For example, investors can access market news, get real-time quotes, and conduct online trading. In a distributed computing environment, investors can access these services without knowing the detailed configurations of the system. Moreover, a distributed system can provide a fault-tolerant environment that will greatly reduce the possibility of system failures.

This chapter begins with an overview of electronic trading networks. We then discuss various technology tools for developing online applications, including HTML, CGI, common object request broker architecture (CORBA), Java, active server pages (ASP), Java server pages (JSP), and XML. Transaction securities are also reviewed. Further, we outline the architecture of an object-based financial trading system and describe the various services and applications components of the system. Distributed computing issues such as concurrent processing, synchronization, asynchronous communication, and fault tolerance are discussed as well.

12.1 ELECTRONIC TRADING NETWORKS

Figure 12.1 is a diagram of an electronic trading and clearing network, in which we have an electronic exchange, clearinghouse, and traders linked together with high-speed communication networks. Traders can access the market from

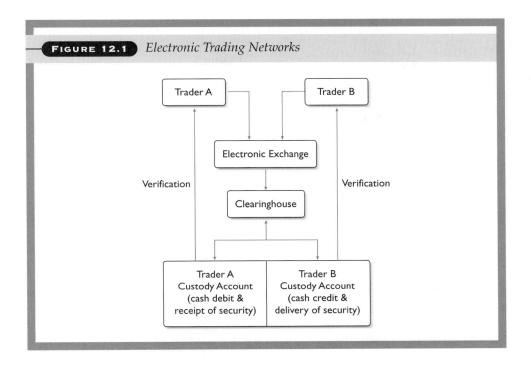

FIGURE 12.1 *Electronic Trading Networks*

virtually any place at any time by using all kinds of devices such as wireless phones and computers. Communication between traders and an exchange will use secure communication protocols. The traders and the electronic exchange identify and authenticate each other through their digital signatures and digital certificates issued by trusted certification authorities. Using this setup, orders can go directly from traders to the exchange. The only requirement is that an order has to be electronically verified against the trader's custody account to make sure that the order is valid. For example, to submit a sell order, a trader has to have the financial security. For a buy order, the trader has to have enough cash or margin requirement. After the validation process, the order simply bears a digital certificate so that it can be transmitted directly from the trader to the exchange.

Trading in the electronic exchange is fully automated. A computerized automated market not only transmits orders electronically but also matches orders by using a computerized algorithm. Computerized order matching and execution significantly improve market efficiency. By fully automating the trading process, the electronic exchange can conduct sophisticated matches (e.g., matching bundle or combinational orders) that human market makers are unable to do. In addition, electronic trading can handle a large trading volume and speed up the whole trading and clearing process. A speedy clearing process will substantially reduce default risks in the market.

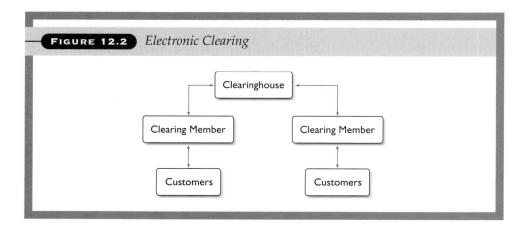

FIGURE 12.2 *Electronic Clearing*

The electronic exchange is linked with a global clearinghouse. Trading data from the exchange can be transferred to the clearinghouse electronically. The clearinghouse settles the trade by transferring the ownership of the security from the seller's custody account to that of the buyer and then by debiting the transaction price to the buyer's account and crediting it to the seller's account. To reduce risks and clearing volume, the clearinghouse does not clear transactions from all the customers directly (Figure 12.2). Only the members of the clearinghouse (exchange) can settle their transactions through the clearinghouse directly. Nonmember customers can settle their transactions through clearinghouse members.

12.2 INTERNET-BASED DEVELOPMENT TOOLS

Traditionally, the trading system uses proprietary client-server technology. The next-generation electronic trading and clearing network will adopt Internet-based open technologies to have a worldwide reach. Here, we discuss technologies for developing future financial applications.

12.2.1 HTML and CGI

HTML is a simple markup language containing text and a few dozen tags that tell a browser exactly how to format the text and specify the hypertext links to other Web pages. HTML language is in ASCII format, and it is easy to use different text editor tools to create HTML files. Hypertext transport protocol

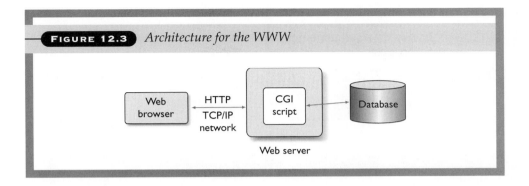

FIGURE 12.3 *Architecture for the WWW*

(HTTP) is the communication protocol that transfers HTML files from Web servers to Web browsers. Figure 12.3 displays the architecture of the WWW. When one wants to visit a particular Web site, the Web browser first locates the site through the site's uniform resource locator (URL). For example, the URL for Yahoo!'s home page is http://www.yahoo.com. Then, the browser issues a request to the Web server, and the server sends the HTML file to the browser by using HTTP. After that, the browser and Web server disconnect, and the transaction ends.

The initial Web applications focus on sending information from server to browser. The demand is gradually increasing for interactive Web-based applications that allow the server to respond to requests coming from clients. These applications often have to involve corporate databases and business applications. Examples include Internet searches and filling out registration forms and order forms. The HTML "form" tag and CGI have been introduced to handle this type of interactive application. An HTML form is delimited by using the <form>...</form> tags and is displayed on the client's Web browser. The data creating databases and that a user enters into data and communicates with other applications creating the form are captured and sent to the Web server. The CGI script interprets the data, interacts with databases, and generates dynamic Web pages. CGI is a widely used standard interface between Web servers and applications. CGI scripts can be written in many languages that conform to the CGI standard. The most common choices are Perl, Tcl, C++, and Java. For a long time, CGI was the only available approach for developing online interactive applications. Figure 12.4 represents National Discount Broker's WebStation, an online trading application. The application is developed by using an HTML frame. The following are some of the features provided by WebStation:

- Get real-time quotes on stocks, indexes, warrants, options, and mutual funds.
- Submit buy or sell orders.
- Cancel any open orders.

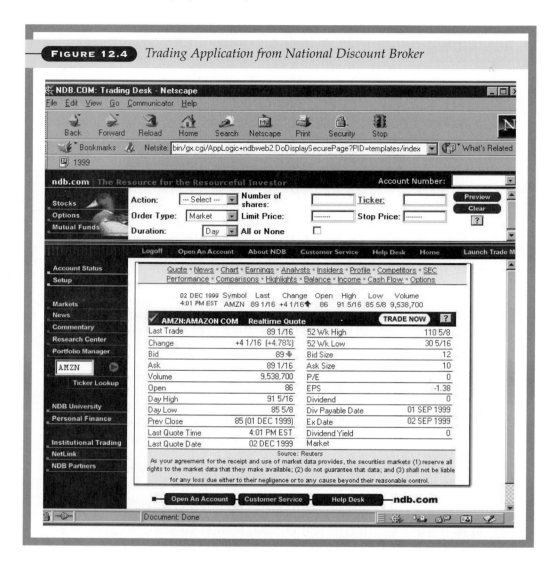

FIGURE 12.4 *Trading Application from National Discount Broker*

- View a list of open orders.
- View account's value and balances.
- View order execution history.
- View news summaries from Reuters.
- View an options chain (a list of all options and their symbols) for a stock or index.

12.2.2 CORBA

CORBA is a distributed object-oriented computing standard proposed by the Object Management Group (OMG). It provides an infrastructure that allows objects to communicate independent of the specific platforms and techniques used to implement the addressed objects. There are four key elements of the OMG's object management architecture (Figure 12.5):

- *The Object Request Broker (ORB).* The ORB is the object interconnection bus. CORBA provides an interface definition language (IDL), which can be used to define object interfaces independent of implementation. Clients and servers in a CORBA environment do not need to know the details of each other's implementation. IDL tells which methods can be invoked on an object. Using CORBA, we can create object interfaces and implement objects by using different programming languages. Once these objects are implemented and registered with the system, they can communicate with each other through ORB.

- *Object Services.* These services extend the capabilities of the ORB. The common object services include naming and directory, event notification, persistence, life-cycle management, transactions, concurrency control, relationships, and externalization. Other services proposed by OMG include query, licensing, properties, security, and time.

- *Common Facilities.* These facilities are a collection of higher-level services broadly applicable to many high-value capabilities for specific domains. Common facilities for most applications include user interface, information storage and retrieval, system management, and task management. Domain-specific

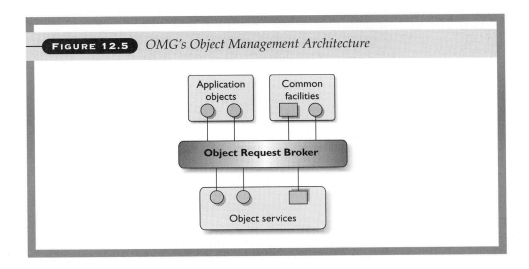

FIGURE 12.5 *OMG's Object Management Architecture*

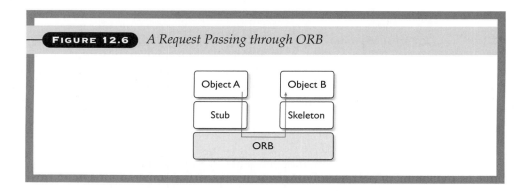

FIGURE 12.6   *A Request Passing through ORB*

facilities represent technology that supports various specialized applications, such as health care, retailing, financial systems, and manufacturing.

- *Application Objects.* These objects are components specific to end-user applications and build on top of ORB, object services, and common facilities. Application objects have IDL-defined interfaces and interact with other application objects.

Language neutral is one of the biggest advantages of CORBA. CORBA objects can be programmed by using different languages and are still able to operate with each other. For example, a Java applet can communicate with a server application that is implemented in C, C++, or Java. The developer has to define properly the object interfaces by using IDL and select an ORB product that supports the different languages. The job of OMG is to develop standards for CORBA, and the implementation of CORBA is left for private companies. There are a few commercial ORB products, such as DAIS from PeerLogic, Orbix from Iona, and DSOM from IBM. Sun Microsystems has developed an ORB product that can support the distributed communication of Java objects. It has the *idltojava* compiler that can generate portable client stubs and server skeletons. When object A invokes a method on object B, A's stub code uses the ORB for a connection to B's server and locates object B through the naming service (Figure 12.6). If interactive communication is needed, A has to export its reference to B at its initial contact. Then, object B can call back A through ORB.

Figure 12.7 is a Java applet application using a CORBA communication model. The application broadcasts live prices for all the stocks that are traded in Easdaq (European Association of Securities Dealers Automated Quotation). Easdaq lists many high-tech companies in biotechnology, telecommunications, and computer technologies. The Java application displays the trading volume as well as different market prices, such as the mid, high, low, bid, ask, and last traded prices. A user can customize a portfolio of companies that he or she wants to follow. The prices will update constantly and reflect the price movements in the real market. This

---

FIGURE 12.7 *Live Price Information from Easdaq*

Code	Company	U/D	Curren	Mid Price	High	Low	Bid	Ask	Last Trade	Volume
ACTV	ACTIVCARD	D	USD	+2.315	+2.4	+2.32	+2.26	+2.3700	+2.32	+9000
AWSG	ARTWORK SYSTEMS	U	USD	+16.75	+17.125	+16.5	+16.5	+17	+17	+11320
CHMX	CHEMUNEX S A	D	FRF	+7.45	+7.78	+7.4	+7.3	+7.6	+7.5	+125700
DEBA	DEBONAIR HLDGS	D	GBP	+1.515	+1.5	+1.5	+1.48	+1.55	+1.5	+2900
EPIQ	EPIQ NV	U	DEM	+4.9375	+5.125	+4.77	+4.875	+5	+4.875	+24450
ESAT	ESAT TELECOM GRP	D	USD	+33	+33.75	+33.75	+32	+34	+33.75	+50
ESPR	ESPRIT TELECOM	U	USD	+27.75	+28.125	+26.875	+26.875	+28.625	+28.125	+1290
FLVF	F.L.V.FUND	D	USD	+14.375	+14.5	+14	+14.25	+14.5	+14.25	+18165
GLGR	GLOBAL GRAPHICS	U	FRF	+252	+250	+249	+250	+254	+250	+2480
GRAN	GRANGER TELECOM	U	USD	+11.5	+12	+10.375	+11	+12	+12	+1385
IVIS	ICOS VISION SYS	U	USD	+13.6875	+14	+14	+13.375	+14	+14	+323
LHSP	LERNOUT & HAUSP	D	USD	+36.3125	+37.5	+33.75	+36	+36.625	+34.125	+190512
OPIN	OPTION INTL NV	D	USD	+31.1875	+31.375	+31	+31	+31.375	+31	+26829

© EASDAQ European Association of Securities dealers Automated Quotation
Unsigned Java Applet Window

application successfully uses a distributed object model that supports interactive communication between an applet object and a server.

12.2.3 Java

Java is an important technology for implementing the electronic trading network that we have discussed. Started as a research project at Sun Microsystems in the early 1990s, Java is becoming one of the most popular programming languages today. One of the most important reasons for the great success of Java is that it integrates well with the WWW and can be deployed virtually anywhere over the Internet. Besides, Java is simple compared with languages such as C++, which leads to quicker project development. Many companies, including banks, investment companies, and exchanges, are developing client applications using Java. Compared with other programming languages, Java has more useful features. Next, we describe these features in the framework of developing electronic market applications.

Object-Oriented Language

Java is an object-oriented programming language. According to Bjarne Stroustrup, the designer of C++, a programming language serves two purposes. It provides a tool for programmers to specify computation actions to be executed, and it provides a set of concepts for developers to use when thinking about what can be done. The first purpose ideally requires a language that is "close to the machine," so that the instructions to the computer are executed simply and efficiently. The second purpose requires a language that is "close to the problem," so that the concepts of a solution can be modeled directly and concisely. The C language was designed primarily for the first purpose. Object-oriented languages such as Java and C++ serve the second purpose well. Objects that represent hierarchical orders in the real world are powerful conceptual tools for modeling real-world problems. In contrast with earlier procedural and modular programming paradigms, which focused on algorithmic procedures and modules, object-oriented programming allows programmers to define a set of classes with a clear hierarchical structure to solve a particular problem. Object-oriented programming and software engineering provide many advantages. Object-oriented design provides a clearer model of real-world problems. Object-oriented libraries, which contain many existing classes, make programming a much simpler job. Overall, object-oriented software engineering promises faster project development and cheaper maintenance cost.

Now, we discuss the concepts of object and class in more detail. Object is the fundamental concept of objected-oriented programming and is the building block of Java applications. Simply put, an object is an instance of the same class that has similar behavior. A class is a user-defined type, which has predefined behaviors. The key characteristics of an object are its identity, state, and behavior. An object has its unique identity and its own state. The latter is described by a set of state variables that stores the information about the object. Let us look at an order in stock trading. In theory, individual orders in the market are instances of the class *order*, and they always have different identities and most likely have different states. Some of the state variables of an order in the stock market are owner name, security symbol, type of order, number of shares, executed price, and order status. The behavior of an order is normally represented by its methods. For example, the two fundamental methods of an order are "submit" and "cancel." An object integrates data and functions and hides the details of the implementation to other objects. This property is called encapsulation.

Another important property of object-oriented programming is inheritance. This means that one class (subclass) can inherit a superclass by receiving the data structures and functions defined in the superclass. The subclass can extend the superclass and be customized to have some special behavior. This property has proven extremely convenient and efficient in developing financial market applications. For example, we can create market order, limit order, and stop order by extending the superclass order (Figure 12.8).

Distributed Applications

Traditionally, network application development is difficult. Programmers have to understand the details of the network as well as the network protocols. They also

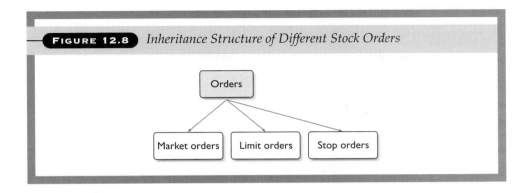

FIGURE 12.8 *Inheritance Structure of Different Stock Orders*

have to know the hardware platform where the software will be deployed to develop network applications. Java has changed all that. Compared to C or C++, Java provides a much easier environment for network application development. This is one of the great strengths of Java. Java has an extensive library of routines for coping with TCP/IP. The core Java API comes with a standard set of classes that provide uniform access to networking protocols such as TCP/IP and user datagram protocol (UDP) across all the platforms to which the Java virtual machine (JVM) has been ported. The *java.net* package provides basic network classes, and the *java.io* package provides a uniform streams-based interface to communication channels. Classes in both packages can be extended to develop sophisticated Internet applications for messaging services and information searching and retrieval.

Another important network function of Java is RMI, which can be used to develop a distributed object application. RMI enables interactive communication between objects distributed over the network. Data and even objects can be transmitted in the network environment. Currently, RMI is suited for distributed applications developed in Java. In the future, new protocols will be introduced to provide compatibility between RMI and CORBA so that RMI objects will become interoperable with CORBA objects. These functions are crucial to developing electronic markets, which are, in effect, distributed applications.

Multithreading

We discuss *multitasking* before explaining multithreading. Multitasking is the ability to have more than one program working at the same time. For example, one can edit a document while downloading and printing a file. A multiple-processor computer can naturally carry out multiple tasks simultaneously. In a single-processor machine, multitasking is realized by alternate or shared CPU time for different programs, giving the impression of simultaneity.

Multithreading takes the idea of multitasking a step further. In multithreading, an individual program operates multiple tasks simultaneously. Each individual

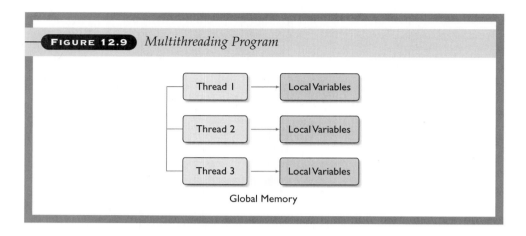

FIGURE 12.9 *Multithreading Program*

task within a process is controlled by a thread, which is a single sequential flow of control within a computing process. Thus, multithreading allows one program to launch multiple threads to do multiple tasks at the same time. Compared with a *computational process*, which has its own address space, threads share the same address space (Figure 12.9). Therefore, a thread uses less system resources. In addition, inter-thread communication is much faster than interprocess communication. In a multiprocessor workstation, multiple threads can operate in parallel to utilize different processors. In a single-processor machine, multiple threads run in an interleaved manner and enable different tasks to be performed simultaneously. However, risks exist for multithreaded programs. Because threads share the same memory space, different threads may interfere with one another. The solution to this problem is called concurrency control, which is discussed later in the chapter.

Java has built-in functions for developing multithreaded programs. The benefits of multithreading are improved interactive responsiveness and performance for real-time applications. For example, using multithreading, the message server at the electronic market can provide concurrent access for many clients. Multithreading also allows traders' applications to perform multiple tasks simultaneously. For example, while a trader submits an order, the application can download market information and real-time price updates.

12.2.4 Java and the WWW

Applications developed in Java can run on different computer platforms without modifications. To be platform independent, the Java compiler precompiles the program into an architecture-neutral byte code that is executable in the Java Virtual Machine (JVM). The JVM is a Java run-time environment, running on top of a particular operating system and interpreting the Java byte code into the native machine instruction. This enables applications developed in Java to be architecture-neutral and deployed through the Internet. Users can download Java programs and run them on their own machines. This guarantees that applications are "developed once and run everywhere."

Java programs that can run on Web pages are called applets and can be downloaded and executed. Unlike regular software applications that have to be installed and reside in local computers, applets can be obtained when they are needed. After use, the applets are simply deleted from the computer memory. There are many other advantages of using applets for Web-based applications.

Applications developed using applets can be accessed from virtually anywhere at any time. This has fundamentally changed the way software and, more importantly, real-time business applications such as financial trading systems are deployed. Users can use all kinds of devices such as computers and hand-held wireless devices to execute the applications.

Different from other Web-based applications such as CGI scripts and ASP, applets are full-fledged applications that have sophisticated graphical user interface (GUI) and are easy to operate. Applets also support client-side computing. Therefore, not every request has to go through the Web server as in the case of using HTML and CGI scripts.

Applets provide a new approach in distributing software. By imbedding applets within the WWW, end-users will be able to use the most updated application every time they access the market without worrying about the version or obsolescence of the application.

Figure 12.10 displays the general layout of a trading applet that we implemented by using Java Swing, which is a new set of user interface components of the Java foundation classes (JFC). When Java was first released, it had weak user-interface facilities named the abstract window toolkit (AWT). AWT provides frames, menus, buttons, lists, and a few other objects but does not have more sophisticated graphical components such as tables and progress bars, which are useful in financial applications development. AWT is therefore inadequate for advanced business applications. Another problem with AWT is that it relies heavily on the run-time platform's native user-interface components, and its appearance is not platform independent. Swing, considered by many to be the next-generation GUI toolkit to enable large-scale business application development in Java, was initially released in 1997. It is now a part of the Java development kit. The following are the new features of Swing:

- *Pluggable Look and Feel.* A pluggable look and feel means that end-users can choose at run time the style of their applications. If a user wants an application to look and behave like a typical Windows application, he or she can have that. He or she can also choose to switch to a different look, such as UNIX motif or Macintosh.

- *Support for People with Disabilities.* The JFC will be able to interoperate with software such as screen readers, screen magnifiers, and speech recognition.

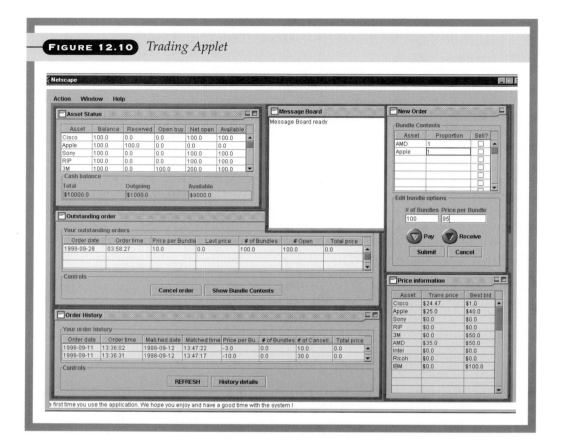

FIGURE 12.10 *Trading Applet*

- *A New Set of Components.* Swing provides a new set of graphical components such as tables, trees, sliders, progress bars, internal frames, tool bars, and labels with images.

There are many advantages in using Java and Swing components to develop a trading interface. First, the user interface is more standardized and has a more professional look. It provides the trader with rich market and personal information that is organized in a hierarchical way. Moreover, the interface is flexible. Users can open multiple windows, or they can minimize or close some windows as they please. By contrast, a Web page does not have the same versatility. Finally, information displayed in the applet is truly interactive. Information will be updated automatically on the applet, and it does require users to reload or refresh the applet.

The applet shown in Figure 12.10 contains six blocks of information: the current asset holdings, the message board, the new order submission form, the open order table, the order history table, and the current market prices. The Asset Status window displays the current holdings information for the trader. The Message Board window displays the messages that are sent from the exchange. The New Order window allows the trader to submit new orders. The Trade History window displays the orders that have been either filled or canceled. If the trader wants to find more information about a particular past order, he or she can select the order and click on the History Details button; then, a new History Detail window will open. The last window displayed in the applet is the current Market Price window, which contains information such as the last traded price and the best bid and ask prices.

12.2.5 RMI and IIOP

RMI is a Java-based framework for distributed object application. It is a significantly easier and lighter-weight approach to developing distributed objects. If Web-based applications are implemented in a pure Java environment, it is efficient to implement distributed object models using RMI. The electronic market can be implemented as an RMI remote object server. The client-side application can be implemented by using a Java applet. Through the naming service, the client locates the exchange and sends it information by invoking the exchange's method. To implement interactive communication, the server call-back function has to be implemented. The following are the steps in developing an interactive communication model between an applet and a server application:

- Create a remote interface for the client applet, and define a method that can be invoked by the exchange.
- Before contacting the RMI server on the exchange, the applet has to export itself by implementing *UnicastRemoteObject.exportObject(this)*, in which the word *this* stands for the applet object. By exporting itself, the applet makes itself available to receive remote calls.
- While contacting the exchange by invoking a remote method on the server-side, the applet passes itself by using object serialization to the exchange. The exchange can then call back the applet by invoking the method defined in the applet interface and send it data.

Currently, Java RMI cannot support communication between Java objects and objects written in other languages, but the situation will soon change. Sun Microsystems is working with OMG to implement RMI over IIOP. IIOP is a part of CORBA, and it enables objects implemented using different commercial ORB packages to communicate with each other by using a unified protocol. Expanding IIOP to support RMI will allow Java distributed objects based on RMI to be able to communicate directly with CORBA-based objects. This will expand the possibilities for Java platform developers.

Despite the differences in implementation, Java RMI and CORBA offer similar functionality. Distributed object framework has demonstrated great advantages over applications that are based solely on HTTP and CGI approaches. Web-based applications that use a server-centric model based heavily on CGI scripts have many limitations of system performance. For example, communications between clients and a Web server cannot be interactive. By contrast, when using CORBA or Java RMI, communications between the traders and the exchange are interactive. Therefore, market information such as trade execution and price will be updated dynamically for traders. If CGI is used for trade applications, the trader has to re-load the Web page or resubmit the requests to get the real-time market information. Such variance in time this process creates makes a big difference in real-time financial trading situations, because static market information could be misleading and cause errors in fast-paced trading.

Moreover, information transmission between traders and the market is more efficient using the Java/CORBA model, which passes the values of the variables between different applications. By contrast, the CGI program has to recreate a Web page and send the whole HTML file back to the browser every time the server responds to a request.

Finally, the development and maintenance of a distributed object system is much more efficient than a system that uses a CGI program. To upgrade the system, we can make changes at the individual object level instead of at the entire system level. As long as the interfaces among the objects remain constant, the implementations of those objects can be changed as needed.

12.2.6 ASP and JSP

Although Java provides rich functionality in developing Web-based applications, we have to admit that it is still a complicated technology. Companies and system developers do value simplicity besides functionality. Sometimes, we are willing to sacrifice some functionality for simplicity. ASP is a typical example. ASP is a Microsoft technology that provides a simple yet powerful way to develop e-commerce applications. ASP was officially introduced by Microsoft in 1996. Since then, it has gained wide recognition in the industry.

ASP uses VBScripts that resides on the server-side to generate dynamic Web pages according to the user's specific requests. Together with the database technology, ASP can be used to develop all kinds of e-commerce applications that process transactions on the server and send dynamic HTML pages to the users.

An ASP program is a combination of both an HTML document and an ASP script (Figure 12.11). While the HTML tells the browser how to display the information, ASP statements instruct the Web server to run certain processes and to create the portion of the page to be sent out. The following is a simple ASP program. ASP statements are in the <% %> delimiters. <% = Time( ) %> calls VBScript function Time to get the current time on the server. After a user submits a request, the corresponding ASP program will be processed by the ASP script engine on the Microsoft Internet Information Server. The resulting HTML document will then be sent to the browser.

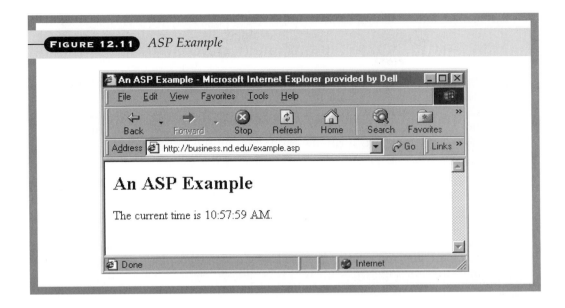

FIGURE 12.11 *ASP Example*

```
<HTML>
<HEAD>
<TITLE>An ASP Example</TITLE>
</HEAD>
<BODY>
<H2>An ASP Example</H2>
The current time is
<%=Time()%>.
</BODY>
</HTML>
```

To a large extent, JSP is a product developed by Sun in response to the great success of ASP. JSP uses the same philosophy of combining HTML and scripts. When a JSP program is requested by a user, it will be processed by a JSP engine to generate a Java class, and then, a dynamic page is sent to the browser. In comparison to ASP, the biggest advantage of JSP is that it can work with various Web servers on different platforms while ASP is usually only compatible with the Microsoft operating system.

12.2.7 XML

XML is another approach to address the limitations of HTML and CGI computing. Microsoft has already shipped XML support in Internet Explorer 4.0, and Netscape supported XML in its Netscape 6. Although HTML provides an outstanding mechanism to deliver and display simple documents over the WWW, its simplicity imposes many limitations in deploying complex distributed applications over the Internet. XML tries to improve the following limitations of HTML:

- *Presentation-Oriented Publishing.* The primary goal of HTML is to provide a simple markup language for delivery and presentation of documents over the Web. Therefore, HTML needs only a limited number of tags and does not allow users to define new tags. This approach becomes inadequate when users have to define attributes and values for their documents.

- *Lack of Structure.* HTML does not support the specification of deep structures needed to represent database schema or object-oriented hierarchies. This creates significant barriers to using HTML for data interchange and efficient processing.

- *Validation.* HTML does not support the kind of language specification that allows applications to check data for structural validity. Almost everything has to be done on the server-side. XML is derived from standard generalized markup language (SGML), which is defined by ISO Standard 8879 (1986). SGML lets users describe document structures and can handle large and complex documents. However, the full SGML contains many optional features that are not needed for Web applications. The World Wide Web Consortium (W3C) has been developing a subset of SGML-XML that retains the basic features of SGML, including user extensibility, complex structures, and validations, but does not have the complexity of SGML. As a result, the applications to support XML will be much easier to develop compared with SGML.

Although XML combines the functionality of document presentation and data exchange, there has been a shift from simple document display to transaction-oriented data exchange for Web-based application development. The following are the two areas in which XML can enhance financial applications development:

- *Database Interchange.* XML can enable structured data interchange between different clients and different markets. Different industries have created consortia to specify the standards or ontology for data exchange. For example, several companies including CyberCash, MasterCard, and Mondex are developing the open trading protocol (OTP) for financial data exchange. OTP messages are XML documents that can be exchanged between different organizations. An OTP trading message is defined to include an XML ID, trading components, and digital signature components. In addition to using XML to transfer payment information, a market performance database can also be transferred and saved in local database systems for analysis.

- *Distributed Processing.* The platform- and application-independent character of XML allows the data to be processed efficiently at different locations. For example, financial databases can be downloaded and analyzed by applications located on local computers. Alternatively, both the data and Java applets can be downloaded from the Web site. They will run on the clients' Web pages and provide decision support for the traders.

XML provides another approach in developing interoperable distributed applications. It is important to compare this approach with the approach of CORBA and Java RMI as discussed earlier. First, data exchange and interoperability using CORBA and Java RMI have to apply more complex programs relative to XML, which is basically simpler. XML focuses on platform- and application-independent data exchange and does not worry about the details of application software implementation. Further, to achieve true interoperability, CORBA and RMI rely on a distributed object infrastructure such as IIOP and a wide availability of business objects. By contrast, XML can reach a wider audience in the near future. XML still has its limitations, though. For example, similar to HTML, it only supports limited interactivity. To overcome this weakness, Microsoft has proposed a channel definition format (CDF) that allows a Web site use of XML to push content into a channel for CDF-compliant client browsers. CDF also permits a Web publisher to offer frequently updated collections of information from different Web servers for automatic delivery to receiving browsers. This may revolutionize the way that financial information is disseminated. Furthermore, there exists synergy between XML and Java. XML provides universally compatible data, whereas Java provides platform-independent applications. A combination of both XML and Java will provide more robust and powerful applications for financial applications.

12.3 SECURE TRANSACTIONS

12.3.1 Internet Security Issues

Security is one of the most important issues for electronic commerce, especially for online trading and other financial transactions over the Internet. Without great confidence in security, traders are unwilling to conduct financial transactions over a public network. In fact, security is a broad issue ranging from transaction security over the Internet to secure corporate databases and networks. Some of the security threats include invasion of individuals' privacy and theft of valuable confidential information. Here, we only discuss the issues related to secure transaction. Transaction security has to meet the following three requirements:

- *Identification and Authentication.* Identification and authentication ask the question, "Are you who you say you are?" Financial transactions must bear unambiguous identifications of the different parties involved in the transaction, including individual customers and financial institutions. On the

Internet, the identification of a financial institution often takes the form of the known URL or the Internet provider (IP) address, while a customer is generally identified by his or her log-in identification and password. More advanced identification methods involve the use of public-key cryptography. Both clients and companies have to identify themselves and be authenticated to each other. Authentication is a mechanism that makes sure that the other party of the transaction can be confident of the identity of the other party. It verifies the identity of a user or company by using cryptographic methods, which we discuss later.

- *Privacy and Confidentiality.* Privacy and confidentiality make sure that messages and sensitive transaction data such as identification, password, social security number, and credit card number are kept private and are able to sustain security attacks. In one security case, hackers systematically gathered system identifications and passwords over the Internet by inserting a network monitoring tool to capture passwords sent at the beginning of each communication session. As a result, hundreds of thousands of Internet user passwords were compromised. The incident happened in 1994 and caused a major panic in the Internet community.

- *Integrity.* Transaction integrity ensures that the contents of transaction data remain unmodified during the transmission process between the client and the company. Data transmission must be tamper-proof in the sense that no one can add, delete, or modify any part of the message during transport. Methods for ensuring information integrity include error detection codes, checksums, and some other encryption techniques.

12.3.2 Basic Cryptographic Techniques

Cryptographic techniques such as encryption and digital signature are fundamental building blocks of the infrastructure of electronic commerce. The goal of using different cryptographic methods is to make sure that a hacker cannot view a message and compromise the integrity of it, even if the message is intercepted. The cryptographic techniques include private-key and public-key encryption and digital signature.[1]

12.3.3 Secure Socket Layer

Secure socket layer (SSL) is the encryption protocol implemented for Web servers and Netscape browsers. It is a protocol between TCP/IP and applications layers so that users can add SSL transparently to different Web-based communication protocols, such as Telnet, HTTP, and FTP. SSL delivers a powerful security solution to Web-based transactions. It provides solutions for authentication, confidentiality, and integrity. Since its introduction, SSL has gained wide support from the industry.

SSL uses a hybrid cryptographic method, with both secret-key and public-key encryption algorithms. This is because using public encryption alone has some shortcomings:

- Public-key algorithms are slow. It is estimated that symmetric encryption methods are generally at least 1,000 times faster than public-key algorithms. In a real-time computing environment with a large amount of information exchange, it could make a big difference.

- Using public-key encryption can be vulnerable to chosen plain-text attacks. If a hacker knows that the original message can only be a number of possible choices, he or she can easily figure out the original message by simply encrypting all the possible messages and comparing the results with the encrypted message.

The way SSL works can be summarized as follows:

- Bob, the online broker, sends Alice his public key certified by a trusted third party.
- Alice generates a random secret session key, encrypts it by using Bob's public key, and sends it to Bob.
- Bob decrypts Alice's message by using his private key to recover the session key.
- Bob and Alice encrypt their messages by using the secret session key.
- The secret session key will be destroyed after the transaction.

SSL provides authentication for the merchant. Authentication for the client is also available by using SSL, but it is optional. The difficulty of cracking an encrypted SSL message is a function of the length of the secret session key. With a long session key, even if the key is eventually found out after many hours of computation, the transaction is most likely over by then, and the key will be of no use. This has greatly reduced the risks of security breach during transactions.

12.4 DISTRIBUTED COMPUTING AND FINANCIAL TRADING SYSTEMS

From a computing point of view, the trading and clearing network is, in effect, a distributed computing system, which can be defined as a collection of autonomous computers linked by a communication network. The software applications in such a system form an integrated computing facility that enables resource sharing and provides users with access to various system resources that the system maintains. The advantages of a distributed system range from speedy computation to improved system availability and reliability. Meanwhile, a distributed system has to deal with many computing issues such as remote procedure calls that are not encountered in a centralized system.

12.4.1 ATM: Example of a Distributed System

Before we discuss the basic concepts of distributed systems, let us look at a common distributed system example. An automated teller machine (ATM) is a good example of a distributed system (Figure 12.12). The main function of an ATM is cash withdrawal for bank customers. To withdraw money, a user first has to be validated based on his or her bank card and pin number before the transaction. Validation and the subsequent transactions involve the local computer and account servers at the bank's headquarters. If the user does not belong to the local bank that owns the ATM, the local computer has to communicate with another bank's account server. After the transaction, the customer's account has to be updated to reflect the transaction. Although ATM is a specific application, it demonstrates the complexity of distributed computing. First, to successfully accomplish the task, an ATM requires the collaboration of different computing resources, including the local machine and different bank servers. Second, security and reliability are the top concerns of the application. The system has to provide a series of security measures and has to be highly reliable in terms of communication and availability of the central account database.

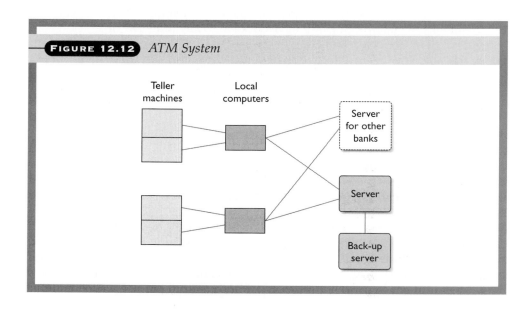

FIGURE 12.12 *ATM System*

12.4.2 Characteristics of a Distributed Computing System

From a resource-sharing point of view, a distributed system contains systems resources that are provided by resource managers and are used by users. For example, the bank account server is the resource manager and the teller machine is the resource user in the ATM network. Two popular models of distributed systems exist today: client-server model and distributed object model.

Client-Server Model

With the increasing use of PCs, the client-server computing model has become an important new computing architecture for businesses in the early 1990s. Today, it is still the best-known and most widely used distributed system model. In the client-server system, computing resources such as database and transaction processing are provided centrally by servers, whereas clients access system resources and present results to end-users. Typically, clients operate on PCs that have graphical display and carry out some local computation. Servers often run on UNIX workstations or mainframe computers.

The client-server model has served as an effective approach to sharing system information, application programs, and other resources in a distributed computing environment. Most enterprise systems today are implemented in the form of the client-server model. The ATM, as mentioned, is a typical client-server example and so are the many banking and financial trading systems. They tend to operate on corporate private communication networks. With the advent of the Internet and the WWW, client-server computing has evolved into Web-based Internet or intranet applications. The user interface has moved from proprietary GUI programs to platform-independent Web browsers. Web-based online banking and trading systems are such examples.

One drawback of the client-server model is that client software communicates directly with server programs without an intermediate layer. This results in a monolithic client-server software package. It is therefore extremely difficult to re-configure the existing client-server setting and include another application development by other vendors. Distributed object model and component-based software engineering have been introduced to deal with the problem.

Distributed Object Model

The distributed object model follows the general idea of an object-oriented approach, as discussed in an earlier chapter. In the distributed object model, each computing resource, either the resource provider or the resource user, is an object. The distinction between clients and servers is not important. An object can be a server and a client at the same time. In the system, objects are uniquely identified throughout the system by the naming and directory services. Therefore, objects can move around in the system, depending on the efficient hardware and software configuration, and can still be identified. CORBA is the industrial standard distributed object architecture. Enterprise JavaBeans is another distributed object model based on Java technology.

Accompanied with the distributed object model is component-based software engineering. Objects are straightforward abstractions of real-world entities. Software components are similar to objects, but there are some differences. Whereas object-oriented programming focuses on hierarchy structure, object inheritance, and code reusability, the component model looks at how to build software systems by combining predeveloped software objects or components. The emphasis of the component model is not on inheritance but on combination and integration of different software components. The benefits of the component approach range from rapid software development to increased customization and enhanced software quality.

Whether it is a client-server or a distributed system, there are some common characteristics for a distributed system. Here, we discuss some of the major properties:

- *Resource Sharing.* Resources including both hardware and software can be shared in a distributed system. In earlier systems, hardware resources such as hard disk space and printer devices were shared in the system to reduce system cost. In a multiuser system (e.g., a time-sharing computer system), a central computer's CPU time is shared among different users. With the rapid decrease of hardware costs, resources shared in a distributed system are largely application programs and databases. For example, in a distributed banking system, the customers' account database is basically the shared resource.

- *Concurrent Processing.* In a distributed system, many users may execute different programs simultaneously. Naturally, a distributed system has multiple processes running simultaneously or in parallel. This is common for real-world distributed system applications (e.g., financial stock trading, banking, or airline reservation). Even for a single application program, multiple processes may run at the same time. This is because multiple users may access a particular system resource that is operated on a single workstation. This brings up the issue of concurrency control. In a multithreaded environment, as discussed earlier, an application program can launch multiple threads to handle the requests of multiple users. Because these threads may share global memory, many processes have to be synchronized to avoid conflicts. Therefore, a distributed system must provide parallel computing as well as maintain the consistency of information in the system. This issue is discussed in more detail later in this chapter.

- *Transparency.* Transparency is defined as the concealment of the details of the system implementation and the different parts of the system. To the users, the system should be perceived as a whole piece rather than as applications and services located on different computers. Distributed system transparency exists at different levels. First of all, the system should provide access transparency, which means that applications programs or objects can be accessed uniformly without users knowing their exact hardware locations. Naming and directory services help to achieve access transparency. Further, the system should maintain its access transparency when the system is reconfigured. For example, applications programs or the database server should still be accessible by using previous names even if they have changed their locations due to increasing service demands.

- *Fault Tolerance.* There are two approaches to increasing the reliability of a system: fault prevention and fault tolerance. Although systems should be designed to prevent as many faults as possible, total fault prevention is impossible. Fault tolerance is therefore necessary for systems with a high requirement of reliability, such as financial, air traffic control, and military systems. A system fault could happen to system hardware or software. A fault-tolerant system should continue to function even when facing some system faults or failures. Depending on the level of fault tolerance, systems may function in a degraded form when faults happen. To implement fault tolerance, there are generally two approaches: hardware redundancy and software recovery. We discuss these issues in detail later.

12.4.3 Financial Trading Systems

The world's financial markets are undergoing fundamental changes. Financial barriers between different countries are being eliminated, and geographic boundaries are becoming less important. One of the driving forces behind the changes is technology. In addition to the common properties of a distributed system, including resource sharing, concurrency, transparency, and fault tolerance, a financial trading system has to have other requirements.

Global Accessibility

The world we are living in today is increasingly becoming a global village where information and financial resources can be exchanged freely. The design and development of the next generation of financial trading systems have to recognize this trend. Financial trading systems should be able to be accessed by persons from virtually any place at any time, using all kinds of computer platforms and devices. Developing the system based on proprietary technology and interfaces will not be successful. The Internet and the WWW have provided a technical infrastructure for developing global-accessible systems. The tremendous development of online trading is the evidence. Therefore, tomorrow's trading systems have to continue building on open technology and take advantage of many new online computing tools such as XML, Java, and CORBA.

Simplicity

The users of a financial trading system have diversified backgrounds; their system is different from most corporate information systems that are used by some specialized companies on a daily basis. Therefore, one of the principles in developing a system for such users is simplicity. Comprehensibility and user-friendliness are some of the most important requirements for a financial trading system. Earlier Web-based trading systems based on HTTP/CGI provided global accessibility, but they failed to deliver some functionality because of the limitation of the technology. For example, GUI design is limited using HTML, and so the system supports limited interactivity. Users have to "reload" the Web page to update the price quotes. More advanced tools that we discussed earlier will help design more simplistic systems with more embedded functionality.

Scalability

Scalability is the capability of a system to adapt to increased service load. Any system has limited system resources in the short term and can become completely overwhelmed by increased use. Storage space, RAM, and the CPU could function in a degraded form if they are overloaded. In financial trading, scalability is extremely important because an unexpectedly large number of orders and users may arrive on the market in some usual situations (e.g., during a major market correction). During these events, a highly scalable system will function properly or degrade much more moderately than a nonscalable system. The development of a highly scalable system is challenging. In fact, the ability to scale up easily is an important property of a distributed system. A central system's performance is essentially a function of the system's size or processing speed. Therefore, the capacity of any central system limits the scale of its performance. By contrast, in distributed systems, demand load can be dynamically balanced, and some resources can even be added to the system.

The issue of scalability is highly related to fault tolerance. A heavily loaded component in a system is likely to cause fault. System redundancy is essential for developing scalable and fault-tolerant systems. When a fault is detected or when there is a big increase of service demand, services can be automatically routed to the system's back-up components.

Real Time

The operation of a financial trading system has to happen in real time. There are rigid time requirements for the performance of the system. The correctness of the system depends not only on the logical result of computation but also on the time at which the results are produced. Some real-time systems have more restrictive time constraints than others. For example, air traffic control systems and military weapon control systems have to guarantee the time for the completion of tasks; otherwise, the results would be catastrophic. Implementing real-time systems is difficult. Real-time systems have to meet the time requirements in addition to being fault tolerant. Methodologies in designing a real-time system include the decomposition of a complicated system into subsystems and the allocation of the whole system load into different subsystems. Sometimes, there is confusion between the concepts of computing quickly with real-time computing. In a real-time system, the goal is not only to compute quickly but also to provide the predictability and explicit assurance of the time requirements for the computing task.

Security

We have discussed transaction security issues for financial trading and clearing. In addition, there are other security-related issues in financial trading and clearing (e.g., system security and access control). Because a financial trading system operates in the open Internet environment and contains a large amount of sensitive and important financial information and transaction data, the system has to be shielded from possible attacks to make sure information is safely guarded once it reaches its destination. One common practice today is to create "fire walls." For financial trading, creating fire walls does not prohibit users from interacting with the exchange. Rather, the fire wall monitors and controls the traffic going through the exchange. There are many methods for building fire walls. One viable way is to control the destination for different applications. For example, trading orders can go only through certain ports. Another popular method is to create proxy servers, which are application gateways that sit between the open Internet and the internal exchange computer network. The proxy server shields the internal information and computer network from the outside world. Outside applications have to go through the proxy server to reach the internal applications. There are many advantages to using the proxy service. First, it hides the internal information. Second, it can provide a consistent naming service to different applications or components. Therefore, outside applications can communicate with the trading system by using the same name and address even though the internal configuration has been changed. Third, it helps to implement the security policies such as authentication and encryption consistently for the whole application.

12.4.4 A Component-Based Trading System Architecture

After discussing the general properties of distributed systems and special requirements for financial trading systems, we describe the architecture for a financial trading system that is globally accessible, secure, scalable, and fault tolerant. Figure 12.13 is a diagram of component-based trading system architecture.

Component-based system design enhances the object-oriented approach that we discussed earlier in this chapter. Component is an extension of the object concept. Whereas objects are created from classes, which are defined in a specific language, a component is a precombined unit of code that is language independent and may consist of a collection of objects to carry certain functions with well-defined interface. The advantages are rapid software development and high scalability.

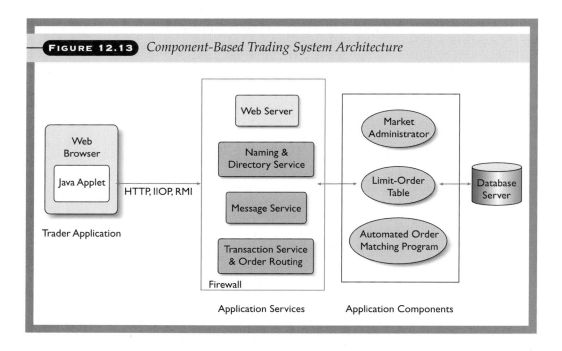

FIGURE 12.13 *Component-Based Trading System Architecture*

In the model, the client trading application combines Web pages with a Java applet. Users have access to increased functionality based on this design. They can submit orders as well as view and cancel open orders. Real-time prices of selected portfolios can also be displayed with dynamic price updates. In addition, users can view messages sent from the exchange through a message board. The application uses both HTTP and IIOP to communicate with the exchange.

The exchange application has both application services and application components. This model supports a more generic object-based distributed system design. Instead of letting client applications directly communicate with application modules, as is often implemented in client-server architecture, the combination of different application services serves as a middleware, interfacing client requests with exchange application components. Therefore, components implemented by different vendors can be flexibly assembled together without reinventing the wheel. Other advantages include scalability and transparency. As the functionality and demand for services grow, more computers can be added to the system. Different services represented by objects/components can be distributed among different computers, balancing the workload and increasing system performance. For example, the limit-order table and the matching program can operate from different workstations. The architecture ensures that the application program does not need to change when the scale of the system increases, thus providing location and access transparency throughout the system.

We provide an overview of the services and applications in this object-based trading system model.

- *Web Server.* The Web server publishes the information and instructions for the trading application. A traditional Web server handles CGI calls as well. It is the center, or could be a potential bottleneck, of all the application requests. In this model, much of the application traffic has been directed to other object services, such as message and transaction processing.

- *Naming and Directory Service.* With the naming and directory service, the system provides location and service transparency. First, the trading applications do not have to know exactly on which machine the limit-order table is located. The naming and directory service will present a coherent electronic market to traders and hide the internal configuration of the system. Second, application components for the exchange can also locate other components consistently through the naming services.

- *Message Service.* The message service provides a systemwide asynchronous message exchange. In an asynchronous communication mode, messages accumulate in the message queue and will be processed at the time that is most convenient for the receiver. The message service for financial trading systems provides a flexible and reliable way of communication between clients and the exchange. In addition to traditional communication modes such as e-mail, the message server also provides communication services such as news subscription and newsgroups. Technically, both "pull" and "push" technology will be used.

- *Transaction Service.* Transaction service is a critical service for financial trading. It controls the interactions between clients and the exchange and routes the orders to their destinations for execution. Different from message services, communication for transactions is channeled through remote procedure calls. In the Java and CORBA framework, protocols such as IIOP and RMI are used. Transaction service has to satisfy the basic transaction properties (e.g., atomic, consistent, isolated, and durable). Atomic means that the transaction executes completely or not at all. For example, when a user submits a trading order through the Internet, errors could happen due to traffic congestion or some other technical problems. Atomicity requires that either the order is submitted or canceled. In either case, the trader has to get a clear response. Consistency means that the transaction has to maintain the consistency for the database, whereas isolation requires each transaction to be executed with no interference from other transactions. Durability is the property requiring that the transaction results will not be lost due to system failure.

- *Market Monitor.* A financial trading system has to offer surveillance functions. It allows exchange personnel or legislative bodies to monitor the trading behavior and to make sure that trading regulations and rules are followed. It should allow both real-time and historic monitoring. Programs to detect unusual trading behaviors are installed to alert exchange officials. Meanwhile, the market monitor should also keep audit trails for all transactions information.

- *Limit-Order Table.* The limit-order table, or limit-order book, is one of the most important application components of financial exchange. It records all the open orders, from which we can easily figure out the supply and demand situation, and subsequently the future trend of market movement. The order book updates in real time as new orders come in and existing orders are either filled or canceled. Depending on the market design and configuration, selected information from the limit-order table is released to the public.

- *Automated Order-Matching Program.* The matching program, which basically implements a mathematical matching algorithm, is the core of the whole financial exchange. It specifies the rules and priorities on how orders are matched in the exchange. Different order-matching programs will produce drastically different order execution results. In a market in which humans are market makers, even though there are specified order-matching rules, the real implementation becomes somewhat arbitrary many times. In an automated order-matching and execution market, the rules are computerized. Traditionally, exchange members, traders, and software engineers design matching algorithms. However, to a large degree, a financial exchange market is an institution that has to follow the rules of economics. Therefore, we believe that many exchanges will use economic efficiency as one of the most important criteria in designing order-matching programs. Market efficiency is thus measured by the total trading surplus resulting from the trades.

- *Real-Time Database.* The real-time database provides timing constraints for database transactions. The database has to record all transaction information including both historic as well as the real-time limit-order table. To achieve a quick response, sometimes the whole database has to be memory resident. Therefore, operations on the database do not have to access the disk storage. It was different to achieve memory residence earlier, but now the main computer memory can be expanded to gigabytes and is thus able to store all the database information. Meanwhile, the database has access to external devices. When there are any changes in the tables, the data will be sent to external devices and recorded. In case of system failure, all transaction data will not be lost. A fault-tolerant real-time database will typically have two copies of the database residing on separate computers. The standby database will have an up-to-date copy of the information in the master database and will be ready to swap to master mode when the other database crashes. When the database that was previously master is next restarted, it will then be set up as a standby for the new master database, in case the other one crashes for any reason.

12.5 CONCURRENT PROCESSING AND SYNCHRONIZATION

12.5.1 Concurrent Processing

In the case of a single computer, concurrent processing means that many computing processes exist concurrently. If the computer has only one CPU, then these computing processes are being executed in an interleaving mode. If the computer has multiple processors, then different processes can be distributed among different processors, enabling true parallel computing. In a distributed computing system, multiple computers exist, each with at least one processor. We can see that concurrent processing in a distributed system exists in the following cases:

- Many users simultaneously submit different requests and execute different applications. The whole system is in a mass-parallel processing situation. For example, some traders are submitting orders while some are checking or canceling their open orders. Meanwhile, the exchange is matching orders and notifying traders of their execution reports. All these processes are occurring simultaneously. A single user operating on a single workstation can invoke several programs simultaneously. For example, a trader can use the trading application to compute the optimal portfolio while downloading the latest news and stock prices.

- Different clients may invoke a single server application simultaneously, resulting in multiple processes running concurrently on a single computer. For example, the server's order submission application may be invoked by many different traders simultaneously.

12.5.2 Threads

From the concurrent processing cases just discussed, we can see that concurrent or parallel processing arises naturally within a distributed system. Threads, which we discussed earlier, are excellent tools for implementing concurrent processing. On the server-side, multiple threads can be spawned to handle multiple requests from clients simultaneously (Figure 12.14). This is much more efficient than a single-threaded program. For a multiprocessor computer, the benefit is obvious because different processors can execute multiple threads to exploit the multiprocessor feature. Otherwise, some processors would be idle, and thus system resources would be wasted. Why is using threads still a better solution for a uniprocessor computer? Let us assume there are two client requests, and each takes 6 msec of processing and 4 msec of delay for input-output delay, such as

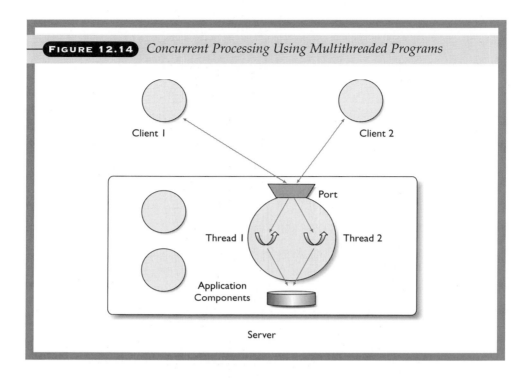

FIGURE 12.14 *Concurrent Processing Using Multithreaded Programs*

updating database tables. On average, the total processing time for a request using a single-thread program is 10 msec. Any new requests submitted while the server is processing a request have to wait until the server is free. In a multi-threaded server, while one thread is waiting for the input-output, another thread can process the new request. On average, the total processing time for a request will be less than that in a single-threaded program, and the overall server throughput will be much higher.

Multiple threads can also be implemented for client applications, especially for applications with window-type user interface. Users can open one window and conduct some calculation. While waiting for the results, the user can then switch to another window to look at the price changes or latest breaking news on the screen.

Multithreaded programs can be implemented easily by using Java programming language. Unlike many programming languages such as C and C++ that do not have built-in multithreading tools and must make calls to operating system multithreading primitives, Java provides a multithreaded environment as a part of the language itself. Thus, it is much more convenient to develop efficient and highly scalable multithreaded applications using Java.

12.5.3 Synchronization

In multithreaded programs, multiple threads often share the same memory space. These threads are not protected from each other and can access the same data item. Thus, we have to make sure that an application is free from interference from other applications so as to avoid inconsistencies in the same data. The most common way to implement concurrency control is to use exclusive locks. By locking the data, the application is, in effect, synchronizing or serializing the access to the data. For example, using multithreading, each time a trader sends a new order to the exchange, he or she is launching a new thread at the exchange. The thread contains the following parts of operations:

- Assigning the current *OrderID* to the new order.
- Increment *OrderID.*
- Add the order into the limit-order table.

Suppose the following situation happens:

- Trader A starts to submit an order. Thread A begins to execute.
- Thread A executes part one of the order submission method and is interrupted by thread B.
- Trader B starts to submit an order. Thread B begins to execute.
- Thread B executes part one of the order submission method and is interrupted by thread A.
- Thread A continues to finish parts two and three of the order submission method.
- Thread B finishes parts two and three of the order submission method.

The above scenario will cause the two orders sent by traders A and B to have the same *OrderID.* The problem can be solved by adding the synchronized keyword to the *SubmitOrder()* method. It serves as a mutually exclusive lock for the method, allowing only one thread to call the method. On completion of the method, the thread will automatically release the lock.

While applying locks, we have to make sure that the portion of the data to be serialized is kept as small as possible. By applying unnecessary locks, the program performance will become less efficient. Let us look at the cancel order example: A trader is canceling an order right after the order has been routed to the matching program. Suppose that the cancel operation deletes the order from the limit-order table. Suppose also that the matching program finds a match for the particular order that results in a trade. The exchange will then try to update information for that order in the limit-order table but will find that the order has already been deleted. To solve this problem, we could lock the limit-order table while matching is being conducted. However, this lock would be expensive and would freeze the limit-order table constantly. As a result, the order submit method would have to wait on many occasions. In this case, an asynchronous processing is a better way to solve the problem. We discuss it next.

12.6 SYNCHRONOUS COMMUNICATION

In a synchronous remote call, object A sends a message to object B and waits for the feedback. Thus, in synchronous communication, the sending and receiving processes synchronize at every message. The sending process at object A has to wait for feedback from object B to continue. On the object B side, it has to respond instantaneously to object A's request as well as to other remote calls. Otherwise, there would be serious delays for object A and other objects that are waiting for replies. By contrast, with asynchronous communication, the server can schedule its operations more efficiently because it does not have to reply to each order immediately. Meanwhile, the client application does not have to wait for an immediate reply to conduct the next task.

To implement the cancel order function mentioned earlier, asynchronous communication can be used, because we do not want the trade process to wait for the replies of the cancel process (Figure 12.15). Normally, the order cannot be

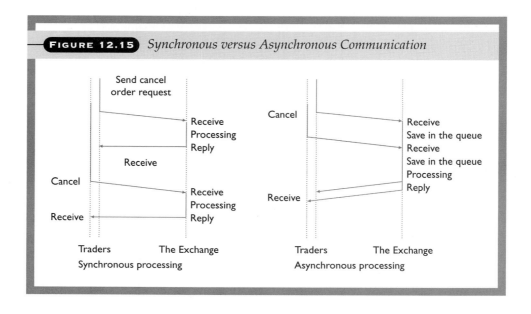

FIGURE 12.15 *Synchronous versus Asynchronous Communication*

canceled immediately if matching is going on. If synchronous cancel requests are implemented, there would be delays at both the trader and the exchange side. Using asynchronous communication, the cancel requests are stored in a queue at the exchange side. After submitting the cancel requests, the trader application can proceed without waiting for the reply. At the exchange, the cancel queue will be emptied each time before the matching program restarts.

The asynchronous communication mode is, in fact, a queued transaction processing method. In addition to the advantages for concurrency control and load balancing as discussed earlier, queued transaction is useful in situations when faults happen for either clients or servers. Suppose errors occur at the server. Using remote method calls such as RMI or IIOP, either the client application is blocked and has to wait for the server reply or the client is prompted with an error message. Users would have to resubmit requests at a later time. The same problem could happen for a server application when it wants to contact the client. An alternative is to let the client (server) send the requests to the queue rather than to the server (client). The queue acts as a buffer between clients and server. Requests are accumulated in the queue and will be sent to the destination even if the network or the destination applications suffer some problems. Asynchronous communication is an important communication type to implement message-based transactions mentioned earlier.

12.7 FAULT TOLERANCE

In a fully automated electronic financial market, failure of the computer system would be disastrous. The down time of a stock market could result in turmoil in the financial market and possibly result in losses amounting to hundreds of millions of dollars. Many types of faults could happen in a trading system:

- *Hardware Faults.* Computer hardware, including the processors, memory management, or storage devices, could crash.
- *Software Faults.* Software faults could originate from a single error in a segment code. The faults could also come from an erroneous reaction of the software to some imperfection in hardware or other software segments.
- *Communication Faults.* Communicating in an open network, messages could be lost, duplicated, or corrupted. Techniques such as checksum or digital signature could detect corrupted messages, but the original messages would still have to be resubmitted.

In a distributed computing system, the fault model is different from that of a centralized computing system in which the system behaves like a monolithic unit and either functions well or fails entirely. In a distributed trading system, we have to understand the possible ways a system might fail. An understanding of the fault model in a distributed system helps to design better fault-tolerant systems.

First, in a distributed system, the trading process depends on many different processes that run on different computers. If one process fails to function, it will likely affect the function of the whole system. In this sense, the likelihood of faults increases in a distributed system. In addition, fault detection in a distributed environment will also be challenging. It is important to take into account the interdependencies of different components in the trading system and develop fault recovery strategies.

Second, in a distributed architecture, we can design and develop systems that can be combined in a way such that the joint probability of failure will be significantly reduced. This can generally be achieved by letting application components detect errors in the system automatically and switch the operation from failed components to back-up components.

The following are two basic fault-tolerance approaches:

- *Hardware Redundancy.* For example, to use additional computers and storage devices.
- *Software Redundancy.* For example, to provide software that will take over when errors are detected.

Traditional fault tolerance is achieved by supplying a stand-by system, which keeps an archive of the database of the master system. If the master system fails, the back-up system will take over. Fault tolerance relies on roll-back recovery to reconstruct the correct transaction information based on the back-up data in the back-up system. This method is good for batch processing systems. Even though the roll-back recovery may delay the batch processing, the system could tolerate any failures short of those damaging both the archive and active copies of the database. For a financial market that is operated as a call market, roll-back recovery is a straightforward way to implement fault tolerance. A back-up trading system creates an archive of the limit-order database and all the trading information. If the master trading system fails for some reason, the back-up system should take over and restart the process. It is not appropriate to use this approach for a market that operates continuously and in real time. The lack of service during system roll-back in a continuous stock market is just intolerable.

Another fault-tolerance approach for systems that have to be operating continuously is to use replication in a distributed computing environment.

- *Active Replication.* All replication components are executed concurrently, and their internal states are closely synchronized. Active replication uses the fault masking to hide the occurrence of faults. One fault-masking technique is to use a group of servers, each running on a different computer. It uses a group management mechanism. The group output is determined from the outputs of individual members. If the system does not incur errors, then only one output from the multiple components will be picked. If there are errors in the system, a majority vote is used to determine the correct output. For example, suppose we have three replicated components running concurrently. If we have a single error, then two components will produce the correct value and the other one will not. The result of the majority will be used for the output. This mechanism will not work if we have only two replicated components. When one component produces the correct output and the other one the wrong one, then it is not possible to tell which component has gone wrong.

- *Passive Replication.* In passive replication, only one master component is active, but other replication components' internal states are regularly updated by means of checkpoints from the active component. Passive replication achieves fault tolerance by detecting the existence of faults and performing certain actions to remove faulty components from the system.

12.8 SUMMARY

This chapter discussed the emerging technologies for implementing financial market applications. First, we discussed the advantages of using Java from a business point of view. The functionality provided by Java is ideal for interactive financial trading applications in electronic markets. We have reviewed the different approaches in developing Web-based interactive applications. HTML/CGI is the traditional method in developing online applications. Although Java and CORBA provide rich functionality in developing interactive and dynamic online applications, tools such as ASP and JSP offer solutions that are simple to develop without much compromise of functionality. In the meantime, HTML is also evolving. XML will be the next generation of HTML language used for Web browser and online application development. The focus of XML is more on information and data exchange rather than on simple document display.

Transaction security is critical to online financial applications. We have discussed the security requirements for online financial applications, and we reviewed existing security techniques, including secret-key and public-key encryption, digital signature, and Netscape's SSL.

From a computing point of view, an electronic financial market is a large-scale distributed computing system with a large number of clients interacting with the electronic exchange and the clearinghouse. As a distributed computing system, the trading system has many characteristics such as resource sharing, concurrent processing, transparency, and fault tolerance. In implementing a distributed financial trading system, many computing issues have to be discussed, but here, we have selected only some of the most important. We discussed in detail concurrent processing, multithreads, and synchronization. In addition to synchronized communication, a trading application also supports asynchronous communication. In many situations, the latter exhibits big advantages. Finally, we discussed fault-tolerant computing. It is critical to have fault tolerance for a financial trading application. The two basic fault-tolerance approaches are hardware redundancy and software redundancy. Practical implementation methods include roll-back recovery and process replications.

13

CREATIVE

DESTRUCTION

Approximately half a century ago, Joseph Schumpeter, an Austrian-born econo-mist, used the term *creative destruction* to describe the evolutionary process of capitalism. According to Schumpeter, capitalism is "by nature a form or method of economic change and not only never is but never can be stationary." The changing process "incessantly revolutionizes the economic structure *from within,* incessantly destroying the old one, incessantly creating a new one. The process of Create Destruction is the essential fact about capitalism."[1]

Half a century after Schumpeter wrote those words, technology is profoundly changing our economic system. The Internet is tearing apart the old financial institutions and creating new ones that were unimaginable just a few years ago. Online trading, online information dissemination, and ECNs are just some of the examples. The new electronic marketplace has reduced information asymmetry and improved transaction efficiency. However, the existing marketplace is far from perfect. The same competitive forces will continue creating new institu-tional structure and improving the overall market efficiency.

13.1 BARRIERS TO A FRICTIONLESS MARKETPLACE

As mentioned in the first chapter of the book, the fundamental functions of finan-cial systems are relatively stable over time. But the institutional structure that carries those functions will go through major transformations from time to time. The underlying motivation for this never-ending creative destruction process is to build a frictionless marketplace by incessantly reducing information asymmetry and transaction cost, the two biggest barriers to market efficiency.

The efficiency of a market critically depends on the amount and the quality of information available to both buyers and sellers. When market participants are not endowed with proper information, the market can be inefficient and even break down. Information asymmetry is closely linked to the incentive problem. Adverse selection and moral hazard are two examples. The lemons problem, first discussed by Akerlof, is a case of adverse selection in which bad products can eventually drive quality products out of the market.[2] This happens when one party to a transaction has private information that is not revealed to the other party. Take, for example, multiple firms offering financial services of varying quality. Although the firms know their service quality, investors do not. Because investors could get poor services, they may not be willing to pay high prices for quality services any more even though there are high-quality service providers in the market. Eventually, firms that offer high-quality services may be driven out of the market—a classic case of adverse selection.

Moral hazard, however, occurs after a contractual relationship has been established between market participants. For example, after an investor has established an account with a brokerage firm, the investor expects the broker to execute his or her orders in his or her best interest. But the broker may route the orders to its favored market center, which might not offer the best execution. The problem of moral hazard happens when a contracted agent's behavior is difficult to monitor.

Market efficiency suffers when incentive problems such as adverse selection and moral hazard occur as individuals seek personal gain at the expense of the aggregate market optimality. This is made possible by the presence of high information asymmetry. Technology can expedite information dissemination and improve the quality of information in the market. Although this may never solve the incentive problem, which is inherent in human behavior, a more transparent marketplace will certainly reduce opportunistic behavior and improve market efficiency. Information disclosure encourages fair competition and increases the accountability of market participants' behavior.

Information asymmetry and the incentive problem are closely associated with transaction costs in the marketplace. Different from production costs or other internal costs that firms incur, transaction costs include the time, effort, and money that are involved to complete transaction between different agents in the market. Transaction costs for online trading, for example, include trade commissions, which are disclosed to investors, and stock bid-ask spreads, which are relatively more difficult to measure. For example, although the order submission and routing technologies affect the direct cost of trading, the way markets are organized affects bid-ask spread. As mentioned earlier, if incentives are not well aligned, opportunistic behavior, contract negotiation, and disputes will significantly increase transaction costs. Therefore, transaction cost, the economic equivalent of friction in physical systems,[3] is a major factor affecting the efficiency of a market system.

13.2 IMPACT OF TECHNOLOGY

Information technology, particularly the Internet and electronic commerce, has reduced information asymmetry and transaction cost in the financial market. Here, we summarize some of the major developments.

Information Dissemination—Financial Portals

Portals, the gatekeepers to the Internet, are a highly specialized type of Internet business. As portals tend to be the first online stop, they help users to find the network resources that are most relevant to them. Some of the best-known portals are Yahoo!, Excite, Google, and America Online. These generic portals offer a directory service, a search engine, and current news. Generic portals have recently taken their business one step further by creating specialized and personalized portals. Yahoo!Finance, for example, is one of most popular financial portals. It does almost everything related to finance and investment. It offers up-to-the-minute business news, market overviews, company and mutual fund research, and tools and services related to personal finance. Yahoo!Finance offers investment information to Internet users that was unheard of earlier. It offers quotes, stock charts, and news for customized portfolios. Information on institutional holders and insider trades is also available. Registered users can also participate in online discussion forums for individual stocks. Yahoo! also has online personal financial services including bill payment, insurance, tax, and loan services.

Financial portals such as Yahoo!Finance aggregate investment information on industrial sectors and individual companies from a variety of research sources. Potentially, financial portals allow unlimited information disclosure over the Internet. This development has already had a tremendous impact on the market and has benefited millions of investors who participate in capital markets. It allows individual investors to access information that was only available to large institutional investors a few years ago. Without a large amount of quality information, individual investors are always in a disadvantageous position in trading with informed institutional traders. Although large institutions may still have many advantages, the gap in information access has been narrowed significantly due to the Internet. Already unprecedented numbers of individual investors in the United States are participating in the equity market. Potentially, in a world without information asymmetry, retail investors could compete perfectly with large institutional investors.

High market transparency will also make financial institutions be more accountable to their customers and function more efficiently. The disclosure of mutual fund prospectus and performance, for instance, makes fund managers more accountable to fund investors. Similarly, disclosure of their order routing operations will make brokerage firms more accountable to their customers. With highly informed investors, financial services companies have to compete more vigorously by focusing on delivering values to their customers' firms while reducing costs. This process drives the whole market toward greater efficiency.

Competing Exchange Markets

Market efficiency has also been increased through recent developments in exchange markets, which now provide more alternatives for trading stocks. Today, investors' orders can be traded at any of the following venues:

- *Exchanges.* For a stock that is listed on the New York Stock Exchange (NYSE), the brokerage firm can send the order to the floor of NYSE or other regional exchanges. The brokerage firm can also direct the order to firms called "third market makers," who buy and sell stocks listed on an exchange at publicly quoted prices. Most of the trading of NYSE-listed stocks happens at the NYSE, which has consistently captured more than 80 percent of the orders.[4]

- *Market Makers.* There are two types of market makers. The first type is the Nasdaq market makers, who are dealers ready to buy or sell stocks traded on the Nasdaq market. The other type is the "third market makers" mentioned above.

- *ECNs.* ECNs now account for about 30 percent of the total share volume traded on the Nasdaq market. So far, the impact of ECNs on the NYSE has not been significant. ECNs now account for approximately 3 percent of the total share-trading volume of exchange-listed stocks. However, due to their cheaper and faster trading technology, ECNs pose a growing threat to the organized exchanges.

- *Internalization.* Finally, the brokerage firm can route orders to a market maker that is an affiliate of the brokerage firm for execution.

Now that the competition in the exchange markets is higher than ever before, trading costs have dropped significantly. According to a recent study, the bid-ask spread, a key measure of trading cost, has declined an impressive 30 percent in Nasdaq since the emergence of ECNs.[5] The competition has clearly benefited investors and has provided individual markets with stronger incentives to innovate, which will further improve the overall efficiency of the equity markets. As discussed earlier, the NYSE and Nasdaq are determined to change their organizational structure to for-profit exchanges to better compete with the electronic trading networks. New, innovative trading systems such as Primex are also being developed to provide better trading services.

Competitive Products

Not only has competition between trading venues heated up, competition for products has also grown tremendously. As discussed in previous chapters, an increasing number of products is being traded in markets today. Hurricane insurance, electricity, presidential elections, and Hollywood movies are just some of the examples. In the financial market, investors have a growing selection of products from which to choose. Investors can buy individual stocks, mutual funds, and derivative products such as options and futures. For investors who want to participate in the equity market but would like to avoid the risk of individual stocks, mutual funds used to be the only choice. Now, they can trade exchange-traded funds (ETF) such as cubes (QQQ), which track the Nasdaq 100 index, spiders (SPDRS), which track the Standard & Poor's 500 stock index, or diamonds (DIA), which follow the Dow Jones industrials. These funds can be bought and sold just like stocks. Some analysts believe that QQQ is one of the most successful new products in the history of the modern security industry.[6]

Competing products offer investors alternative ways to participate in the financial markets. Investors favor products that match their preferences with lower transaction costs. The introduction of new financial products has increased competition between firms that offer different products and services. This is the key to the viability of the marketplace.

13.3 NEW PROBLEMS AND THREATS

While technologies are reducing information asymmetry and transaction cost on a broad scale, new problems associated with technologies have also emerged.

13.3.1 Online Fraud

One wonderful aspect of the Internet is that it transfers control from large organizations to the individuals. As discussed in earlier chapters, the Internet has rendered the financial markets more democratic. Individual investors no longer rely on their broker for the latest stock prices and investment information. Numerous online services such as Yahoo! and others provide millions of investors the opportunity to express their opinions on any given stock. But this empowerment of the individuals comes at a cost. It exposes the investors to the possibility of fraud.

Fraud is no stranger to the financial markets. The financial services sector is the most heavily regulated sector in the United States. But no matter how comprehensive the regulations or how strict the enforcement, as the legend goes, "robbing a bank is still one of the fastest ways to become rich." In the securities markets, "robbing" takes the form of selling titles to ownership of assets at highly inflated prices.

Everyone Is a Publisher

The Internet is repeatedly referred to as a decentralized network. Firms and individuals use the Internet to exchange information with each other. They can publish information on their Web sites, providing material that can potentially be accessed by anyone on the Internet. But Web pages are not the only publishing medium. From the perspective of the financial markets, chat rooms and bulletin boards are an important media in which the average investor can "publish" his or her views, opinions, expectations, questions, and answers on every aspect of the investment process.

These publishing venues have made it possible for the average Joe to transform him- or herself from a consumer of published information to a publisher of information. The Merrill Lynches and Fidelity Investments are no longer indispensable. Instead of calling a broker for investment advice and related information and instead of subscribing to research from Merrill Lynch, individual investors can log on to various discussion sites on the Internet to share and exchange information.

The interesting aspect of this development—and at this stage an unanswered question—is whether these media can effectively replace existing sources of fee-based investment information vendors. In other words, will the average investor be better off following and participating in discussions about stocks in a chat room than calling a stock broker at Merrill Lynch for investment advice?

The essential nature of the Internet and the Web is that they are "open platforms" that evolved in a noncommercial research environment and took off among avid hobbyists and scientists long before marketers had ever heard of them. Participation is in the Internet's DNA. Anyone can build a Web site; the tools are free or nearly so, the "how to's" are easy to find, and today even the hosting space can be had for free, thanks to companies that have built whole businesses by selling ads in "build your own site" communities. With a do-it-yourself site, you can run a small business, contribute to the Web's vast pool of information, express yourself, and have a blast.

Everyone Is an Entrepreneur

If a firm wishes to raise funds to finance some productive business opportunity, the managers of the business have to communicate its prospects to potential investors. Before the advent of the Web, a firm would have had to print promotional literature (termed a prospectus in legal jargon) and have it mailed to hundreds of potential investors. As we saw in our discussion of the Internet-based initial public offerings, a prospectus published over the Internet can, at least in theory, reach a much wider audience and at a fraction of the original cost. Borrowers, both large and small, can access the Internet for funds. They can use this medium to raise capital directly from individual investors. This facility changes the dynamics of the financial markets. It is surely a threat to the traditional role of intermediaries such as investment banks.

By making it potentially easier to raise money, the medium expands the pool of both borrowers and lenders. And in the process it dilutes the quality of both those who want capital and those who have capital. Bogus get-rich-quick offers existed long before there was an Internet. The telephone and the postal service simply served as the communication media. But because the global computer network allows anyone with a computer to become a publisher, the medium has breathed new life into age-old scams. The Internet is full of schemes designed to dupe the unwary. It is surprising that people fall for schemes that sound—and often are—too good to be true.

Online Fraud

On April 8, 1998, Matthew Bowin was arrested for allegedly defrauding roughly 150 investors out of $190,000 in a scheme to sell stock in his company over the Internet.[7] The front for this scheme was a company titled Interactive Products and Services, Inc., which claimed to be designing a computer keyboard that would make it easier for users to navigate the Internet. According to the Securities and Exchange Commission (SEC), Bowin posted a prospectus—a document detailing his company's business—on the Internet and received payments from investors as far away as Hong Kong. Bowin had promised that he would hold investors' money in escrow until he had raised $500,000, at which point he would issue stock certificates. But the SEC said Bowin spent the money on himself, buying groceries and stereo equipment. The company did not make any products, did not have a team of design and marketing consultants as it had claimed, and had accrued $300,000 in unpaid advertising debts.

In August 2000, the FBI arrested 23-year-old Mark Jakob for manipulating the stock of computer products maker Emulex. The fake release warned of an earnings restatement and an executive resignation for Emulex. In the first hour of trading, Emulex shares plunged more than 60 percent, knocking roughly $2.5 billion off its total market capitalization.[8] This time, the bogus news was released through Internet Wire, a company that offers Internet-based press releases.

A few weeks later, in September 2000, the SEC charged Jonathan Lebed, a 15-year-old boy, with stock fraud. According to the SEC, the teenager, on several occasions, purchased a block of a thinly traded micro-cap stock and within hours sent hundreds of false messages on message boards touting the stock by using fictitious names. He then allegedly sold his shares at a profit.[9] On January 5, for example, he bought 18,000 shares of Man Sang Holdings Inc., a Chinese jewelry company, at prices between $1.37 and $2. He then posted false messages over the Internet. The next day, trading volume of the company soared to more than a million shares at a peak price of $4.68. That day Lebed sold his shares for a profit of more than $34,000.

Chat rooms, by their very nature, offer a convenient forum for sharing financial information and opinions. A person posting a message to a chat room is not required to reveal his or her true identity. Federal law prohibits chat room hosts from disclosing online members' identities without a court order. In addition, it might be difficult to convict someone merely for opining that a particular stock may be a good or bad buy.

The relative anonymity, plus the protection provided by law, could potentially encourage a person to be direct and honest in appraising a company's performance and expressing one's opinion. At the same time, the lack of transparency provides a convenient environment for individuals to mislead other investors. For instance, a person can claim to have access to insider information from a particular company. As others in the chat rooms have no way of verifying the authenticity of information presented by any individuals, they ought to discount any such claims to privileged access. But given human frailties, there are sufficient numbers of gullible investors who suspend their judgment and get taken in by spurious statements posted either as pranks or as efforts to deliberately mislead.

By allowing millions of individuals to share their information and expectations with each other, the Internet discussion forums live up to the original spirit of the Internet. Chat rooms are in a sense a microcosm of the original vision of the founders of the Internet. They have freed the individual from the confines of a small group of like-minded peers. They allow millions of widely dispersed investors to exchange information and in the process have permanently altered the financial markets. However, the success or failure of this medium depends on the level of trust among its users.

13.3.2 Computer Glitches

As we become increasingly reliant on technology, so reliant that Internet connections and cellular phones have become more necessity than luxury, we expose ourselves to the more significant consequences of technical failures.

For example, on the morning of October 8, 1998, the Dow Jones Industrial Average (DJIA) was erroneous for the first 12 minutes. It turned out that the merger between Citicorp and Travelers Group, which led to the creation of a new entity, Citigroup, using Citicorp's ticker symbol, CCI, was the reason. In calculating the value of the DJIA, the NYSE's computers used the previous night's closing price of Citicorp ($70 approximately), instead of the Citigroup opening price of $31.75.[10]

In another instance, on November 25, 1998, the Tokyo Stock Exchange's (TSE) futures and options trading system failed for a second successive day as a programming error shut down trading in the last minute of business. A computer programming glitch prevented the exchange from setting a closing price on Japanese government bond futures for December delivery. The glitch caused the bond futures trading screen to black out. Once this happened, traders were unable to view market quotes. Without proper price information, trading stopped immediately. The previous day, trading had been halted for most of the trading period; there was a glitch in the computer program that controlled transmissions between the exchange's host server and client servers at member brokers.

Finally, on February 18, 2000, updated quotes for Nasdaq composite index were unavailable for more than 2.5 hours due to a computer communications glitch at Nasdaq's Connecticut office.

These breakdowns are not costless. In an increasingly competitive environment, a persistent systems failure would be a serious blow to the market. Customers tired of dealing with unreliable systems can route their trades to other trading systems. In the case of the TSE, the exchange is in the process of developing a strategy to compete with privately run electronic trading systems that will soon be allowed to operate under the government's financial market reform.

13.3.3 Market Fragmentation

Rapid advances in technology have dramatically lowered the costs of developing electronic trading systems. As a result, the exchange markets once dominated by a handful of markets such as the NYSE and Nasdaq have seen new competitors. There is no question that competition has made individual markets more efficient. However, competition has also led to a certain degree of market fragmentation as more market centers are competing for order flows. Today, ECNs account for about 30 percent of the total share volume traded on the Nasdaq market.[11]

As discussed earlier, one of the most important functions of an exchange market is to provide liquidity to buyers and sellers. As more markets are competing for order flow for the same security, markets could get more fragmented as orders are channeled to different trading venues. This may isolate orders in individual markets and reduce the opportunity for interaction of all buying and selling interest in that security. This will reduce a market's ability to aggregate orders and reduce competition on price, which is one of the most important benefits of a market.[12]

Without the ability to aggregate buying and selling interests in a market system, the market will, in effect, pose higher transaction costs for its participants. Let's assume, for instance, that a buyer uses a market order to purchase a security. Under a more fragmented market, the buyer is less likely to get the best possible price in the market because sell interests are spread at different markets. In addition, the depth of each market center is reduced. If the buyer has a large order size, the impact on the stock price from the large order could further increase the transaction cost for the buyer. For an investor who uses a limit order, the chance of getting the order executed is lowered as incoming orders are scattered among multiple markets.

13.4 PROCESS OF CREATIVE DESTRUCTION

According to Schumpeter, every 50 years or so, waves of technological revolutions will cause creative destruction that will destroy old institutional structures and create new ones. Information technology is revolutionizing our economy and vastly transforming the society we are living in. The financial market is just one example of how the Internet is shaping the current industry.

If technology is the exogenous force for this revolution, then the motivation to reduce information asymmetry and lower transaction cost is the internal force within the market system. Competitive forces are reducing information asymmetry and driving down transaction costs. This process is benefiting millions of consumers and is changing the balance of power between existing players. Financial institutions that constantly innovate and offer values to customers will be able to survive this creative destruction process. Those who stand still will fall far behind and disappear.

Admittedly, we are still on the verge of this revolution. One of the most challenging tasks of this revolution is to establish an institutional infrastructure to support new ways of doing business. Although we have some infrastructure in place, the task is far from accomplished. As technology is in the process of creating the new economy, there are ample examples of temporary imbalances. But in the long run, competitive forces within our economic system will destroy those inefficiencies. As we expect new trust models in the online world will eventually control cyberspace fraud, we believe competition in financial markets will lead to an industry model with a socially desirable balance of market consolidation and competition.

13.5 SUMMARY

Schumpeter is right in that capitalism is never stationary. But in the age of the Internet and electronic commerce, changes are taking place at a pace much faster than Schumpeter predicted. This dynamic marketplace offers opportunities and challenges. New entries are creating new business models that threaten the incumbents. It is natural during this process for new problems to emerge and imbalances to occur, which in turn become the stimulus for new innovations. To a certain extent, this book offers a snapshot of the financial markets at a time of rapid changes. We have no doubt that many institutions described in this book will soon change beyond recognition.

NOTES

CHAPTER 1

1. D. Crane *et al.*, *The Global Financial System: A Functional Perspective*. Boston, MA: Harvard Business School Press, 1995.
2. See Network Wizard's Web site: http://www.nw.com.
3. D. Crane *et al.*, *The Global Financial System: A Functional Perspective*. Boston, MA: Harvard Business School Press, 1995.
4. Source: L. Allen, *Capital Markets and Institutions: A Global View*. New York: John Wiley & Sons, 1997.
5. S. Mason *et al.*, *Cases in Financial Engineering: Applied Studies of Financial Innovation*. Upper Saddle River, NJ: Prentice Hall, 1995.
6. M. Porter, *Competitive Advantage*. New York: The Free Press, 1985.

CHAPTER 2

1. R. Buckman, Merrill says online trading is bad for investors. *Wall Street Journal*, September 23, 1998.
2. In 1998, John Steffens, chief of Merrill's brokerage division, openly criticized online trading as a threat to the financial health of the average investor.
3. See, Big brokerage firms inch online. *Industry Standard*, May 7, 1999.
4. The eInvesting report, eMarketer, November 2000; http://www.emarketer.com.
5. Jupiter Communications: $3 trillion in assets by 2003 in online brokerage accounts, but customer services still lacking. September 1, 1999; http://www.jup.com.
6. See, Your egalitarian net broker sets high hurdles for perks. *Wall Street Journal*, June 21, 1999.
7. Data mining goes online. CNNfn, September 24, 1999.
8. See, L. Trager, Portals garnering most online investment traffic. Interactive Week Online, July 23, 1998.
9. There are a large number of studies attempting to study Internet usage. Their findings and estimates tend to vary considerably.
10. See, B. Lipton, E*Trade launches portal site. CNET News.com, September 10, 1998.
11. Why should anyone charge money for real-time price information? After all, does it belong to anyone in particular? As it is determined in the marketplace through trades among thousands of investors, how can any single entity claim ownership to it? Well, the reality is different. If a trade takes place on the floor of the NYSE (technical term here is *printed at the NYSE*), then the price at which the transaction took place and the number of shares that were traded belongs to the NYSE. Anyone who wants real-time access to it has to buy it from the NYSE.
12. Well, not really free. When signing up with E*Trade, one will have to supply some personal information, stuff that can be used by the firm to market its services. Information is wealth, and personal information is of great value in the business world.
13. In October 1999, the U.S. Congress passed the Financial Services Modernization: Gramm-Leach-Bliley Act. It was signed by the President in November 1999. The new law allows for one-stop shopping for financial services, with banking, insurance, and securities activities being available under one roof.
14. See, E*Trade goes shopping, and might get more than it banked on, MSNBC.com, June 1, 1999, for an interesting view on the merits of this takeover of an online bank.

CHAPTER 3

1. There is an exception to this rule. On the Nasdaq market, investors can buy or sell small quantities of shares of any particular stock; order sizes as small as five shares are executed at regular prices. This is possible because most of the orders from small investors are pooled and executed through electronic trading systems. But at the average price of $40 per share, buying even five shares each in 20 stocks will cost $4,000. This amount is still much larger than the average monthly investment by an individual investor in his or her retirement account. If we include NYSE-listed stocks, it is nearly impossible for the average investor to acquire a diversified portfolio of stocks with even a full year's savings.

2. Chapter 5 presents some numbers and other relevant details of individuals who populate the NYSE floor.

3. Chapter 5 describes how large investors are reluctant to send orders for very large numbers of shares, say, hundreds of thousands, to the NYSE floor. Such orders either get split into smaller orders or, increasingly, get routed to alternative trading institutions.

4. See H. Chen and J. R. Ritter, The seven percent solution. *Journal of Finance* June 2000: 55(3), 1105–1131.

5. Underwriters discourage their customers from flipping the stock; insiders have to sit through minimum holding periods before becoming eligible to sell the stock.

6. See, In pioneering online "auction" for IPO, Ravenswood Winery gets cool response. *Wall Street Journal*, April 12, 1999.

7. See, Market savvy investor's journal: a toast to OpenIPO from the "little guy." *Los Angeles Times*, April 13, 1999.

8. See, Banks are scrambling to offer Web-wise ways to do business. *Business Week*, May 10, 1999.

9. Flipping is a practice of selling a stock immediately after buying it at the IPO price.

10. See, Banks are scrambling to offer Web-wise ways to do business. *Business Week*, May 10, 1999.

11. A hashing algorithm translates one message into another set of bits in a way that (1) a message yields the same result every time the algorithm is used. (2) It is computationally infeasible for a message to be derived from the result produced by the algorithm; (3) it is computationally infeasible to find two different messages that produce the same hash result by using the same algorithm.

12. Secure socket layer, a protocol developed by Netscape for transmitting private documents via the Internet. See details in Chapter 12.

CHAPTER 4

1. D. Friedman and J. Rust, eds., *The Double Auction Market: Institutions, Theories, and Evidence.* Addison-Wesley: 1993.

2. L. Harris and J. Hasbrouck, Market vs. limit orders: the SuperDOT evidence on order submission strategy. *Journal of Financial and Quantitative Analysis* 1996: 31(2), 213–231.

3. See I. Domowitz and J. Wang, Auctions as algorithms. *Journal of Economic Dynamics and Control* 1994: 18, 29–60.

4. S. Grossman and M. Miller, Liquidity and market structure. *Journal of Finance* 1988: 43, 617–633.

5. M. Pagano and A. Roell, Transparency and liquidity: a comparison of auction and dealer markets with informed trading. *Journal of Finance* 1996: 57, 579–612.

6. See Chapter 7 of R. A. Schwartz, *Reshaping the Equity Markets.* HarperBusiness: 1991.

7. See Chapter 20 of K. Garbade, *Securities Markets*. McGraw-Hill: 1982.
8. See http://www.itginc.com for an example of one such service.

CHAPTER 5

1. DJIA is an index made up of 30 large stocks. Until late 1999, membership in this index was restricted to the largest U.S. corporations listed on the NYSE. In 1999, stocks issued by Microsoft and Intel, two large technology firms that trade on the Nasdaq market, were included in the DJIA.
2. This is obviously an extreme example. Another more reasonable scenario would be when there is considerable uncertainty regarding the fortunes of a particular company. Market-maker quotes and limit orders are available, but the spread between the highest bid and the lowest offer is so wide, say, $10.00 on a stock that otherwise trades in the $20.00 per share range, that brokers refuse to execute their clients' orders. In the case of the NYSE, the specialist has the authority to suspend trading in such circumstances.
3. Some firms are also linked to their floor booths through SuperDOT or through proprietary communications systems. Nonmembers can telephone orders directly to floor broker booths.
4. SuperDOT also handles order cancellations and administrative inquiries. Order cancellations become effective as soon as they are received and processed by SuperDOT. Cancellation is not contingent on approval by the specialist. Through SuperDOT, member firms may also request order status reports at any time.
5. The specialist may also use the ITS to get the order executed on another market that displays a better quote.
6. This is not against SEC regulations as long as the specialist is not trading ahead of a customer order routed to him or her.
7. A street scandal that may not die. *Business Week,* August 9, 1999.
8. See, http://www2.nyse.com/press/NT00024196.html.
9. See, NYSE agrees to monitor floor traders more carefully. *New York Times,* June 30, 1999. See also, NYSE regulator says broker profit-sharing not seen as illegal. *Bloomberg News,* October 21, 1999.
10. Institutional investors will be required to set up prearranged credit and order-size parameters with an NYSE member firm prior to using XPress Routing. Although a member firm will thus be sponsoring an institutional client, it will not get to see an order routed through it.
11. See, Trading in the dark: pros, cons of big board's longer session. *Barrons,* May 27, 1991.

CHAPTER 6

1. A series of sales of shares and warrants by the NASD in 2000 and 2001 has seen its ownership in Nasdaq diluted to less than 40%. The plan is to eventually divest balance holdings by mid-2002.
2. The terms *broker-dealer* and *market makers* are used interchangeably throughout this book.
3. The Chicago Stock Exchange is categorized as an unlisted trading participant (UTP) and supports electronic trading in Nasdaq stocks.
4. Automatic execution was not guaranteed in the original proposal. It was only in 1988 that market-maker participation in SOES was made mandatory.
5. See, Tough time in electronic trading. *Business Week,* October 23, 2000, pp. 142–143.

6. W. Christie and P. Schultz, Why do NASDAQ market makers avoid odd-eighth quotes? *Journal of Finance* December 1994: 1813–1840.

7. Security Exchange Act Release No. 37619A (September 6, 1996), 61 FR 48290 (September 12, 1996).

8. See, P. Handa and R. A. Schwartz, Limit order trading. *Journal of Finance* December 1996: 51(5), 1744–1752.

9. See, L. Harris and J. Hasbrouck, Market vs. limit orders: the SuperDOT evidence on order submission strategy. Working paper, USC/UCLA/NYSE Conference on Market Microstructure, 1992.

10. See, Volatility isn't what it used to be (it's worse). *New York Times,* October 19, 1999.

11. See, With IPOs, Web firms find fewer shares can be better. *Wall Street Journal,* April 19, 1999.

12. See, G. Ip, Nasdaq's trading problems make it vulnerable to rivals. *Wall Street Journal,* June 10, 1999.

13. See, T. Wilson, Nasdaq puts stock in the Web. *InternetWeek,* at CMPnet.com, July 2, 1998.

14. Stock prices have traditionally been quoted in fractions: fourth, eighth, 16th (6.25 cents), and so on. By the 1990s, there was a worldwide move to quote prices in decimals.

15. Message traffic is expected to grow with decimalization. The reason for this is simple. If stocks trade in increments of one to two cents as expected, market makers will have to update their quotes more frequently. Every change will result in one or more messages sent over Nasdaq's networks.

16. See, The rocky road to decimalization. *Wall Street & Technology,* June 15, 2000.

17. The first round was completed as of January 2001.

18. This flexibility is important, as with decimal pricing spreads need not be in five-cent increments. And with one-cent spreads, it is not necessary that quotes be made at every one-cent increment. For example, there might be bids at $9.77, $9.79, and $9.80 but not at $9.78.

19. An order that is either a market order or has a limit price greater than or equal to the best offer in case of a buying interest, and vice versa, in case of a selling interest.

20. Technically, all orders will be nondirected by default, unless the broker specifically directs an order toward another broker's quote/order.

21. This fee will be waived if the broker is signed up with the ECN and sends the order directly to its order book, instead of through the Nasdaq network.

22. For purposes of the discussion here, we have ignored the fact that an ECN might not have a single pricing policy for all market participants.

23. There is a second issue that has worried Nasdaq's opponents and that has to do with the fact that Nasdaq's parent, the NASD, is trying to compete with those whom it also regulates. We examine this issue a bit later.

24. See, Madoff voices next Nasdaq concern to SEC. *Wall Street Letter,* March 30, 1998.

25. See, Nasdaq's technology.

CHAPTER 7

1. See Chapter 6 (Section 6.6.5) for an interesting discussion on the impact of such fees on the treatment of ECN quotes under the SuperMontage proposal.

2. There are multiple views on the correct definition of the term *best execution.* Kenneth Pasternak, the president and CEO of the Knight/Trimark Group, one of the largest market makers on the Nasdaq market defines it, for instance, as, "best execution is

what the customer says it is." See, Online trading, ECNs prove hot topics at SIA meeting. *Wall Street Journal*, November 8, 1999.

3. See, Market quality monitoring overview of 1997 market changes. *NASD Economic Research*, March 17, 1998. Also, M. Barclay *et al.*, Effects of market reform on trading costs and depths of Nasdaq stocks. *Journal of Finance* 1999: 54(1), 1–34.

4. See, ECNs look for strength in numbers, *Industry Standard News*, September 16, 1999, for a report on a proposal to link a bunch of ECNs (for after-hours trading) such that "submit an order on one system but see it executed on a different system—one that offers a better price." At the time of writing, it is not clear that such a link has been successfully implemented.

5. This system has now been replaced by an electronic trading system from the Swiss Stock Exchange.

6. As with so many other fads that follow stock price levels, with a sharp drop in various stock indices through 2000–01, by April 2001 Instinet had decided to shelve its retail plan for the time being. So, the discussion above is sort of academic, but the issues themselves are relevant to any evolving marketplace.

7. Island was once a division of Datek Securities, a brokerage firm that focused on the day-trading segment.

8. See, Reuters' Instinet sets acquisition of discount broker Lynch Jones. *Wall Street Journal*, November 18, 1999.

9. See, Another threat to Nasdaq—four firms launch electronic stock trading system. *Associated Press*, July 22, 1999.

10. See, Electronic networks revolutionize trading—traditional markets compete with new kid to keep investors. *Associated Press*, August 29, 1999.

11. Archipelago Holdings LLC, the owner of the Archipelago ECN, has come up with an innovative strategy to "buy" order flow: Investors and brokers who route their orders to the ECN will receive the rights to ownership of the ECN. See, Bids & offers—what's in a domain? *Wall Street Journal*, November 19, 1999.

12. See, Electronic networks hook up—shakeout among ECNs just round the corner. *Associated Press*, October 15, 1999.

13. The SuperMontage proposal discussed in Chapter 6 is the latest incarnation of this idea. Fortunately for Nasdaq, and unfortunately for ECNs, this proposal has received the SEC's approval.

14. It is not clear if some of the newer entrants to the ECN business have any profitable business models in mind. For example, the December 2, 1999, issue of the *Wall Street Journal* quoted the CEO of a potential entrant as saying that he had no idea if his new ECN will make any money and that he had not really given that issue much thought. See, G. Ip, Electronic trading firms generate buzz, few bucks.

15. See, Valuation issues stall ECN deal, *Industry Standard*, October 8, 1999, for a report on the problems plaguing the alliance between Waterhouse and Island discussed above.

16. See, NYSE allows member firms to trade on competing venues. *Wall Street Journal*, December 3, 1999. Also, SEC plans moves to lift barriers shielding big board from rivals. *Wall Street Journal*, December 1, 1999.

CHAPTER 8

1. See, http://www.azx.com.

2. "OptiMark system gets reality check as challenges, restrictions continue. *Wall Street Journal*, October 14, 1999.

3. See Primex Web site (http://*www.primextrading.com*) for details.

CHAPTER 9

1. Tradepoint was renamed virt-x in 2001.
2. See, Swedish surprise. *Business Week,* September 11, 2000.
3. Jiway means "wisdom" in Chinese.
4. The OM CLICK Exchange System, OM Group, 1998.
5. *The Swiss Exchange: From Vision to Reality.* The Swiss Exchange, 1996.
6. Australia stock exchange to go public. *New York Times,* October 14, 1998.

CHAPTER 10

1. Source: The Bond Market Association, 2001, http://www.bondmarkets.com.
2. Source: Federal Reserve Bank of New York, 2001, http://www.ny.frb.org.
3. Source: The Bond Market Association, 1999.
4. Source: The Bond Market Association, 2000, and independent research conducted by the authors.

CHAPTER 11

1. See, D. C. North, *Institutions, Institutional Change, and Economic Performance.* Cambridge, NY: Cambridge University Press, 1990.
2. I. Moore *et al., Introduction to the New California Power Market.* California Power Exchange White Paper, 1998.
3. California woes cloud electricity deregulation prospects. *American Gas,* October 2000.
4. The future of California. *Business Week,* April 30, 2001.
5. Testimony of Curt L. Hebert, Jr., Chairman, Federal Energy Regulatory Commission before the Committee on Energy and Commerce Subcommittee on Energy and Air Quality, U.S. House of Representatives, March 20, 2001.
6. *ComEd and TVA Hub Electricity Futures and Options: The Reference and Applications Guide.* Chicago Board of Trade, 1999.
7. Source: http://www.dailyrocket.com/willard/willard14.html.
8. For latest trading at IEM, see http://www.biz.uiowa.edu/iem.
9. R. Forsythe *et al.,* Anatomy of an experimental political stock market. *The American Economy Review* 1992: 82(5), 1142–1161.
10. See, http://www.hsx.com.

CHAPTER 12

1. Refer to Chapter 3 for a detailed discussion.

CHAPTER 13

1. J. Schumpeter, *Capitalism, Socialism and Democracy.* New York: Harper, 1942, pp. 82–83.
2. See, G. Akerlof, The market for lemons: quality uncertainty and the market mechanism. *Quarterly Journal of Economics* 84, 488–500.
3. See, O. Williamson, *The Economic Institutions of Capitalism.* New York: The Free Press, 1985.
4. *Fact Book.* New York Stock Exchange, 2000; see http://www.nyse.com/about/about.html.
5. M. Barclay, W. G. Christie, J. H. Harris, E. Kandel, and P. H. Schultz, The effects of market reform on the trading costs and depths of Nasdaq stocks. *Journal of Finance* 1999: 54(1), 1–34.
6. See, Cube stake: why the Nasdaq 100 sizzles. *Fortune,* September 18, 2000.

7. See, Man charged with net stock fraud. CNET News.com, April 8, 1998.
8. See, FBI nabs Emulex suspect. CNNFN.com, August 31, 2000.
9. See, Teenage trader runs afoul of the SEC as stock touting draws charges of fraud. *Wall Street Journal,* September 21, 2000.
10. M. Kane, Computer glitch trips up Dow Jones industrial average. ZDNet, October 8, 1998.
11. *Market Data.* National Association of Securities Dealers, May 2000. See, http://www.marketdata.nasdaq.com/mr6d.html.
12. SEC release 34-42450, file no. SR-NYSE-99-48.

Photo Credits

INDEX